Lecture Notes in Artificial Intelligence 862

Subseries of Lecture Notes in Computer Science
Edited by J. G. Carbonell and J. Siekmann

Lecture Notes in Computer Science

Edited by G. Goos, J. Hartmanis and J. van Leeuwen

Rafael C. Carrasco   Jose Oncina (Eds.)

Grammatical Inference
and Applications

Second International Colloquium, ICGI-94
Alicante, Spain, September 21-23, 1994
Proceedings

Springer-Verlag
Berlin Heidelberg New York
London Paris Tokyo
Hong Kong Barcelona
Budapest

Rafael C. Carrasco   Jose Oncina (Eds.)

Grammatical Inference and Applications

Second International Colloquium, ICGI-94
Alicante, Spain, September 21-23, 1994
Proceedings

Springer-Verlag
Berlin Heidelberg New York
London Paris Tokyo
Hong Kong Barcelona
Budapest

Series Editors

Jaime G. Carbonell
School of Computer Science, Carnegie Mellon University
Schenley Park, Pittsburgh, PA 15213-3890, USA

Jörg Siekmann
University of Saarland
German Research Center for Artificial Intelligence (DFKI)
Stuhlsatzenhausweg 3, D-66123 Saarbrücken, Germany

Volume Editors

Rafael C. Carrasco
Jose Oncina
Departamento de Tecnología Informática y Computación
Universidad de Alicante
E-03071 Alicante, Spain

CR Subject Classification (1991): I.2, F.4.2-3, I.5.1, I.5.4, J.5

ISBN 3-540-58473-0 Springer-Verlag Berlin Heidelberg New York

CIP data applied for.

© Springer-Verlag Berlin Heidelberg 1994
Printed in Germany

Typesetting: Camera ready by author
SPIN: 10481826   45/3140-543210 - Printed on acid-free paper

Preface

This book contains the papers presented during the Second International Colloquium on Grammatical Inference (ICGI-94), held in Alicante, Spain, September 21–23. Grammatical Inference (GI) is broadly understood as the task of learning grammars from data. Traditionally, GI has been studied within several contexts: information theory, formal language theory, computational linguistics, machine learning, pattern recognition, computational learning and neural networks, and many others. This multidisciplinary perspective, however, has not led so far to a focussed research community. A first attempt to correct this started with the "First Colloquium on Grammatical Inference: Theory, Applications and Alternatives" held in the University of Essex, U.K., in April 1993. Following the success of this colloquium, the ICGI-94 provided a forum for discussion of principles, theory, and applications of all those aspects of automatic learning that explicitly focus on grammars and languages. The topics covered were:

- theory and algorithms.

- learning paradigms (identification in the limit, stochastic approaches, genetic algorithms).

- pattern recognition.

- neural networks.

- computational linguistics.

- machine learning.

- applications to natural language processing, language translation, speech and image processing.

This colloquium was co-sponsored by the Universidad Politécnica de Valencia (UPV), the Universidad de Alicante (UA), the Asociación Española de Reconocimiento de Formas y Análisis de Imágenes (AERFAI), the Asociación Española Para la Inteligencia Artificial (AEPIA), the Asociación Española de Informática y Automática (AEIA), the Institute of Electrical Engineers (IEE), and the International Association for Pattern Recognition (IAPR).

As the editors of these proceedings, we wish to thank all those who submitted papers for consideration, as well as the program committee members for their help in evaluating the contributions.

Alicante   Rafael C. Carrasco
September 1994   Jose Oncina

Conference Chairmen

P. García, Univ. Politécnica de Valencia
J. Oncina, Univ. de Alicante

Program Commitee

D. Angluin, Yale University
R. Damper, Univ. Southampton
J. Feldman, ICSI Berkeley
C. L. Giles, NEC Princeton
J. Gregor, Univ. Tennessee
F. Gruau, CENG Grenoble
D. Luzeaux, ETCA-CREA-SP Arcueil
E. Mäkinen, Univ. Tampere
L. Miclet, IRISA-ENSSAT Lannion
G. Nagaraja, IIT Bombay
F. Pereira, ATT Bell Labs. New Jersey
L. Pitt, Univ. Illinois
Y. Sakakibara, Fujitsu Labs.
A. Sanfeliu, Univ. Politécnica de Cataluña
R. Sharman, IBM United Kingdom
A. Stolcke, ICSI Berkeley
Y. Takada, Fujitsu Labs.
E. Vidal, Univ. Politécnica de Valencia
P.S.P. Wang, Northeastern Univ. Boston
J. Wright, Bristol Univ.
P. Wyard, British Telecom
T. Yokomori, Univ. of Electro-Comm. Tokio
S. J. Young, Univ. Cambridge

Organizing Committee

S. Lucas, Essex Univ.
R. Alquézar, Univ. Politécnica de Cataluña
F. Casacuberta, Univ. Politécnica de Valencia
A. Castaño, Univ. Politécnica de Valencia
A. Castellanos, Univ. Politécnica de Valencia
R. Carrasco, Univ. de Alicante
A. Corbí, Univ. de Alicante
M. Forcada, Univ. de Alicante
I. Galiano, Univ. Politécnica de Valencia
L. Micó, Univ. de Alicante
P. Pastor, Univ. de Alicante
E. Segarra, Univ. Politécnica de Valencia
J. Sempere, Univ. Politécnica de Valencia

Table of Contents

Grammatical Inference: An Introductory Survey

Enrique Vidal

Dpto. Sistemas Informáticos y Computación

Universidad Politécnica de Valencia, 46020 Valencia, SPAIN

Grammatical Inference (GI) encompasses theory and methods for learning grammars from training data. It is a well established discipline that dates back to the sixties. Perhaps the most traditional field of application of GI has been Syntactic Pattern Recognition [8, 14, 21]; but there are many other possible applications, including Speech and Natural Language processing, Gene Analysis, Sequence Prediction, Cryptography, etc. A number of papers of this volume deal with some of these applications. Ahonen et al. and Lucas et al., present applications of GI in Image Processing, while applications to Natural Language problems are covered in the papers by Jardino, Marcken, Della Pietra et al., Castellanos et al., Wright et al., Osborne, Dennis and Young & Shih

The most classical formalization of GI is known as Language Identification in the Limit, originally introduced by Gold in 1967 [12]. Here, a finite set $R+$ of strings known to belong to an unknown language L (positive training set) and, possibly, another finite set $R-$ of strings that do not belong to L (negative training set) are given. Identification of L in the Limit can be stated as finding a grammar G such that $R+$ is included in the language of G, $L(G)$, $R-$ is disjoint with $L(G)$ and, in the limit, for sufficiently large $R+$ and $R-$, $L(G) = L$. Identification in the Limit has traditionally been strongly affected by two fundamental decidability results, due to Gold [12].

The first result is negative in nature and states that no superfinite class of languages can be identified in the limit from only positive presentation. A superfinite class of languages is one that contains all finite languages and at least one that is infinite. Intuitively speaking the problem is one of over-generalization: if in a given inference step a language is produced that is larger than the unknown target language, this is irreversible, since no further positive string will ever supply information to detect this error. Since the class of Regular Languages is superfinite, not even this simple class is identifiable in the limit from only positive data.

The second result is more positive and states that any ennumerable class of recursive languages (context-sensitive and below) can be identified in the limit from complete presentation (both positive and negative data).

However, the interest of this result is strongly weakened by the fact that negative samples are not always available and, furthermore, it has been argued that their use may lead to probably intractable problems, even for Regular Languages. More specifically, given fixed finite samples $R+$ and $R-$ the problem of finding the smallest deterministic finite automaton, A, such that $R+$ is included in $L(A)$ and $R-$ is disjoint with $L(A)$ has been shown to be NP-HARD [13, 1]. Nevertheless, we can still attempt identification in the limit by trying to obtain adequate finite automata, A', such that $R+$ is in $L(A')$ and $R-$ is disjoint with $L(A')$, but without insisting that the size of A' strictly be the smallest possible for $R+$ and $R-$. This idea has recently led to an algorithm that can be shown to identify the whole class of Regular Languages in the limit [24, 25] and, moreover, it can achieve very accurate "approximate identification" (in the sense to be discussed below) with high efficiency [16]. An alternative technique for Regular GI from complete presentation is proposed in this volume by Dupont and formal issues concerning the search space underlying this problem appear in the paper by Dupont et al.

In any case, the difficulties with negative data have traditionally led practitioners to attempt escaping from negative theoretical evidence by (a) using only positive data and (b) either infer adequate non-superfinite classes of languages or apply convenient a-priori knowledge to explicitly limit the class of languages of interest. Following Angluin [4], GI methods that seek inferring adequate classes of languages are known as Characterizable [2, 3, 29, 10] of those using a-priori knowledge are referred to as Heuristic [7], [20], [22], [31], [9], etc.

Apart from these two basic paradigms for the development of GI algorithms using only positive data, there has been (and currently are) other more fundamental efforts trying to make the negative GI results milder. An interesting early work is due to Wharton who established a theoretical setting for *approximate language identification* in the limit and showed that approximate identification is possible with dense classes of languages using only positive presentation [37]. Dense classes are those in which for any given language one can find arbitrary close languages in the class, according to any properly defined distance between languages. Many classes of languages in which strings are assigned membership figures can fall into this category, an interesting example being the class of Stochastic Regular Languages [5].

This idea is being followed in recent and promising techniques that explicitly assume the stochastic nature of the grammars to be inferred and directly adopt learning schemes based on probabilistic criteria [27, 33]. The aim is to supply the lack of the negative information (that would control overgeneralization) with statistical information gathered from the positive data. This approach is particularly interesting since learning stochastic languages is in fact the final target of any GI approach that should deal with real tasks such as Pattern Recognition, Language Modeling, etc. Former works in this direction [27, 33] are further developed in this volume by Stolke & Omohundro and Carrasco & Oncina.

Using probabilistic information to discover rules has in fact been a basic paradigm in the field of Information Theory and it was very early established by Shannon that language learning can be properly seen as a problem of estimating probabilities of sequences of N symbols, or "N-Grams", with $N \rightarrow infinity$. This approach has recently proved to be particularly appropriate for Language Modeling in Automatic Speech Recognition. Contributions in this volume that are more or less directly related with this approach are those of Jardino, Della Pietra et al., Wright et al., and Dennis et al.

Also within the framework of Information Theory, and perhaps not sufficiently recognized in the specific field of GI, is the probability estimation technique of Hidden Markov Models (HMM) known as Backward-Forward [15, 17]. It can be used as the basis of a rather straightforward, probabilistically motivated regular GI technique: if some information about the appropriate number of states or non-terminals, n, is available, we can obtain a locally optimal estimate of the $O(n^2)$ probabilities of a fully connected n-state HMM from a sequence of training strings [17]. Then, by (optionally) pruning out zero or low probability transitions, a (stochastic) finite automaton or regular grammar can be obtained. In the paper by Sanchez and Benedi in this volume this technique is used in combination with other heuristic GI methods.

Another interesting framework for approximate learning is that recently introduced by Valiant [35] in which a learning method is asked to find models which, with arbitrarily high probability, are arbitrarily precise approximations to the unknown data source; hence the name: Probably Approximately Correct identification or PAC. This framework is currently being (theoretically) developed in many directions [23] and it is often argued that the PAC criterion can be closer to the practical requirements of real situations than other settings like Gold's Identification in the Limit.

While most GI work has traditionally been devoted to regular grammars, there is no doubt of the interest of trying to go beyond these simple models. In particular, the motivations for developing learning methods for Context-Free Languages (CFL) are clear: First, CFLs are much more powerful than Regular Languages. They can properly account for subtle language constraints and admit very compact representations in the form of Context Free Grammars

(CFG). Also, well known (moderately) efficient parsers exist for CF Grammars. Finally, we should remember that using both positive and negative examples, identification of CFLs in the limit is theoretically possible (though no efficient algorithm is known so far). However, we should also take into account that learning CFLs from positive data only is undecidable.

The situation here is somewhat worse than in the case of Regular Languages and only few non-regular (and non-superfinite) classes of CFLs are known to be learnable from positive data only [34, 30]. Learning other interesting classes of CFL (or general CFLs) seems to require more than just raw positive examples; namely, positive strings accompained with their corresponding unlabeled derivation trees or "skeletons". These descriptions can be obtained by adequately adding brackets to the strings. Techniques using this form of presentation are based on a well known result that states that, for any CFG, G, the set of skeletons of all the strings of $L(G)$ is a Regular Tree Language [32, 19, 11].

Two papers of this volume, those by Takada and Sempere & Garcia, deal with the inference of classes of CF languages, while the topic of inference using bracketed strings or skeletons is covered by Ruiz & Garcia.

As in the case of Regular Languages, another possibility is to rely on probabilistic information. Within the Information Theory framework, this idea led to the well-known Inside-Outside algorithm [6, 17, 18, 28] which is the Context-Free counterpart of the previously mentioned Backward-Forward reestimation technique of HMM. The papers by Casacuberta and Young & Shih in this volume are directly related with this approach.

A particularly interesting issue of GI is that of Transduction Learning. A transducer is a formal device which inputs strings from a given input set or language and outputs strings belonging to another (usually different) language. Perhaps the most important motivation for studying the learning of these devices from input-output training pairs comes from the fact that simple transducers are often adequate enough to deal with useful mappings between complex languages. A classical hierarchy of transductions include Sequential, Subsequential and Finite State or Rational Transductions, as well as other more complex classes. Rational Transducers, in general, seem to be hard to learn and, in fact, no method is known so far to approach the learning of these devices. Sequential Transducers, on the other hand, constitute a very constrained class that can hardly find convenient application in the fields where GI is usually applied. But Subsequential Transducers overcome many of these constraints, making these transducers very useful in real applications. This has risen the interest in the learning of this class of transducers for which a quite effective algorithm has been recently introduced [24, 26].

The difficulty of learning Rational Transducers in general is discussed in this volume in the paper by Itai, while an application of Subsequential Transducer learning to Language Translation is presented by Castellanos et al.

Grammatical Inference has so far been approached through a great diversity of algorithmic techniques, including Heuristic and Genetic Search. Also, many researchers have adopted the Neural Network framework and specific network architectures and learning algorithms have been developed more or less directly oriented to approach GI problems. Genetic and Heuristic search techniques are covered in this volume by the papers of Dupont, Wyard and Giordano, while NN techniques appear in those of Roques and Alquezar & Sanfeliu.

References

[1] D.Angluin: On the Complexity of Minimun Inference of Regular Sets Inf.& Control, 39, pp.337-350, 1978.

[2] D.Angluin: Inductive Inference of Formal Languages from Positive Data Inf.& Contr.,45,pp.117-135, 1980.

[3] D.Angluin: Inference of Reversible Languages J.ACM,29,3, pp.741-765.

[4] D.Angluin, C.H.Smith: Inductive Inference: Theory and Methods. Comp. Surveys, 15,N3, pp.46-62, 1983.

[5] D.Angluin: Identifying Languages from Stochastic Examples. YALEU/DCS/RR-614. 1988.

[6] J.K.Baker: Trainable Grammars for Speech Recognition. In Speech Communication Papers, 97th Meeting of the ASA (Klatt, D.H. and Wolf, J.J. eds). pp.547-550.

[7] A.W.Biermann and J.A.Feldmann: On the Synthesis of Finite-State Machines from Samples of their behavior. IEEE Trans. Compt., C-21, pp.592-597.

[8] K.S.Fu, Booth: Grammatical Inference: Introduction and Survey. Parts 1 and 2, IEEE Trans. SMC, 5, 5, pp.95-11, 409-423, 1975.

[9] P.Garcia, E.Vidal, F.Casacuberta: Local Languages, the Successor Method, and a step towards a General methodology for the Inference of Regular Grammars. IEEE Trans. PAMI,9,6 pp.841-845. 1987.

[10] P.Garcia, E.Vidal: Inference of K-Testable Languages In the Strict Sense and Application to Syntactic Pattern Recognition. IEEE Trans. on PAMI, 12, 9, pp.920-925, 1990.

[11] P.Garcia,J.Oncina: Learning General Context-Free Grammars form positive structural samples and negative strings. DSIC Research Report, 1993.

[12] E.M.Gold: Language Identification in the Limit. Inf. and Control, Vol.10, pp.447-474, 1967.

[13] E.M.Gold: Complexity of Automaton Identification from Given Data. Inf. and Control,37, pp.302-320, 1978.

[14] R.Gonzlez and M.Thomason: Syntactic Pattern Recognition. An Introduction. Addison-Wesley, 1978.

[15] X.D.Huang, Y.Ariki, M.A.Jack: Hidden Markov Models for Speech Recognition. Edinburgh U. Press. 1990.

[16] K.J.Lang: Random DFAs can be Approximately Learned from Sparse Uniform Examples. COLT92.

[17] K.Lari, S.J.Young: The Estimation of Stochastic context-free grammars using the Inside-Outside Algorithm. Comp. Speech and Language, 4, pp.35-36, 1990.

[18] K.Lari, S.J.Young: Applications of Stochastic Context-Free Grammars Using the Inside-Outside Algorithm. Comp. Speech and Language, 5, pp.237-257, 1991.

[19] E.Makinen: Remarks on the structural grammatical inference problem for context-free grammars. Inf. Proc. Letters 44, pp.125-127, 1992.

[20] L.Miclet: Regular Inference with a Tail-Clustering Method. IEEE Trans. SMC,10, pp.737-743. 1980.

[21] L.Miclet: Grammatical Inference. In Syntactic and Structural Pattern Recognition and applications. H.Bunke, A.Sanfeliu (eds.), pp.237-290. World Scientific, 1990.

[22] S.Muggleton: Induction of Regular Languages from Positive Examples. Tech. Rep, Turing Institute Research Memoranda, Glasgow. 1984.

[23] B.K.Natarajan.: Machine Learning. A theoretical approach. Morgan Kaufmann, 1991.

[24] J.Oncina: Aprendizaje de Lenguajes Regulares y Funciones Subsecuenciales. Phd diss. Universidad Politecnica de Valencia. 1991.

[25] J.Oncina, P.Garcia: Inferring Regular Languages in Polynomial Updated Time. In Pattern Recognition and Image Analysis. N.Perez de la Blanca, A.Sanfeliu and E.Vidal (eds). pp.49-61. World Scientific Pub, 1992.

[26] J.Oncina, P.Garcia, E.Vidal: Learning Subsequential Transducers for Pattern Recognition Interpretation Tasks. IEEE Trans. on PAMI, Vol.15, No.5, pp.448-458, May, 1993.

[27] J.Oncina: Inference of Probabilistic Automata. Tech. Rep. DSIC Polyt. Univ. of Valencia, 1993

[28] F.Pereira, Y.Schabes: Inside-Outside Reestimation from Partially Bracketed Corpora. 30 Annual Meeting of the ACL, pp.128-135, 1992.

[29] V.Radhakrishnan, G.Nagaraja: Inference of Regular Grammars via Skeletons. IEEE Trans. SMC, 17,6, 1987.

[30] V.Radhakrishnan, G.Nagaraja: Inference of Even Linear Grammars and its Applications to picture Description Languages. Pattern Recognition, 21,1, 55-62.

[31] H. Rulot, E.Vidal: Modeling (sub)string-length-based constraints through a Grammatical Inference Method, Devijver and Kittler, eds. Springer, Berlin 1987.

[32] Y. Sakakibara : Efficient Learning of Context-Free Grammars from Positive Structural Examples. Inf. and Comput. 97, pp.23-60, 1992.

[33] A.Stolke, S.Omohundro: Hidden Markov Model Induction by Bayesian Model Merging. In C.L.Giles, S.J.Hanson, and J.D.Cowan, eds., Advances in Neural Information Processing Systems 5, San Mateo, CA, Morgan Kaufman, 1993.

[34] Y.Takada: Grammatical Inference for Even Linear Languages Based on Control Sets. Inf. Proc. Letters, 28,4,pp.193-199, 1988.

[35] L.G.Valiant: A Theory of the learnable. Communications of the ACM, 27, 11, pp.1134-1142, 1984.

[36] E.Vidal, F.Casacuberta, P.Garcia: Syntactic Learning Techniques for Language Modeling and Acoustic-Phonetic Decoding. Speech Recognition and Coding: New Advances and Trends, J.Rubio and J.M.Lopez (eds.), Springer-Verlag, 1994.

[37] R.M.Wharton: Approximate Language Identification. Inf. and Control, 26, pp.236-255. 1974

Learning Morphology – Practice Makes Good

Alon Itai

Computer Science Department

Technion, Haifa, Israel

email: itai@cs.technion.ac.il

– Extended Abstract –

Abstract

A model for learning morphological transformations is given. The model is based upon Koskenniemi's Two Level Morphology model. It is shown that while the number of examples required for learning is polynomial, the computational problem associated with learning is intractable.

Learning homomorphisms is a simple special case of the general model. While a general method for learning homomorphisms is not known, it is shown that even if the target language is over a single letter alphabet, learning within the minimum number of examples is computationally intractable. If, however, additional examples are given, learning can be achieved in time polynomial in the size of the morphological transformation.

1 Introduction

In linguistics, morphology is the theory of the construction of words. Words are constructed from more basic units called *morphemes*. To construct a word the appropriate morphemes are concatenated then *morphological transformations* are applied to yield the final form. For example, in English the word *friendliness* is derived from the morphemes *friend*, *ly* and *ness*. A morphological transformation changes the morpheme *ly* to *li*.

English morphology is quite simple. However, other languages, such as Finnish and Hebrew, have very rich morphology. The richness can manifest itself in either the number and complexity of the morphemes involved in constructing a word (Finnish or Turkish), or the complexity of the transformations (Hebrew). We shall be concerned in the transformations, and more specifically in how they are learned.

In order to develop a theory for learning one must have a concrete model of the morphological process. We shall adopt the *Two Level Morphology* model suggested in 1983 by Koskenniemi, which has gained a lot of popularity and is the most widely accepted model for morphological transformations. The model is language independent, and permits an automatic generator and analyzer from language dependent transition rules. Koskenniemi constructed a analyzer and generator, KIMMO, and then specified the rules for Finnish

[10] and other languages [8] to obtain efficient and simple morphological tools. Several other authors used the same system for additional languages.

This approach has drawn criticism on two accounts: the computational complexity of the model [2, 7], and the appropriateness'for languages whose morphology is not of a concatenative nature [11]. Rather than entering this controversy we wish to examine the learning problems associated with the model.

According to Koskenniemi's Two Level Morphology model, words are constructed in two phases: first, one constructs the lexical level consisting of a sequence of stems and affixes then morphological transformations are applied. Koskenniemi modelled these transformations by a finite state transducer (see formal definitions in Section 2.1).

Assuming that the two level model is indeed an appropriate model of morphological transformations, we concentrate on the problem of learning the transducer.

Our learning model is the bounded error model of Littlestone [12] (see Section 2.2). We feel that in the context of learning a language it is more natural than, say, the PAC model [16], since normally we receive only positive examples, and a probabilistic distribution does not seem natural. Moreover, learning according to this model implies PAC learnability [13], and learning in the limit [1].

We show that the general problem of learning a transducer is computationally infeasible. However, even for the case that the transducer has a single state, and the output language has only one letter, we show that minimizing the number of errors is an NP-Complete problem. However, in this case, if we allow more errors, then we can learn such that the number of errors is linear in the "size" of the transducer. The computation time is polynomial in the number of errors. Thus the computational problem is hard only if we insist on minimum information. If we allow redundant information, then the task becomes manageable. We show how to learn a homomorphism in time that is polynomial in the size of the training sequence, however, the length of the training sequence depends on the length of the longest example, and the degree of the polynomial is equal to the size of the input alphabet.

A similar situation occurs for learning general transducers: under reasonable cryptographic assumptions, there is no polynomial time algorithm that learns transducers from polynomial length training sequences. Oncina et al. [14] show how to learn another variant of transducers, subsequential transducers, in the limit, and each error requires work that is polynomial in the length of the current training sequence.

The rest of the paper is organized as follows: Section 2 describes the linguistic and computational learning models. Section 3 discusses learning homomorphisms, Section 4 learning transducers, and finally Section 5 contains the conclusions and further research areas.

2 The Model

This section consists of two parts. The first describes the linguistic background, and the second the Computational Learning model.

2.1 The Two Level Model

Koskenniemi's two level model for morphology considers two representations of a word: the *lexical representation* consisting of a sequence of the morphemes that constitute the word, and the *surface representation* the written (or spoken) presentation. The relationship between these two presentations is governed by the *two level rules*. These rules may be used to transform the lexical representation to the surface representation, as well as to get the lexical representation from the surface one.

From a mathematical point of view, a lexical representation is a word over some finite alphabet Σ. Koskenniemi assumed that this representation can be constructed from a *lexicon* (or from several lexicons). In this paper we do not address the problem of this construction. We assume that the lexical representation is a word v over a finite alphabet Σ and that $v \in \Sigma^*$ is given. The surface representation is also a word over a (different) alphabet Γ.

The two level rules may be viewed as a finite state transducer [4], which is a generalization of a nondeterministic finite state acceptor. The transition function, δ, not only determines the next state, but also the output. Formally, a finite state transducer is a quintuple $M = (Q, \Sigma, \Gamma, \delta, q_0)$, where Q is a finite set of *states*; Σ and Γ are finite alphabets, called the input alphabet and output alphabet respectively; δ, the transition function, is a subset of $Q \times \Sigma \times \Gamma^* \times Q$, it may be viewed as a partial function from $Q \times \Sigma$ to subsets of $\Gamma^* \times Q$, i.e., if $(q, a, w, q') \in \delta$ then if M is in state $q \in Q$ and received input $a \in \Sigma$ it may produce output $w \in \Gamma^*$ and move to state $q' \in Q$; $q_0 \in Q$ is the *initial state*.

Given a word $v = c_1...c_n \in \Sigma^*$, M *transforms v to w* if there exits a sequence of states $s_0, ..., s_n$ and $w_1, ..., w_n \in \Gamma^*$ such that:

1. $s_0 = q_0$.

2. $(s_{i-1}, c_i, w_i, s_i) \in \delta$, (for $i = 1, ..., n$).

3. $w = w_1...w_n$ (the concatenation of all the outputs).

Note that since δ is nondeterministic, there may be inputs for which the transducer produces zero, one or more output words. The case that M produces no output corresponds to rejection by a finite state acceptor.

Example 1: *The following finite state transducer properly transforms the suffix LY to li when it occurs before the end of the word.*
$\Sigma = \{A, B, ..., Z, +, \$\}$.
$\Gamma = \{a, b, ..., z\}$.
$Q = \{q_0, q_1\}$

$\delta = \{(q_0, A, a, q_0), ..., (q_0, Z, z, q_0),$
$\quad (q_0, A, a, q_1), ..., (q_0, X, x, q_1), (q_0, Y, i, q_1), (q_0, Z, z, q_1),$
$\quad (q_0, \$, \wedge, q_2), (q_1, +, \wedge, q_0)\}$.

Take the lexical level word FRIEND+LY+NESS. *After D the output is* friend *and the transducer is in state q_1, the first + is therefore transformed to $\wedge$ and the transducer reverts to q_0. When seeing the Y, the transducer produces i and moves to q_1, as before, + is transformed to $\wedge$. (The transition after Y to q_0 involves transforming Y to y, but then*

there will be no transition for +, so there is no sequence that produces (*)friendlyness).
□

Koskonniemi described his system somewhat differently, and provided default rules for transforming the lexical level to the surface one. The current formulation is mathematically equivalent to his system, and generalizes his only in the respect that Koskonniemi has imposed the restriction that in δ the output consists of zero or one character, i.e., $w_i \in \Gamma \cup \{\Lambda\}$, where Λ denotes the empty word (the word of zero length). This restriction is natural for Finnish and simplifies the the implementation, but is unnatural for other languages (Hebrew [11] and Arabic). (In these languages, one sometimes has to insert vowels that do not exist in the lexical level. To implement these languages in KIMMO, the lexical level has to have a place-holder in every place that such a vowel can be inserted, and the transition rules have to erase them most of the time. The resultant system is redundant and unnatural.)

A finite state transducer is *deterministic* if $(q, a, w, p), (q, a, w', p') \in \delta$ implies that $w = w'$ and $p = p'$. A *homomorphism* is a deterministic finite state transducer which has only one state.

2.2 The Bounded Error Model

We now describe the learning model. Following Littlestone [12] we assume the following setting. A triple $L = (X, Y, \mathcal{F})$ is a *learning problem* if X and Y are sets and $\mathcal{F}$ a set of functions from X to Y. Learning is a game played by two agents, the *teacher* and the *student*. Initially, the teacher chooses a function $f \in \mathcal{F}$.

The game consists of an infinite number of rounds. In each round the teacher presents the student with an element $x \in X$, and the student responds with a hypothesis for $f(x)$. If the hypothesis is correct, the teacher indicates this, and otherwise, it provides $f(x)$. The goal of the teacher is to maximize the number of errors, and that of the student to minimize them.

Let b be a natural number, and $L = (X, Y, \mathcal{F})$ a learning problem. L can be *learned within b errors*, if there exists an algorithm such that for every $f \in \mathcal{F}$ and every training sequence $x_1, x_2, ... \in X$ when presented with $x_1, x_2, ...$, if the student applies the algorithm it will make at most b errors.

To address issues of computational complexity, we partition $\mathcal{F}$ into an infinite sequence of disjoint sets, i.e., $\mathcal{F} = \bigcup_n \mathcal{F}_n$. Thus, each target function $f \in \mathcal{F}$ belongs to a distinct $\mathcal{F}_n$. We allow the number of errors b to be a function of n, i.e., $b(\cdot)$ is an integer function. Then $\mathcal{F}$ can be *learned with bounded error $b(\cdot)$* if for all n, $\mathcal{F}_n$ can be learned within $b(n)$ errors. Learning is *polynomial* if $b(\cdot)$ is bounded by a polynomial. Learning is *polynomial time* if the time complexity of the student's algorithm, is also bounded by a polynomial in the bit length of the training sequence. Note that in this definition $b(n)$, the number of examples of the training sequence E, is polynomial in n, but $||E||$ the number of bits of E is not necessarily bounded by a polynomial of n. The reason for this definition is that the teacher might provide a very long example, then just reading it might take super-polynomial time.

In our setting, the set X is the lexical level, and Y the surface level. Thus, the student receives the surface level, and has to "guess" the lexical level. This models the situation where a child understands the lexical level from the context, and tries to generate the surface level. Correct transformations are reinforced, while erroneous ones are corrected. In the more realistic context of unsupervised learning (no explicit corrections), the student would eventually hear the correct form, and thus receive the correction.

The partition of $\mathcal{F}$ can be done several ways, either according to the number of states of the transducer, or according to the size of its descriptions (its Kolmogorov complexity). We shall indicate the partition when appropriate.

3   Learning Homomorphisms

In Section 4 we'll show that learning a general transducer is hard. We first consider a simple case where the transducer is deterministic and consists of a single state. In this case the transducer is a homomorphism.

3.1   A Polynomial Algorithm for $|\Gamma| = 1$.

We first consider the simple case that the output alphabet Γ consists of a single letter, i.e., $\Sigma = \{c_1, c_2, ..., c_n\}$, $\Gamma = \{a\}$.

In this case, we can learn within n errors. Let $x_i = |h(c_i)|$ and $n_i(v)$ be the number of occurrences of c_i in v. Every example $(v_j, h(v_j))$ induces an equation in the unknowns $x_1, ..., x_n$:

$$\sum_{i=1}^{n} n_i(v_j)x_i = |h(v_j)|.$$

Thus, once we have n linearly independent equations, we can compute the x_i's.

Consider the kth round. If the equation associated with v_k is linearly dependent on those of $v_1, ..., v_{k-1}$, then we can calculate $h(v_k)$ from the available data, without introducing any additional errors. Otherwise, we might introduce an error, but this case can occur at most n times, since there can be at most n linearly independent equations in n unknowns. The computation time is that of solving a system of linear equations – $O(n^3 + ||E||)$, where $||E||$ is the bit length of the training sequence E.

Also n is a lower bound on the number of errors: For $i = 1, ..., n$, let $v_i = c_i$. There is no way to predict $h(v_i)$ before seeing it.

3.2   Learning within the Minimum Number of Errors

Consider the problem of learning a homomorphism. Sometimes after N rounds the student has enough information to avoid any further errors. However, the computational effort might be prohibitive.

Let TWO HOMOMORPHISMS be the following decision problem:
INPUT: $(v_1, w_1), ..., (v_N, w_N) \in \Sigma^* \times \Gamma^*$, $v_{N+1} \in \Sigma^*$.
QUESTION: Do there exist homomorphisms h_1, h_2, such that for $i = 1, ..., N$, $h_1(v_i) = h_2(v_i) = w_i$, and $h_1(v_{N+1}) \neq h_2(v_{N+1})$.

Theorem 1: *TWO HOMOMORPHISMS is NP-Complete, even if Γ consists of a single letter.*

Proof: We show a reduction from 3-Exact Cover (3XC):

INPUT: Sets $S_1, ..., S_m \subseteq \{1, ..., 3n\}$, each set S_i has cardinality 3.

QUESTION: Does there exist a subset of indices $I \subseteq \{1, ..., n\}$, such that every element is covered exactly once by $\bigcup_{i \in I} S_i$, i.e., for all $j \in \{1, ..., 3n\}$ there exist a unique $i \in I$ for which $j \in S_i$.

Given an instance of 3XC, we construct an instance of TWO HOMOMORPHISM as follows: $\Sigma = \{c_0, c_1, ..., c_n\}$, $\Gamma = \{a\}$. For $j = 1, ..., 3n$ let $w_j = a$, and if $S_{j_1} S_{j_2} ... S_{j_{k_i}}$ are all the sets that contain j then $v_j = c_0 c_{j_1} c_{j_2} ... c_{j_{k_i}}$. Finally, let $v_{3n+1} = c_0$.

Let $I = \{i_1, ..., i_n\}$ be a solution to 3XC. Then define h_1, as follows

$$h_1(c_i) = \begin{cases} a & \text{if } i \in I \\ \wedge & \text{otherwise.} \end{cases}$$

(In particular $h_1(c_0) = \wedge$.) The assumption that every j is covered by exactly one $S_i, i \in I$, implies that $h_1(v_j) = a = w_j$. Thus h_1 satisfies all the $N = 3n$ constraints $h(v_j) = a$.

Define h_2:

$$h_2(c_i) = \begin{cases} a & \text{if } i = 0 \\ \wedge & \text{otherwise.} \end{cases}$$

However, $h_1(c_0) = \wedge \neq a = h_2(c_0)$. Thus, h_1 and h_2 differ on v_{N+1}.

In the other direction: Obviously, h_2, as defined above, satisfies all the constriants. Let h_1 be another homomorphism that satisfies the constraints. Since c_0 appears in all the v_i's and $h(v_i) = a$ ($i \leq 3n$), $|h_1(c_0)| \leq 1$. Thus, since $h_1(c_0) \neq h_2(c_0)$, we must have $h_1(c_0) = \wedge$.

Define $I = \{i : h_1(c_i) \neq \wedge\}$. Since for all $j \leq 3n$, $h_1(v_j) = a$, for each j, v_j contains a letter c_{i_j} ($i_j \geq 1$) for which $h_1(c_{i_j}) = a$. Thus, $i_j \in I$. Also, we cannot have $j \in S_i, S_{i'}$ for distinct $i, i' \in I$, since then $h_1(v_j)$ would contain at least two a's.   □

Thus if there is only one homomorphism, the student need not make an error after the first N rounds. And if there is more than one homomorphism, an adversary may force the student to make an error in round $N + 1$. However, the student must solve an NP-complete problem in order to know that there is only one answer.

3.3   Discussion

The proofs of Sections 3.1 and 3.2 seem to contradict each other. The first states that learning requires polynomial time, and the second that learning a homomorphism is NP-Complete. The difference is that the positive result allows more examples than necessary from an Information Theoretic point of view, while the negative result holds only when we insist on the minimum number of examples. Thus, if we allow more examples, learning becomes feasible, i.e., practice makes good.

3.4   Larger Output Alphabets

When $|\Gamma| = 1$ every error introduced a new independent linear equation. This does not hold for larger output alphabets.

Example 2: *Consider the training sequence* $((c_1c_2, ababab), (c_2c_1, ababab))$. *Both examples yield the the same equation:* $x_1 + x_2 = 6$. *There are 7 homomorphisms consistent with the first example, (define* h_i *by* $|h_i(c_1)| = i$, $i = 0, \ldots 6$*) and four homomorphism consistent with the second one (*h_i, $i = 0, 2, 4, 6$.*) Thus, in this training sequence we might make two errors, and still not find* h.

Thus this case seems more difficult, and we have not found a bounded error learning algorithm. We will resort to finding algorithms that are polynomial in the size of the training sequence but exponential in the size of the input alphabet.

Let $|\Gamma| \geq 1$ and let n be the size of the input alphabet Σ. It is trivial to learn a homomorphism within n errors if in every example (v_j, w_j), v_j consists of a single letter. Therefore, we shall consider the the number of examples in the training sequence as a function of the length (in characters) of the *longest* example. A learning algorithm A is *example sensitive* if there exists a function $f(\cdot)$ such that if given r examples the longest of which is of length k and $r \geq f(k)$, then A learns. Learning is polynomial if f is a polynomial. As before, the learning algorithm is polynomial time if the time complexity is bounded by a polynomial in the (number of bits of the) training sequence. This definition is weaker than the one we had before, since now the number of errors depends on the size of the examples, while beforehand the number of errors depended only on the parameter n, (in this case the size of the input alphabet Σ).

In this section we show an example sensitive algorithm to learn homomorphisms, within $O(k^n)$ errors, the time complexity is polynomial in $\|E\| k^n$, where $\|E\|$ is the bit complexity of the training sequence. For fixed sized alphabets this learning algorithm is polynomial in the size of the training sequence.

In the course of the learning process, the student is presented with a training sequence $(v_1, w_1), (v_2, w_2), \ldots$. Let us order the letters of $\Sigma = \{c_1, \ldots, c_n\}$ by their order of occurrence in $v_1 v_2 v_3 \ldots$; i.e., c_1 appeared first, c_2 second etc. Let (v_{q_i}, w_{q_i}) be the first example containing c_i, and $\ell_i = |w_{q_i}|/n_i(v_{q_i})$. (Recall that $n_i(v)$ denotes the number of occurrences of c_i in v.) Obviously, $0 \leq |h(v_{c_i})| \leq \ell_i$. And hence the number of homomorphisms consistent with $E_i = ((v_1, w_1), \ldots, (v_{q_i}, w_{q_i}))$ is at most $L = \prod_{i=1}^{n}(1 + \ell_i)$. The hypothesis of our algorithm is the homomorphism consistent with all the examples seen so far and whose lengths are lexicographically minimum, i.e., the consistent homomorphism for which $(|h(c_1)|, |h(c_2)|, \ldots, |h(c_i)|)$ is lexicographically minimum.

Since a hypothesis is updated only on making an error or seeing a new letter, the number of errors is also bounded by L. Consequently, if k is the length of the longest example v_q, then the number of errors is $b \leq L \leq (1 + k)^n = O(k^n)$.

A straightforward implementation of the above ideas requires $O(\|E\|^2 k^n)$ time. However, with suitible data structures we illustrate how this can be done in $O(\|E\| k^n)$ time.

A *length vector* is a sequence of length $i \leq n$ of nonnegative integers. Given a finite training sequence, $E = ((v_1, w_1), \ldots (v_q, w_q))$ over $\{c_1, \ldots, c_i\} \subseteq \Sigma$, a length vector $\lambda^i = (\lambda_1, \ldots, \lambda_i)$ is *consistent* with E if there exists a homomorphism h consistent with E such that $|h(c_j)| = \lambda_j$, $(j = 1, \ldots, i)$. We can check if a length vector λ^i is consistent with a training sequence E in $O(\|E\|)$ time.

During the course of the algorithm we check length vectors for consistency. However, not all vectors need be checked separately, since if $\lambda^i = (\lambda_1, \ldots, \lambda_i)$ is inconsistent then for all $j \geq i$ so is $\lambda^j = (\lambda_1, \ldots, \lambda_j)$. Thus we need not keep inconsistent length vectors that have a prefix which is also inconsistent. This observation suggests that we keep the inconsistent length vector in a *trie*. In our context, a trie is a labelled tree of depth $\leq n$. Its root is labelled by the empty word, all vertices at depth i are labelled with a value for λ_i. Thus a vertex of depth $i-1$ can have at most $1 + \ell_i$ children, labelled $0, ..., \ell_i$, (in the sequal we will bound the maximum degree by ℓ_i). Therefore, each path from the root to a leaf at level i spells out an inconsistent length vector of length i (see Figure 1 (a)).

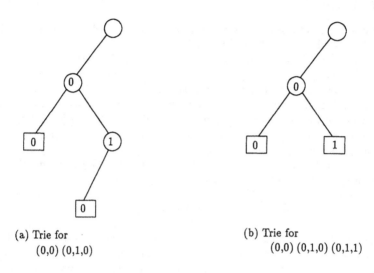

(a) Trie for
(0,0) (0,1,0)

(b) Trie for
(0,0) (0,1,0) (0,1,1)

Figure 1: Tries with upper bounds: $\ell_1 = 1$, $\ell_2 = 2$, $\ell_3 = 1$.

Instead of looking for a homomorphism directly, we look for a consistent length vector. Thus when we find that a length vector $\lambda = (\lambda_1, ..., \lambda_i)$ has become inconsistent, we insert it into the trie. Let $\pi = (\lambda_1, ..., \lambda_{i-1})$ be the parent of λ. If π has $1 + \ell_{i-1}$ children, then π itself is inconsistent, so we can remove all its children and turn π into a leaf (see Figure 1 (b)). Otherwise, we check $\lambda' = (\lambda_1, ..., 1 + \lambda_i)$ for consistency.

This process ensures that every length vector considered is either inconsistent or corresponds to the lexicographically minimum consistent homomorphism. Since checking whether a length vector is consistent requires at most time proportional to $O(\|E\|)$, and there are at most L infeasible length vectors, the entire process requires $O(\|E\|L) = O(\|E\|k^n)$ time.

4   Learning Transducers

In general, learning transducers is difficult, since it generalizes learning finite state machines.

The following problem has been shown by Gold [6], (see also [5, AL8]) to be NP-complete:

MINIMUM INFERRED FINITE STATE AUTOMATON
INSTANCE: Finite alphabet Σ, two finite subsets $S, T \subseteq \Sigma^*$, positive integer K.
QUESTION: Is there a K-state deterministic finite automaton A that recognizes a language $L \subseteq \Sigma^*$ such that $S \subseteq L$ and $T \subseteq \Sigma^* - L$?

Theorem 2: *The problem of learning a transducer from m positive and negative examples is NP-Complete.*

Since the problem is obviously in NP, it suffices to show a reduction from MINIMUM INFERRED FINITE STATE AUTOMATON.

Let $+, -, @ \notin \Sigma$, $\Sigma' = \Sigma \cup \{@\}$ and $\Gamma = \Sigma \cup \{+, -\}$. For each $s \in S$ give the pair $(s@, s+)$, and every in $t \in T$ the pair $(t@, t-)$, i.e., @ is transformed to either $+$ or $-$ depending on whether the preceding word belongs to L.

Let $M_R = (Q, \Sigma, \delta_R, q_0, F)$ be a finite state machine that accepts all words of S and rejects all words of T. We construct a finite state transducer $M_T = (Q, \Sigma', \Gamma, \delta_T, q_0)$. We define δ_T as follows: for every triple $(q, a, q') \in \delta_R$, δ_T contains the quadruple (q, a, q', a). In addition δ_T contains the quadruples $(q, @, q, +)$ for all $q \in F$ and $(q, @, q, -)$ for $q \notin F$. Both M_R and M_T have the same number of states, and M_T performs the correct transformation, iff M_R accepts S and rejects T.

The reverse construction of M_R from M_T is similar. Thus finding a K state transducer is equivalent to finding a K state finite state machine. □

We can use the above construction to show that learning transducers is difficult in the following sense: Let R_n be the set of regular languages accepted by n-state finite automata. Since the VC-dimension of R_n is polynomial [3], then from an information theoretic point of view, R_n can be PAC-learned within polynomially many examples.

Kearns and Valiant [9] have shown that subject to reasonable cryptographic assumptions, there exist learning problems that cannot be learned in polynomial time, even if randomized algorithms are allowed.

Warmuth and Pitt [15] have shown that regular languages are the most hard to learn. Thus, subject to the same cryptographic assumptions, there does not exist an algorithm to learn a the language of an arbitrary n-state finite automaton whose computation time is polynomial in n. This results holds even if we allow an arbitrary number of examples.

The transformation used in the previous theorem shows that learning the transformation of a transducer is just as hard. Thus there probably is no polynomial time algorithm to PAC-learn the transformation of a transducer. Since bounded error learning implies PAC learning [13], there is no polynomial time algorithm to learn transducers in the bounded error model.

5 Conclusions

We have shown a model to discuss the problem of learning morphology. However, the general model (transducers) is computationally intractable. We therefore considered a special case, homomorphisms into a single letter alphabet. In this context we exhibited a tradeoff between computational time and the number of examples.

More work should be done on learning homomorphisms into larger alphabets. More importantly, it would be interesting to find natural linguistic limitations of the type of morphological transformations such that the resultant learning problem would become tractable.

References

[1] Angluin, D. and C. Smith, "Inductive inference: theory and methods". Comput. Surveys, 15, 237-269, (1983)

[2] Barton, G. E., "Computational complexity in two-level morphology". ACL '86, 53-59.

[3] Blumer A., A. Ehrenfeucht, D. Haussler and M. Warmuth, *Learnability and the Vapnik-Chervonenkis dimension*, J. ACM, 36(4), 929-965, (1989).

[4] Harrison, M. A., *Introduction to Formal Language Theory*, Addison-Wesley, 1978.

[5] M.R. Garey and D.S. Johnson, *Computers and Intractability, A Guide to the Theory of NP-Completeness*, W.H. Freeman and Company, (1979).

[6] Gold, E. M., "Complexity of automaton identification from given data". Information and Control, 37, 302-320, (1978).

[7] Koskenniemi, K. and K. W. Church. "Complexity, Two-level morphology, and Finnish". COLING '88.

[8] Kataja, L., and K. Koskenniemi, "Finite-state description of Semitic morphology: A case study of Ancient Akkadian".

[9] Kearns, M., and L. Valiant, "Cryptographic limitations on learning Boolean formulae and finite automata". Proc. 21st STPC, 433-444, (1989).

[10] Koskenniemi, K., "Two-level morphology: A general computational model for word-form recognition and production". Publication No. 11, University of Helsinki, Dept. of General Linguistics, Hallituskata 11-33, SF-00100 Helsinki 10, Finland.

[11] A. Itai, A. Lavie, U. Ornan and M. Rimon, "On the applicability of Two Level morphology to the inflection of Hebrew verbs". ALLC June 1988, Jerusalem, (TR 513, CS Department Technion).

[12] Littlestone, N., "Learning quickly when irrelevant attributes abound: a new linear threshold algorithm". Machine Learning 2, 285-318, (1987).

[13] Littlestone, N., "Mistake bounds and logarithmic linear-threshold learning algorithms", Ph.D. Thesis, U.C. Santa Cruz, March 1989.

[14] Oncina, J., P.García, and E. Vidal, Learning subsequential transducers for pattern recognition interpretation tasks". IEEE Trans. Pattern Anal. and Machine Intell., 15, 448-458, (1993)

[15] Pitt, L., and M. K. Warmuth, "Reduction among prediction problems: on the difficulty of predicting automata". Proc. of 3rd annual structure in complexity theory, (1988).

[16] Valiant L.G., *A Theory of the Learnable*, Comm. ACM, 27(11), 1134-42, (1984).

A Hierarchy of Language Families Learnable by Regular Language Learners

Yuji Takada

Institute for Social Information Science (ISIS)
FUJITSU LABORATORIES LTD.
140 Miyamoto, Numazu-shi, Shizuoka 410-03, JAPAN

Abstract

We shall establish the existence of a hierarchy of language families, in which the learning problem for each family is reduced to the learning problem for regular languages. Thus this boosts the learnability of learning algorithms for regular languages.

Keywords: Learning from examples, hierarchy of language families, even linear grammars, regular languages, control sets.

1 Introduction

In this paper, we shall establish the existence of a hierarchy of language families, in which the learning problem for each family is reduced to the learning problem for regular languages. The hierarchy starts with the family of regular languages and each family in it is properly contained in the family of context-sensitive languages and has a nontrivial language such as $\{a_1^n a_2^n \cdots a_{2k}^n \mid n \geq 0\}$, where k is a nonnegative integer and each a_i is a symbol. Thus this boosts the learnability of learning algorithms for regular languages such as [Ang87] and [OG92].

The hierarchy is defined inductively by controlling certain type of even linear grammars with languages in one family to yield languages in the next larger family. An even linear grammar, proposed by Amar and Putzolu [AP64], is a linear grammar whose nonterminal productions are of the form $A \rightarrow uBv$ such that the length of u is the same as the one of v, where u, v are terminal strings and A, B are nonterminals. An even linear language is the language generated by an even linear grammar. The family of even linear languages properly contains the family of regular languages and is properly contained in the family of linear languages.

Radhakrishnan and Nagaraja [RN88] have presented a learning algorithm for even linear grammars and its application to picture description languages. We have shown in [Tak88] that the problem of learning even linear languages is reduced to the problem of learning regular languages; we have given an algorithm that reduces the learning problem for even linear languages to the one for regular languages. This makes any algorithm for regular languages applicable to learning even linear languages. Furthermore, the correctness and time complexity of a learning algorithm for even linear languages are immediately obtained. In this paper, we shall show that these also hold for the hierarchy.

2 Preliminaries

Let Σ denote an alphabet and Σ^* denote the set of all strings over Σ including the null string λ. A *language* is a subset of Σ^*. A language is called *regular* if it is accepted by a finite automaton. $lg(u)$ denotes the length of a string u.

For any two sets A and B, $A \subset B$ means that A is a *proper* subset of B. Then $A \subseteq B$ means that $A \subset B$ or $A = B$.

An *even linear grammar*, abbreviated *ELG*, is a four-tuple $G = (N, \Sigma, \Pi, S)$. N is a finite nonempty set of *nonterminals*. Π is a finite nonempty set of *productions*; each production in Π is of the form

$$\pi_n : A \rightarrow uBv \quad \text{or} \quad \pi_t : A \rightarrow w,$$

where $A, B \in N$, $u, v, w \in \Sigma^*$, and $lg(u) = lg(v)$. Each production is labeled by its unique label symbol and therefore uniquely referred with its label. S is a special nonterminal called the *start symbol*. We assume that N, Σ, and Π are disjoint.

Let $G = (N, \Sigma, \Pi, S)$ be an *ELG*. We write $x \xRightarrow[G]{\pi} y$ to mean that y is derived from x using the production π. Let $x_0, x_1, \ldots, x_n$ be strings over $N \cup \Sigma$. If

$$x_0 \xRightarrow[G]{\pi_1} x_1, \ x_1 \xRightarrow[G]{\pi_2} x_2, \ \ldots, \ x_{n-1} \xRightarrow[G]{\pi_n} x_n,$$

then we denote $x_0 \xRightarrow[G]{\alpha} x_n$, where $\alpha = \pi_1 \pi_2 \cdots \pi_n$, that is called a *derivation from x_0 to x_n with the associate word α in G*. The *language generated by G* is the set

$$L(G) = \{w \mid S \xRightarrow[G]{\alpha} w \text{ and } w \in \Sigma^*\}$$

and the *associate language of G* is the set

$$A(G) = \{\alpha \mid S \xRightarrow[G]{\alpha} w \text{ and } w \in \Sigma^*\}.$$

An *even linear language* is the language generated by an *ELG*.

Definition 2.1 Let $G = (N, \Sigma, \Pi, S)$ be an *ELG* over Σ. A subset C of Π^* is called a *control set on G* and

$$L(G, C) = \{w \in \Sigma^* \mid S \xRightarrow[G]{\alpha} w \text{ and } \alpha \in C\}$$

is called the *language generated by G with the control set C*.

Definition 2.2 A *universal ELG* over an alphabet Σ is an *ELG* $U = (\{S\}, \Sigma, \Psi, S)$ such that Ψ consists of the following productions;

$$\Psi = \{\psi_n : S \rightarrow aSb \mid a, b \in \Sigma\} \cup \{\psi_t : S \rightarrow a \mid a \in \Sigma\} \cup \{\psi_\lambda : S \rightarrow \lambda\}.$$

Remark 2.3 For any alphabet Σ, a universal ELG U has the following properties;

1. $L(U) = \Sigma^*$,

2. U is unique up to renaming of the start symbol,

3. if the cardinality of Σ is k then U has $k^2 + k + 1$ number of productions,

4. U is unambiguous, that is, for any $w \in \Sigma^*$, $S \xRightarrow[U]{\alpha} w$ and $S \xRightarrow[U]{\beta} w$ imply $\alpha = \beta$.

The following is the central definition of this paper.

Definition 2.4 Let $\mathbf{U}$ denote the collection of all universal ELGs and $\mathcal{R}$ denote the family of regular languages. Define $\mathcal{L}_i$ for any integer $i \geq 0$ inductively as follows

$$\mathcal{L}_0 = \mathcal{R}$$
$$\mathcal{L}_i = \{L(U, C) \,|\, U \in \mathbf{U} \text{ and } C \in \mathcal{L}_{i-1}\} \quad \text{for any integer } i \geq 1.$$

By Remark 2.3, for any alphabet, a universal ELG is unique up to renaming of the start symbol. Therefore, given an integer $i \geq 1$ and an alphabet Σ, we have a unique sequence of universal ELGs $U_1, U_2, \ldots, U_i$, where $U_j = (\{S\}, \Psi_{j-1}, \Psi_j, S)$ for any j $(1 \leq j \leq i)$ with $\Psi_0 = \Sigma$, and with a regular language R over Ψ_i, these $U_1, U_2, \ldots, U_i$ specify exactly one language $L(U_1, L(U_2, \ldots, L(U_i, R) \ldots))$ in $\mathcal{L}_i$.

3 Hierarchy

In this section, we shall prove the existence of the hierarchy of language families.

Lemma 3.1 $\mathcal{L}_0 \subset \mathcal{L}_1$.

Proof. We have shown in [Tak92] that $\mathcal{L}_1$ is the family of even linear languages, that properly contains the family of regular languages as shown in [AP64]. $\square$

Lemma 3.2 $\mathcal{L}_{i-1} \subseteq \mathcal{L}_i$ for each integer $i \geq 1$.

Proof. We prove this by induction on i. Lemma 3.1 establishes the base of the induction. Assume that the assertion is true for $j \geq 1$. Let $L \in \mathcal{L}_j$. Then there exist $U \in \mathbf{U}$ and $C \in \mathcal{L}_{j-1}$ such that $L = L(U, C)$ holds. By the inductive hypothesis, $C \in \mathcal{L}_j$ and therefore $L \in \mathcal{L}_{j+1}$. $\square$

Lemma 3.3 *For each integer $i \geq 1$ and any language $L \in \mathcal{L}_i$, there exists C in $\mathcal{L}_{i-1}$ such that $L = L(U, C)$ and $C \subseteq A(U)$ for a universal ELG U.*

Proof. [Tak92] has shown the case $i = 1$. Suppose that $i \geq 2$ and $L = L(U_1, C')$ for $C' \in \mathcal{L}_{i-1}$. Let $U_2, U_3, \ldots, U_i$ be universal ELGs and R be a regular language such that $C' = L(U_2, L(U_3, \ldots, L(U_i, R) \ldots))$. Since $A(U_1)$ is regular, $A(U_1)$ is in $\mathcal{L}_{i-1}$ by Lemma 3.2. Then there exists a regular language $R_{A(U_1)}$ such that

$$A(U_1) = L(U_2, L(U_3, \ldots, L(U_i, R_{A(U_1)}) \ldots))$$

holds. Let $R' = R \cap R_{A(U_1)}$ and $C = L(U_2, L(U_3, \ldots, L(U_i, R') \ldots))$. Since each U_j and U_1 are unambiguous by Remark 2.3, $C \subseteq A(U_1)$ and $L = L(U_1, C)$. $\square$

Lemma 3.4 *For each integer $i \geq 1$, $\mathcal{L}_i$ is contained in the family of context-sensitive languages.*

Proof. In the case $i = 1$, $\mathcal{L}_i$ is the family of even linear languages and [Tak88] establishes the base of the induction.

Assume that the assertion holds for any integer $j \geq 1$. Let $U = (\{S\}, \Sigma, \Psi, S)$ be a universal ELG and $G = (N, \Psi, \Pi, S_G)$ be a context-sensitive grammar that generates $C \in \mathcal{L}_j$. Define the context-sensitive grammar $G' = (N \cup \Psi \cup \{S, S_G, S_{G'}\}, \Sigma, \Pi', S_{G'})$, where Π' is defined as follows;

$S_{G'} \to SS_G$ is in Π',

$u \to v$ is in Π' if $u \to v$ is in Π,

$a\psi \to \psi a$ is in Π' if $a \in \Sigma$ and $\psi \in \Psi$,

$S\psi_n \to aSb$ is in Π' if $\psi_n : S \to aSb$ is in Ψ,

$S\psi_1\psi_2\psi_t \to a_1a_2cb_2b_1$ is in Π' if $\psi_1\psi_2\psi_t$ is derived from $A \in N$ in G
                                         for $\psi_1 : S \to a_1Sb_1$, $\psi_2 : S \to a_2Sb_2$,
                                         and $\psi_t : S \to c$ in Ψ,

$S_{G'} \to acb$ is in Π' if $\psi_n\psi_t$ is generated in G
                                         for $\psi_n : S \to aSb$ and $\psi_t : S \to c$ in Ψ,

$S_{G'} \to c$ is in Π' if ψ_t is generated in G for $\psi_t : S \to c$ in Ψ.

It is not hard to see that for any $w \in \Sigma^*$, $w \in L(U, C)$ if and only if w is generated in $L(G')$; by using productions of type $a\psi \to \psi a$, derivations in U with C can be simulated by G' and derivations in G' can be arranged into ones in U with C. Hence $L(U, C)$ is context-sensitive and this completes the proof. □

Definition 3.5 For each integer $i \geq 1$, let

$$L_i^e = \{b_1a^nb_2a^n \cdots a^nb_{2^i+1} \mid n \geq 0\}.$$

That is,

$$
\begin{aligned}
L_1^e &= \{b_1a^nb_2a^nb_3 \mid n \geq 0\} \\
L_2^e &= \{b_1a^nb_2a^nb_3a^nb_4a^nb_5 \mid n \geq 0\} \\
L_3^e &= \{b_1a^nb_2a^nb_3a^nb_4a^nb_5a^nb_6a^nb_7a^nb_8a^nb_9 \mid n \geq 0\} \\
&\vdots \quad \vdots
\end{aligned}
$$

Lemma 3.6 $L_i^e \in \mathcal{L}_i$ for each integer $i \geq 1$.

Proof. Let $U_i = (\{S\}, \Sigma_i, \Psi_i, S)$ be a universal ELG where

$$\Sigma_i = \{a, b_1, b_2, \ldots, b_{2^i+1}\}$$

$$
\begin{aligned}
\Psi_i \supset \quad & \{b_j : S \to b_jSb_{2^i+2-j} \mid 1 \leq j \leq i\} \\
& \cup \ \{b_{2^{i-1}+1} : S \to b_{2^{i-1}+1}\} \\
& \cup \ \{a : S \to aSa\}.
\end{aligned}
$$

Let $R = \{b_1 a^n b_3 \mid n \geq 0\}$. Then clearly $L_1 = (U_1, R) = L_1^e = \{b_1 a^n b_2 a^n b_3 \mid n \geq 0\}$.

Inductively assume that $L_j^e \in \mathcal{L}_j$ for any integer $j \geq 1$. Then it is easy to verify that $L(U_j, L_j^e) = L_{j+1}^e$. Hence $L_{j+1}^e \in \mathcal{L}_{j+1}$. $\square$

The following lemma is easily obtained by modifying the result in [Kha74].

Lemma 3.7 *For each integer $i \geq 1$, if $L \in \mathcal{L}_i$, there exists positive integers p, q depending on L such that if $z \in L$ and $lg(z) > p$ then*

$$z = \prod_{j=1}^{2^{i-1}} u_j v_j w_j x_j y_j, \quad \prod_{j=1}^{2^{i-1}} v_j x_j \neq \lambda, \quad lg(\prod_{j=1}^{2^{i-1}} v_j w_j x_j) < q,$$

and for any integer $k \geq 0$

$$z_k = \prod_{j=1}^{2^{i-1}} u_j v_j^k w_j x_j^k y_j$$

is an element of L, where $\prod$ denotes concatenation.

Proof. Since $\mathcal{L}_1$ is the family of even linear languages, a subfamily of context-free languages, the base of the induction is easily shown.

Inductively assume that the assertion holds for $l \geq 1$. Let $L = L(U, C)$ be in $\mathcal{L}_l$. By Lemma 3.3, we assume that $C \subseteq A(U)$. Let p_l and q_l be natural numbers associated with the inductive hypothesis for C. Choose $p_{l+1} > 3p_l$ and $q_{l+1} > 3q_l$. Let $z \in L(U, C)$ such that $lg(z) > p_{l+1}$. Then $S \xRightarrow[U]{\alpha} z$ and $\alpha \in C$. Since $lg(z) > p_{l+1}$, we have

$$lg(\alpha) \geq \frac{lg(z)}{3} > \frac{p_{l+1}}{3} > \frac{3p_l}{3} = p_l.$$

Hence, by the inductive hypothesis for C,

$$\alpha = \prod_{j=1}^{2^{l-1}} \mu_j \nu_j \omega_j \chi_j \varphi_j, \quad \prod_{j=1}^{2^{l-1}} \nu_j \chi_j \neq \lambda, \quad lg(\prod_{j=1}^{2^{l-1}} \nu_j \omega_j \chi_j) < q_l,$$

and for any integer $k \geq 0$

$$\alpha_k = \prod_{j=1}^{2^{l-1}} \mu_j \nu_j^k \omega_j \chi_j^k \varphi_j$$

is an element of C. Thus we have

$$S \quad \xRightarrow[U]{\mu_1 \nu_1 \omega_1 \chi_1 \varphi_1} \quad s_1 S t_1$$

$$\xRightarrow[U]{\mu_2 \nu_2 \omega_2 \chi_2 \varphi_2} \quad s_1 s_2 S t_2 t_1$$

$$\vdots$$

$$\xRightarrow[U]{\mu_{2^{l-1}} \nu_{2^{l-1}} \omega_{2^{l-1}} \chi_{2^{l-1}} \varphi_{2^{l-1}}} \quad s_1 s_2 \cdots s_{2^{l-1}} t_{2^{l-1}} \cdots t_2 t_1.$$

Now expanding further each indicated segment of the above derivation, we have

$$S_{r-1} \xrightarrow[U]{\mu_r} s_{1,r} S_r t_{1,r}$$

$$\xrightarrow[U]{\nu_r} s_{1,r} s_{2,r} S_r t_{2,r} t_{1,r}$$

$$\xrightarrow[U]{\omega_r} s_{1,r} s_{2,r} s_{3,r} S_r t_{3,r} t_{2,r} t_{1,r}$$

$$\xrightarrow[U]{\chi_r} s_{1,r} s_{2,r} s_{3,r} s_{4,r} S_r t_{4,r} t_{3,r} t_{2,r} t_{1,r}$$

$$\xrightarrow[U]{\varphi_r} s_{1,r} s_{2,r} s_{3,r} s_{4,r} s_{5,r} S_r t_{5,r} t_{4,r} t_{3,r} t_{2,r} t_{1,r}$$

$$= s_r S_r t_r,$$

for all $r = 1, \ldots, 2^{l-1}$, where it is understood that $S_{2^{l-1}} = \lambda$ or $S_r = S$ otherwise.

Now since $C \subseteq A(U)$, every associate word in C derives an element in $L(U, C)$. Hence when ν_r and χ_r iterate we still have strings in $L(U, C)$. Since U is a universal ELG, implying the existence of the single nonterminal S in each sentential form (except the last), this allows the derivations to proceed after iteration as they did before iteration. Thus we conclude

$$z = (\prod_{r=1}^{2^{l-1}} s_{1,r} s_{2,r} s_{3,r} s_{4,r} s_{5,r})(\prod_{r'=0}^{2^{l-1}-1} t_{5,2^{l-1}-r'} t_{4,2^{l-1}-r'} t_{3,2^{l-1}-r'} t_{2,2^{l-1}-r'} t_{1,2^{l-1}-r'})$$

and because α_k is in $C \subseteq A(U)$,

$$z_k = (\prod_{r=1}^{2^{l-1}} s_{1,r} s_{2,r}^k s_{3,r} s_{4,r}^k s_{5,r})(\prod_{r'=0}^{2^{l-1}-1} t_{5,2^{l-1}-r'} t_{4,2^{l-1}-r'}^k t_{3,2^{l-1}-r'} t_{2,2^{l-1}-r'}^k t_{1,2^{l-1}-r'})$$

is in $L(U, C)$ for all $k \geq 0$.

Since $\prod_{j=1}^{2^{l-1}} \nu_j \chi_j \neq \lambda$ and since U has no rule of the form $S \to S$, it immediately follows

$$(\prod_{r=1}^{2^{l-1}} s_{2,r} s_{4,r})(\prod_{r'=0}^{2^{l-1}-1} t_{4,2^{l-1}-r'} t_{2,2^{l-1}-r'}) \neq \lambda.$$

Also since $lg(\prod_{j=1}^{2^{l-1}} \nu_j \omega_j \chi_j) < q_l$, it is clear that

$$lg((\prod_{r=1}^{2^{l-1}} s_{2,r} s_{3,r} s_{4,r})(\prod_{r'=0}^{2^{l-1}-1} t_{4,2^{l-1}-r'} t_{3,2^{l-1}-r'} t_{2,2^{l-1}-r'})) < 3q_l$$

that is less than q_{l+1}. Now a simple change of notation completes the induction and proves the lemma. $\square$

Theorem 3.8 (Hierarchy Theorem)

$$\mathcal{R} = \mathcal{L}_0 \subset \mathcal{L}_1 \subset \mathcal{L}_2 \subset \cdots \subset \mathcal{CS}$$

where $\mathcal{CS}$ denotes the family of context-sensitive languages.

Proof. Lemmas 3.2 and 3.4 establish the inclusions. It remains to show that these are proper.

Let $L_p = \{a^p \mid p \text{ is a prime}\}$. It is known that $L_p \in \mathcal{CS}$. By Lemma 3.7 and the argument being the same as that used in showing L_p is not context-free with the use of the pumping lemma for the context-free family, $L_p \notin \mathcal{L}_i$ for each integer $i \geq 0$.

Lemma 3.1 ensures that $\mathcal{L}_0 \subset \mathcal{L}_1$. We shall show that $L_i^e \notin \mathcal{L}_{i-1}$ for any integer $i \geq 2$. By Lemma 3.7, if $L_i^e \in \mathcal{L}_{i-1}$ then we can pump nontrivially within 2^{i-1} bounded segments. By choosing n large enough, we can force each of these bounded segments to be contained within a substring of the form $ab_j a$. Hence at most $2^{i-1} + 1$ number of b_j's can be involved, thus affecting at most 2^{i-1} number of a^n's. Since we have 2^i number of a^n's, some a^n's will not be changed. Thus we arrive at a contradiction because we can pump nonempty segments within some a^n's while leaving others unchanged, thereby introducing strings not in L_i^e. This shows $L_i^e \notin \mathcal{L}_{i-1}$ and, with Lemma 3.6, completes the proof of the theorem. $\square$

4 Learnability

In this section, we consider the problem of learning each family in the hierarchy.

Let $U = (\{S\}, \Sigma, \Psi, S)$ be a universal *ELG*. Then define $A(U, \alpha)$ as follows; for any string α over Ψ,

$$A(U, \alpha) = \begin{cases} w & \text{if } S \overset{\alpha}{\underset{U}{\Longrightarrow}} w \text{ and } w \in \Sigma^* \\ \infty & \text{otherwise} \end{cases}$$

and $A(U, \infty) = \infty$, where ∞ means "undefined".

Definition 4.1 For any integer $i \geq 1$ and any alphabet Σ, let L be a language over Σ in the family $\mathcal{L}_i$. Then a language C is called a *canonical control set* for L if and only if

1. $L = L(U_1, L(U_2, \ldots, L(U_i, C) \ldots))$ for universal ELGs $U_1, U_2, \ldots, U_i$, and

2. for any $\alpha \in C$, $A(U_1, A(U_2, \ldots, A(U_i, \alpha) \ldots)) \neq \infty$.

Lemma 4.2 *For each integer $i \geq 1$ and any language $L \in \mathcal{L}_i$, a canonical control set for L is unique and regular.*

Proof. Let $L = L(U_1, L(U_2, \ldots, L(U_i, C) \ldots))$ for universal ELGs $U_1, U_2, \ldots, U_i$. Repeated applications of Lemma 3.3 ensure that there exists a regular canonical control set for L. Since $U_1, U_2, \ldots, U_i$ are unambiguous by Remark 2.3, C is unique. $\square$

From this lemma, we have the following corollaries, that show that each family in the hierarchy has similar properties to the family of regular languages.

Corollary 4.3 *For each integer $i \geq 1$, $\mathcal{L}_i$ is closed under Boolean operations.*

Corollary 4.4 *For each integer $i \geq 1$, the following problems are solvable for two languages L_1 and L_2 in $\mathcal{L}_i$; (1) $L_1 \subseteq L_2$ and (2) $L_1 = L_2$.*

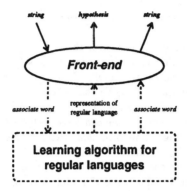

Figure 1: A configuration of learning algorithm for $\mathcal{L}_i$

Let i be a fixed integer greater than or equal to 1. Lemma 4.2 implies that, to identify a language $L \in \mathcal{L}_i$, a learning algorithm has only to identify its unique regular canonical control set for L.

To construct a learning algorithm for the family $\mathcal{L}_i$, we have only to prepare a front-end processing algorithm and add it to a learning algorithm for regular languages. In general, a learning algorithm for $\mathcal{L}_i$ gets strings, outputs strings and outputs representations of languages. Here we assume that it outputs a sequence of universal ELGs and a representation of a regular language as a representation of a language in $\mathcal{L}_i$. A learning algorithm for regular languages gets associate words, outputs associate words and outputs representations of regular languages. Hence the front-end processing algorithm has the following two tasks;

- converting a string to an associate word by iteratively parsing in universal ELGs, and

- converting an associate word to a string by iteratively generating in universal ELGs.

A configuration of learning algorithm is illustrated in Figure 1.

The front-end processing algorithm reduces the problem of identifying a language in $\mathcal{L}_i$ to the problem of identifying a regular canonical control set for the language. Hence we have the following theorem.

Theorem 4.5 (Learnability Theorem) *For each integer $i \geq 1$, the problem of learning $\mathcal{L}_i$ is reduced to the problem of learning the family of regular languages.*

We note that, since any universal ELG U is unambiguous, the time complexity of parsing a string in U is $O(n^2)$, where n is the length of the string. the time complexity of generating a string from an associate word in U may be bounded by a polynomial in the length of the associate word and the size of U that is bounded by the cardinality of the alphabet by Remark 2.3. These observations immediately give the time complexity of a learning algorithm for $\mathcal{L}_i$. Hence, with a polynomial time learning algorithm for regular languages such as [Ang87] and [OG92], for each integer $i \geq 1$ we have a polynomial time learning algorithm for $\mathcal{L}_i$.

5 Conclusions

In this paper, we have established the existence of a hierarchy of language families, in which the learning problem for each family is reduced to the problem for regular languages. A key idea of our result is using control sets on grammars; by defining the next larger family inductively by controlling grammars with languages in one family, we uniformly have a learning method for any family in the hierarchy and boosts the learnability of learning algorithms for regular languages. This partially shows that regulated rewritings [Sal73] such as control sets are one of promising way for the learning problem for formal languages.

One of open problems is learning with a variable i. In this case, a learning algorithm may be required to find a suitable i so that the target language is in the class $\mathcal{L}_i$. This may be not so easy; suppose a strategy that begins with some i and increases or decreases i only after finding that the target is not in $\mathcal{L}_i$. It may be difficult to decide whether the target is not in $\mathcal{L}_i$ only from examples.

Acknowledgements

This work has been done while the author is visiting Department of Computing, Imperial College of Science, Technology and Medicine, United Kingdom.

References

[Ang87] Dana Angluin. Learning regular sets from queries and counter-examples. *Information and Computation*, 75:87–106, 1987.

[AP64] V. Amar and G. Putzolu. On a family of linear grammars. *Information and Control*, 7:283–291, 1964.

[Kha74] Nabil A. Khabbaz. A geometric hierarchy of languages. *Journal of Computer and System Sciences*, 8:142–157, 1974.

[OG92] José Oncina and Pedro García. Identifying regular languages in polynomial time. In H. Bunke, editor, *Advances in structural and syntactic pattern recognition*, pages 99–108. World Scientific, Singapore, 1992.

[RN88] V. Radhakrishnan and G. Nagaraja. Inference of even linear grammars and its application to picture description languages. *Pattern Recognition*, 21(1):55–62, 1988.

[Sal73] Arto Salomaa. *Formal Languages*. Academic Press, New York, 1973.

[Tak88] Yuji Takada. Grammatical inference for even linear languages based on control sets. *Information Processing Letters*, 28(4):193–199, 1988.

[Tak92] Yuji Takada. *Algorithmic Learning Theory of Formal Languages and its Applications*. Doctoral thesis, Hokkaido University, 1992. Also published as IIAS Research Report RR-93-6E.

What is the search space of the regular inference ?

P. Dupont [1], L. Miclet [1,2] and E. Vidal [3]

(1) France Télécom - CNET/LAA/TSS/RCP
2, route de Trégastel 22301 Lannion Cedex (France)
(2) Ecole Nationale Supérieure de Sciences Appliquées et Technologie - IRISA
6, rue de Kérampont 22305 Lannion Cedex (France)
(3) DSIC - Universidad Politécnica de Valencia
Camino de Vera s/n, 46071 Valencia (Spain)

E-mail: dupont@lannion.cnet.fr

Abstract

This paper revisits the theory of regular inference, in particular by extending the definition of *structural completeness* of a positive sample and by demonstrating two basic theorems. This framework enables to state the regular inference problem as a search through a boolean lattice built from the positive sample. Several properties of the search space are studied and generalization criteria are discussed. In this framework, the concept of *border set* is introduced, that is the set of the most general solutions excluding a negative sample. Finally, the complexity of regular language identification from both a theoritical and a practical point of view is discussed.

1   Introduction

Regular inference is the process of learning a regular language from a set of examples, consisting of a positive sample, i.e. a finite subset of a regular language. A negative sample, i.e. a finite set of strings not belonging to this language, may also be available.

This problem has been studied as early as the growth of the theory of formal grammars. It has an obvious theoritical interest and also an important range of applications, in particular in the fields of *Identification of Sequential Processes*, *Pattern Recognition*, *Speech* and *Natural Language Processing*. The theoretical complexity of this problem is now well established [17] and many empirical algorithms have been also devised, most of them using only a positive sample [6]. However, regular inference as a "generalization as search" problem has not yet been stated in a comprehensive manner. This is the point of view that we develop throughout this paper.

We recall in section 2 the basic algebraic notions which will be necessary to define the space of possible solutions to the inference problem: regular languages, finite automata, partitions of a finite set, derivation of an automaton with respect to a partition of its state set, lattices of automata. We revisit the notion of *structural completeness* of a sample with respect to an automaton by extending its definition.

Section 3 is devoted to the detailed description of the search space of the inference problem. We review here the basic theorems which characterize this space and demonstrate them consistently with our definition of structural completeness. It follows that the search space is a boolean lattice of automata built from a positive sample. We state some properties of this lattice. In particular, we show that building the lattice from the *maximal canonical automaton* of a positive sample is more general than from the *prefix tree acceptor*.

We present in section 4 some generalization criteria which may be used to guide the search. In particular, if a negative sample is available, the inference problem may be viewed as the *minimal DFA consistency problem* (section 4.1). Along the same lines, we define in section 4.2 the concept of *border set*, that is the set of the most general solutions consistent with some given positive and negative samples, and we study some properties of this set.

Finally, we recall in section 5 the theoritical complexity results of regular language identification and point out that, while the exact identification of a regular language from a positive and a negative sample is a probably intractable problem, an approximate identification, in some sense, can be achieved in polynomial time.

2 Definitions and notations

The reader familiar with the classical definitions of automata theory may omit section 2.1. We introduce these notions here for the sake of completeness.

2.1 Languages, automata and partitions

2.1.1 Basic definitions

Let Σ denote a finite alphabet, let u, v, w denote elements of Σ^*, i.e. strings over Σ, and let λ denote the empty string. Let $|u|$ denote the length of the string u. We say that u is a *prefix* of v if there exists w such that $uw = v$. We say that u is a *suffix* of v if there exists w such that $wu = v$. A language L is any subset of Σ^*. Let $Pr(L) = \{u | \exists v, uv \in L\}$ denote the set of prefixes of L. Let $L/u = \{v | uv \in L\}$ denote the *left-quotient* of L by u. We have $L/u \neq \phi$ iff $u \in Pr(L)$.

2.1.2 Finite automata

A *finite automaton* is a 5-tuple $(Q, \Sigma, \delta, q_0, F)$ where Q is a finite set of *states*, Σ is an *alphabet*, δ is a *transition function*, i.e. a mapping from $Q \times \Sigma$ to 2^Q, q_0 is the *initial state* and F is a subset of Q identifying the *final* or *accepting states*. If for any q in Q and any a in Σ, $\delta(q, a)$ has at most one member, respectively exactly one member, the automaton A is said to be *deterministic*, respectively *complete*. In the sequel, we shall denote DFA, respectively NFA, a deterministic, respectively a non-deterministic, finite automaton.

2.1.3 Language accepted by a finite automaton

An *acceptance* of a string $u = a_1 \ldots a_l$ by a (possibly non-deterministic) automaton A defines a (possibly non-unique) sequence of $l + 1$ states $(q^0, \ldots, q^l)$ such that $q^0 = q_0$, $q^l \in F$ and $q^{i+1} \in \delta(q^i, a_{i+1})$, for $0 \leq i \leq l - 1$. These $l + 1$ states are said to be *reached* for this acceptance and the state q^l is said to be *used as accepting state*. Similarly, the l transitions (i.e. elements of δ) are said to be *exercized* by this acceptance.

An automaton A is said to be *ambiguous* if there exists at least one string u for which there are several acceptances. In that case, the automaton A is necessarily non-deterministic. A set of transitions being exercized by a set of strings S_s is the union of the sets of transitions exercized by some acceptance of each string in S_s. The corresponding states are said to be *reached* for some acceptance of S_s.

The language $L(A)$ accepted by a finite automaton A is the set of strings accepted by A. A language L is accepted by a finite automaton A if and only if it is a regular set, that is it may be defined by a regular expression [1]. In the sequel, an automaton will denote a *finite* automaton and a language will denote a *regular* language.

A state q of an automaton A is said to be *useful* if there exists a string u in $L(A)$ for which the state q may be reached for some acceptance of u. Otherwise, the state is said to be *useless*. An automaton that contains no useless state is said to be *stripped*.

Let $A(L) = (Q, \Sigma, \delta, q_0, F)$ denote a DFA which has the minimal number of states for a given language L. $A(L)$ is also called the *canonical automaton* of L and may be defined as follows:

$Q = \{L/u \mid u \in Pr(L)\}$,
$q_0 = L/\lambda$,
$F = \{L/u \mid u \in L\}$,
$\delta(L/u, a) = L/ua$ where $u, ua \in Pr(L)$.

$A(L)$ is unique up to a renumbering of its states, that is, every deterministic automaton which exactly accepts L and contains the minimal number of states for this language, is *isomorphic* to $A(L)$ [1].

2.1.4 Derived automata

For any set S, a partition π is a set of pairwise disjoint nonempty subsets of S whose union is S. Let s denote an element of S and let $B(s, \pi)$ denote the unique element, or *block*, of π containing s. We say that π_i *refines*, or *is finer than*, π_j if and only if every block of π_j is a union of one or several blocks of π_i.

If $A = (Q, \Sigma, \delta, q_0, F)$ is an automaton, the automaton $A/\pi = (Q', \Sigma, \delta', B(q_0, \pi), F')$ *derived from A with respect to the partition π of Q*, also called the *quotient automaton* A/π, is defined as follows:

$Q' = Q/\pi = \{B(q, \pi) | q \in Q\}$, $F' = \{B \in Q' | B \cap F \neq \phi\}$,
$\delta' : Q' \times \Sigma \to 2^{Q'} : \forall B, B' \in Q', \forall a \in \Sigma, B' \in \delta'(B, a)iff\exists q, q' \in Q, q \in B, q' \in B'$ and $q' \in \delta(q, a)$.

The states of Q belonging to the same block B of the partition π are said to be *merged* together.

2.2 Language samples and associated automata

Let I_+ denote a finite subset, called *positive sample*, of any language L. Let I_- denote a finite subset, called *negative sample*, of the complementary language $\Sigma^* - L$. Consequently, I_+ and I_- are two disjoint finite subsets of Σ^*.

2.2.1 Structural completeness

A sample I_+ is said to be *structurally complete* with respect to an automaton A accepting L, if there exists an acceptance $AC(I_+, A)$ of I_+ such that:
(1) every transition of A is exercized.
(2) every element of F (the final state set of A) is used as accepting state.
Remark that the classical definitions [4, 12, 13, 3] of structural completeness did not include the second condition. We shall see in section 3.1 that this second condition is also necessary.

2.2.2 Maximal Canonical Automaton, Prefix Tree Acceptor and Universal Automaton

Let $I_+ = \{u_1, \ldots, u_M\}$ be a positive sample, where $u_i = a_{i,1} \ldots a_{i,|u_i|}$, $1 \leq i \leq M = |I_+|$.

Let $MCA(I_+) = (Q, \Sigma, \delta, q_0, F)$ denote the *maximal canonical automaton with respect to* I_+ [12]. It is constructed as follows:
   Σ is the alphabet on which I_+ is defined.
   $Q = \{v_{i,j} | 1 \leq i \leq M, 1 \leq j \leq |u_i|, v_{i,j} = a_{i,1} \ldots a_{i,j}\} \cup \{\lambda\}$, $q_0 = \lambda$, $F = I_+$,
   $\delta(\lambda, a) = \{v | v = a_{i,1}, a = a_{i,1}, 1 \leq i \leq M\}$,
   $\delta(v_{i,j}, a) = \{v_{i,j+1} | v_{i,j+1} = v_{i,j}a_{i,j+1} \text{ and } a = a_{i,j+1}\}, 1 \leq i \leq M, 1 \leq j \leq |u_i| - 1$.
Consequently, $L(MCA(I_+)) = I_+$ and $MCA(I_+)$ is the largest stripped automaton, i.e. the automaton having the largest number of useful states, with respect to which I_+ is structurally complete. Note that $MCA(I_+)$ is generally non-deterministic.

Let $PTA(I_+)$ denote the *prefix tree acceptor* of I_+ [3]. It is the quotient automaton $MCA(I_+)/\pi_{I_+}$ where the partition π_{I_+} is defined as follows:
   $B(q, \pi_{I_+}) = B(q', \pi_{I_+})$ iff $Pr(q) = Pr(q')$.
That is, the $PTA(I_+)$ is obtained from the $MCA(I_+)$ by merging states sharing the same prefixes. Note that $PTA(I_+)$ is deterministic.

Let UA denote the *universal automaton*. It accepts all the strings defined over the alphabet Σ, i.e. $L(UA) = \Sigma^*$, and it is the smallest automaton with respect to which every sample of Σ^* is structurally complete.

2.3 Lattices of automata

Let $P(A)$ denote the set of partitions of the state set of an automaton A. Let $r(\pi_i)$, or simply r_i, denote the number of blocks of the partition π_i. Let $\pi_1 = \{B_{11}, \ldots, B_{1r_1}\}$ and π_2 be two partitions of $P(A)$. We say that π_2 *directly derives from* π_1 if the partition π_2 is constructed from π_1 as follows: $\pi_2 = \{B_{1j} \cup B_{1k}\} \cup (\pi_1 \setminus \{B_{1j}, B_{1k}\})$, for some j, k between 1 and r_1, $j \neq k$. Consequently, $r_2 = r_1 - 1$.

This derivation operation defines a partial order relation on $P(A)$, which we shall denote $\preceq$. In particular, we have $\pi_1 \preceq \pi_2$. Let $\ll$ denote its transitive closure. In other words, $\pi_i \ll \pi_j$ if and only if π_i is finer than π_j. By extension, we say that A/π_i is *finer than* A/π_j and that A/π_j *derives from* A/π_i. By construction of a quotient automaton, we have the language inclusion property [4] which may be reformulated as follows:

$$A/\pi_i \ll A/\pi_j \text{ if } L(A/\pi_i) \subseteq L(A/\pi_j).$$

The set of automata partially ordered by the relation $\preceq$ is a boolean lattice, that we shall denote $Lat(A)$, of which A and UA (i.e. the universal automaton) are respectively the null and universal elements.

The *depth* of an automaton A/π in $Lat(A)$ is given by $N - r(\pi)$, where N is the number of states of A. Consequently, the depth of the automaton A in $Lat(A)$ is equal to 0 while the depth of the universal automaton UA is equal to $N - 1$.

3 The search space of the regular inference problem

Regular inference may be defined as the discovery of an unknown automaton A from which an observed positive sample I_+ is supposed to have been generated. Given the additional hypothesis of structural completeness of I_+, this problem may be considered as a search through a boolean lattice built from the positive information. This property follows from two (partially demonstrated) theorems [12, 3], that we revisit in section 3.1.

3.1 Basic theorems

Theorem 1 *Let I_+ be a positive sample of any regular language L and let A be any automaton accepting exactly L. If I_+ is structurally complete with respect to A then A belongs to $Lat(MCA(I_+))$.*

Proof.
We shall construct the $MCA(I_+)$ from an acceptance of I_+ by A. This construction defines a partition π such that A is isomorphic to $MCA(I_+)/\pi$.
Let $I_+ = \{u_1, \ldots, u_M\}$, where $u_i = a_{i,1} \ldots a_{i,|u_i|}$, $1 \leq i \leq M$, be a positive sample which is structurally complete with respect to A.
The acceptance $\mathcal{AC}(I_+, A)$ defines for each string u_i a sequence $(q_A^{i,0}, \ldots, q_A^{i,|u_i|})$ of $|u_i| + 1$ states, where $q_A^{i,0} = q_{0_A}$, $q_A^{i,|u_i|} \in F_A$ and $q_A^{i,j+1} \in \delta_A(q_A^{i,j}, a_{i,j+1})$, $1 \leq i \leq M, 0 \leq j \leq |u_i| - 1$. We start the construction of the MCA by considering its initial state, $q_{0_{MCA}}$ and let define $q_{MCA}^{i,0} = q_{0_{MCA}}$, $1 \leq i \leq M$. Each time a transition of A is exercized, we add a new state in Q_{MCA} and we adapt the transition function δ_{MCA} as follows:

$$q_A^{i,j+1} \in \delta_A(q_A^{i,j}, a_{i,j+1}) \Leftrightarrow q_{MCA}^{i,j+1} \in \delta_{MCA}(q_{MCA}^{i,j}, a_{i,j+1}), 1 \leq i \leq M, 0 \leq j \leq |u_i| - 1.$$

Moreover, we construct the final state set F_{MCA} as follows:

$$F_{MCA} = \{q_{MCA}^{i,|u_i|}, 1 \leq i \leq M\}.$$

We also define a function φ which maps the states of MCA over those of A:

$$\varphi: Q_{MCA} \to Q_A : \varphi(q_{MCA}^{i,j}) = q_A, \text{ whenever } q_A = q_A^{i,j}, 1 \leq i \leq M, 0 \leq j \leq |u_i|.$$

Finally, let the partition π be defined as follows:

$$B(q_{MCA}^l, \pi) = B'(q_{MCA}^k, \pi) \text{ iff } \varphi(q_{MCA}^l) = \varphi(q_{MCA}^k).$$

The very definition of the partition π implies that A is isomorphic to MCA/π, since the structural completeness of I_+ implies that $\delta_{MCA/\pi}$ exactly corresponds to δ_A. The second condition on the structural completeness of I_+ imposes that

$$\forall q_A \in F_A, \exists i, 1 \leq i \leq M \text{ such that } q_A^{i,|u_i|} = q_A.$$

Consequently, $F_{MCA} = \{q_{MCA}|\varphi(q_{MCA}) \cap F_A \neq \phi\}$ and $F_{MCA/\pi}$ exactly corresponds to F_A. $\square$

Theorem 2 *Let I_+ be a positive sample of any regular language L and let $A(L)$ denote the canonical automaton accepting L. If I_+ is structurally complete with respect to $A(L)$ then $A(L)$ belongs to $Lat(PTA(I_+))$.*

Proof.
We may follow the same proof than in the theorem 1, except that the acceptance of I_+ by $A(L)$ is now unique since $A(L)$ is deterministic. Similarly, each entry of the transition function of the $PTA(I_+)$ contains at most one member, since the $PTA(I_+)$ is deterministic. $\square$

To illustrate the last part of the demonstration of the theorem 1, we consider the following example. According to our definition, the sample $I_+ = \{ab\}$ is not structurally complete with respect to the automaton A of figure 1, where q_1 and q_2 are both final states. For this reason, the automaton A may not be derived from the $MCA(I_+)$, and obviously neither from the $PTA(I_+)$. Indeed, it is not possible to define a partition π of the state set Q_{MCA} such that A corresponds to $MCA(I_+)/\pi$ with $q_1 \in F_{MCA/\pi}$. On the contrary, the sample $\{ab, a\}$ is structurally complete with respect to the automaton A which may thus be derived from the MCA, or from the PTA, associated with this last sample.

Figure 1: Automaton A and the $MCA(I_+)$.

Theorem 3 *Let I_+ be a positive sample. Let $\mathcal{A}$ be the set of automata such that I_+ is structurally complete with respect to any automaton belonging to $\mathcal{A}$. The set $\mathcal{A}$ is equal to $Lat(MCA(I_+))$.*

Proof.
(1) If I_+ is structurally complete with respect to an automaton A, then A belongs to $Lat(MCA(I_+))$. This is exactly the theorem 1.
(2) If an automaton A belongs to $Lat(MCA(I_+))$ then I_+ is structurally complete with respect to A [4]. By construction, I_+ is structurally complete with respect to $MCA(I_+)$. Since every automaton in $Lat(MCA(I_+))$ may be derived from the $MCA(I_+)$ for some partition π, the result follows directly from the definition of a quotient automaton. $\square$

3.2 Some properties of the search space

From the section 3.1 we know that if we have a positive sample I_+ of an unknown language L and if we suppose that I_+ is structurally complete with respect to an unknown automaton A accepting exactly L, we may derive A for some partition π of the state set of $MCA(I_+)$. The inference problem may thus be seen as a search through a boolean lattice for the partition π.

Let us first mention that the theorem 1 of section 3.1 is more general than the theorem 2 in the sense that it only supposes the structural completeness of I_+ with respect to any automaton accepting a language L, not necessarily with respect to the canonical automaton[1] for L. Moreover, we have the property 1.

Property 1 $Lat(PTA(I_+)) \subseteq Lat(MCA(I_+))$.

This is clear since $PTA(I_+)$ may be defined as a quotient automaton of $MCA(I_+)$. Besides as the $Lat(PTA(I_+))$ is generally *properly* included in $Lat(MCA(I_+))$, searching in $Lat(PTA(I_+))$ instead of $Lat(MCA(I_+))$ allows for reducing the search space. We shall now detail other properties of these search spaces.

The first important feature is that each element in the lattices corresponds to a particular automaton, but many different automata represent the same language. Therefore, we might think of restricting the search to deterministic automata. However, we have the property 2.

Property 2 *There exist positive samples I_+ for which some languages are only represented by NFA's in $Lat(MCA(I_+))$.*

Note that the same property holds for $Lat(PTA(I_+))$ as a consequence of the property 1. Consider the NFA of figure 2. It accepts the language L_1 defined by the regular expression $(ba^*a)^*$. The sample $I_+ = \{baa\}$ is structurally complete with respect to this automaton. However, this sample is not structurally complete with respect to the minimal DFA for the same language, and thus the same holds for any DFA accepting the language L_1. Consequently, we may not identify the language L_1 if we restrict the search to DFA's.

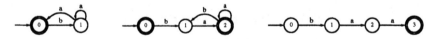

Figure 2: $NFA(L_1)$, $A(L_1)$ and $MCA(I_+)$, with $L_1 = (ba^*a)^*$.

Property 3 *There exist positive samples I_+ for which the set of languages which may be identified from $Lat(PTA(I_+))$ is properly included in the set of languages which may be identified from $Lat(MCA(I_+))$.*

By the property 1 we know that the set of automata which may be derived from the $MCA(I_+)$ includes the set of those which may be derived from the $PTA(I_+)$. The property 3 follows from the fact that sometimes this inclusion is proper and that the automata

---

[1]A structurally complete sample with respect to $A(L)$ is sometimes called *representative* for L [15].

which belongs to $Lat(MCA(I_+))$ and not to $Lat(PTA(I_+))$, have no equivalent automaton, i.e. any automaton accepting the same language, in $Lat(PTA(I_+))$.

Let us consider the language $L_2 = (ba + b(aa)^*)$, which may be represented by the NFA of figure 3 and its corresponding canonical automaton $A(L_2)$. Let the positive sample I_+ be equal to $\{ba, baa\}$. The associated $MCA(I_+)$ and $PTA(I_+)$ are represented in the figure 4. We may clearly derive $NFA(L_2)$ from the $MCA(I_+)$ while not from the $PTA(I_+)$. This is due to the fact that the states q_1 and q_2 of the MCA, respectively q_3 and q_4, are merged together in the PTA. Moreover, since I_+ is structurally complete with respect to $NFA(L_2)$ but not with respect to $A(L_2)$, this last automaton may not be derived from the PTA and neither any deterministic automaton accepting the same language.

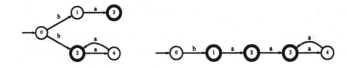

Figure 3: $NFA(L_2)$ and $A(L_2)$, with $L_2 = (ba + b(aa)^*)$.

Figure 4: $MCA(I_+)$ and $PTA(I_+)$, with $I_+ = \{ba, baa\}$.

4 Guiding the search for the unknown automaton

4.1 Generalization criteria

Given a positive sample I_+ of a regular language, the criterion which will guide the search for some unknown automaton A accepting I_+ has to be defined. Indeed, we want to generalize in some sense the information contained in this sample.

We know, by construction, that any automaton derived from the $MCA(I_+)$ accepts a language including I_+. In that sense, any automaton belonging to $Lat(MCA(I_+))$ constitutes a possible generalization of the positive sample. Therefore, one may be interested in finding an automaton identifying a language belonging to a particular subclass of regular languages, for example, the class of k-reversible languages [3] or the class of k-testable languages [5].

Suppose now that a negative sample of the unknown language L is available. Then, the inference problem may be stated as the discovery of an automaton which is *compatible*, or *consistent*, with the positive and negative sample. That is, we look for an automaton A such that $I_+ \in L(A)$ and $I_- \cap L(A) = \phi$. There are many such automata in $Lat(MCA(I_+))$ and, in particular, the MCA satisfies these requirements. However, it does not generalize the positive learning data in the sense that the language accepted strictly corresponds to the positive sample. For this reason, we may look for the DFA, consistent with the positive and negative sample, which moreover contains the minimal number of states. This is the so-called *minimal DFA consistency problem*. The simplicity of the inferred automaton is here chosen as generalization criterion. Remark, however, that this problem has been proved to be NP-Hard (see section 5).

4.2   Border Set

Relating the minimal DFA consistency problem with the characterization of the search space given in section 3, gives rise to the concept of *border set*.

Definition 4.2.1 *An antistring $\overline{as}$ in a lattice of automata is a set of automata such that any element of $\overline{as}$ is not related by $\preceq$ with any other element of $\overline{as}$.*

Definition 4.2.2 *An automaton is said to be at a maximal depth in a lattice of automata, if there is no automaton A' which may be derived from A such that $L(A') \cap I_- = \phi$.*

Definition 4.2.3 *The border set $BS_{MCA}(I_+, I_-)$ is the antistring in $Lat(MCA(I_+))$, of which each element is at a maximal depth.*

Definition 4.2.4 *The border set $BS_{PTA}(I_+, I_-)$ is the antistring in $Lat(PTA(I_+))$, of which each element is at a maximal depth.*

Consequently, the border set of a lattice is the set of automata which correspond to the limit of the generalization under the control of the negative sample. The minimal DFA consistency problem may now be viewed as the discovery of the smallest DFA in a border set.

Property 4 $BS_{PTA}(I_+, I_-) \subseteq BS_{MCA}(I_+, I_-)$.

This is a direct consequence of the property 1.

Property 5 *There may be several distinct languages represented by the automata belonging to $BS_{MCA}(I_+, I_-)$.*

This property follows from the fact that the partial order relation introduced in section 2.3 applies to automata but not to languages.

Property 6 *There may exist NFA's belonging to $BS_{MCA}(I_+, I_-)$ which contain less states than the minimal consistent DFA.*

In particular, this is the case when the minimal consistent DFA corresponds to a language which may be represented by an NFA having less states.

Property 7 *All deterministic automata belonging to $BS_{MCA}(I_+, I_-)$ are necessarily minimal for the language they accept.*

Note that the same property holds for $BS_{PTA}(I_+, I_-)$ as a consequence of the property 4.
Proof.
Let A be a DFA accepting the language L and consistent with I_+ and I_-. Let A be not isomorphic to the canonical automaton $A(L)$. We may construct the partition π of the state set of A in such a way that A/π is obtained from A by merging states sharing the same suffixes (or tails). By construction, $A/\pi = A(L)$. Hence, $A \ll A(L)$ and the depth of $A(L)$ is higher than the depth of A. Consequently, whatever the belonging of $A(L)$ to $BS_{MCA}(I_+, I_-)$, A may not belong to it. □
This property states that any deterministic automaton which is not minimal for the language it accepts, may not belong to $BS_{MCA}(I_+, I_-)$. On the other hand, there exist canonical automata which do not belong to $BS_{MCA}(I_+, I_-)$ since, firstly, all such automata are not necessarily compatible with I_- and, secondly, it may be possible to derive from some canonical automaton another automaton which belongs to $BS_{MCA}(I_+, I_-)$.

An algorithm to construct the border set by enumeration under the control of I_- has been given in [14]. Its computational cost is obviously not tractable and several approximations have been proposed [14].

5   The complexity of regular language identification

In section 4.1, we have essentially limited the discussion to the minimal DFA consistency problem. The relation of this problem with the most general problem of learning a (regular) language needs some clarification. For this purpose, we recall the most classical paradigm of language learning that is *the identification in the limit* proposed by Gold [7]. Next, we mention the computational complexity results of automaton identification and, finally, we discuss the feasibility of approximate identification from sparse data.

5.1   Automaton identification in the limit

There are two closely related variations of identification in the limit [8]. The first one corresponds to the case of *requested data* in which as much data as needed is supposed to be available, that is, may be requested. Here, the learning algorithm is supplied with a growing sequence of data $D_1, D_2, \ldots, D_i, \ldots$ compatible with an arbitrary target machine A. At each discrete time step i the learning algorithm must propose an hypothesis (a DFA, e.g.) $H(D_i)$ representing the guessed solution at step i. The algorithm is said to have the *identification in the limit* property if, after some finite time index t, all the guessed solutions $H(D_i)$, with $i \geq t$, are the same and $L(H(D_i)) = L(A)$.

In the case of *given data*, i.e. the set D of available learning data is fixed, the learning algorithm must propose an hypothesis $H(D)$. This algorithm is said to have the identification in the limit property if, for any target machine A, it is possible to define a set D_A^r as follows [8]:

$$D_A^r \text{ is a subset of } \Sigma^* \text{ such that } \forall D \supseteq D_A^r, \ L(H(D)) = L(A).$$

We call the set D_A^r a *representative sample*[2] for $L(A)$ (see section 4.2). Note that the representative sample not only depends on the language to be identified but also on the learning algorithm.

---

[2]This term has not to be confused with the definition of Muggleton [15].

Gold showed that, using both positive and negative examples, all the *recursively enumerable* classes of languages, the regular one in particular, can be identified in the limit. In contrast, no *superfinite* class of languages, i.e. one that contains all finite languages and at least one that is infinite, can be identified in the limit using only positive examples [7].

5.2 Theoritical and practical complexity of automaton identification

An excellent overview on the *computational complexity of DFA learning* is given by Pitt [17]. We will not discuss in deep these topics here but rather we will briefly present some facts that may perhaps help seeding new light into the long controversial theme of the *practical* tractability of learning DFA's from positive and negative examples.

The key negative theoretical evidence can be summarized as follows :

- Finding the smallest DFA consistent with I_+ and I_- is NP-Hard [2, 8].

- The minimal DFA consistency problem can not be approximated within any polynomial of the size of the optimal solution [18].

- Approximate inference of finite automata from sparse labeled examples is NP-Hard if an adversary chooses both the target machine and the training set [10].

On the other hand, Trakhtenbrot and Barzdin proposed an $\mathcal{O}(mn^2)$ state-merging algorithm [19] for building the smallest DFA consistent with a *complete* labeled learning sample, where m is the size of the PTA built from the positive information and n is the size of the target DFA. This complete learning sample is made of all the strings up to the length l, each of them being labeled either as positive or negative. The length l depends on some features[3] of the target automaton and has been shown to be equal to $2n - 1$, in the *worst case* [19]. Whenever n is large, the size of the learning sample becomes prohibitive. Furthermore, Angluin has shown that, in the worst case, the exact automaton identification is not feasible if a vanishingly small fraction of the complete learning sample is lacking [2].

Fortunately enough, the computational complexity seems to be better in the *average case*. For DFA's randomly drawn from a well defined probability distribution, the expected value of the complete sample size is given by [19]:

$$|S|_{complete} = (|\Sigma|^2 n^C \log_2 n - 1)/(|\Sigma| - 1).$$

where C only depends on $|\Sigma|$.

The expected average size of a complete learning sample, at least for small alphabets, might suggest that exact identification of average DFA's is feasible. However, there is no practical guarantee to have a complete sample available, whatever its size. One should only assume the availability of *sparse* data. In this framework, Lang has empirically shown [11] that highly accurate *approximate* identification may be achieved by using a

---

[3]Those features are the *degree of distinguibility* of the automaton and its *depth* in the sense defined in [19].

(randomly drawn) vanishingly small fraction of the complete learning sample; that is, a fraction which decreases as the size of the target automaton increases.

The polynomial algorithm proposed by Lang [11], and independently by Oncina and Garcia [16], is reminiscent of the Trakhtenbrot and Barzdin's algorithm [19]. In this technique, a greedy search in $Lat(PTA(I_+))$ yields a "locally optimal" solution to the consistency problem. Indeed, the solution produced by this algorithm is a DFA belonging to $BS_{PTA}(I_+, I_-)$. By the property 7, we know that this DFA is a canonical automaton. However, it is not necessarily the smallest DFA consistent with the data except if the data contain a representative sample. In other words, when the learning data are sufficiently representative, this algorithm is proved to produce the canonical automaton of the language to be identified. Moreover, this automaton is also the solution to the minimal DFA consistency problem in that particular case. Note, finally, that Oncina and Garcia have shown that the size of a representative sample proper to this algorithm is $\mathcal{O}(n^2)$ [16].

References

[1] A. Aho and J. Ullman, *The Theory of Parsing, Translation and Compiling, Vol. 1: Parsing*, Series in Automatic Computation, Prentice-Hall, Englewood, Cliffs, 1972.

[2] D. Angluin, *On the Complexity of Minimum Inference of Regular Sets*, Information and Control, Vol. 39, pp. 337-350, 1978.

[3] D. Angluin, *Inference of Reversible Languages*, Journal of the ACM, Vol. 29, No. 3, pp. 741-765, 1982.

[4] K.S. Fu and T.L. Booth, *Grammatical Inference: Introduction and Survey*, IEEE Transactions on SMC, Part 1: Vol. 5, pp. 85-111, Part 2: Vol. 5, pp. 409-423, 1975.

[5] P. Garcia and E. Vidal, *Inference of K-testable languages in the strict sense and applications to syntactic pattern recognition*, IEEE Transactions on PAMI, Vol. 12, No. 9, pp. 920-925, 1990.

[6] J. Gregor, *Data-driven Inductive Inference of Finite-state Automata*, International Journal of Pattern Recognition and Artificial Intelligence, Vol. 8, No. 1, pp. 305-322, 1994.

[7] E.M. Gold, *Language Identification in the Limit*, Information and Control, Vol. 10, No. 5, pp. 447-474, 1967.

[8] E.M. Gold, *Complexity of Automaton Identification from Given Data*, Information and Control, Vol. 37, pp. 302-320, 1978.

[9] M.A. Harrison, *Introduction to Formal Language Theory*, Addison-Wesley, Reading, Massachusetts, 1978.

[10] M. Kearns and L. Valiant, *Cryptographic Limitations on Learning Boolean Formulae and Finite Automata*, Proc. of the 21st ACM Symposium on Theory of Computing, pp. 433-444, 1989.

[11] K.J. Lang, *Random DFA's can be Approximately Learned from Sparse Uniform Examples*, Proc. of the 5th ACM workshop on Computational Learning Theory, pp. 45-52, 1992.

[12] L. Miclet, *Inférence de Grammaires Régulières*, Thèse de Docteur-Ingénieur, E.N.S.T., Paris, France, 1979.

[13] L. Miclet, *Regular Inference with a Tail-Clustering Method*, IEEE Trans. on SMC, Vol. 10, pp. 737-743, 1980.

[14] L. Miclet and C. de Gentile, *Inférence Grammaticale à partir d'Exemples et de Contre-Exemples : deux Algorithmes Optimaux (BIG et RIG) et une Version Heuristique (BRIG)*, Actes des JFA-94, Strasbourg, France, pp. F1-F13, 1994.

[15] S. Muggleton, *Induction of Regular Languages from Positive Examples*, Turing Institute Report, TIRM-84-009, 1984.

[16] J. Oncina and P. Garcia, *Inferring Regular Languages in Polynomial Update Time*, Pattern Recognition and Image Analysis, N. Perrez de la Blanca, A. Sanfeliu and E. Vidal (editors), Series in Machine Perception and Artificial Intelligence, Vol. 1, pp. 49-61, World Scientific, 1992.

[17] L. Pitt, *Inductive Inference, DFA's, and Computational Complexity*, Lecture Notes in Artificial Intelligence, K.P. Jantke (editor), No. 397, Springer-Verlag, Berlin, pp. 18-44, 1989.

[18] L. Pitt and M. Warmuth, *The Minimum Consistent DFA Problem Cannot be Approximated Within any Polynomial*, Tech. Report UIUCDCS-R-89-1499, University of Illinois, 1989.

[19] B. Trakhtenbrot and Ya. Barzdin, *Finite Automata: Behavior and Synthesis*, North Holland Pub. Comp., Amsterdam, 1973.

A Characterization of Even Linear Languages and Its Application to the Learning Problem *

Jose M. Sempere   Pedro García

Departamento de Sistemas Informáticos y Computación
Universidad Politécnica de Valencia
Camino de Vera s/n, 46071 Valencia (Spain)
email:jsempere@dsic.upv.es email:pgarcia@dsic.upv.es

Abstract

Even Linear Language class is a subclass of context-free class. In this work we propose a characterization of this class using a relation of finite index. Theorems are provided in order to prove the consistence of the characterization. Finally, we propose a method to learn this class using a reduction to the problem of learning regular languages.

1   Introduction.

Formal Language Theory has been applied to learning under the Grammatical Inference paradigm. A survey of this approximation can be found in [2]. Under this paradigm, one way of obtaining good learning algorithms is by providing some characteristics of the formal language class to be learned and by taking advantage of these characteristics to design the algorithms. Typically, the language classes used in grammatical inference have been the context-free class, the regular class or any context-free subclass which could or could not contain the regular class. Some learning algorithms have been proposed to learn some of these classes from information that consisted of given data as strings or skeletons, or different queries.

The Even Linear Language class (ELL) was initially introduced by Amar and Putzolu [1] as a subclass of the more generic Linear Language class. In their work, Amar and Putzolu provided a Nerode-type characterization [4] of the ELL. Under this characterization, a language is even linear iff it is saturated by a finite index quasi-congruence. Informally, a quasi-congruence is similar to a congruence in the sense that given two words, its equivalence implies the equivalence of the words obtained by including the previous words in right and left equal length contexts.

Some works have focused on the learning problem of even linear languages. For example, the work done by Radhakrishnan and Nagaraja [6] deals with a finite and positive

---

*Work partially supported by the Spanish CICYT under grant TIC93-0633-CO2

sample for carrying out the learning task. In their work, they used sample strings to obtain even linear grammars from the structural information that the string skeletons could give in terms of which subskeletons were similar and which were not. This algorithm has been applied to the Picture Description Language (PDL) to recognize simple symmetrical objects as established in the same work. Another study in learning even linear languages is by Takada [7]. In his work, Takada established that every even linear language can be generated by a universal grammar provided with a certain *control set* that regulates the application of its rules. Takada proved that the *control set* of every even linear grammar is a regular language. This allows us to reduce the problem of learning even linear languages to the problem of learning regular languages. With this purpose, the input data are analyzed through the universal grammar and converted into strings of rules from which the *control set* is learned using any regular language inference algorithm. Finally, an even linear grammar can be obtained from the inferred *control set* which generates the same language as the universal grammar with the *control set*.

In the present work, we propose a new characterization of the ELL which allows us to define a canonical grammar associated to an even linear language. This grammar is the minimal size grammar of a set of even linear grammars in a standard form which generates the language and is unique except for those which are isomorphic to it.

The Even Linear Languages learning problem is posed, as in [7], through a reduction to the Regular Languages learning problem. The input data are submitted to a transformation, and a regular language learning algorithm is applied to the transformed data. The inverse transformation provides a hypothesis which consists of an even linear grammar for the input sample, from the inferred automata.

2 Basic concepts and notation.

Let Σ be a finite alphabet and Σ^* the free monoid generated by Σ. For every $x \in \Sigma$, $| x |$ denotes the length of x and λ denotes the string of length zero. Given a language $L \subseteq \Sigma^*$ and $x \in \Sigma^*$, then $x^{-1}L$ and Lx^{-1}, respectively, denote the right quotient and the left quotient of x in L, i.e. $x^{-1}L=\{u \in \Sigma^* \mid xu \in L\}$, $Lx^{-1}=\{u \in \Sigma^* \mid ux \in L \}$.

A finite automaton (FA) over Σ is denoted by a five-tuple $M=(Q,\Sigma,\delta,q_0,F)$, where Q is the set of states, $q_0 \in Q$ the initial state, $F \subseteq Q$ the final states, Σ the input alphabet, and δ the transition function. The language accepted by M is denoted by L(M).

The four tuple $G=(N,\Sigma,P,S)$ denotes a grammar where N and Σ are the nonterminal and the terminal alphabets respectively, P is the set of rules of G and $S \in N$ is the start symbol. L(G) denotes the language generated by G.

An Even Linear Grammar (ELG) is a context-free grammar [4] $G=(N,\Sigma,P,S)$ where all the rules in P are of the following forms

- $A \rightarrow xBy$, where $x,y \in \Sigma^*$, $A,B \in N$ and $| x |=| y |$.

- $A \rightarrow x$, where $x \in \Sigma^*$, $A \in N$.

A language L is an even linear language if there exists an ELG which generates L. The class of Even Linear Languages is a proper subclass of the context-free languages and properly includes the class of regular languages.

Given an ELG, there exists an equivalent ELG where every production is in one of the following standard forms [1]

- $A \rightarrow aBb$, where $a, b \in \Sigma$, $A, B \in N$.

- $A \rightarrow a$, where $a \in \Sigma \cup \{\lambda\}$, $A \in N$.

3   A characterization of the Even Linear Languages.

We are going to propose an alternative characterization that could serve as a base in the learning problem. In the first place, we will establish that given any even linear grammar in the standard form defined above, we can find an equivalent deterministic even linear grammar using a transformation on the strings of the language through the following definition.

Definition 1. Let Σ be an alphabet and let the string $x = a_1 a_2 ... a_{k-1} a_k a_{k+1} ... a_{n-1} a_n$, where $\forall\ 1 \leq i \leq n$, $i \neq k$, $a_i \in \Sigma$ and $a_k \in \Sigma \cup \{\lambda\}$. We define the *joined extreme of x* and we denote it by $\sigma(x)$ as the string $a_1 a_n \mid a_2 a_{n-1} \mid ... \mid a_{k-1} a_{k+1} \mid a_k$. We can define the *joined extreme* of a string in an inductive way through the following two definitions:

$\sigma : \Sigma^* \rightarrow (\Sigma^2 \cup \Sigma)^*$

- $\sigma(a) = a$, $\forall\ a \in \Sigma \cup \{\lambda\}$.

- $\sigma(axb) = ab \mid \sigma(x)$, $\forall\ a, b \in \Sigma$, $\forall\ x \in \Sigma^*$.

We can extend this definition to languages and provide the *joined extremes* of a language L defined as $\sigma(L) = \{\ \sigma(x) \mid x \in L \}$.

In the same way we can define the inverse transformation as follows

- $\sigma^{-1}(a) = a$, $\forall\ a \in \Sigma \cup \{\lambda\}$.

- $\sigma^{-1}(ab \mid x) = a\sigma(x)b$, $\forall\ a, b \in \Sigma$, $\forall\ x \in \Sigma^*$.

In this case, $\sigma^{-1}(L) = \{\sigma^{-1}(x) \mid x \in L\}$ and $\sigma^{-1}(\sigma(x)) = x$, so $\sigma^{-1}(\sigma(L)) = L$.

From the last definition, we can enunciate a theorem which establishes that the transformation σ defined above obtains a regular language from an even linear language, and from this fact, we can define a relation of finite index that characterizes the even linear languages.

Theorem 1 *If $L \subseteq \Sigma^*$ is an even linear language, then $\sigma(L)$ is a regular language.*

Proof

Let the language $L = L(G)$, where $G = (N, \Sigma, P, S)$ is an even linear grammar in the standard form. We define the finite automaton $A = (Q, \Sigma', \delta, q_0, F)$, where $Q = N \cup \{q_f\}$, $q_f \notin N$, $\Sigma' = \Sigma^2 \cup \Sigma$, $q_0 = S$, $F = \{q_f\}$, δ is defined by the rules:

- If $A \rightarrow aBb \in P$, then $B \in \delta(A, ab)$

- If $A \rightarrow a \in P$, then $\delta(A, a) = \{q_f\}$.

41

So, through an induction process we can prove that

$$\forall A \in N \; A \Longrightarrow_G^* x \text{ iff } \delta(A, \sigma(x)) \cap F \neq \varnothing.$$

Let us observe that if we take a finite automaton like the one constructed in the previous theorem as input, then we can build an equivalent even linear grammar maintaining the inverse process of the theorem, and the equivalence proof is trivial. In this case, given an automaton A, the obtained grammar generates the language $\sigma^{-1}(L(A))$. In Figure 1, we can observe an example of an even linear grammar and its associated finite automaton.

Once we have shown a correspondence between an even linear language L and its regular transformed language $\sigma(L)$, we can establish certain relationships between the regular language theory and similar results for even linear languages to obtain a relation of finite index which produces an equivalent result to the Myhill-Nerode Theorem [4]. In order to do this, we will give another definition.

Definition 2. Given an even linear grammar in the standard form $G=(N,\Sigma,P,S)$, we will say that this grammar is *deterministic* if $A \to aBb \in P$ and $A \to aCb \in P$ imply that $C=B$.

Theorem 2 *Given an even linear grammar in the standard form $G=(N,\Sigma,P,S)$, then a deterministic even linear grammar in the standard form G' exists such that $L(G)=L(G')$.*

Proof

Given G we can obtain a FA A which accepts $\sigma(L(G))$ as established in Theorem 1. Using operations on this automaton [4], we can obtain an equivalent deterministic FA A'. Keeping similar rules to those used in the previous theorem, the grammar that we associate to A' accepts $\sigma^{-1}(\sigma(L(G))=L(G)$.

Finally, we can establish an equivalence relation taking $(\Sigma x \Sigma)^*$ as the relationship domain.

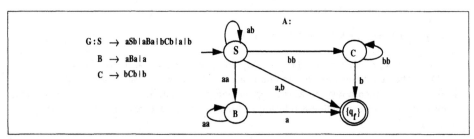

Figure 1:   An Even Linear Grammar G and its associated FA A. $L(A)=\sigma(L(G))$.

Definition 3. Given a language L, we will say that the string pairs (u_1,v_1) and (u_2,v_2) are related (they are *undistinguishable*) under the language L and we denote it by $(u_1,v_1) \equiv_L (u_2,v_2)$ iff

- $\mid u_1 \mid = \mid v_1 \mid, \mid u_2 \mid = \mid v_2 \mid$

- $\forall \; w \in \Sigma^* \; u_1 w v_1 \in L$ *iff* $u_2 w v_2 \in L$ or, using an alternative notation, we will say that $(u_1,v_1)L=(u_2,v_2)L$, where $(u,v)L=u^{-1}(Lv^{-1}) = (u^{-1}L)v^{-1}$.

From the above definition, we can establish the definitive result to characterize the Even Linear Language class. We will do this by the following theorem.

Theorem 3 $L \subseteq \Sigma^*$ *is an even linear language iff* $\equiv_L$ *has a finite index.*

Proof

- Necessary condition proof.

  Let the language $L=L(G)$, where $G=(N,\Sigma,P,S)$ is a deterministic even linear grammar as established in Theorem 2. We define the relation $\equiv_G$ over $(\Sigma x \Sigma)^*$ as follows. $(u_1,v_1) \equiv_G (u_2,v_2)$ *iff*

  - $\mid u_1 \mid = \mid v_1 \mid, \mid u_2 \mid = \mid v_2 \mid$
  - $S \Longrightarrow_G^* u_1 A v_1$ *iff* $S \Longrightarrow_G^* u_2 A v_2$

  Obviously, $\equiv_G$ has a finite index, given that it will have as many equivalence classes as nonterminal symbols of the grammar. We will prove that if $(u_1,v_1) \equiv_G (u_2,v_2)$, then $(u_1,v_1) \equiv_L (u_2,v_2)$, and therefore $\equiv_L$ has a finite index.

  $(u_1,v_1) \equiv_G (u_2,v_2) \Rightarrow \forall\ w \in \Sigma^*\ u_1 w v_1 \in L$ iff $u_2 w v_2 \in L \Leftrightarrow (u_1,v_1) \equiv_L (u_2,v_2)$.

- Sufficient condition proof.

  Then, let us suppose that $\equiv_L$ has a finite index. Let us define the grammar $G=(N,\Sigma,P,S)$, where $N=\{(u,v)L \mid u,v \in \Sigma^*$ and $\mid u \mid = \mid v \mid\}$, $S=(\lambda,\lambda)L$ and P is defined through the following rules

  - If $(u,v)L=A$ and $(ua,bv)L=B$, then $A \rightarrow aBb \in P$.
  - If $a \in A \cap \{\Sigma \cup \{\lambda\}\}$, then $A \rightarrow a \in P$.

  Then let us see that $L(G)=L$. In the first place, we could prove that $(u,v)L=A$ *iff* $S \Longrightarrow_G^* uAv$, through an induction process.

  Once this has been proved, we can see that $L(G)=L$, through a double inclusion proof.

  - $L(G) \subseteq L$
    Let us take $x \in L(G)$. Then $S \Longrightarrow_G^* uAv \Longrightarrow_G uav=x$ with $\mid u \mid = \mid v \mid$ and $a \in (\Sigma \cup \{\lambda\})$, then $(u,v)L=A$ and $a \in A$, so $uav=x \in L$.
  - $L \subseteq L(G)$
    Let $x=uav \in L$ with $\mid u \mid = \mid v \mid$ and $a \in (\Sigma \cup \{\lambda\})$, then $a \in (u,v)L=A$. So, it is clear that $A \rightarrow a \in P$ and $S \Longrightarrow_G^* uAv$, so $S \Longrightarrow_G^* uAv \Longrightarrow_G uav=x \in L(G)$.

Let us see an example of how to construct an even linear grammar from the equivalence relation as established in the previous theorem.

Example

$L=aa^*b^*b$

$$(a,a)L=\oslash \qquad (a,a)A=a^*=B \qquad (a,a)B=a^*=B \qquad (a,a)C=\oslash$$
$$(a,b)L=a^*b^*=A \qquad (a,b)A=a^*b^*=A \qquad (a,b)B=\oslash \qquad (a,b)C=\oslash$$
$$(b,a)L=\oslash \qquad (b,a)A=\oslash \qquad (b,a)B=\oslash \qquad (b,a)C=\oslash$$
$$(b,b)L=\oslash \qquad (b,b)A=b^*=C \qquad (b,b)B=\oslash \qquad (b,b)C=b^*=C$$

so, the obtained grammar (maintaining the construction of Theorem 3) will be the following one:

$$S \rightarrow aAb \qquad A \rightarrow aBa \mid aAb \mid bCb \mid a \mid b \mid \lambda$$
$$B \rightarrow aBa \mid a \mid \lambda \quad C \rightarrow bCb \mid b \mid \lambda$$

Finally we can enunciate a result related to the minimum size of the even linear grammars.

Theorem 4 *The constructed grammar of Theorem 3 is the minimal deterministic grammar which generates L and is the only one except for isomorphic ones.*

Proof

As seen in Theorem 3, given a grammar G, the induced relation $\equiv_G$ is a refinenment over the relation $\equiv_L$, so the number of auxiliary symbols induced by $\equiv_G$ is greater than the number of those induced by $\equiv_L$.

4 Application to the learning problem.

Once we have presented a characterization of the class of the even linear languages, our purpose is to apply it to its learning. It can easily be seen that learning an even linear language L can be solved by learning its associated regular language $\sigma(L)$, so the problem of learning even linear languages is obviously resolved. The characterization of the Even Linear Languages proposed in this work is different from the characterization used in [7] but allows us to obtain a result over the learning of the even linear languages which is completely equivalent.

Thus, the scheme to be carried out to learn any even linear language could be the one proposed in Figure 2.

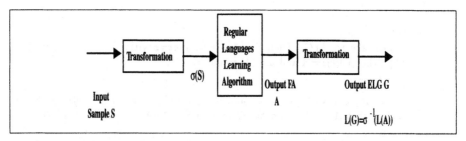

Figure 2: A scheme to learn Even Linear Languages.

The proposed scheme is easy to understand. Given a sample of an even linear language, the transformation σ is applied and it obtains a regular language sample. Then, any regular language learning algorithm can be applied over the transformed sample and, last, the transformation that obtains even linear grammars from finite automata is made by the inverse result of Theorem 1. Let us note that in the module that uses any regular language learning algorithm, an algorithm like the one proposed in [5] could be used which uses a complete presentation sample as input and obtains finite automata as a hypothesis. This algorithm identifies any regular language in the limit [3], so, in such a case, any even linear language can be identified.

Another way of carrying out the identification of any even linear language in the limit could be done by providing algorithms that work without making a reduction of this problem to the regular language identification problem. It could be done by providing a nonterminal merging technique in a similar way of that applied in [5] and [8]. The results of Theorem 3 and Theorem 4 will help to prove the convergence of the algorithm.

5 Acknowledgements

We would like to thank Manuel Vázquez de Parga for his helpful suggestions and his original contribution to the transformation of Even Linear Languages to Regular Languages.

References

[1] V. Amar, G. Putzolu On a Family of Linear Grammars. *Information and Control* 7, pp 283-291. 1964.

[2] D. Angluin, C. Smith Inductive Inference: Theory and Methods. *Computing Surveys* 15, No. 3 pp 237-269. 1983.

[3] M. Gold Language Identification in the Limit. *Information and Control* 10, pp 447-474. 1967.

[4] J. Hopcroft, J. Ullman *Introduction to Automata Theory, Languages and Computation*. Addison-Wesley Publishing Company. 1979.

[5] J. Oncina, P. García Inferring regular languages in polinomial update time. *Pattern Recognition and Image Analysis. Selected Papers from the IVth Spanish Symposium.* Series in Machine Perception Artificial Intelligence. Vol. 1. World Scientific. 1992.

[6] V. Radhakrishnan and G. Nagaraja Inference of Even Linear Grammars and Its Application to Picture Description Languages. *Pattern Recognition* 21, No. 1 pp 55-62. 1988.

[7] Y. Takada Grammatical Inference of Even Linear Languages based on Control Sets. *Information Processing Letters* 28, No. 4 pp 193-199. 1988.

[8] B. Trakhtenbrot, Y. Barzdin *Finite Automata: Behavior and Synthesis*. North Holland Publishing Company. 1973.

Object-Oriented Inferences
in a Logical Framework for Feature Grammars

Liviu-Virgil Ciortuz
Department of Computer Science
"A. I. Cuza" University of Iasi
6600 Iasi, Romania
e-mail: ciortuz@orion.uaic.ro

July, 1994

Abstract: This paper deals on defining object-oriented inferences by desining a new unification procedure called χ-*unification* (which leads to a sound and complete resolution) in DF-logic, a significant subset of F-logic [KLW,1990], an useful frame-based logical framework that enables the declarative implementation of feature grammars like LFGs, GPSGs, HPSGs, etc.

0. Introduction:

DF-logic is the sub-set of F-logic (defined by M. Kifer and his colleagues from SUNY at Stony Brook in [KLW,1990]) obtained by imposing the use Datalog terms (instead of Prolog terms) as 'identification terms' in the atom defintions.

We provide DF-logic with an effective procedural semantics by replacing the unification procedure originally designed for F-atoms such that most things previously intended to be done at the resolution level sould be placed at the unification level (thus drastically reducing the number of resolution rules).

This idea was previously used in the framework of the first-order predicate logic by H. Ait-Kaci in [AKN,1986] (only) for the type-inheritance principle. He defined LOGIN as a logic programming language which extends Prolog by incorporating inheritance at a "built-in" level, namely in the unification procedure. This was called ψ-unification and it extends the well-known unification in the first-order predicate calculus.

The χ-unification procedure here proposed involves not only (type) inheritance, but also other object-oriented principles like argument sub-typing, range super-typing, functionality and the (so called) well-typing conditions. Moreover, while ψ-unification in LOGIN leads to uncomplete resolution, our approach preserves both soundness and completeness of implied inference in DF-logic.

The work here reported could be naturally redone for F-logic (see [Cio,1994]). So, the F-logic restriction to DF-logic is intended only for gaining more effectiveness in implementing a top-down inference procedure in these settings, and is motivated by reasons of immediate practical sufficiency.

1. Syntax:

DF-atoms in DF-logic define frames of methods characterizing classes (and objects as well). Their syntactic form is

$$\text{id[method}_1; \text{method}_2; \dots ; \text{method}_n]$$

where id is the "identification" term for that atom, and each method$_i$, for i = 1,2, ..., n has one of the following syntactic forms:

name@a_1, a_2, ... , a_k -> v	- functional (or: single valuated) method;
name@a_1, a_2, ... , a_k => t_1, t_2, ... , t_m	- function-typing method;
name@a_1, a_2, ... , a_k ->> v_1, v_2, ... , v_s	- set-valuated method;
name@a_1, a_2, ... , a_k => t_1, t_2, ... , t_r	- set-typing method;
name@a_1, a_2, ... , a_k	- predicative method.

Is-a atoms, having the syntactic form t_1:t_2 are seen as *class constraints*: the object (represented by) t_1 must belong to the class t_2, or (equally valid): the class t_1 is a sub-class in (or, better: is derived* from) the class t_2. And these are *explicit* class constraints. Other, *implicit* class constraints will be infered using object-oriented principles like well-typing conditions and functionality.

The antisymmetry of is-a relations leads to the necessity of introducing *equations* having the syntactic form t_1=t_2.

Well-formed formulas in DF-logic are defined quite naturally starting from the atom definitions given above, following the classic way (see [Llo,1987]). The same will be true for other notions like literals, clauses, Horn clauses, definite programs, etc. For examplification, we suggest the reader to see the section 3 ("A Simple Example").

2. Semantics:

The declarative semantics of DF-logic is given in the Appendix at the end of this paper. Herbrand semantics of DF-logic is naturally definable and a Herbrand-like theorem is valid in these settings.

Now we will concentrate on presenting the object-oriented inference rules in the DF-logic procedural semantics.

Definition 1:

A *conditioned term hierarchy* in a DF-logic is a tuple $\mathfrak{K}$ = <T,ρ,Δ,Γ>, where T is a set of terms, ρ is a relation on T, and Δ and Γ are application defined on ρ and {(A,m)| A∈F, m∈ methods(A)} respectively, and taking as value formulas. (So, for each pair (a,b) in ρ, Δ(a,b) will denote the condition under which a "is a" b, i.e., the object a belongs to the class b, or: a is subclass of the class b.)

If (A,B)∈ρ, then A is called a *parent* of A. B is a *proper parent* of A if it is parent of A but they do not belong to a same cycle in $\mathfrak{K}$. A term B∈T is an *ancestor* of A in $\mathfrak{K}$ if (A,B) ∈ trans-closure(ρ) in $\mathfrak{K}$, where trans-closure(ρ) denotes the reflexive and transitive closure of ρ in $\mathfrak{K}$. A term B∈T is a *meta-term* of A in $\mathfrak{K}$ if there is A'∈T, which is both an ancestor of A in $\mathfrak{K}$ and a parent of B, A is an instance of B, and for any proper parent of B is an acestor of A.

Remark: Because every formula in DF-logic could be equivalently written in the disjunctive normal form, the value taken by Δ and Γ could be seen as a set of atom conjunctions, and so will be in the subsequent. The empty set should be interpreted as T, the formula always true. If

---

* This is why we will cal l class constraints as *derivation constraints*.

Δ and Γ are always T (true), then $\mathcal{K}$ in the above definition is in fact a un-conditioned hierarchy.

Definition 2:

Two terms t_1 and t_2 in a DF-logic language unify wrt a conditioned given term hierarchy $\mathcal{K} = <T,\rho,\Delta,\Gamma>$, under the condition δ, σ being one of their unifying substitutions, (and we will denote this fact by unify(t_1,t_2,σ,δ)), if they unify as Datalog terms modulo the conditional equality relation induced on T when considering Trans-closure(ρ) as antisymmetric relation, δ being the underlying equality condition.[1]

Note: If $\mathcal{K}$ does not contain any cycle, then term unification wrt $\mathcal{K}$ is just Datalog term unification, i.e. two constant symbols unify iff they are the same, and any variable unifies with any term, either constant or variable.

If $\mathcal{K} = <T,\rho,\Delta>$ is a conditioned term hierarchy, and a and b are terms, then (a,b)$\in$trans-closure(ρ) in $\mathcal{K}$, under the condition δ, if there are a_1, a_2, ... , a_k in T, with a = a_1, and a_k = b, such that $(a_i,a_{i+1})\in\rho$, for i = 1, ... , k-1, and $\delta = \delta_1 \wedge$ ... $\wedge\delta_{k-1}$, where $\delta_i\in\Delta(a_i,a_{i+1})$, for i = 1, ... , k-1.

Definition 3:

Two elementary methods

$\quad$ m_1: $\qquad$ name$_1$ @ $a_{11},a_{12},...,a_{1n_1}$ [q_t$_1$ [value$_1$]]
$\quad$ m_2: $\qquad$ name$_1$ @ $a_{21},a_{22},...,a_{2n_2}$ [q_t$_2$ [value$_2$]]

unify wrt the conditioned term hierarchy $\mathcal{K} = <T,\rho,\Delta>$, and σ is one of their unifying substitutions, under the condition δ (we will denote this fact by χ-unify (m_1,m_2,σ,δ)), if

i. q_t$_1$ and q_t$_2$ are the same (i.e., the two methods are of the same quasi-type), and $n_1 = n_2$;

ii. if m_1 and m_2 are (they both) functional, set-valued or predicative methods, then the term arrays
$\quad$ <name$_1$,a_{11},a_{12},...,a_{1n_1},[value$_1$]>
$\quad$ <name$_2$,a_{21},a_{22},...,a_{2n_2},[value$_2$]>
unify, σ being one of their unifying substitution, and
δ is the conjunction of the corresponding unifying conditions (on equalities);

iii. if m_1 and m_2 are (they both) function-typing or set-typing methods, then[2]
$\quad$ unify (name$_1$,name$_2$,σ,δ_0),
$\quad$ ($a_{1i}\sigma$,$a_{2i}\sigma$), for i = 1, ... , n_1, and (value$_1\sigma$,value$_2\sigma$) are instances of tuples in trans-closure(ρ) in $\mathcal{K}$, under the δ_i, respectively δ_{n_1+1} conditions, and
$\quad$ $\delta = (\delta_0\wedge\delta_1\wedge$... $\wedge\delta_{n_1}\wedge\delta_{n_1+1})\sigma$.

Remark: In the case iii. of the above definition, the unifying order m_1, m_2 is important; it may not be reversible. This is why it is said that m_1 unifies "into" m_2 wrt $\mathcal{K}$.

Note: Method unification wrt $\mathcal{K}$ could be defined by adding $a_{1i}\sigma = a_{2i}\sigma$, respectively $a_{1i}\sigma : a_{2i}\sigma$ to the underlying condition. (So, the "early" binding of veriables determined by Defintion 3 is replaced by "latter" binding, which is more efficient.) Also, if If $\mathcal{K}$ does not contains any cycle, $a_{1i}\sigma = a_{2i}\sigma$ will be replaced by a corresponding unit substitution in the mgu construction, if one

---

[1] $\quad$ Here is the point where we substitute the Paramodulation resolution rule in [KLW,1990].

[2] $\quad$ Here is the point where we substitute the Argument Sub-Typing and Range Super-Typing resolution rules in [KLW,1990].

of $a_1_i\sigma$ and $a_2_i\sigma$ is variable. In these new settings the results which follows in the present paper do maintain their validity.

Definition 4:

Let m_1 and m_2 be methods, and $\mathcal{K}$ a conditioned term hierarchy. The substitution σ is one of the m_1 and m_2 most general unifiers wrt $\mathcal{K}$ if

  i. σ is one of the m_1 and m_2 unifiers wrt $\mathcal{K}$, and

  ii. for each unifier θ of m_1 into m_2 wrt $\mathcal{K}$, with $\theta \leq \sigma$, it follows that $\sigma \leq \theta$.

Definition 5:

Let m_1 and m_2 be methods, and $\mathcal{K}$ a conditioned term hierarchy. A set Ω of most general unifiers of m_1 into m_2 wrt $\mathcal{K}$ is said to be complete if for any χ-unifier θ of m_1 into m_2 wrt $\mathcal{K}$ there is $\sigma \in \Omega$, such that $\sigma \leq \theta$.

Method Conditional χ-Unification Algorithm

Input: m_1 and m_2, two elementary methods

  m_1: $name_1$ @ $a_{11}, a_{12}, ..., a_{1n_1}$ [q_t_1 [$value_1$]]
  m_2: $name_2$ @ $a_{21}, a_{22}, ..., a_{2n_2}$ [q_t_2 [$value_2$]]

and H = <T,ρ,Δ> a conditioned term hierarchy.

Output: Ω, a complete set of most general unifiers of m_1 into m_2 wrt H, together with the underlying conditions.

Procedure:

```
if q_t1=q_t2, n1=n2 and mgu(name1, name2, θ, δ0)
    if m1 and m2 are non-typing methods
        Ω = { (σ,δ) | mgu(<a11,a12,...,a1n1,value1>,<a21,a22,...,a2n2,value2>,σ,δ) };
    else (m1 and m2 are typing methods)
        {
        Ω = ∅;
        for each application
            λ:{a11,a12,...,a1n1,a1n1+1=value1}∪{a21,a22,...,a2n2,a2n2+1=value2}→T
                such that a is an instance of λ(a) for every a in the domain of λ
            {
            σλ = θ, and δλ = δ0;
            for i=1, ... , n1+1
                if (λ(a1i),λ(a2i)) belongs to trans-closure(ρ)
                    σλ = σλσi, with mgu(<a1iσλ,a2iσλ>,<λ(a1i)σλ,λ(a2i)σλ>,σi,δi), and
                    δλ = δλ∧δi;
                else
                    jump out the inner loop to select another λ;
            Ω = Ω ∪ {σλ};
            }
        }
    else Ω = ∅;
return Ω.
```

Theorem 1:

Let m_1 and m_2 be methods, and $\mathcal{K}$ = <T,ρ,Δ> a conditioned term hierarchy. The above algorithm returns a complete set of most general unifiers of m_1 into m_2 wrt $\mathcal{K}$ (together with the corrspondinf underlying conditions).

Definition 6:

A *conditioned DF-atom hierarchy* (or, simply: a conditioned DF-hierarchy) in a DF-logic language L is a tuple $\mathcal{K} = <F,\rho,\Delta,\Gamma>$, where F is a set of DF-atoms in L, ρ is a relation on term(F), and Δ and Γ are applications defined on ρ respectively $\{(A,m)|\ A\in F,\ m\in methods(A)\}$, and taking as value formulas in the disjunctive normal form. ($\Gamma(A,m)$ will denote the condition under which the method m belonging to the atom A could be applied.)

Notes:

1.The notions of parent, descendent, ancetsor and meta-atom in a DF-hierarchy are immediately definable starting from their conterparts for conditioned term hierarchies.

2. A term hierarchy could be easily extended to a Df-atom hierarchy by considering t[] the ("empty") DF-atom associated to each term t in the hierarchy). Also, some notions introduced above, like method χ-unification extend naturaly to DF-hierarchies.

Definition 7:

Let A and B be DF-atoms, and $\mathcal{K}$ a conditioned DF-hierarchy. A unifies into B wrt $\mathcal{K}$, and σ is one of their unifying substitution, under the condition δ, (simply said: A χ-unifies into B under δ), and this fact will be denoted by χ-unify (A, B, σ, δ), if

   i.   unify (id(A), id(B), σ, δ_0);

   ii. for each method m in A

           there is an atom B_m in $\mathcal{K}$ such that

               if m is not-typing method then B_m is meta-atom of B (under the condition

                   δ_m) and

               if m is typing method then B_m is ancestor[3] of B (under the condition δ_m),

           there is a method m' in B_m in $\mathcal{K}$ such that

           unify (id(B), id(B_m), σ, δ_m'), and

           χ-unify (m, m', σ, δ_m'');

   iii. $\delta = (\delta_0 \wedge \bigwedge_{m\in methods(A)}(\delta_m \wedge \delta_m' \wedge \delta_m'')\ )\sigma$.

Note: The definition of most general unifier and complete set of most general unifiers for two DF-atoms (wrt a DF-hierarchy $\mathcal{K}$) are natural versions of the corresponding definitions given in the case of methods.

The following algorithm gives a constructive way to obtain a complete set of χ-mgus for two DF-atoms wrt a given DF-hierarchy. This algorithm will use the following notations:

   i. for a DF-atom A, methods(A) denotes the set of all methods in A;

   ii. for A in a DF-hierarchy $\mathcal{K} = <T,\rho,\Delta,\Gamma>$, meta-atoms(A) and ancestors(A) will denote the set of all meta-atoms of A, respectively the set of all ancestors of A in $\mathcal{K}$.

DF-Atom Conditional χ-Unification Algorithm

Input: A and B, two DF-atoms, and

        H = $<F,\rho,\Delta,\Gamma>$ a conditioned DF-hierarchy.

Output: Ω, a complete set of most general unifiers of A into B wrt H, together with the unification

        underlying conditions.

Procedure:

        $\Omega = \varnothing$;

        if (mgu(id(A), id(B), θ, δ_0))

---

[3]   Here is the point where we substitute the Type Inheritance resolution rule in [KLW,1990].

if A has no methods,

  return $\Omega = \{(\theta, \delta_0)\}$.

else

for each λ:methods$(A\theta) \to \bigcup_{B_m \in meta\text{-}atom(B\theta, \mathfrak{X})}$methods$(B_m) \cup \bigcup_{B_m \in ancestor(B\theta}$
)methods(B_m)

  such that $\lambda(m) \in$ methods$(B\theta) \cup \bigcup_{B_m \in meta\text{-}atom(B\theta, \mathfrak{X})}$ methods(B_m) for each
  not-typing method $m \in$methods$(A\theta)$

{

$\sigma_\lambda = \varepsilon$ (the empty substitution), and $\delta_\lambda = \delta_0$;

for each method m in $A\theta$

  if $(\chi\text{-mgu}(m\sigma_\lambda, \lambda(m)\sigma_\lambda, \sigma_m, \delta_m))$

   $\sigma_\lambda = \sigma_\lambda \sigma_m$, and $\delta_\lambda = \delta_\lambda \wedge \gamma_m \wedge \delta_m \wedge \Gamma(B_m, \lambda(m))$, with γ_m the condition under
   which B_m involved in the range of λ is a meta-ancestor of B in $\mathfrak{X}$;

  else

   jump out the inner loop to select another λ;

$\Omega = \Omega \cup \{(\theta\sigma_\lambda, \delta_\lambda \theta\sigma_\lambda)\}$;

}

 return Ω.

Theorem 2:

Let A and B be DF-atoms, and $\mathfrak{X} = \langle F, \rho, \Delta, \Gamma \rangle$ a conditioned DF-hierarchy.
The above algorithm returns a complete set of most general unifiers of A into B wrt $\mathfrak{X}$
(together with the corrspondinf underlying conditions).

Now, speaking about DF-logic program P (set of Horn clauses), one could easily associate it
in a natuaral way a unique DF-hierarchy:

Definition 8:

  Let P be a set of Horn clauses apart standardized in DF-logic language. *The canonical
DF-hierarchy* associated to P is the conditioned DF-hierarchy $\mathfrak{X}(P) = \langle F, \rho, \Delta, \Gamma \rangle$ defined by
starting from (the "base" hierarchy):

 $F = \{\top\} \cup \{A | A$ is DF-atom, head of a clause C in P$\}$,

   where $\top$ is a special symbol, the "top" element in the hierarchy,

 ρ is the minimal relation which satisfy the following two conditions:

   i. $\rho \supseteq \{(a,b) | a{:}b$, or $a{=}b$, or $b{=}a$ is head of a clause C in P$\}$;

   ii. $\rho \supseteq \{(X,b) |$ there is a clause C in P such that the variable X is id(head(C))
     and X:b, with b constant symbol, appears in body(C)$\}$, C having been
     written as head(C):-body(C),

 $\Delta(a,b) = \{$body(C)$|a{:}b$, or $a{=}b$, or $b{=}a$ is head of a clause C in P$\}$, and

 $\Gamma(A,m) = $ body(C)$\backslash \{$id(A):b in body(C)$|b$ is constant symbol$\}$, for each method m in A
   $\in$F, if m comes into A (by merging) from the head of the clause C.

and then closing it through well-typing conditions and the functionality rules (paramodularity
being enclosed into unification), i.e.,

   iii.ρ is extended with $(v,t)\sigma$ if[4]

    there are two DF-atoms in F

    $o[... ; m@a_1, a_2, ... a_k \to v ; ...]$ and

    $o'[... ; m'@a_1', a_2', ... a_k' => t ; ...]$,

     or

---

[4]   Here is the point where we substitute the Well-Typing inference rule in [KLW,1990].

$o[\ldots ; m@a_1,a_2, \ldots a_k ->> v ; \ldots]$ and
$o'[\ldots ; m'@a_1',a_2', \ldots a_k' =>> t ; \ldots]$, such that
$(o,o') = (\alpha_0,\beta_0)\sigma_0$, where $(\alpha_0,\beta_0) \in$ trans-closure(ρ) under the condition δ_0,
$(a_i,a_i') = (\alpha_i,\beta_i)\sigma_i$, where $(\alpha_i,\beta_i) \in$ trans-closure(ρ) under the condition δ_i, for $i = 1, \ldots , n$, and
$\sigma = \sigma_0\sigma_1 \ldots \sigma_n$; and, in this case Δ is extended with $\Delta(v\sigma,t\sigma) \supseteq \{\delta\sigma\}$, and

iv. $\rho \supseteq \{(v,w), (w,v)\}$ if[5]
there are two DF-atoms in F
$o[\ldots ; m@a_1,a_2, \ldots a_k -> v ; \ldots]$ and
$o'[\ldots ; m'@a_1',a_2', \ldots a_k' -> w ; \ldots]$, such that
$(o,o') = (\alpha_0,\beta_0)\sigma_0$, where α_0 and β_0 belong to a same cycle in $\mathcal{K}(P)$, or one is meta-atom of the other, under the condition δ_0,
$(a_i,a_i') = (\alpha_i,\beta_i)\sigma_i$, where $(\alpha_i,\beta_i) \in$ trans-closure(ρ) under the condition δ_i, for $i = 1, \ldots , n$, and
$\sigma = \sigma_0\sigma_1 \ldots \sigma_n$; and, in this case Δ is extended with $\Delta(v\sigma,w\sigma) \supseteq \{\delta\sigma\}$.

Finally, ρ will be extended such that any maximal acyclic chain γ in ρ ends up in T.
Optionally, the atoms in F which have the same identification part (up to a renaming substitution) and the same proper parents could be merged.

Furthermore, we define the *χ-inference rules*, which are intended to be applied (using χ-unification) wrt a given DF-hierarchy. In the case of a DF-logic program P, we will see, it should be the canonical DF-hierarchy $\mathcal{K}(P)$ just defined above, in order to provide a sound and complete resolution in DF-logic.

1. χ-Resolution:
   If $\neg A \lor C$ and $B \lor C'$ are two clauses standardized apart in a DF-logic language, and θ is a χ-mgu of A into B under the condition δ, then derive $(C \lor C' \lor \neg \delta)\theta$.

2. χ-Factoring:
   If $\neg A \lor \neg B \lor C$ is a clause, and θ is a χ-mgu of A into B under the condition δ, then derive $(\neg B \lor C \lor \neg \delta)\theta$. If $A \lor B \lor C$ is a clause, and θ is a χ-mgu of A into B under the condition δ, then derive $(A \lor C \lor \neg \delta)\theta$.

3. χ-Is-A Trans-Closure (or: "built-in" Is-A Trans-Closure)[6] :
   Derive $(X:Y \lor \neg \delta \lor \neg \delta')\theta$, if there are X' and Y' in $\mathcal{K}$ such that unify($<X,Y>,<X',Y'>,\theta,\delta$), and $(X',Y') \in$ trans-closure(ρ) in $\mathcal{K}$ under the condition δ'.

4. χ-Is-A Antisimetry (or: "built-in" Is-A Antisimmetry):
   Derive $((X=Y) \lor \neg \delta \lor \neg \delta')\theta$, if there are X' and Y' in $\mathcal{K}$ such that unify($<X,Y>,<X',Y'>, \theta,\delta$), and X' and Y' belong to a same cycle in $\mathcal{K}$ under the condition δ'.

5. Merging:
   If $A \lor C$ and $B \lor C'$ are two clauses standardized apart, and θ is a mgu of the identification parts of A and B under the condition δ, then derive $R \lor (C \lor C' \lor \neg \delta)\theta$, were R is the canonical union of $A\theta$ and $B\theta$.

---

[5]   Here is the point where we substitute the Functionality inference rule in [KLW,1990].
[6]   Here is the point where we substitute the Is-A Reflexivity and Is-A Transitivity inference rules in [KLW,1990].

6. Elimination:

From ¬A[]∨C, derive C.

The following two results give the soundness and completeness of χ-deduction rules on Horn clauses:

Theorem 3 (Soundness):

Let S be a set of Horn clauses in a DF-logic language, and C_1, ... , C_n a finite sequence of clauses such that $C_n = C$ and, for $1 \le k \le n$, $C_k \in S$ or C_k is derived from C_i and (possibly) C_j, with i, j < k, by one of the χ-deduction rules, wrt the canonical DF-hierarchy associated to S. C is a logical consequence of S.

Theorem 4 (Completeness):

Let S be an unsatisfiable set of clauses in a DF-logic language. There is a refutation (i.e. a derivation of the empty clause) from S using the χ-deduction rules working wrt the canonical DF-hierarchy associated to S.

The above theorems are proven in a natural manner by reference to the corresponding results in [KLW,1990].

Finally, we give a top-down inference procedure in DF-logic:

A Top-Down Inference Algorithm in DF-Logic

Input: P, a definite program written in a DF-logic language,
      G, a goal ← A_1, A_2, ... , A_k.,
      R, a selection rule, R(G) = A_i.
Output: σ, an answer substitution, if there is a substitution θ such that P ⊢ Gθ, and
      'Fail', otherwise.
Procedure (identified in the following as 'top-down'):
    if G = □ (the null list)
        return σ = ε (the empty substitution);
    compute $\mathcal{K}(P)$ = <F,ρ,Δ,Γ>, the canonical hierarchy associated to P;
    eliminate the empty DF-atoms in G;
    factorize the DF-atoms in G having the same identification part;
    rename the variables in G into new variables, distinct from those in P;
    A_i = R(G);
    if (A_i is DF-atom)
        $\mathcal{B}$ = {B∈F | mgu(A_i,B,θ,δ,) and, under the condition γ, (id(Bθ),b)∈trans-closure(ρ), for
            any ground term b such that id(A_i):b is is-a atom in G}, and
        G' = (G \ ({A_i}∪{id(A_i):b | b is ground term in G}))∨¬δ';
    else
    if (A_i is is-a atom)
        $\mathcal{B}$ = {B_1:B_2 | B_1,B_2∈F and unify(A_i,B_1:B_2,θ,δ)}, and
        G' = G \ {A_i};
    else (A_i is equality atom)
        $\mathcal{B}$ = {B_1=B_2| B_1 and B_2 belong to a same cycle in F, and unify(A_i,B_1=B_2,θ,δ)}, and
        G' = G \ {A_i};
    if (∃B∈$\mathcal{B}$, χ-mgu(A_i,B,σ,δ))
        if (top-down(P,G=(G'∧¬δ)θ,σ))
            return θσ;
        else;
    else;
    return 'Fail'.

3. A Simple Example

We suppose the example we give now ilustrates to some extend the ideas exposed in this paper.

Let be the DF-logic program (inspired by [CL,1990]):

```
X[happy] :- X:person[friend -> _ ].
person[friend => person].
X[F -> Y] :- Y[F:symmetric -> X].
friend:symmetric.
albert:person[friend -> lucy].
```

and the goal

```
?- lucy[happy].
```

After (de)applying the easily understandable syntactic conventions used above, the first, the third, and the fifth clauses will be written:

```
X[happy] :- X:person, X[friend -> Z].
X[F -> Y] :- F:symmetric, Y[F -> X].
albert:person.
albert[friend -> lucy].
```

Inspired by the idea of definite feature atoms in [Abr,1990], the canonical DF-hierarchy associated to the above logic program could be visualized as it follows:

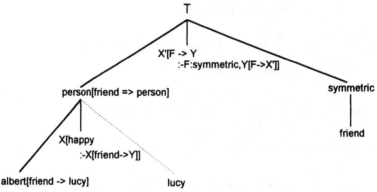

Remarks: The above hierarchy is in fact a non-conditioned one, due to the simplicity of the considered program. The dotted line corresponds to the is-a relationship added in the second phase of the canonical DF-hierarchy associated to the DF-logic program.

The χ-resolution produces the following goal lists:

G0:	lucy[happy].	χ-unifier: $\sigma_0 = \{X/lucy\}$;
G1:	lucy[friend -> Z].	χ-unifier: $\sigma_1 = \{X/lucy, F/friend, Z/Y\}$;
G2:	friend:symmetric, Y[friend -> lucy].	
G3:	Y[friend -> lucy].	χ-unifier: $\sigma_3 = \{Y/albert\}$;
G4:	$\square$.	

Remarks:
1. One could backtrack after G3, but no more solutions will be found.
2. We could enhance χ-unification in DF-logic taking into accound fully bounded class variables. Namely, each variable X in the expressions to be unified is characterized by a set of

"boud" constraints X:b, with b constant symbol. In these new settings, the above resolution could be done in four steps, instead of five, by eliminating G2.

Conclusion

We have defined a way for doing object-oriented inferences in DF-logic, a data frame-based logic obtained from F-logic (a frame-based logic introduced in [KLW,1990]) by restricting identification terms to variables and constant symbols. The :-a atoms in DF-logic are treated as class/object derivation relationships. We deal with these constraints in a dynamic way, i.e. we infer new derivation relationships starting from the given ones, through the so-called well-typing conditions, the is-a reflexivity, is-a transitivity, and functionality principles, and using a special unification procerdure called χ-unification. This computation on feature frames represented by DF-atoms involves type-inheritance, argument sub-typing, and range super-typing wrt a given (conditioned) hierarchy of DF-atoms.

Further Work

This work is the theoretical base for further implementing HPSGs for the Romanian language syntax.

Bibliography

[Abr,1990] H.Abramson, *Definte Feature Grammars for Natural Language Processing*, in Logic Programming and Natural Language Understanding, vol. III, 1990.

[Cio,1994] L.-V.Ciortuz, Logic Programming with Built-in Object-Orientation, Annals of "Ai.I. Cuza" University of Iasi, Computer Science Section, 1994 (to appear).

[Hen,1989] P. van Hentenrick, *Constraint Satisfaction in Logic Programming*, MIT Press, 1989.

[KLW,1990] M.Kifer, G.Lausen, J.Wu, *Logical Foundations of Object-Oriented and Frame-Based Languages*, Technical Report 90/14, SUNY at Stony Brook, 1990.

[Llo,1987] J.W.Lloyd, *Foundations of Logic Programming*, Springer-Verlag, second edition, 1987.

Appendix: Declarative Semantics of DF-Logic

Definition 1:

The *semantic structure* (or: interpretation) of an DF-logic language L is a tuple

$$I = <U, \leq, I_C, I_{\_>}, I_{=>}, I_{\_>>}, I_{=>>}, I_P>$$

where:

- U - the universe of interpretation - is a non-empty set;
- $\leq$ is a partial order relation on U;
- I_C is the interpretation function for constant symbols, with $I_C(c)$ being an element c' in U, for each constant symbol c in the language alphabet;
- $I_{\_>}:U \rightarrow \prod Partial(U^{n+1},U)$ $n \geq 0$, is the interpretation of functional methods.
  Partial(A,B) is the set of all partially defined functions from A to B.
  When $I_{\_>}(m)$ $(u,u_1,u_2,...,u_n)$ is defined, it denotes the value of the method m applied to the object/class u in the context of the $u_1,u_2,...,u_n$ objects/classes;
- $I_{=>}:U \rightarrow \prod_{n \geq 0} PartialAntimonotone(U^{n+1},2_\uparrow^U)$ is the interpretation of function-typing methods.
  Here $2_\uparrow^U$ denotes the set of all upward-closed subsets of the U (i.e., $A \subseteq U$ is in $2_\uparrow^U$ iff y $\in A$ for all $y \geq x$, if $x \in A$). A function $f:A \rightarrow B$ is antimonotone if and only if whenever f(x) is defined, then for all $y \in A$ with $y \leq_A x$, f(y) is defined too, and $f(x) \leq_B f(y)$. Obviously, $\leq_A$ and $\leq_B$ are partial order relations on A and B, respectively. (The antimonotone property will be used for type inheritance.)
  When $I_{=>}^{(n)}(m)(u,u_1,u_2,...,u_n)$ is defined, it will say that the value of the functional method m applied to the object/class u in the context defined by the $u_1,u_2,...,u_n$ objects/classes belongs to each one of the classes in the set denoted by $I_{=>}^{(n)}(m)(u,u_1,u_2,...,u_n)$;
- $I_{\_>>}:U \rightarrow \prod_{n \geq 0} Partial(U^{n+1},2^U)$ is the interpretation of set-valued methods.
  2^U denotes the powerset of U, i.e. the set of all subsets of the U set.
  When $I_{\_>>}^{(n)}(m)(u, u_1, u_2, ... , u_n)$ is defined, it denotes that subset of U which is the value of the set-valued method m applied to the object/class u in the context of the $u_1,u_2,..., u_n$ objects/classes;
- $I_{=>>}:U \rightarrow \prod_{n \geq 0} PartialAntimonotone(U^{n+1},2_\uparrow^U)$ is the interpretation of set-typing methods.
  When $I_{=>>}^{(n)}(m)(u,u_1,u_2,...,u_n)$ is defined, it will be used to say that each element in the value of the set-valued method m applied to the object/class u in the context defined by the $u_1,u_2,...,u_n$ objects/classes belongs to every class in the set denoted by $I_{=>>}^{(n)}(m)(u,u_1,u_2,...,u_n)$;
- $I_P:U \rightarrow \prod_{n \geq 0} 2^{U^{n+1}}$ is the interpretation of predicative methods.
  For each $n \geq 0$, the $I_P^{(n)}(m)$ component of $I_P(m)$ denotes the set of all (n+1)-uples $<u,u_1,u_2,...,u_n>$ belonging to m, when m is interpreted as a (n+1)-ary relation.

Two *well-typing conditions* link the interpretations of method values and types:

    i. if $I_{\_>}^{(n)}(m)(a,a_1,a_2,...,a_n)$ is defined, then $I_{=>}^{(n)}(m)(a,a_1,a_2,...,a_n)$ is defined, and
      if $I_{\_>>}(m)(a,a_1,a_2,...,a_n)$ is defined, then $I_{=>>}^{(n)}(m)(a,a_1,a_2,...,a_n)$ is defined too;

    ii. if $q = I_{\_>}^{(n)}(m)(a,a_1,a_2,...,a_n)$, then $q \leq r$ for each $r \in I_{=>}^{(n)}(m)(a,a_1,a_2,...,a_n)$, and
      if $q \in I_{\_>>}^{(n)}(m)(a,a_1,a_2,...,a_n)$, then $q \leq r$ for each $r \in I_{=>>}^{(n)}(m)(a,a_1,a_2,...,a_n)$.

We define a *variable assignment* in the language L a mapping that applies to each variable X an element u in the semantic universe U. The mapping could be naturally extended to the set of terms in the language L.

The *truth values* for the two *special predicates* used in the DF-logic settings, namely the *is-a* relation and the *equality* relation are defined (in the semantic structure I and the variable assignment as) as it follows.

Definition 2:

$I \vdash_{as} a{:}b$ iff $as(a) \leq as(b)$ in U, and
$I \vdash_{as} a{=}b$ is true iff $as(a) = as(b)$ in U.

Here $I \vdash_{as} F$ stands for: the formula F is true in the semantic structure I and the variable assignment as, and $I \vdash F$ will say that F is true in the structure I (and every assignment as).

The truth values for non-compound DF-atoms (i.e. DF-atoms containing only one method) are given by the following equivalence relations.

Definition 3:

$I \vdash_{as} a[m a_1, a_2, ..., a_n \text{->} v]$ iff
$\quad I_{\text{->}}{}^{(n)}(m')(a', a_1', a_2', ..., a_n')$ is defined and $I_{\text{->}}{}^{(n)}(m')(a', a'_1, a'_2, ..., a'_n) = v'$, where $m', a', a_1', a_2', ..., a_n',$ and v' are respectively the $m, a, a_1, a_2, ..., a_n,$ and v images through as.

$I \vdash_{as} a[m a_1, a_2, ..., a_n \text{=>} t_1, t_2, ..., t_r]$ iff
$\quad I_{\text{=>}}{}^{(n)}(m')(a', a_1', a_2', ..., a_n')$ is defined and $I_{\text{=>}}{}^{(n)}(m')(a', a'_1, a'_2, ..., a'_n) \supseteq \{t'_1, t'_2, ..., t'_r\}$, where $m', a', a_1', a_2', ..., a_n',$ and $t'_1, t'_2, ..., t'_r$ are respectively the $m, a, a_1, a_2, ..., a_n,$ and $t_1, t_2, ..., t_r$ images through as.

$I \vdash_{as} a[m@a_1, a_2, ..., a_n \text{->>} v_1, v_2, ..., v_m]$ iff
$\quad I_{\text{->>}}{}^{(n)}(m')(a', a_1', a_2', ..., a_n')$ is defined, and $I_{\text{->>}}{}^{(n)}(m')(a', a'_1, a'_2, ..., a'_n) \supseteq \{v'_1, v'_2, ..., v'_m\}$ where $m', a', a_1', a_2', ..., a_n',$ and v' are respectively the $m, a, a_1, a_2, ..., a_n,$ and $v_1, v_2, ..., v_m$ images through as.

$I \vdash_{as} a[m@a_1, a_2, ..., a_n \text{=>>} t_1, t_2, ..., t_r]$ iff
$\quad I_{\text{=>>}}{}^{(n)}(m')(a', a_1', a_2', ..., a_n')$ is defined and $I_{\text{=>>}}{}^{(n)}(m')(a', a'_1, a'_2, ..., a'_n) \supseteq \{t'_1, t'_2, ..., t'_r\}$, where $m', a', a_1', a_2', ..., a_n',$ and $t'_1, t'_2, ..., t'_r$ are respectively the $m, a, a_1, a_2, ..., a_n,$ and $t_1, t_2, ..., t_r$ images through as.

$I \vdash_{as} a[m@a_1, a_2, ..., a_n]$ iff
$\quad I_p{}^{(n)}(m') \ni (a', a'_1, a'_2, ..., a'_n)$, where $m', a', a_1', a_2', ..., a_n'$ are respectively the $m, a, a_1, a_2, ..., a_n$ images through as.

Finally, the truth value of an atom (1.1) is given by

Definition 4:

$I \vdash_{as} id[method_1; ...; method_k]$ iff $I \vdash_{as} id[method_1] \& ... \& I \vdash_{as} id[method_k]$

For a non-compound atom

$a[m@a_1, a_2, ..., a_n \text{ q\_t } v_1, v_2, ... v_m]$

with q_t being ->>, =>, or =>>, we consider its *elementary sub-atoms*

$a[m@a_1, a_2, ..., a_n \text{ q\_t } v_k]$ for $k = 1, ..., m$.

Any other atom like $a[m@a_1, a_2, ..., a_n \text{ -> } v]$ or $a[m@a_1, a_2, ..., a_n]$ is its own elementary sub-atom.

The *elementary sub-atom set* of an atom (1.1) is the union of the elementary sub-atom set of all non-compound sub-atoms of the given atom. Using the above truth relations, it follows that an atom (1.1) is true in the semantic structure I (and the variable assignment as) iff all its elementary sub-atoms are true in I (and as). So, any atom could be written under elementary form, i.e. it could be equivalently replaced by an atom having only elementary methods.

The other semantic definitions in DF-logic extend in a natural way the corresponding definitions in the first-order predicate calculus.

AUTOMATIC DETERMINATION OF A STOCHASTIC BI-GRAM CLASS LANGUAGE MODEL

Michèle Jardino
Gilles Adda
LIMSI-CNRS
B.P. 133
F-91403, ORSAY Cedex, FRANCE
E-mail: jardino@limsi.fr, gadda@limsi.fr

ABSTRACT

As pointed out by Jelinek [1] the n-gram word model is a very efficient model but not well adapted for highly inflected languages such as French. So we have developed a class-based bigram model determined entirely automatically from written text corpora. The classes are not defined, the words are not tagged, the solely assumption is the number of classes.

We get a robust model which insures a more complete coverage of the succession probabilities. Here we present results on new classifications of 2 millions of words of a French text [2], obtained with allowing more than one possible class for each word, as well as optimised combinations of word and class bigram models.

I- INTRODUCTION

The design of probabilistic grammars is strongly affected by the determination of nonterminals which is generally carried out by hand. Especially in the case where rules are automatically built [3,4], this hand-made initialisation can give sub-optimal results.

In the simple case of n-gram class based grammars [5], statistical methods permit the entirely automatic classification of words of written texts [2,6,7,8]. Here we present a special taxonomy obtained with this kind of procedure which distributes, after optimisation, words into unlabelled classes. These classes are not defined in advance, they are merely word clusters built by the automatic process.

Description of the method and detailed results of the classification are given for large corpora.

II- CLASSIFICATION METHOD

Words are classified in order to get the maximum probability P_T of a given text. We will demonstrate below how this probability depends on the classification.

II-1 Text probability

With a text of N words: $\omega_1 \, \omega_2 \ldots \omega_N$, P_T is, ideally:

$$P_T = P(\omega_1) \prod_{n=2}^{N} P(\omega_N \mid \omega_{N-1} \ldots \omega_1)$$

In other terms, the probability to get the last word of a text depends on all the previous words, which is not really true. We must reduce the history of each word, first because we don't need all the history and secondly because we have not enough data to estimate reliable probabilities, and finally because machines can't manage such huge information quantities. For example, at present, the recognition tasks involved in ARPA evaluations [9], take into account an history reduced to one or two words .

Here, only the previous word is kept, so P_T becomes:

$$P_T = P(\omega_1)\prod_{n=2}^{N} P(\omega_n \mid \omega_{n-1})$$

But even with this restriction, huge sizes of texts are required to get a sensible evaluation of the parameters. A text of vocabulary size V, needs the estimation of V^2-1 probabilities of word pairs to reach the complete coverage of all the possibilities.

A more robust procedure is to put words into C classes. With this approach, the estimation of C^2+V-1 parameters insures a full coverage of all the possibilities, when only one class is assumed for each word. When V is greatly higher than C, the reduction of the number of parameters to be estimated is about $(V/C)^2$ and less training texts are required to train these parameters.

When words are distributed among classes, the succession probability of two words, $P(\omega_n \mid \omega_{n-1})$, can be written :

$$P(\omega_n \mid \omega_{n-1}) = \sum_{C(\omega_n)} P(\omega_n \mid C(\omega_n)) \sum_{C(\omega_{n-1})} P(C(\omega_n) \mid C(\omega_{n-1})) \, P(C(\omega_{n-1}) \mid \omega_{n-1})$$

where $C(\omega_n)$ and $C(\omega_{n-1})$ are the classes which contain respectively the words ω_n and ω_{n-1} .

II-2 PERPLEXITY

It is clear that the text probability P_T decreases when the size of the text increases. A much more tractable parameter has been defined [10]: the perplexity PP_T :

$$PP_T = \exp(-1/N \log P_T)$$

which realises a weighting of P_T by N, the number of words of the text.

In the very unfavourable case where the text contains N independent and equally probable words, PP_T is merely equals to N. More generally, PP_T could be regarded as the average number of words which can follow each word of the text.

II-3 CLASSIFICATION PROCESS USING SIMULATED ANNEALING

Starting from a training text and a given number of classes we get an optimised classification of the words of this text by minimising PP_T, its perplexity. The estimation of PP_T is calculated from maximum likelihood estimates of the probabilities, counting the relative frequencies of the class pairs and the relative frequencies of the words in their class. The simulated annealing process is used as the optimisation method. This method has already been used in this type of problem [11] to get for instance the shorter travelling salesman route or the best implementation of circuitry in computers.

The process starts with a state of the system (or a configuration), for instance a possible route for the traveller or a particular partition of the words of a text into classes, and then automatically choose successive states depending from the preceding ones, in order to reduce a characteristic value : the length of the route in the first case, the perplexity of the text in the second one. This a Markov process.

Assumptions
Here, we will consider only the case of a classification in which each word is only put into one class. Classifications with more than one class per word follow the same scheme.The initial configuration or initial classification must be one of the worse configurations of the system which corresponds to one of the highest value of the perplexity. Then configurations are successively modified by moving only one word from its initial class to a new one, both word and class are randomly chosen (Monte Carlo selection). The new configuration is accepted under conditions which depend on the new value of the perplexity and on a control parameter (Metropolis algorithm [12]).

Metropolis algorithm
In classical Monte Carlo minimizations a new configuration is only accepted if the perplexity decreases; with the Metropolis algorithm a worse configuration, with a higher perplexity, can be accepted depending on the value of the control parameter cp.
Assuming a perplexity value PP_i at step i and a perplexity value PP_{i+1} at step i+1, we compare $\exp((PP_i - PP_{i+1})/cp)$ with a random number contained between 0 and 1. If it is higher the new configuration is accepted and denied in the opposite case.

Acceptance ratio χ
At the beginning of the optimisation all the transitions must be accepted. This condition gives an initial value cp_0 for the control parameter which is directly related to the average of the fluctuations of the perplexity δPP_j such that :

$$\exp(-\delta PP_i/cp_0) = 1$$

Different approaches [13] calculate pp_0 assuming an acceptance ratio χ slightly less than 1. In fact this value can be easily determined experimentally .

Iterative procedure
The optimisation is carried out in a double iterative procedure: first for a fixed value of the control parameter an important number of configurations are tried (for example in [13] a multiple of the number of different words of the text is prescribed) then the control parameter is slightly decreased and the process is repeated until there is no more change or until a very low value (near 0) of the control parameter is reached.
The choice of the initial value of the control parameter must allow an important proportion of accepted solutions (typically higher than 80%) .
It has been demonstrated [14] that if the control parameter decreases like a logarithm during the process and if an infinite number of changes are made at each step a global minimum is reached.

Any written text can be treated using this method, without any knowledge of the language, of its syntax or semantics...

III- CLASSIFICATION RESULTS ON TRAINING

We began to classify texts of some thousands of words [2,7] of French and German language; now we are processing texts with millions of words. Words are merely strings between blanks, so in this framework, punctuation signs are regarded as words.

Here we present different experiments on texts extracted from the French newspaper "Le Monde". The training text has about 2 millions of words with a vocabulary of 65 000 words. The results of different trainings will be seen both from the angle of the succession probabilities of classes and from the one of their contents.

In the two following parts, we describe results assuming one possible class for each word (case 1). In the third part, we present results assuming two possible classes for each word (case 2).

III-1 OBSERVED CONTENTS OF SOME CLASSES

The following results come from a word distribution into 1000 classes. They reflect the short range context which has been taken into account (memory reduced to one word). Nevertheless, sensible classifications are obtained; this is illustrated by the examples :

- *classes with only one very common word*:
    - punctuations
    - grammatical words (*de, pour, le...*)
- *syntactical classes* which respect agreement in gender and number:
    - feminine singular nouns: *affaire, exposition, harmonie, idéologie, impulsion, intimité, utopie, épreuve, étude, abstraction, autoroute, infection, interrogation, odeur.*
    - feminine singular adjectives: *fausse, mauvaise, seule, vraie, franche, sainte.*
    - masculine singular past participle: *cassé, disparu, défendu, ignoré, introduit, lancé, marqué, organisé, renversé, salué, tué, abandonné, adopté, attaqué, commandé, contesté, divisé, dégagé, déposé, identifié, intégré, opéré, paralysé, récupéré, transformé, plongé, chassé, fabriqué.*
    - infinitive verbs: *croire, apporter, approuver, prétendre, supporter, écarter, citer, confirmer, considérer, imaginer, interpréter, nier, regretter, indiquer, signifier, estimer.*
    - adverbs: *normalement, librement, totalement, uniquement, exclusivement, fermement, franchement, pleinement, successivement, indéfiniment, différemment, mutuellement, considérablement, obligatoirement.*
- *semantic classes*
    - last names: *Calvet, Fabius, Aubert, Chancel, Chérèque, Curien, Damette, Dietrich, Febvre, Frey, Havel, Horn, Jospin, Lapautre, Léotard, Moussa, Pelletier, Prost.*
    - first names: *François, Lionel, Vaclav, Daniel, Louis, Maria, Hans, Fouad, Jean-Yves, Gaston.*
- *semantic classes combined with syntactical classes*
    - masculine singular adjectives characterizing countrys: *finlandais, français, iranien, panaméen, brésilien, indien, israélien, lituanien, ouest-allemand, sud-africain.*

Other classes are not so well defined, but they contribute as the previous ones, to the distribution which insures the lowest perplexity value.

III-2 CLASS PAIR PROBABILITIES

A result of a classification is a matrix which gives the probability of class pairs. For example the classification of the 2 millions of words into 1000 classes gives a filling rate of about 10%. As this matrix is not easy (nor interesting) to show as a whole we give one histogram of the occurrences of class pairs with the respective contents of some involved classes in figure 1. Classes are numbered from 1 to 1000. In our example, the first class is numbered 269, it contains the words: *François, Lionel, Vaclav, Daniel, Louis, Maria, Hans, Fouad, Jean-Yves, Gaston.* The main following classes are the class 242 containing words: *Vuitton, XIV, Bérégovoy, Lawson, Mermaz, Mitterrand, Bouteiller, Genoud, Krasucki, Lacroix, Ligatchev, Mauroy, Modrow;* the class 10 : *Calvet, Fabius, Aubert, Chancel, Chérèque, Curien, Damette, Dietrich, Febvre, Frey, Havel, Horn, Jospin, Lapautre, Léotard, Moussa, Pelletier, Prost,* and the class 18 : *Renault, Tjibaou, Rothschild, Airways, Bram, Bull, Chargeurs, Columbia, Dassault, Ford, Rhône-Poulenc, Schneider, Stewart, Suzuki, Aveline...*

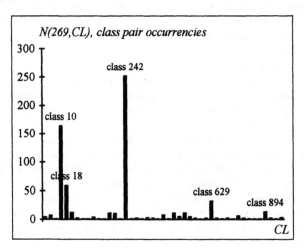

Figure 1: class pair occurencies of (269, CL).

A possible analysis of the contents of these classes is that the class 269 contains first names or words with a similar behaviour, and the classes 242, 10 and 18 contains corresponding last names or words with a similar behaviour. For instance for the word pair *Louis XIV, Louis* could be regarded as a first name and *XIV* as a last name.

III-3 IMPROVED CLASSIFICATIONS

The preceding qualitative results (quantitative results will be exhibited at the end of the paper) were obtained assuming that each vocabulary word belongs only to one class. With this assumption the different possible classifications of a graphemic word are not taken into account: for instance the French word *le* which could be either a pronoun or an article belongs to only one class. This assumption is harmful, as the words following *le* will tend to go in the same class with no difference between the verbs and the nouns. Thus, we are now developing a more refined model with the possibility for each vocabulary word to belong to different classes.

In a first step, one vocabulary word can be put into two different classes, with a context dependent division: the first class contains the subset of words whith the highest left bigram, the second one the rest of the words in other left contexts. Other strategies are obviously possible, but this is one of the easiest. Results are shown and compared with the previous classification in figure 2 (the number of different classes equals 1000).

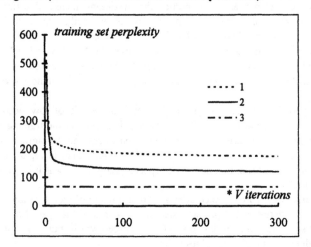

Figure 2: Evolution of perplexity during training: 1 - one word belongs to one class, 2 - one word can belong to two classes, 3 - limiting case: C=V

Perplexity values in the second case are reduced by 25%, compared with perplexity in the first case. The third case corresponds to the bigram word perplexity calculated on the same training text.

Interesting new classifications emerge using this new method. For instance, words like *le, la, les* which stand each alone in one class in the former classification, belong now to two classes, according to the difference between their use as an article or as a pronoun. Other ambiguous words have also been split depending on the context: the word *dure* which means "hard" as an adjective and "last" as a verb can be found in two classes. One other satisfactory observation is that a lot of words have not been split: the method does not seem to produce unuseful classes.

IV-LANGUAGE MODEL, EVALUATION

IV-1 EVALUATION

A held-out text, which has not been used for training, is used both to evaluate the perplexity of the classifications obtained and to fix the optimum values of some interpolation parameters. This held-out text is referred to as the test set in the remaining of the paper.

A test set of 200 000 words has been used to evaluate the model. It contains sentences randomly chosen in the original corpus and not contained in the training part.

The evaluation has been carried out in both cases when one vocabulary word belongs either to one class or to two classes.

IV-2 UNSEEN WORDS AND UNSEEN CLASS PAIRS

Although large training texts are used to estimate probabilities, there remain unseen events with zero probability when the probabilities are kept equal to the maximum likelihood estimations. So interpolation methods are needed to deduce more realistic distribution probabilities: the general process is to reduce the maximum likelihood estimations and to redistribute the corresponding "mass" according to the probability rules. In [15], different methods have been compared, here we will only use the best one.

A fixed quantity δ is subtracted from class pair occurrences $N(C_iC_j)$ and the corresponding mass $M_i(\delta)$ is uniformly redistributed among all possible bigrams associated with C_i. The value of δ is optimised directly on the test set but it is possible to determine its value from the training text [16].

Furthermore a special class has been created, containing words of low occurrence in the training text. This class is meant to deal with test words unseen in the training set. With this process non-zero probabilities are given for these unseen words and the bigram associated with them. This way to deal with unseen words is not the optimal one, in regard of the test set perplexity, but is more realistic, in a context of speech recognition, which is the main purpose of these classifications.

The number of unknown words is fixed arbitrarily to a fraction of words of lower occurencies; with 25%, we get underestimated probabilities for the words of the special class in regard of the analysed test set which contains less than 10% of unseen words; but this approximation has a very small incidence on perplexity values (1%).

IV-3 TEST SET PERPLEXITY AGAINST THE NUMBER OF CLASSES

In figure 3, we show the test set perplexities for the two classifications (a single class per word vs two possible classes per word).

As shown in figure 3, a minimum value of perplexity, depending on the number of classes is obtained. The aim of the classification is to share probabilities among words with the same behaviour. When the number of classes is too low, we have an over-generalization, and the probabilities are not specific enough. When the number of classes is too high, we have an over-specialisation on the training text: the estimation is too close to the training text, and does not permit enough generalization. This explains increasing perplexity values for the highest values of the number of classes.

The optimum number of classes is relatively high: about 1500 classes in case 1, for a training text of 2 millions of words. This number is directly related to the size of the training text, and does not exhibit any "optimal" number of classes for the French language.

In case 2, when a word may belong to two classes, the optimum number of classes is higher (about 2000) and lower perplexity values are reached : we observe a decrease of 20% of the perplexity on the test set., the perplexity decreasing from about 230 in the best case with classification 1 to 185 with classification 2.

64

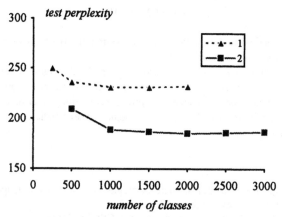

Figure 3: Perplexity of a test set (200000 words, 20000 vocabulary words) against the number of classes; case 1: one word belongs to one class, case 2: one word can belong to two classes.

IV-4 COMPARISON BETWEEN BIGRAM CLASS MODEL AND BIGRAM WORD MODEL

The probabilities given by the bigram class model can be compared with those of the bigram word model which merely counts the word pair occurrences. In figure 4, we present a linear combination of the two models depending on α, the interpolation parameter. When $\alpha=0$ we obtain the test perplexity evaluated from the bigram word model, when $\alpha=1$ the test perplexity evaluated from the bigram class model.

In both cases, large improvements are obtained when combining of the word bigram model with the class bigram model (more than 15% of perplexity decrease). When one word can have two classes, the bigram class model performs better than the bigram word model.

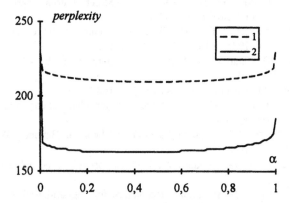

Figure 4: Perplexity of the test set when bigram class model is combined with bigram word model for different values of α ($\alpha=0$ corresponds to the word bigram model, $\alpha=1$ to the class bigram model), case 1: one word belongs to one class, case 2: one word can belong to two classes.

V- CONCLUSION

We have described a method to automatically classify words of large texts in order to evaluate probabilities of class pairs and of word pairs.

As we exhibit significantly lower test set perplexity values, for the bigram class model and for the interpolated class-word bigram models, as compared to the classical word-bigram model, this kind of language model should be able to improve recognition performance of continuous spoken language. It could also provide a powerful method to automatically determine parts of speech of texts before parsing.

REFERENCES:

[1] F. Jelinek, "Up from trigrams! The struggle for improved language models", EUROSPEECH'91 Proc., Geneva, Italy, 1991, p.1037

[2] M. Jardino, G. Adda, "Language modelling for CSR of large corpus using automatic classification of words", EUROSPEECH'93, Proc., Berlin, Germany, 1993, p.1191

[3] R. Bod. "Monte Carlo parsing", 1993. Proceedings, Third International Workshop On Parsing Technologies. Tilburg, the Netherlands and Durbuy, Belgium.

[4] D. Magerman. "Parsing as statistical pattern recognition", 1993. IBM Technical Report, IBM TJ. Watson Research Center, New York, USA.

[5] P.F. Brown, V.J. Della Pietra, P. V. de Souza, J.C. Lai, R.L. Mercer. "Class-based n-gram models of natural language", Dec. 1192. Computational Linguistics, vol 18, n°4, p.467.

[6] G. Maltese, F. Mancini. "A technique to automatically assign parts-of-speech to words taking into account word-ending information through a probabilistic model", Proceedings, EUROSPEECH 91, Genova, Italy, p.753.

[7] M. Jardino, G. Adda. "Automatic word classification using simulated annealing", 1993. Proceedings, ICASSP-93, Minneapolis, USA, p.II 41.

[8] H. Ney, U. Essen, R. Kneser. "On structuring probabilistic dependences in stochastic langage modelling", 1994. Computer Speech and Language, vol 8, p.1.

[9] J.L. Gauvain, L.F. Lamel, G. Adda, M. Adda-Decker. "The LIMSI continuous speech dictation system: evaluation on the ARPA Wall Street Journal Task". Proceedings, ICASSP'94, Adelaide, South Australia, p.I-557.

[10] F. Jelinek, R.L. Mercer, L.R. Bahl. "The development of an experimental discrete dictation recognizer", Nov. 1985. IEEE, vol 73, n°11, p.1616.

[11] S. Kirkpatrick, C.D. Gelatt Jr and M.P. Vecchi. "Optimization by simulated annealing", Science, 220 (1983) p671-680

[12] Metropolis et al. J. Of Chemical Physics,21 (1953) 1087-1092

[13] P.J.M. van Laarhoven and E.H. Aarts. "Simulated Annealing: Theory and Applications", D. Reidel Publishing Company, 1987

[14] M. Mezard, G. Parisi, M.A. Virasoro. "Spin Glass Theory an Beyond", World Scientific Lectures Notes in Physics, vol 9, 1987

[15] M. Jardino. "A class bigram model for very large corpus", to be published in Proc. of ICSLP'94, Japon.

[16] H. Ney, U. Essen. "On smoothing techniques for bigram-based natural language modelling", 1991. Proceedings, ICASSP-91, Toronto, Canada, p. 825.

The Acquisition of a Lexicon from Paired Phoneme Sequences and Semantic Representations

Carl de Marcken

MIT Artificial Intelligence Laboratory

545 Technology Square

Cambridge, MA 02139, USA

cgdemarc@ai.mit.edu

Abstract

We present an algorithm that acquires words (pairings of phonological forms and semantic representations) from larger utterances of unsegmented phoneme sequences and semantic representations. The algorithm maintains from utterance to utterance only a single coherent dictionary, and learns in the presence of homonymy, synonymy, and noise. Test results over a corpus of utterances generated from the Childes database of mother-child interactions are presented.

1 Introduction

This paper is concerned with the machine-learning of a lexicon from utterances that consist of an unsegmented phoneme sequence paired with a semantic representation of what those phonemes collectively mean. The problem is modeled after the environment that a child learns in, presented with a continuous speech signal[1] and potentially hypothesizing a meaning for that signal based upon visual stimuli. We radically simplify the problem the child encounters for the computer by pre-digesting the speech stream into a sequence of phonemes, and by providing an exact, transparent, and unambiguous semantic representation.

For instance, the computer might be presented with the utterance[2] "OK, here's the big ball":

Phoneme Sequence	Sememe Set
/ɑkhirzðəbɪgbɔl/	{ BE THE OK BALL HERE BIG }

---

[1]Children do in fact hear some pause information, and thus restricting our algorithm to totally unsegmented speech is somewhat unnatural. But, as data in [1] suggests, short utterances often are pauseless, and many sentences children hear are quite short (5.6 words on average in our test database, with little embedding).

[2]The particular phonemes used in the paper are the output of a public domain text-to-phoneme converter, which is frequently inaccurate (witness "OK" → /ɑk/). It's mislabelings do not have any effect on the work presented here.

From this and other utterances our goal is to produce an algorithm that learns a lexicon containing:

/ɑk/　{ OK } | /hir/　{ HERE } | /z/　{ BE }
/ðə/　{ THE } | /bɪg/　{ BIG } | /bɔl/　{ BALL }

It is not sufficient for our algorithm to learn any mapping from phoneme sequences to semantic symbols that explains the training data. Many mappings will do so, including the trivial one in which the final lexicon contains the training utterances themselves. We ask that the algorithm learn a lexicon that generalizes well, and does so without recourse to cognitively implausible mechanisms, such as off-line algorithms that access large amounts of the corpus at once.

This problem is interesting for several reasons. Although considerable study has been devoted to the acquisition of formal and natural grammars, grammatical categories for words, and even phonological processes, the acquisition of the lexicon has been largely neglected by the computational linguistics and machine learning communities, despite growing agreement that most language variation stems from there. Thus from a cognitive science and artificial intelligence viewpoint, this problem is a fundamental but relatively unstudied part of the process of learning a natural language, and a prerequisite to the acquisition of grammar. It also is a task where model complexity must be traded against global coverage in an environment where only a small proportion of the data is available at any one time to the algorithm.

Of course, the work presented here presumes a gross simplification of the real task faced by a computer or child that seeks to learn from sound pressure waveforms and sensory stimuli. Children may well not have the innate capability to segment a speech stream into discrete alphabetic sound units like phonemes (this is a matter of some debate in the field) and even if they do, word pronunciation is highly context-dependent. This is not necessarily an insurmountable problem; the methods used here can easily be extended to handle some sound variation in words, and section 6 discusses more recent work that accepts input closer to what current technology could derive from sound waves. A bigger assumption is the uniqueness and simplicity of the semantic representation for each utterance; the simplicity of our semantic representation both complicates the learning process for our algorithm by eliminating information that could constrain the search (in conjunction with grammar, for example) and simplifies the task by reducing the complexity of the information to be learned. The unambiguous interpretation we implicitly assume the child can give an utterance in an environment may or may not be trivializing the task: given our limited knowledge of child psychology it is difficult to tell. But some methods for increasing the ambiguity of semantic interpretation for an utterance are discussed in the next section and in section 6.

2　Previous Work

Olivier [8] and Cartwright and Brent [3] present simple algorithms that segment text and phoneme sequences by learning from statistical irregularities. In particular, they place phoneme sequences in a dictionary if those phonemes occur consecutively more often than they would if phonemes were selected by a memoryless random process with identical aggregate distribution. Olivier's algorithm is on-line, extremely efficient, and incorporates no priors. Cartwright and Brent's is a batch description-length formulation [9] that uses the size of the dictionary as a prior. Their algorithms perform with minimal adequacy, unable to distinguish correlations due to the dictionary from correlations due to syntax and semantics.

Siskind has presented a series of algorithms [10], [11], [12] that learn word-meaning associations when presented with paired sequences of tokens and semantic representations. Our model of our problem is based on his work. His work differs from ours in two principle ways: first, Siskind learns more complex semantic representations (Jackendoff-style semantic formulae [6] rather than simple symbol sets[3]), in an environment where his algorithms are presented with many ambiguous semantic representations (one of which is correct); and second, Siskind's work assumes pre-segmented tokens as input. So, his algorithm receives *ok here is the big ball* rather than our /ɑkhirzðəbɪgbɔl/. Siskind's work has tended to rely on classical search methods, and maintains a dictionary that may contain a variety of concurrent hypotheses for any given word.

See the above papers for references to other related work, and a further discussion of the motivation for this line of research.

3   The Algorithm

The algorithm presented here maintains a single dictionary, a list of words. Each word is a triple of a phoneme-sequence, a set of sememes (semantic symbols), and a confidence factor called the temperature. The temperature affects the likelihood that the word will be spontaneously deleted from the dictionary and also the ability of the word to participate in the creation of new words. Thus a high temperature (near 1) implies that a word is likely to be involved with new word creation and to be deleted, and a low temperature (near 0) implies that the word is static and unlikely to be deleted.

When the algorithm is presented with an utterance, it performs a local variation of the expectation-maximization (EM) procedure [5]: it attempts to parse the utterance using the words in its dictionary, resulting in values for hidden word-activation variables. By parse we mean that the algorithm attempts to find a set of words that collectively cover all the phonemes and sememes of the utterance, without overlap or mismatched elements. After the parse is complete, the maximization step occurs, with modification of the dictionary to reduce the error of activated words: new (warm) words are added to the dictionary to account for unparsed portions of the utterance, and variations of words used in the parse are added to the dictionary to fix mismatched or overparsed[4] portions of the utterance. Periodically words are deleted from the dictionary if they have not been

---

[3]In recent work Siskind has separated the learning of the set of semantic primitives associated with a word from the learning of the relations between those primitives. Borrowing from his work, it would not be difficult to extend our algorithm to learn semantic formulae rather than merely sets of semantic primitives. Similarly, the method Siskind uses to disambiguate between multiple ambiguous semantic interpretations for an utterance is equally applicable here. He essentially uses Bayes theorem to calculate the probability of a meaning given a word sequence from the probability of the word sequence given the meaning, which can be very effective if the proper definitions of some of the words in the utterance are known.

[4]By *overparsed* we mean portions of the utterance that are accounted for by more than one word.

cooled by being used, a brand of prior that favors a minimal-size dictionary.

```
PROCESS-UTTERANCE(u, d) = {
            let words = DICTIONARY-WORDS(d)
(§3.1)      let matches = MATCH-WORDS(u, words)
(§3.2)      let E¹, < α^{1w} >, < ΔP_i^1 >, < ΔS_j^1 > = PARSE(u, matches)
(§3.3)      let new-words = CREATE-NEW-WORDS(u, matches, < α^{1w} >, < ΔP_i^1 >, < ΔS_j^1 >)
(§3.1)      let new-matches = MATCH-WORDS(u, new-words)
(§3.2)      let E², < α^{2w} >, < ΔP_i^2 >, < ΔS_j^2 > = PARSE(u, matches+new-matches)
(§3.4)      COOL-WORDS(matches+new-matches, E², < α^{2w} >, < ΔP_i^2 >)
(§3.4)      ADD-COOLED-WORDS(new-matches, d)
(§3.5)      GARBAGE-COLLECT-DICTIONARY(d)
(§3.5)      REDUCE-DICTIONARY(d)
}
```

Figure 1: Pseudocode for the procedure the learning algorithm applies to each utterance. u is an utterance, d is the dictionary, E is an error scalar, $< \alpha^w >$ is a vector of word activations, $< \Delta P_i >$ is a vector of phonemic deviances, and $< \Delta S_j >$ is a vector of semantic deviances. Subroutines are described below in the sections listed.

Figure 1 presents pseudocode for the algorithm. The subroutines used by this algorithm are described in more detail below.

3.1 Matching

A word may occur at different points in a phonemic utterance. The MATCH-WORDS function of the algorithm finds places in an utterance that a word might occur and generates an evaluation of how closely it matches there. It does this by creating a vector (the *phonemic-match*, or PM vector) that describes in terms of numbers from 0 to 1[5] how well a word accounts for each phoneme in the utterance, and a similar SM vector for the sememes. It also computes two scalars, $\overline{PM}$ and $\overline{SM}$ that represent mismatched phonemes and sememes (such as a sememe in the word but not in the utterance).

Figure 2 contains a sample of what the MATCH-WORDS function produces for the utterance *the men*, assuming the dictionary contains reasonable definitions for the words *the*, *them* and *man*. The match with the word *the* offset into the utterance by 1 has a sufficiently poor phonemic match that MATCH-WORDS would filter it out. The function returns a list of these matches and the associated vectors and scalars.

3.2 Parsing

In order to evaluate how well the current dictionary accounts for an utterance, the algorithm attempts to fully parse the utterance with words from the dictionary, placing

---

[5]Right now only 0 or 1 are used, 1 for a perfect match and 0 for anything else. This scheme anticipates using intermediate values to represent phonemes likely to be related by phonological processes, such as /t/ and /d/.

Word		Position	PM /ðəmɛn/	SM { THE MAN }	$\overline{PM}$	$\overline{SM}$
/ðə/	{ THE }	0	< 11000 >	< 10 >	0	0
/ðə/	{ THE }	1	< 00000 >	< 10 >	2	0
/ðɛm/	{ THEM }	0	< 10100 >	< 00 >	1	1
/man/	{ MAN }	2	< 00101 >	< 01 >	1	0
⋮	⋮	⋮	⋮	⋮	⋮	⋮

Figure 2: Some of the data produced by MATCH-WORDS to evaluate how well the words *the, them,* and *man* match up with the utterance *the men*. The position reflects the offset of the phonemic word into the utterance. Thus the word /ðə/ matches well phonetically when offset 0 and poorly when offset 1.

words in such a fashion that each phoneme of the utterance is covered by a phoneme from exactly one dictionary word (with no extra phonemes being contributed by any word), and each sememe from the utterance is covered by a sememe from exactly one dictionary word (with no extra sememes being contributed by any word).

These desiderata can be modeled by giving each word match w an activation coefficient α^w between 0 and 1. If $\alpha^w = 0$, the word does not participate in the parse. If $\alpha^w = 1$, the word participates fully. A perfect parse meets the following conditions using non-fractional activations:

$$\sum_w \alpha^w PM^w = <1\ldots1>, \quad \sum_w \alpha^w SM^w = <1\ldots1>$$

$$\sum_w \alpha^w \overline{PM}^w = 0, \quad \sum_w \alpha^w \overline{SM}^w = 0$$

The first two conditions guarantee that every phoneme and sememe is covered exactly once by the words in the utterance.[6] The second two guarantee that these words are not also contributing any extraneous phonemes or sememes. Of course, it may not be possible to meet these conditions given the available dictionary, at least not without fractional activations. So we parse with the goal of minimizing a global error function. If we let $\Delta P_i = 1 - \sum \alpha^w PM_i^w$, the distance between the current total activation of the ith phoneme and its target of 1, and similarly for sememes ΔS_j, our global error function is

$$E = c_1 \sum_i f(\Delta P_i) + c_2 \sum_j f(\Delta S_j) + c_3 \sum_w \alpha^w \overline{PM}^w + c_4 \sum_w \alpha^w \overline{SM}^w$$

Here i sums over the length of the phonemic utterance, j over the number of different sememes in the utterance, and w over the word matches. The f function must be carefully chosen to result in a concentration of error in single phonemes or sememes rather than a distribution over the parse, and to penalize over-parsing a phoneme or sememe.[7]

---

[6]Actually, the semantic target is not necessarily a uniform 1 vector, since some sememes may occur multiple times in the utterance. One might alternatively leave the target vector at a uniform 1 and adjust the success requirement to $\sum \alpha_i^w SM_i^w \geq 1$. A pause can be represented with a 0 phonemic target.

[7]The following function performs adequately:

We can minimize E by varying the activation vector $< \alpha^w >$. A simple gradient-descent search from a randomly placed starting vector performs adequately for the particular vectors that arise here. The end result of the parsing process is a tuple of the final minimized error E, the activation vector $< \alpha^w >$, and the deviation vectors $< \Delta P_i >$ and $< \Delta S_i >$. Thus at the end of the parsing process we know not only how much each word participates in the parse (α^w) but also which phonemes and sememes are under or over-parsed (ΔP_i and ΔS_j). In the terms of the EM framework we now have an estimate of the hidden variables: the word activations.

3.3 Creating New Words

Once a parse of an utterance has been completed, the algorithm has some sense of what words participated in the utterance and what was misparsed; it now can perform the maximization step of modifying the dictionary. It creates new words, using a variety of methods that have proven successful but are not in any way the only ones that might work. Some of the methods used in this process are similar to those used by Siskind [12]. We can divide the methods into two parts: fixing words that participated in the parse and creating wholly new words. Fixes include deleting and adding phonemes and sememes from a definition.

Words participate in fixes with some probability. In the case of semantic fixes, that probability is proportional to the word's activation and its temperature. This prevents a cold word from participating in any semantic changes. In the case of phonemic fixes, the probability is proportional only to the word's activation. This makes it easy for a fully frozen word (say *cucumbers*) to create a new word *cucumber* with the same meaning, but difficult for *cucumbers* to change its meaning to { AVOCADO }. The fixes that a word can participate in are:

- Remove sememes from the word if they do not occur in the utterance sememe set or are overparsed ($\Delta S_i < -c$).

- Add underparsed sememes ($\Delta S_i > c$) to the word if there are no underparsed phoneme sequences in the utterance (as then the misparse would most likely be due to a missing word).

- Alter the word's phoneme sequence so as to eliminate phonemes that mismatch with the utterance, and to eliminate phonemes that are overparsed ($\Delta P_i < -c$).

- Extend the word's phoneme sequence so as to incorporate neighboring underparsed phonemes ($\Delta P_i > c$), up to a certain maximal length of extension.

In all cases the original word remains in the dictionary and a new word is created that incorporates the change.

$$f(\delta) = \left\{ \begin{array}{ll} |\delta| + \epsilon(1 - 4(|\delta| - \frac{1}{2})^2) & \text{if } |\delta| \leq 1 \\ \delta^2 & \text{otherwise} \end{array} \right.$$

It penalizes error and makes it least expensive to concentrate error on some phonemes and sememes rather than to distribute error with partial activations.

Wholly new words are also created to account for unparsed portions of the utterance. A set of sequences of consecutive underparsed phonemes from the original utterance is created. These sequences represent the phonemic components of potential new words. Similarly, a set of the underparsed sememes is created. If there are two or fewer underparsed phoneme sequences and each is below a maximum new-word-length, then each one is turned into a new word, using the set of underparsed sememes as the hypothesized semantic representation.

New words start out with a high temperature, near 1.

3.4   Cooling Words

As can be seen from the pseudocode in figure 1, new words are used in a reparse of the utterance. If the result is a good parse and these words are highly activated, then confidence in the words is increased by cooling the temperature asymptotically towards 0. The COOL-WORDS subroutine of the algorithm cools a word from a parse if it meets each of several conditions:

- It has no phonemic mismatches ($\overline{PM}^{w} = 0$).

- It has no semantic mismatches ($\overline{SM}^{w} = 0$).

- Its neighboring phonemes are well parsed ($\Delta P_{l,r} < c$, where l and r are the left and right phonemic boundaries of the word match).

- Its activation is over a threshold ($\alpha^{w} > c$)

Cooling is a function of the total parse error E. A low error implies more cooling. Words are therefore cooled when they are confidently used in a successful parse. A nearly-frozen word has successfully taken part in a number of good parses. A warm word has not reliably demonstrated its necessity.

New words are not added to the dictionary unless they are cooled after the reparse of the utterance that caused their creation. This minimizes the number of potentially-disruptive changes to the dictionary.

3.5   Removing Words from the Dictionary

As utterances are parsed, new words are created to explain and correct errors, and are added to the dictionary. Many of these new words are unsuccessful and do not participate in many parses; they represent failed branches of the search. If a word remains uncooled for some time period, it is a good indication that adding that word to the dictionary was a mistake. After a certain fixed-length trial number of utterances, a word becomes open for deletion from the dictionary. Periodically words are garbage-collected from the dictionary, with the probability of deletion roughly proportional to the temperature. A fully frozen word (temperature = 0) will never be deleted. A warm word is highly likely to be deleted.[8]

---

[8]This heuristic prevents the algorithm from learning words that only occur once or twice, a problem given Carey's [2] evidence that children can (and need to) acquire some words from a very small number

As the algorithm starts to learn with an empty dictionary, the first words it creates tend to be utterance-encompassing, such as /atsraɪt/ { THAT BE RIGHT }. Later the algorithm learns the components of such words, i.e., /at/, /s/, and /raɪt/. Periodically the dictionary attempts to reduce its size by parsing each of its words. If it can successfully parse a word without recourse to the word itself, that word is eliminated from the dictionary.

The process of removing words from the dictionary is a means of implementing a prior preference for a small dictionary, one with no unnecessary words. The gradual cooling of words used in parses ensures that words remain in the dictionary only if the data necessitate their presence.

4 A Short Example

Here we present a short description of the algorithm's performance on a single example from the test suite, /yukɪktɔffðəsɑk/ paired with { YOU KICK OFF THE SOCK }. At the point that the utterance is encountered, the matching process finds 3 acceptably close matches in the dictionary: /yu/ { YOU } offset 0, /ðə/ { THE } offset 9, and /rsɑk/ { SOCK } offset 10. Notice that *you* and *the* have no mismatches, but *sock* has an extra /r/. *You* and *the* are well cooled (temperature near 0) at this point, but not surprisingly, *sock* is still quite warm (temperature .64).

Parsing with these three words leaves all with activation near 1. Two new words are then created. The first is a fix of the phonemic mismatch in /rsɑk/. It is /sɑk/ { SOCK }, the old word with the one mismatched phoneme removed. The second word is completely new, created to account for the unparsed parts of the utterance: /kɪktɔff/ { KICK OFF }. The sentence is then rematched and parsed. In the new parse, /rsɑk/ is given low activation because the sentence can be parsed with less error using /sɑk/ instead, and /kɪktɔff/ is given activation near 1. The total error is quite low (it would be zero if the gradient descent search had produced correct activations of exactly 0 or 1), and the activated words are cooled. Thus, /sɑk/ and /kɪktɔff/ are cooled but /rsɑk/ is not. Garbage collection will eventually remove /rsɑk/ from the dictionary, which is not likely to be cooled again given the new competition from /sɑk/.

5 Tests and Results

To test the algorithm, we are using 34438 utterances from the Childes database of mothers' speech to children [7],[13]. These text utterances were run through a publicly available text-to-phoneme engine and also used to create a semantic dictionary, in which each root word from the utterances was mapped to a corresponding sememe. Various forms of a root ("see", "saw", "seeing") all map to the same sememe, e.g., SEE . Semantic representations

---

of exposures. One solution would be to speed the cooling process as the majority of the dictionary becomes stable. But the problem has deep roots and needs greater investigation: any on-line algorithm that maintains no explicit memory of previous data points will have a difficult time recovering from some of its mistakes. The usual solution of weight-decay towards a prior (to improve generalization and allow an algorithm to recover from noisy or misinterpreted data) does not work well if the algorithm must maintain perfect memory.

for a given utterance are merely unordered bags of sememes generated by taking the union of the sememe for each word in the utterance. Figure 3 contains the first 6 utterances from the database.

Sentence	Phoneme Sequence	Sememe Set
this is a book.	/ðɪsɪzebuk/	{ THIS BE A BOOK }
what do you see in the book?	/wɑtduyusiɪnðəbuk/	{ WHAT DO YOU SEE IN THE BOOK }
how many rabbits?	/haʊmɛnirabbɪts/	{ HOW MANY RABBIT }
how many?	/haʊmɛni/	{ HOW MANY }
one rabbit.	/wʌnrabbɪt/	{ ONE RABBIT }
what is the rabbit doing?	/wɑtɪzðərabbɪtduɪŋ/	{ WHAT BE THE RABBIT DO }

Figure 3: The first 6 utterances from the Childes database used to test the algorithm.

We describe the results of a single run of the algorithm, trained on one exposure to each of the 34438 utterances. Successive runs tend to result in nearly identical dictionaries. The final dictionary contains 1182 words (some entries are different forms of a common stem). Over the corpus the algorithm has been exposed to 2158 different stems. 82 of the words in the dictionary have never been used in a low-error parse. We eliminate these words, most of which are high temperature, leaving 1100. Figure 4 presents some entries in the final dictionary, and figure 5 presents all 21 of the 1100 entries that could be considered significant mistakes. So 1079 out of the 1100 entries (98%) are correct.

Phoneme Sequence	Sememe Set	Phoneme Sequence	Sememe Set
/yu/	{ YOU }	/bik/	{ BEAK }
/ðə/ /	{ THE }	/we/	{ WAY }
/wɑt/	{ WHAT }	/bukkes/	{ BOOKCASE }
/tu/	{ TO }	/brik/	{ BREAK }
/du/	{ DO }	/fiŋgɜ/	{ FINGER }
/e/	{ A }	/santəklɔs/	{ SANTA CLAUS }
/ɪt/	{ IT }	/tɑp/	{ TOP }
/aɪ/	{ I }	/kɔld/	{ CALL }
/ɪn/	{ IN }	/ɛgz/	{ EGG }
/wi/	{ WE }	/θɪŋ/	{ THING }
/s/	{ BE }	/kɪs/	{ KISS }
/ɑn/	{ ON }	/hi/	{ HEY }

Figure 4: Dictionary entries. The left 12 are the 12 words used most frequently in good parses. The right 12 were selected randomly from the 1100 entries.

The most obvious error visible in figure 5 is the suffix -ing (/ɪŋ/), which should be semanticless (have an empty sememe set). Indeed, a semanticless word is properly hypothesized but a special mechanism prevents semanticless words from being added to the dictionary. This mechanism is necessary because the error function overpromotes semanticless words and results in poor learning of phonological words that happen to contain them as substrings. Without it, the system would chance upon a new word like *ring*, /rɪŋ/, use the semanticless /ɪŋ/ to account for most of the sound, and build a new word /r/ { RING } to cover the rest; witness *something* in figure 5. One solution to such a problem is to incorporate additional linguistic knowledge about word structure and about sound changes that occur at word boundaries[9], a solution discussed to some extent by Cartwright and Brent [3] and Church [4]. Alternatively, as a more immediate workaround, we could provide the test corpus with an explicit semantic clue, such as the following association: /ɪŋ/ { PROGRESSIVE }.

Most other semanticless affixes (plural /s/ for instance) are also properly hypothesized and disallowed, but the dictionary learns multiple entries to account for them (/g/ "egg" and /gz/ "eggs"). The system learns synonyms ("is", "was", "am", ...) and homonyms ("read", "red"; "know", "no") without difficulty.

Phoneme Sequence	Sememe Set	Phoneme Sequence	Sememe Set
/ɪŋ/	{ BE }	/nupis/	{ SNOOPY }
/ɪŋ/	{ YOU }	/wo/	{ WILL }
/ɪŋ/	{ DO }	/zu/	{ AT ZOO }
/ʃiz/	{ SHE BE }	/don/	{ DO }
/wɑthappind/	{ WHAT HAPPEN}	/ɛrɛ/	{ BE }
/dont/	{ DO NOT }	/smʌd/	{ MUD }
/sʌmθ/	{ SOMETHING }	/nidəlɪz/	{ NEEDLE BE }
/wɑtarðiz/	{ WHAT BE THESE }	/drɑnʌðɜwiz/	{ DROWN OTHERWISE }
/shappin/	{ HAPPEN }	/sɛlf/	{ YOU }
/t/	{ NOT }	/ə/	{ BE }
/skɑtt/	{ BOB SCOTT }		

Figure 5: All of the significant dictionary errors. Some of them, like /ʃiz/ are conglomerations that should have been divided. Others, like /t/, /wo/, and /don/ demonstrate how the system compensates for the morphological irregularity of English contractions. The /ɪŋ/ problem is discussed in the text; misanalysis of the role of /ɪŋ/ also manifests itself on *something*.

6 Shortcomings and Future Directions

The most obvious immediate shortcoming of the algorithm is the previously discussed difficulty with semanticless words and affixes. As mentioned in the introduction, a more important issue is the simplicity of the environment the current algorithm assumes. We are building a new and considerably more complex learning architecture to rectify some of the deficiencies. In particular,

---

[9]For instance, in English no stem may be vowel-less, and word boundaries can sometimes be distinguished with the knowledge that word-initial obstruents are aspirated (/t/ is pronounced with an exhalation of air in *top* but not *stop*).

- instead of discrete phonemes, the new system accepts a time series of potentially noisy estimated vocal articulator positions. It attempts to find phoneme sequences from its dictionary that provide the most complete and consistent account for the perceived positions.

- the system incorporates some knowledge of morphology and phonology, selected to enable it to infer some contextual sound-change rules and consequently use sound changes as evidence of word boundaries. This knowledge should help the system learn semanticless words and affixes.

- the system accepts a complex conditional probability distribution over semantic symbols as the child's interpretation of the environment, and uses a Bayesian model to determine which sememes are actually represented by the utterance.

If successful, the improved system will considerably expand the scope and performance of the preliminary work presented here.

7 Acknowledgements

This research is supported by NSF grant 9217041-ASC and ARPA under the HPCC program. David Baggett, Robert Berwick, Jeffrey Siskind, Oded Maron, Greg Galperin and Marina Meila have made valuable suggestions and comments related to this work. A Common Lisp version of the algorithm and the test corpus can be found in ftp:-//ftp.ai.mit.edu/pub/users/cgdemarc/papers/icgi94.

References

[1] J. Bachenko and E. Fitzpatrick. 1990. "A Computational Grammar of Discourse-Neutral Prosodic Phrasing in English," *Computational linguistics* 16, 3, 155-170.

[2] S. Carey. 1978. The Child as a Word Learner. In M. Halle, J. Bresnan and G. Miller (eds), *Linguistic Theory and Psychological Reality*. M.I.T. Press, Cambridge, Massachussets.

[3] T. Cartwright and M. Brent. 1994. Segmenting Speech Without a Lexicon: Evidence for a Bootstrapping Model of Lexical Acquisition, *in Proceedings of the 16th Conference of the Cognitive Science Society, 1994.*

[4] K. Church 1987. "Phonological parsing and lexical retrieval," *Cognition*, 25:53-69

[5] A. P. Dempster and N. M. Laird and D. B. Rubin. 1977. "Maximum Likelihood from Incomplete Data via the EM Algorithm" *Journal of the Royal Statistical Society, B* 39, 1–38.

[6] R. Jackendoff. 1990. *Semantic Structures*. M.I.T. Press, Cambridge, Massachussets.

[7] B. MacWhinney and C. Snow. 1985. "The Child Language Data Exchange System," *Journal of Child Language* 12, 271–296.

[8] D. Olivier. 1968. *Stochastic Grammars and Language Acquisition Mechanisms*. PhD thesis, Harvard University, Cambridge, Massachusetts.

[9] J. Rissanen. 1978. "Modeling by shortest data description," *Automatica* 14, 456–471.

[10] J. Siskind. 1992. *Naive Physics, Event Perception, Lexical Semantics, and Language Acquisition*. PhD thesis, Massachusetts Institute of Technology, Cambridge, Massachusetts.

[11] J. Siskind. 1993. Lexical Acquisition as Constraint Satisfaction. Technical Report IRCS-93-41, University of Pennsylvania Institute for Research in Cognitive Science.

[12] J. Siskind. 1994. Lexical Acquisition in the Presence of Noise and Homonymy. In *Proceedings of the 12th National Conferance on Artificial Intelligence (AAAI-94)*.

[13] P. Suppes. 1973. "The semantics of children's language," *American Psychologist*.

Inference and Estimation of a Long-Range Trigram Model

S. Della Pietra   V. Della Pietra   J. Gillett
J. Lafferty[†]   H. Printz   L. Ureš

IBM T. J. Watson Research Center
P.O. Box 704
Yorktown Heights, NY 10598 USA

Abstract

We describe an implementation of a simple probabilistic link grammar. This probabilistic language model extends trigrams by allowing a word to be predicted not only from the two immediately preceeding words, but potentially from any preceeding pair of adjacent words that lie within the same sentence. In this way, the trigram model can skip over less informative words to make its predictions. The underlying "grammar" is nothing more than a list of pairs of words that can be linked together with one or more intervening words; this word-pair grammar is automatically inferred from a corpus of training text. We present a novel technique for indexing the model parameters that allows us to avoid all sorting in the M-step of the training algorithm. This results in significant savings in computation time, and is applicable to the training of a general probabilistic link grammar. Results of preliminary experiments carried out for this class of models are presented.

1   Introduction

The most widely used statistical model of language is the so-called *trigram model*. In this simple model, a word is predicted based solely upon the two words which immediately precede it. The simplicity of the trigram model is simultaneously its greatest strength and weakness. Its strength comes from the fact that one can easily estimate trigram statistics by counting over hundreds of millions of words of data. Since implementation of the model involves only table lookup, it is computationally efficient, and can be used in real-time systems. Yet the trigram model captures the statistical relations between words by the sheer force of numbers. It ignores the rich syntactic and semantic structure which constrains natural languages, allowing them to be easily processed and understood by humans.

Research supported in part by NSF and ARPA under grants IRI-9314969 and N00014-92-C-0189.

[†]Current address: School of Computer Science, Carnegie Mellon University, 5000 Forbes Avenue, Pittsburgh, PA 15213 USA, E-mail: lafferty@cs.cmu.edu

Probabilistic link grammar has been proposed as an approach which preserves the strengths and computational advantages of trigrams, while incorporating long-range dependencies and more complex information into a statistical model [LST92]. In this paper we describe an implementation of a very simple probabilistic link grammar. This probabilistic model extends trigrams by allowing a word to be predicted not only from the two immediately preceding words, but potentially from any preceding pair of adjacent words that lie within the same sentence. In this way, the trigram model can skip over less informative words to make its predictions. The underlying "grammar" is nothing more than a list of pairs of words that can be linked together with one or more intervening words between them. This paper presents an outline of the basic ideas and methods used in building this model.

Section 2 gives an introduction to the long-range trigram model and explains how it can be seen as a probabilistic link grammar. The word-pair grammar is automatically inferred from a corpus of training text. While mutual information can be used as a heuristic to determine which words might be profitably linked together, this measure alone is not adequate. In Section 3 we present a technique that extends mutual information to suit our needs. The parameter estimation algorithms, which derive from the EM algorithm, are presented in Sections 4 and 5. In particular, we present a novel technique for indexing the model parameters that allows us to avoid all sorting in the M-step of the training algorithm. This results in significant savings in computation time, and is applicable to the training of a general probabilistic link grammar. In Section 6 we present the results of preliminary experiments carried out using this approach.

2 A Long-Range Trigram Model

As a motivating example, consider the picture shown below. This diagram represents a *linkage* of the underlying sentence "Either a rioja ... suckling pig", as described in [ST91]. The important characteristics of a linkage are that the arcs, or *links*, connecting the various words do not cross, that there is no more than one link between any pair of words, and that the resulting graph is connected. Viewed probabilistically, we imagine that each word is generated from the bigram ending with the word that it is linked to on the left. Thus, the first right parenthesis is generated from the bigram (rioja, "(") while the word "suckling" is generated from the bigram (roast, young). The word "or" is generated from the bigram ($\perp$, Either), where $\perp$ is a *boundary word*.

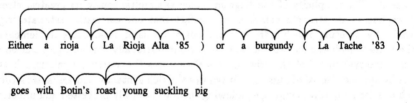

Another valid linkage would connect the first left parenthesis with the last right parenthesis, but this would preclude a connection between the words "Either" and "or" since the resulting links would cross.

To describe the model in more detail, consider the following description of standard trigrams. This model is viewed as a simple finite-state machine for generating sentences. The states in the machine are indexed by pairs of words. Adjoining the boundary word $\perp$ to our vocabulary, we suppose that the machine begins in the state $(\perp, \perp)$. When the machine is in any given state (w_1, w_2) it progresses to state (w_2, w_3) with probability $\mathrm{T}(w_3 \,|\, w_1 w_2)$ and halts with probability $\mathrm{T}(\perp \,|\, w_1 w_2)$, thus ending the sentence.

Our extended trigram model can be described in a similar fashion. Again states are indexed by pairs of words, but a state $s = (w_1, w_2)$ can now either halt, step, or branch, with probability $\mathrm{D}(\mathrm{HALT} \,|\, s)$, $\mathrm{D}(\mathrm{STEP} \,|\, s)$, and $\mathrm{D}(\mathrm{BRANCH} \,|\, s)$ respectively. In case either a STEP or a BRANCH is chosen, the next word w is generated with the trigram probability $\mathrm{T}(w \,|\, w_1 w_2)$. But in the case that BRANCH was chosen for the state s, an additional word w' is generated from the *long-range* trigram distribution $\mathrm{L}(w' \,|\, w_1 w_2)$.

For example, in generating the above linkage, the state indexed by $s = (\mathrm{or}, \mathrm{a})$ chooses to step, with probability $\mathrm{D}(\mathrm{STEP} \,|\, s)$, and the word "burgundy" is then generated with probability $\mathrm{T}(\mathrm{burgundy} \,|\, \mathrm{or\ a})$. On the other hand, the state $s = (\perp, \mathrm{Either})$ branches, with probability $\mathrm{D}(\mathrm{BRANCH} \,|\, s)$, and from this state the words "a" and word "or" are then generated with probabilities $\mathrm{T}(\mathrm{a} \,|\, \perp \ \mathrm{Either})$ and $\mathrm{L}(\mathrm{or} \,|\, \perp \ \mathrm{Either})$ respectively.

This results in linkages, such as the one shown above, where every word is linked to exactly one word to its left, and to zero, one, or two words on its right. If we number the words in the sentence S from 1 to $|S|$, then it is convenient to denote by $\triangleleft i$ the index of the word which generates the i-th word of the sentence. That is, word i is linked to word $\triangleleft i$ on its left. For instance, in the linkage shown above we see that $\triangleleft 8 = 7$, $\triangleleft 9 = 4$, and $\triangleleft 10 = 1$. This notation allows us to write down the probability of a sentence as $P(S) = \sum_{\Lambda \in \mathcal{L}(S)} P(S, \Lambda)$, where $\mathcal{L}(S)$ is the set of all linkages of S, and where the joint probability $P(S, \Lambda)$ of a sentence and a linkage is given by

$$P(S, \Lambda) = \prod_{i=1}^{|S|} \mathrm{D}\left(d_i \,|\, w_i, w_{i-1}\right) \mathrm{T}\left(w_i \,|\, w_{i-1}\, w_{i-1}\right)^{\delta(i-1, \triangleleft i)} \mathrm{L}\left(w_i \,|\, w_{\triangleleft i}\, w_{\triangleleft i - 1}\right)^{1 - \delta(i-1, \triangleleft i)} .$$

(1)

Here $d_i \in \{\mathrm{HALT}, \mathrm{STEP}, \mathrm{BRANCH}\}$, $\delta(i, j)$ is equal to one if $i = j$ and is equal to zero otherwise, and the indices $\triangleleft i$ are understood to be taken with respect to linkage Λ. The indices $\triangleleft i$ determine which words are linked together, and so completely determine a valid linkage as long as they satisfy the no-crossing condition $\triangleleft j \leq \triangleleft i$ whenever $i \leq j$. In particular, specifying the indices $\triangleleft i$ determines the values of d_i, since d_i is equal to HALT, STEP, or BRANCH when $\sum_{j > i} \delta(i, \triangleleft j)$ is equal to zero, one, or two, respectively.

A full description of the model is best given in terms of a probabilistic pushdown automaton. The automaton maintains a stack of states s, where s is indexed by a word bigram, and a finite memory containing a state m. It is governed by a finite control that can read either HALT, STEP, or BRANCH. Initially the stack is empty, the finite memory contains the bigram $(\perp, \perp)$, and the finite control reads STEP. The automaton proceeds by carrying out three tasks. First, the finite control is read and a word is output with the appropriate distribution. If the control reads either STEP or BRANCH, then word w is output with probability $\mathrm{T}(w \,|\, m)$. If the control reads HALT then the automaton looks at the stack. If the stack is empty the machine halts. Otherwise, the state s is popped off the stack and word w is output with probability $\mathrm{L}(w \,|\, s)$. Second, the memory state is changed from $m = (w_1, w_2)$ to $m = (w_2, w)$. Third, the control is set to d with probability $\mathrm{D}(d \,|\, m)$, and state m is pushed onto the stack if the new setting is BRANCH. The probability with which this machine halts after outputting sentence S is precisely the sum $\sum_{\Lambda \in \mathcal{L}(S)} P(S, \Lambda)$ where $P(S, \Lambda)$ is given by equation (1).

In terms of link grammar, there is a natural equivalence between the values HALT, STEP, and BRANCH and three simple *disjuncts*, specifying how a word connects to other words. The value HALT corresponds to a disjunct having a single (unlabeled) left connector, and no right connectors, indicating that a connection can be made to any word on the left, but to no word on the right. The value STEP corresponds to a disjunct having a single left connector and a single right connector, and the value BRANCH corresponds to a disjunct having a single left connector and two right connectors. With this grammar, the probabilistic model described above is a simple variant of the general probabilistic model presented in [LST92].

In terms of phrase structure grammar, the constructive equivalence between link grammar and context free grammars given in [ST91] can be extended probabilistically. This shows how the above model is equivalent to the following standard probabilistic context-free model:

$$
\begin{aligned}
A_{v,w}^u &\rightarrow B_{v,w}^u & \text{D}(\,\text{BRANCH}\,|\,v,w\,) \\
A_{v,w}^u &\rightarrow C_{v,w}^u & \text{D}(\,\text{STEP}\,|\,v,w\,) \\
A_{v,w}^w &\rightarrow \epsilon & \text{D}(\,\text{HALT}\,|\,v,w\,) \\
B_{v,w}^u &\rightarrow C_{v,w}^x\, y\, A_{x,y}^u & \text{L}(\,y\,|\,v\,w\,) \\
C_{v,w}^u &\rightarrow z\, A_{w,z}^u & \text{T}(\,z\,|\,v\,w\,)\,.
\end{aligned}
$$

Here x, y, z are vocabulary words with $x, y \neq \perp$ and A, B, and C are families of nonterminals parameterized by triples of words u, v, w. The corresponding rule probabilities are given in the second column. The start nonterminal of the grammar is $S = A_{\perp,\perp}^\perp$. This view of the model is unwieldy and unnatural, and does not benefit from the efficient link grammar parsing and pruning algorithms.

3 Inferring the Grammar

The probabilistic model described in the previous section makes its predictions using both long-range and short-range trigrams. In principle, we can allow a word to be linked to any word to its left. This corresponds to a "grammar" that allows a long-range link between any pair of words. The number of possible linkages for this grammar grows rapidly with sentence length: while a 10-word sentence has only 835 possible linkages, a 25-word sentence has 3,192,727,797 linkages (see Appendix A). Yet most of the long-range links in these linkages are likely to be spurious. The resulting probabilistic model has far too many parameters than can be reliably estimated.

Since an unrestricted grammar is impractical, we would like to restrict the grammar to allow those long-range links that bring the most improvement to the probabilistic model. Ideally, we would like to automatically discover pairs of words such as "(" and ")" with long-range correlations that are good candidates to be connected by a long-range link. We might find such pairs by looking for words with high mutual information. But if we imagine that we have already included all nearest neighbor links in our model, as is the case for the model (1), there is no point in linking up a pair of words L and R, no matter how high their mutual information, if R is already well-predicted by its immediate predecessor. Instead, we would like to find links between words that have the potential

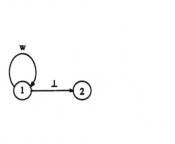

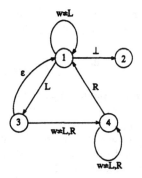

Figure 1: A bigram machine   Figure 2: An (L, R) machine

of improving a model with only short-range links.

To find such pairs we adopt the following approach. Let V be the language vocabulary. For each pair $(L, R) \in V \times V$, we construct a model P_{LR} that contains all the bigram links together with only one additional long-range link: that from L to R. We choose the models P_{LR} to be simple enough so that the parameters of all the $|V|^2$ possible models can be estimated in parallel. We then rank the models according to the likelihood each assigns to the training corpus, and choose those pairs (L, R) corresponding to the highest ranked models. This list of word pairs constitutes the "grammar" as described in the previous section.

The model P_{LR} that we construct for a particular pair (L, R) is a simplification of the model of the previous section; it can be described as a probabilistic finite state automaton (and thus it requires no stack). Before explaining the details of the model, consider the standard bigram model $B(w'|w)$ viewed as a probabilistic finite state machine. This machine maintains a finite memory m that contains the previously generated word, and can be in one of two states, as shown in Figure 1. The machine begins in state 1 with $m = \perp$. The machine operates by making a state transition, outputting a word w, and then setting the memory m to w. More precisely, the machine remains in state 1 with probability $D(\text{STEP}|m) = 1 - B(\perp|m)$. Given that a transition to state 1 is made, the word $w \neq \perp$ is output with probability $B'(w|m)$, where

$$B'(w|m) = \frac{B(w|m)}{1 - B(\perp|m)}.$$

Alternatively, the machine outputs $\perp$ and proceeds to state 2, where it halts, with probability $D(\text{HALT}|m) = B(\perp|m)$.

The machine underlying our probabilistic model P_{LR} is depicted in a similar fashion in Figure 2. Like the bigram machine, our new automaton maintains a memory m of the most recently output word and begins in state 1 with $m = \perp$. Unlike the bigram machine, it enters a special state whenever word L is generated: from state 1, the machine outputs L, sets $m = L$, and makes a transition to state 3 with probability $B(L|m)$. A transition from state 3 back to state 1 is made with probability $D_{LR}(\text{STEP}|L)$. In this case, no word is output, and the memory m remains set to L. Alternatively, from state

3 the machine can output a word $w \neq L, R$ and proceed to state 4 with probability $D_{LR}(\text{BRANCH}|L)\, B_{LR}(w|m)$, where

$$B_{LR}(w|m) = \frac{B(w|m)}{1 - B(L|m) - B(R|m) - B(\perp|m)}.$$

Once in state 4, the machine behaves much like the original bigram machine, except that neither an L nor a R can be generated. Word w is output and the machine remains in state 4 with probability $D_{LR}(\text{STEP}|m)\, B_{LR}(w|m)$; it makes a transition back to state 1 and outputs word R with probability $D_{LR}(\text{HALT}|m)$.

According to this probabilistic finite state machine, words are generated by a bigram model except for the word R, which is generated either from its immediate predecessor or from the closest L to its left. Maximum-likelihood training of this machine yields an estimate of the reduction in entropy over the bigram model afforded by allowing long-range links between L and R in the general model presented in Section 2.

Training of the models P_{LR} for many (L, R) pairs in parallel is facilitated by two approximating assumptions on the parameters. First, we assume that $B_{LR}(w|m) = B(w|m)$. Second, we assume that $D_{LR}(d|m) = D_{LR}(d)$ for $m \neq L$. Under this assumption, the parameter $D_{LR}(\text{HALT})$ encodes the distribution of the number of words between L and R; in the hidden model the number of words between them is geometrically distributed with mean $D_{LR}(\text{HALT})^{-1}$.

Each model P_{LR} can be viewed as a link grammar enhancement of the bigram model in the following way. In the bigram model each non-boundary word w has the single STEP disjunct, allowing only links between adjacent words. In the model P_{LR} we add additional disjuncts to allow long-range links between L and R. Specifically, we give all words the two disjuncts STEP and HALT. In addition, we give L a third disjunct BRANCH_{LR}, which like STEP allows connections to any word on the left and right, and in addition requires a long-range connection to R. Similarly, we give R a third disjunct STEP_{LR} which connects to L on the left and any word on the right. This allows linkages such as

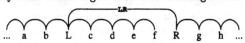

Now suppose that $S = w_1 \cdots w_N$ is a sentence containing a single (L, R) pair separated by at least one word. The probability of S is a sum over two linkages, $\mathcal{L}_{\text{bigram}}$ and $\mathcal{L}_{LR}$: $P_{LR}(S) = P_{LR}(\mathcal{L}_{\text{bigram}}) + P_{LR}(\mathcal{L}_{LR})$. If we let k be the the number of words between L and R, then under the two approximating assumptions made above it is easy to see that

$$P_{LR}(\mathcal{L}_{LR}) = c\, D_{LR}(\text{BRANCH}_{LR}|L)\, D_{LR}(\text{STEP})^{k-1}\, D_{LR}(\text{HALT})$$
$$P_{LR}(\mathcal{L}_{\text{bigram}}) = c\, D_{LR}(\text{STEP}|L)\, B(R|R-1)$$

where c depends only on bigram probabilities. If, on the other hand, S contains a single L and no R then there is a unique linkage for the sentence whose probability is $D_{LR}(\text{STEP}|L)$ times the bigram probability of the sentence. More generally, given the model just described, it is easy to write down the probability $P_{LR}(S)$ of any sentence with respect to the parameters $D_{LR}(d|w)$ and $B(w_2|w_1)$.

We train the parameters of this family of models in parallel, using the forward-backward algorithm. In order to do this, we first make a single pass through the training corpus, accumulating the following counts. For each (L, R) pair, we count $N(k, w|L, R)$, the number of times that L and R are separated by exactly $k \geq 1$ words, none of which is L or R, and the word immediately before R is w. We also count $N(\neg R|L)$, the number of times L appears in a sentence and either is not followed by an R in the same sentence or is followed by an L before an R. In terms of these counts, the increase in log-likelihood for model P_{LR} over the bigram model, in bits of information, is given by

$$\text{Gain}_{LR} = \sum_{k,w} N(k, w|L, R) \log \frac{P_{LR}(k, w, R|L)}{B(R|w)} + N(\neg R|L) \log D_{LR}(\text{STEP}|L)$$

where

$$P_{LR}(k, w, R|L) =$$
$$D_{LR}(\text{BRANCH}_{LR}|L) D_{LR}(\text{STEP})^{k-1} D_{LR}(\text{HALT}) + (1 - D_{LR}(\text{BRANCH}_{LR}|L)) B(R|w)$$

and

$$N(\neg R|L) = c(L) - \sum_{k,w} N(k, w|L, R)$$

with $c(L)$ the unigram count of L. Using this formula, forward-backward training can be quickly carried out in parallel for all models, without further passes through the corpus. The results of this calculation are shown in Section 6.

4 The Mechanics of EM Estimation

In this section we describe the mechanics of estimating the parameters of our model. Our concern is not the mathematics of the inside-outside algorithm for maximum-likelihood estimation of link grammar models [LST92], but managing the large quantities of data that arise in training our model on a substantial corpus. We restrict our attention here to the short-range trigram probabilities $T(z \mid x\ y)$ since these constitute the largest amount of data, but our methods apply as well to the long-range trigrams $L(z \mid x\ y)$ and disjunct probabilities $D(d \mid x\ y)$.

To begin, observe that the trigram probabilities must in fact be EM-trained. In a pure trigram model the quantity $T(z \mid x\ y)$ is given by the ratio $c(x\ y\ z)/\sum_{a \in V} c(x\ y\ a)$ where $c(x\ y\ z)$ is the number of times the trigram $(x\ y\ z)$ appears in the training corpus C. But in our link grammar model the trigram probabilities represent the conditional word probabilities in the case when the STEP linkage was used, and this is probabilistically determined. The same ratio determines $T(z \mid x\ y)$, but the $c(x\ y\ z)$ are now *expected* counts, where the expectation is with respect to trainable parameters.

The EM algorithm begins with some initial set $T(z \mid x\ y)$ of trigram probabilities. For each sentence S of the corpus, the algorithm labels the trigrams $(w_{i-2}\ w_{i-1}\ w_i)$ of S with these probabilities. From these and other parameters, the E-step determines partial estimated counts $\partial(w_{i-2}\ w_{i-1}\ w_i)$. The partial counts for a particular trigram $(x\ y\ z)$, accumulated over all instances of the trigram in the corpus, give the trigram's full estimated count $c(x\ y\ z)$.

Our difficulties occur in implementing the EM algorithm on the desired scale. To explain these difficulties, we will briefly sketch some naïve approaches. We assume the computer we will use has a substantial but not unlimited primary memory, which may be read and written at random, and a much larger secondary memory, which must be read and written sequentially. We will treat the corpus C as a series of words, w_1, w_2, ..., $w_{|C|}$, recorded as indices into a fixed vocabulary V; this series is marked off into sentences. A word index is represented in 2 bytes, and a real value in 4 bytes.

Suppose we try to assign trigram probabilities $T(w_i \mid w_{i-2} \; w_{i-1})$ to the sentence by looking them up in a table, and likewise accumulating the partial counts $\partial(w_{i-2} \; w_{i-1} \; w_i)$ into a table. Both must be randomly addressable and hence held in primary memory; each table must have space for $|V|^3$ entries. For realistic vocabularies of size $|V| \approx 5 \times 10^4$, the two tables together would occupy 10^{15} bytes, which far exceeds the capacity of current memory technologies, primary or secondary.

In a corpus of $|C|$ words, no more than $|C|$ distinct trigrams may appear. This suggests that we maintain the table by entering values only for the trigrams $(x \; y \; z)$ that actually appear in the corpus. A table entry will consist of $(x \; y \; z)$, and its $T(z \mid x \; y)$ and $\partial(x \; y \; z)$. For fast access, the table is sorted by trigram. Unfortunately, this approach is also impractical. For a moderate training corpus of 25 million words, this table will occupy on the order of $25 \times 10^6 \times (6 + 4 + 4) = 350 \times 10^6$ bytes, which exceeds the primary memory of a typical computer.

Thus we are forced to abandon the idea of maintaining the needed data in primary memory. Our solution is to store the probabilities and counts in secondary memory; the difficulty is that secondary memory must be read and written sequentially.

We begin by dividing the corpus into R segments C^1, ..., C^R, each containing about $|C|/R$ words. The number of segments R is chosen to be large enough so that a table of $|C|/R$ real values can comfortably reside in primary memory. For each segment C^i, which is a sequence of words w_1, ..., w_{C_i}, we write an entry file E_i with structure

$$(w_1 \; w_2 \; w_3) \;\; 3, \;\; (w_2 \; w_3 \; w_4) \;\; 4, \;\; \ldots, \;\; (w_{|C^i|-2} \; w_{|C^i|-1} \; w_{|C^i|}) \;\; |C^i|.$$

We sort E_i by trigram to yield SE_i, which has structure

$$(x \; y \; z_1) \; j_1^{(x \; y \; z_1)}, \; \ldots, \; (x \; y \; z_1) \; j_{N(x \; y \; z_1)}^{(x \; y \; z_1)}, \; (x \; y \; z_2) \; j_1^{(x \; y \; z_2)}, \; \ldots, \; (x \; y \; z_2) \; j_{N(x \; y \; z_2)}^{(x \; y \; z_2)}, \; \ldots.$$

Here we have written $N(x \; y \; z)$ for the number of times a trigram appears in the segment, and $j_1^{(x \; y \; z)}$, ..., $j_{N(x \; y \; z)}^{(x \; y \; z)}$ for the sequence of positions where it appears. This sort is done one time only, before the start of EM training.

A single EM iteration proceeds as follows. First we perform an E-step on each segment C^i. We assume the existence of a file AT_i that contains sequentially arranged trigram probabilities for C^i. (For the very first EM iteration, it is easy to construct this file by writing out appropriate uniform probabilities.) Each segment's E-step sequentially writes a file PCT_i of partial estimated counts, $\partial(w_1 \; w_2 \; w_3)$, $\partial(w_2 \; w_3 \; w_4)$, ..., $\partial(w_{|C^i|-2} \; w_{|C^i|-1} \; w_{|C^i|})$.

Next we sum these partial counts to obtain the segment counts. To do this we read PCT_i into primary memory. Then we read SE_i sequentially and accumulate the segment count $c_i(x \; y \; z_1) = \sum_{k=1}^{N(x \; y \; z_1)} PCT_i[j_k^{(x \; y \; z_1)}]$, and so on for each successive trigram of C^i. As each sum completes, we write it sequentially to a file SCT_i of segment counts, of format $c_i(x \; y \; z_1)$, $c_i(x \; y \; z_2)$, ... The trigram that identifies each count can be obtained by sequential inspection of SE_i.

Now we merge across segments, by scanning all $2R$ files SE_i and SCT_i, and forming the complete counts $c(x \; y \; z) = \sum_{i=1}^{R} c_i(x \; y \; z)$. As we compute these sums, we maintain a list $c(x\ y\ z_1)$, $c(x\ y\ z_2)$, ... in primary memory—there will be no more than $|V|$ of them—until we encounter a trigram $(u\ v\ \cdot)$ in the input stream where $x \neq u$ or $y \neq v$. Then we compute $c(x\ y) = \sum_{z \in V} c(x\ y\ z)$, and dump the trigrams $(x\ y\ z)$ and quotients $T'(z \mid x\ y) = c(x\ y\ z)/c(x\ y)$ sequentially to a file ST'. Note that ST' is a sorted list of all the reestimated trigram probabilities.

To complete the process we must write a sequentially ordered file AT'_i of the reestimated trigram probabilities for C^i. First we create a table in primary memory of size $|C^i|$. Then we read SE_i and ST' sequentially as follows. For each new trigram $(x\ y\ z)$ we encounter in SE_i, we search forward in ST' to find $T'(z \mid x\ y)$. Then for each $j_1^{(x\ y\ z)}, \ldots, j_{N(x\ y\ z)}^{(x\ y\ z)}$ listed for $(x\ y\ z)$ in SE_i, we deposit $T'(z \mid x\ y)$ in $AT'_i[j_k^{(x\ y\ z)}]$. When SE_i is exhausted we have filled each position in AT'_i. We write it sequentially to disk and are then ready for the next EM iteration.

5 Smoothing

The link grammar model given by (1) expresses the probability of a sentence in terms of three sets of more fundamental probability distributions T, L and D, so that $P(S) \equiv P(S; T, L, D)$. In the previous sections, we tacitly assumed 2-word history, non-parametric forms. That is, we allowed a separate *free* parameter for each 2-word history and prediction value subject only to the constraints that probabilities sum to one. In the case of the trigram distribution T, for example, there are separate parameters $T(w|w'w'')$ for each triple of words (w, w', w'') subject to the constraints $\sum_w T(w|w'w'') = 1$ for all (w', w''). We will refer to such 2-word history distributions as 3-gram estimators, since they are indexed by triples, and will denote them by T_3, L_3 and D_3. In the previous section we outlined an efficient implementation of EM (inside-outside) training, for adjusting the parameters of T_3, L_3 and D_3 to maximize the log-likelihood of a large corpus of training text.

Unfortunately, we cannot expect the link grammar model using maximum likelihood distributions to work well when applied to new data. Rather, the distributions are likely to be too sharply determined by the training corpus to generalize well. This is the standard problem of overtraining and may be addressed by mixing the sharply defined distributions with less sharp ones to obtain smoother distributions. This procedure is referred to as *smoothing*.

The smoothing we employ in the link grammar is motivated by the smoothing typically used for the trigram language model [BBdSM91]. The idea is to linearly combine the 3-gram estimators T_3, L_3 and D_3 with corresponding 2-gram, 1-gram and uniform estimators to obtain smooth distributions $\tilde{T}_\lambda$, $\tilde{L}_\lambda$ and $\tilde{D}_\lambda$. In the case of $\tilde{T}_\lambda$ we have

$$\tilde{T}_\lambda(w|w'w'') = \lambda_3 T_3(w|w'w'') + \lambda_2 T_2(w|w') + \lambda_1 T_1(w) + \lambda_0 T_0. \tag{2}$$

Here T_3, T_2 and T_1 denote 3-gram, 2-gram and 1-gram estimators for T, and T_0 denotes a uniform distribution. The 2-gram estimator T_2 has a separate parameter $T_2(w|w')$ for each 2-gram $(w\ w')$ subject to the constraint that $\sum_w T_2(w|w') = 1$. The 1-gram estimator T_1 has a separate parameter $T_1(w)$ for each w. In general, an n-gram estimator depends on $n-1$ words of context. The parameters λ_i satisfy the constraint $\sum_i \lambda_i = 1$ to ensure that $\tilde{T}_\lambda$ is a probability distribution. Equation (2) employs the same vector $(\lambda_0, \lambda_1, \lambda_2, \lambda_3)$, for each triple (w, w', w''). In practice, different vectors of λ's are used for different triples. We define $\tilde{L}_\lambda$ and $\tilde{D}_\lambda$ similarly. We then define the smooth link grammar model $\tilde{P}_\lambda$ using these smooth distributions: $\tilde{P}_\lambda(S) \equiv P(S; \tilde{T}_\lambda, \tilde{L}_\lambda, \tilde{D}_\lambda)$.

To completely specify the smooth distributions, we must fix the values of the parameters of the individual n-gram distributions as well as the mixing parameters λ. Estimating all of these simultaneously using maximum likelihood training would defeat the purpose of smoothing: we would find that the only non-zero λ's would be those multiplying the 3-gram estimators, which would ultimately train to their maximum likelihood (and thus unsmooth) values! Instead we adopt the following procedure motivated by the *deleted interpolation* method sometimes used for the trigram model [BBdSM91]. We first divide our corpus of sentences into two parts: a large *training* corpus $\mathcal{T}$, and a smaller *smoothing* corpus $\mathcal{S}$. We estimate the n-gram estimators using the training corpus *only* according to the following scheme. The 3-gram estimators T_3, L_3 and D_3 are chosen to maximize the log-likelihood $\sum_{S \in \mathcal{T}} \log P(S; T_3, L_3, D_3)$ of the training corpus using the EM technique described in the previous section.

The 3-gram estimators are then used to "reveal" the hidden linkages of the training corpus, and the 2-gram and 1-gram estimators are chosen to maximize the likelihood of the training corpus *together with* these revealed linkages. Thus, for $i = 1, 2$, the distributions T_i, L_i and D_i maximize $\sum_{S \in \mathcal{T}} \sum_\Lambda P(\Lambda | S; T_3, L_3, D_3) \log P(S, \Lambda | T_i, L_i, D_i)$. This procedure, while somewhat unwieldy to explain, is simple to implement, as it amounts to obtaining the 2-gram and 1-gram estimators as appropriate conditionals of the EM counts for the 3-gram estimators.

With the n-gram estimators thus determined, we adjust the mixing parameters λ to maximize the probability of the smoothing corpus *only*. The logarithm of this probability is

$$\mathcal{O}_{\text{outer}}(\lambda) = \sum_{S \in \mathcal{S}} \log P(S | \tilde{T}_\lambda, \tilde{L}_\lambda, \tilde{D}_\lambda) = \sum_{S \in \mathcal{S}} \log \sum_\Lambda P(S, \Lambda | \tilde{T}_\lambda, \tilde{L}_\lambda, \tilde{D}_\lambda).$$

This maximization is complicated by the fact that the probability of a sentence now involves not only a sum over hidden linkages, but for each linkage, a sum over hidden λ indices as well. We deal with this by employing *nested* EM iterations, as follows.

1. Begin with some initial λ's.

2. By the inside-outside algorithm described in [LST92] and the previous section, reveal the hidden linkages of the *smoothing* corpus using the smooth distributions $\tilde{T}_\lambda$, $\tilde{L}_\lambda$ and $\tilde{D}_\lambda$ and accumulate the EM counts $c_{T,\lambda}(t)$, $c_{T,\lambda}(l)$ and $c_{D,\lambda}(d)$ for the parameters t, l, d of the distributions T, L and D. These are the counts obtained by maximizing the auxiliary function

$$\sum_{S \in \mathcal{S}} \sum_\Lambda P(\Lambda | S; \tilde{T}_\lambda, \tilde{L}_\lambda, \tilde{D}_\lambda) \log P(S, \Lambda | \tilde{T}_{\lambda'}, \tilde{L}_{\lambda'}, \tilde{D}_{\lambda'})$$

with respect to λ'. Their accumulation is the E-step of the outermost EM iterations.

3. Form the objective function

$$\mathcal{O}_{\text{inner}}(\lambda') = \sum_t c_{T,\lambda}(t) \log \tilde{T}_{\lambda'}(t) + \sum_l c_{L,\lambda}(l) \log \tilde{L}_{\lambda'}(l) + \sum_d c_{D,\lambda}(d) \log \tilde{D}_{\lambda'}(d).$$

Notice that the λ' indices are hidden in $\mathcal{O}_{\text{inner}}(\lambda')$. Use the forward-backward algorithm to find the λ's that maximize $\mathcal{O}_{\text{inner}}(\lambda')$ subject to the appropriate constraints. These nested EM iterations are the M-step of the outermost EM iterations.

4. Using these λ's as new guesses for the λs, return to step 1, and iterate until converged.

Note that the outermost EM steps use the inside-outside algorithm for link grammars; the hidden parses are in general context-free in generative power. However, step 3, which is the M-step for the inside-outside algorithm, is itself an EM estimation problem. Here, however, the hidden structure is regular, so the estimation can be carried out using the forward-backward algorithm for probabilistic finite state machines. The general EM algorithm technology guarantees that each iteration of the above algorithm increases the log-likelihood $\mathcal{O}_{\text{outer}}$ of the smoothing corpus with respect to the smooth model so far. In practice, we have observed that roughly three iterations of the outer EM iterations and 15 iterations of the inner EM iterations suffice to smooth the parameters of our models.

6 Sample Results

This section presents the results of inferring and training our long-range trigram model on a corpus of Wall Street Journal data.

Figure 3 lists examples of the word pairs that were discovered using the inference scheme discussed in Section 3. Recall that these pairs are discovered by training a link grammar that allows long-range links between a single, fixed, pair of words. A given pair is judged by the reduction in entropy that its one-link model achieves over the bigram model. In the table, this improvement, measured in bits of information, is shown in the third column. The first section of the table lists the pairs that resulted in the greatest reduction in entropy. The fourth column of the table gives the values of the probability $\text{D}(\text{BRANCH}_{\text{LR}} \mid L)$ after forward-backward training. This number indicates the frequency with which L generates R from long range, according to the trained model. The second section of the table lists examples of pairs with high $\text{D}(\text{BRANCH}_{\text{LR}} \mid L)$. The fifth column of the table gives the values of the probability $\text{D}_{\text{LR}}(\text{HALT})^{-1}$ after forward-backward training. Recall that since the number of words between L and R is geometrically distributed with mean $\text{D}_{\text{LR}}(\text{HALT})^{-1}$ in the hidden model, a large value in this column indicates that L and R are on average widely separated in the training data. The third section of the table gives examples of such pairs. Finally, the fourth section of the table shows the results of the word-pair calculation applied to the corpus after it was tagged with parts-of-speech. The search was restricted to verb-preposition pairs, and some of the pairs which yielded the greatest reduction in entropy are shown here.

In Figures 4 and 5 we show plots of perplexity as a function of iteration in the EM training of the long-range trigram model described in Section 2, using the word-pair "grammar" that was automatically extracted. These graphs plot the perplexity as a function of iteration, with the trigram perplexity shown as a horizontal line. In the first plot, carried out over a training set of 2,521,112 words, the perplexity falls approximately 12.7% below the trigram perplexity after 9 iterations. After smoothing as described in Section 5, the perplexity on test data was approximately 4.3% below the smoothed trigram

L	R	$\mathrm{Gain_{LR}} \times 10^5$	$\mathrm{D(BRANCH_{LR} \mid} L)$	$\mathrm{D_{LR}(HALT)}^{-1}$
(	)	472.944	0.808	2.277
"	"	80.501	0.089	3.041
between	and	57.097	0.674	2.002
[	]	54.287	0.907	2.644
neither	nor	22.883	0.588	2.030
either	or	16.892	0.496	3.083
both	and	14.915	0.277	1.786
–	–	14.909	0.074	5.309
,	,	14.039	0.117	3.845
from	to	13.021	0.044	1.931
tit	tat	0.344	0.835	2.049
to_preheat	oven	1.663	0.773	1.084
to_whet	appetite	0.521	0.709	1.943
nook	cranny	0.618	0.619	2.426
to_flex	muscle	0.702	0.548	1.784
sigh	relief	0.624	0.411	2.123
loaf	bread	0.434	0.308	2.795
quarterback	touchdown	0.167	0.027	5.715
inning	hit	0.097	0.018	5.673
farmer	crop	0.347	0.023	5.609
investor	stock	0.270	0.014	5.149
firefighter	blaze	0.513	0.071	4.955
whether	or	5.123	0.124	4.925
she	her	9.672	0.078	4.007
to_describe	as	9.022	0.457	3.275
to_rise	to	7.654	0.261	2.437
to_prevent	from	7.491	0.407	3.743
to_turn	into	6.642	0.174	3.566
to_attribute	to	5.679	0.904	4.189
to_view	as	5.193	0.524	3.425
to_bring	to	4.960	0.237	3.836
to_range	to	4.864	0.660	5.356

Figure 3: Sample word pairs

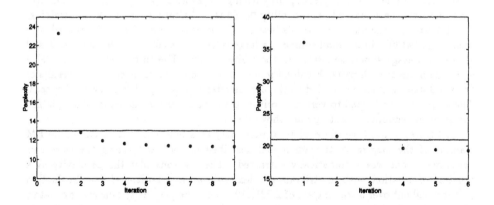

Figure 4: 2.5M corpus   Figure 5: 25M corpus

perplexity. In the second plot, carried out over a training set of 25,585,580 words, the perplexity falls approximately 8% below the trigram perplexity after 6 iterations. After smoothing this model, the perplexity on test data was approximately 5.3% under the smoothed trigram perplexity. The fact that the magnitude of the entropy reduction on training data is not preserved after smoothing and evaluating on test data is an indication that the smoothing may be sensitive to the "bucketing" of the λ's.

These perplexity results are consistent with the observation that for a fixed word-pair grammar, as the training corpus grows in size the long-range trigram model becomes a small perturbation of the standard trigram model. This is because the number of disjunct parameters $D(d \mid w_1 w_2)$ and long-range trigram parameters $L(w \mid w_1 w_2)$ is on the order of the number of bigrams, which becomes negligible compared to the number of trigram parameters as the training set grows in size.

The smoothed models were incorporated into the *Candide* system for machine translation [BBP+94]. When compared with translations obtained with the system using the standard trigram model, our long-range model showed a slight advantage overall. For example, the French sentence "Manille a manqué d'électricité pendant dix heures mercredi," which was translated as "Manila has run out of electricity for ten hours Wednesday" using the standard language model, was translated as "Manila lacked electricity for ten hours Wednesday" using the link grammar model.

While the long-range trigram model that we have described in this paper represents only a small change in the trigram model itself, we believe that the techniques we develop here demonstrate the viability of more complex link grammar models, and show that significant improvements can be obtained using this approach.

References

[BBdSM91] L.R. Bahl, P.F. Brown, P.V. de Souza, and R.L. Mercer. Tree-based smoothing algorithm for a trigram language speech recognition model. *IBM Technical Disclosure Bulletin*, 34(7B):380–383, December 1991.

[BBP+94] A. Berger, P. Brown, S. Della Pietra, V. Della Pietra, J. Gillett, J. Lafferty, R. Mercer, H. Printz, and L. Ureš. The Candide system for machine translation. In *Human Language Technologies*, Morgan Kaufman Publishers, 1994.

[BT73] T. Booth and R. Thompson. Applying probability measures to abstract languages. *IEEE Transactions on Computers*, C-22:442–450, 1973.

[LST92] J. Lafferty, D. Sleator, and D. Temperley. Grammatical trigrams: A probabilistic model of link grammar. In *Proceedings of the AAAI Fall Symposium on Probabilistic Approaches to Natural Language*, Cambridge, MA, 1992.

[ST91] D. Sleator and D. Temperley. Parsing English with a link grammar. Technical Report CMU-CS-91-196, School of Computer Science, Carnegie Mellon University, 1991.

Appendix A: Enumerating Linkages

In this appendix we derive a formula for the number of linkages of the model described in Section 1 when the grammar allows long-range connections between any pair of words.

There is a natural correspondence between the linkages of model (1) and trees where each node has either zero, one, or two children. A node having one child will be called *unary* and a node having two children will be called *binary*. Let $a_{m,n}$ be the number of trees having m unary nodes and n binary nodes. Then $a_{m,n}$ satisfies the recurrence

$$a_{m,n} = a_{m-1,n} + \sum_{0 \le k \le m} \sum_{0 \le l \le n-1} a_{k,l}\, a_{m-k,n-l-1}\,.$$

Thus, the generating function $T(x,y) = \sum_{m,n \ge 0} a_{m,n}\, x^m\, y^n$ satisfies the equation

$$T(x,y) = 1 + x\, T(x,y) + y\, T^2(x,y)\,.$$

Since $T(0,0) = 1$ we have that

$$T(x,y) = \frac{1 - x - \sqrt{(1-x)^2 - 4y}}{2y}\,.$$

The total number of nodes in a tree that has m unary nodes and n binary nodes is $2n + m + 1$. Therefore, if $S(z) = \sum_{k \ge 0} s_k z^k$ is the generating function given by $S(z) = z\, T(z, z^2)$, then

$$s_k = \sum_{2n+m+1=k} a_{m,n}$$

and s_k is the number of trees having a total of k nodes. S is given by

$$
\begin{aligned}
S(z) &= \frac{1 - z - \sqrt{(1-z)^2 - 4z^2}}{2z} \\[2mm]
&= \frac{1 - z - \sqrt{1 - 3z}\sqrt{1 + z}}{2z} \\[2mm]
&= \frac{1}{2z} - \frac{1}{2} - \frac{1}{2z} \sum_{i \ge 0} \binom{1/2}{i}(-3)^i z^i \sum_{j \ge 0} \binom{1/2}{j} z^j \\[2mm]
&= \frac{1}{6} \sum_{k \ge 0} \sum_{0 \le i \le k+1} \binom{1/2}{i} \binom{1/2}{k+1-i}(-3)^{i+1} z^k\,.
\end{aligned}
$$

While we are unable to find a closed form expression for the coefficients

$$s_k = \frac{1}{6} \sum_{0 \le i \le k+1} \binom{1/2}{i} \binom{1/2}{k+1-i}(-3)^{i+1}$$

a few of the values are displayed below.

k	1	2	3	4	5	6	7	8	9	10	20	25
s_k	1	1	2	4	9	21	51	127	323	835	18,199,284	3,192,727,797

Appendix B: Deficiency

We say that a language model is *deficient* if it assigns a probability that is smaller than one to the set of strings it is designed to model. There are several ways in which a probabilistic link grammar can be deficient. One such way is if the total probability of finite linkages is smaller than one. In this appendix we derive conditions under which this type of deficiency can occur for a simplified version of our model. The general analysis is similar, but more intricate [BT73].

Following the notation of Appendix A, suppose that we generate trees probabilistically with a node having zero children with probability p_0, one child with probability p_1, and two children with probability p_2, irrespective of the label of the node. These probabilities correspond to the disjunct probabilities $D(\text{HALT} \mid s)$, $D(\text{STEP} \mid s)$, and $D(\text{BRANCH} \mid s)$. We ignore the short and long-range trigram probabilities in this simplified model. The probability of generating a tree with m unary nodes and n binary nodes is then $p_0^{n+1} p_1^m p_2^n$. The total probability assigned to finite trees is

$$T_{\text{finite}} = \sum_{m,n \geq 0} a_{m,n} \, p_0^{n+1} p_1^m p_2^n = p_0 \, T(p_1, p_0 \, p_2).$$

Using the calculations of Appendix A, this leads directly to the relation

$$
\begin{aligned}
T_{\text{finite}} &= \frac{1 - p_1 - \sqrt{(1 - p_1)^2 - 4 p_0 \, p_2}}{2 p_2} \\
&= \frac{p_0 + p_2 - |p_0 - p_2|}{2 p_2}.
\end{aligned}
$$

In terms of the expected number of children $E[n] = p_1 + 2p_2$, we can state this as

$$T_{\text{finite}} = \begin{cases} 1 & E[n] \leq 1 \\ p_0/p_2 & E[n] \geq 1 \end{cases}.$$

More generally, for n-ary trees with probability p_i of generating i children, with $0 \leq i \leq n$, T_{finite} is the smallest root of the equation

$$T = \sum_{0 \leq i \leq n} p_i \, T^i$$

and $T_{\text{finite}} = 1$ in case $E[n] < 1$. This is a well-known result in the theory of branching processes.

Application of OSTIA to Machine Translation Tasks*

Antonio Castellanos[†], Isabel Galiano and Enrique Vidal

Departamento de Sistemas Informáticos y Computación
Universidad Politécnica de Valencia
Camino de Vera s/n, 46071 Valencia (Spain)
e-mail: `acastell@dsic.upv.es`

Abstract

A new application of the Onward Subsequential Transducer Inference Algorithm (OSTIA) is presented. Limited-domain Machine Translation tasks have been defined from a conceptually constrained task which was recently proposed within the field of Cognitive Science. Large corpora of English-to-Spanish and English-to-German translations have been generated, and exhaustive experiments have been carried out to test the ability of OSTIA to learn these translations. The success of the results show the usefulness of formal learning techniques in limited-domain Machine Translation tasks.

1 Introduction

The *Onward Subsequential Transducer Inference Algorithm* (OSTIA) is an efficient technique for learning an interesting class of mappings between languages [7, 10] which has been recently introduced. These mappings are known as *Subsequential Transductions* (ST). The class of ST is a subclass of the more general class of *Rational* or *Finite-State Transductions* and properly contains the class of *Sequential Transductions* [2]. A Sequential Transduction is one that preserves the increasing length prefixes of input-output strings [2, 6, 14]. While this can be considered as a rather "natural property" of transductions, there are many real-world situations in which such a strict sequentiality is clearly inadmissible. The class of Subsequential Transductions makes this restriction milder, therefore allowing for its application in many practical situations of interest. Apart from this flexibility of subsequential transducers, perhaps more important is the fact that, using OSTIA, these mappings have been recently proved *learnable* from positive presentation of *input-output examples* [7, 8].

ST and OSTIA have been successfully used so far in a variety of applications such as learning to translate Roman numbers into the corresponding Decimal representation, learning to translate (written) English numbers into the corresponding spelling in Spanish,

---

*Work partially supported by the Spanish CICYT, under grant TIC–1026/92–CO2.
[†]Supported by a postgraduate grant from the Spanish "Ministerio de Educación y Ciencia".

etc. [9, 10]. Also, more recently, it has been applied to pseudo-natural *Language Under-standing* [3]. By adapting a basic and theory-free task recently proposed by Feldman et al. [4], a pseudo-natural "English-to-Semantics" transduction task was specified for this latest work. The English sentences within the scope of the task defined by Feldman et al. were associated to logical formulae which represented the semantics of the task. Given a training-set of sentence-meaning pairs, OSTIA quite successfully learnt very accurate transducers for this language understanding task [3].

Following the good results of these previous works, here we study the use of ST and OSTIA in a more challenging task; namely *language-to-language translation*. While one can argue that the kinds of mappings actually underlying general *Machine Translation* (MT) would escape the capabilities of any formal device, we think that in limited domains, useful mappings between complex languages can be properly modeled through ST. In order to study to what extent this idea is correct, a handy pseudo-natural MT task was required, which was also general enough to increase its degree of complexity in a controlled manner for a series of experiments. For this purpose, we have reformulated the previously mentioned task proposed by Feldman et al. [4] as one of limited-domain MT. We show that, given a training-set of English sentences of the task along with their correct translation into both Spanish and German, OSTIA can automatically learn appropriate subsequential transducers that accurately translate previously unseen English sentences into corresponding correct sentences of these target languages.

2 The Onward Subsequential Transducer Inference Algorithm

Formal and detailed descriptions of OSTIA have been presented elsewhere [3, 7, 8, 9, 10]; therefore, only some intuitive ideas about the basic concepts and an outline of the procedures will be presented here.

A *Subsequential Transducer* is a formal device which consists of *states* and *edges*. Each edge connects two states and has an *input symbol* and a *substring of output symbols* associated to it, which belong to certain *input* and *output alphabets*, respectively. Each state also has an output substring associated to it. One of the states is the *initial state* and all the states are *final* or *accepting*. In addition, *determinism* is required; i.e., two outgoing edges from the same state cannot have the same input symbol associated to them.

A string of input symbols is *accepted* if, when starting from the initial state, the successive symbols of the input string match the input symbols associated to a correct (accessible) sequence of edges. When an input string is accepted, an output string is produced, which consists of the concatenation of the output substrings associated to the corresponding correct sequence of edges along with the substring associated to the last state reached with the input string.

A *transduction* from X^* to Y^* is a relation $t \subseteq (X^* \times Y^*)$. A transduction is *subsequential* iff it is carried out by a subsequential transducer. Any subsequential transduction admits different characterizations in terms of different subsequential transducers. Nevertheless, for any subsequential transduction there exists a *canonical subsequential transducer* that has a *minimum number of states* and is *unique* up to isomorphism [8]. This transducer adopts an *"onward" form*. Intuitively, an *Onward Subsequential Transducer* (OST) is one in which the output strings are assigned to the edges in such a way that they are as "close" to the initial state as they can be.

Any nonambiguous or *single-valued* finite sample of input-output pairs T can be properly represented by a *Tree Subsequential Transducer* (TST). A TST can be built as follows:

1. The set of states is the set of *all prefixes* of the input strings. The initial state is the *empty* string (λ).

2. The set of edges consists of edges connecting each prefix (state) with its successors. Each edge will connect the state w with the state wa, having a as the associated input symbol and λ as the associated output substring.

3. States corresponding to complete input strings have associated to them, as the output substrings, the corresponding output strings paired with the input ones in the set of samples. All the other states have the *undefined* string associated to them.

Given T, an *Onward Tree Subsequential Transducer* representing T can be obtained by building the OST equivalent to the TST of T. The procedure consists of moving the longest common prefixes of the output strings, level by level, from the leaves of the tree toward the root.

OSTIA [10] takes a finite single-valued training-set, T, as input and produces an OST compatible with T as output. To this end, OSTIA starts building the Onward Tree Subsequential Transducer which represents T and then tries to merge pairs of states of this transducer. The merging process is carried out in an appropriate order, based on the *lexicographic order* of the names given to the states through the TST construction. Successively, an attempt is made to merge each state with each one of its predecessors, until a merging is acceptable. If no acceptable merging is found, then the next state is considered for merging. For a state merging to be acceptable, the resulting transducer must not be in contradiction with T. This is carried out by testing some conditions on the involved edges and their associated input symbols and output substrings. Sometimes, the *"pushing back"* of some output substrings toward the leaves of the tree is required to try to reach an acceptable state merging.

Every time a pair of states is merged a generalization of T is produced. Thus, at the end of this process, an OST which is a compatible generalization of T is obtained. It has formally been shown that, using this algorithm, the class of subsequential transductions can be identified in the limit from positive presentation of input-output pairs [7, 10]. Therefore, any subsequential transduction can be exactly learnt through OSTIA. However, for this purpose, a set of pairs that contains a (small) *representative set of the transduction* to be inferred is required. The convergence in the limit is guaranteed by the fact that any fair presentation will eventually contain a representative set. On the other hand, in practice, the target transducer is unknown and, thus, no characterization of a representative set of samples is possible. Therefore, the *goodness* of the obtained OST for modelling a given transduction depends upon the set of samples T which is available. This is a fundamental consideration when practical transductions are to be learnt.

3   A Pseudo-Natural Machine Translation Task

From the perspective of Cognitive Science, Feldman et al. recently introduced a compact and theory-free task that presents fundamental challenges to different areas such as

Language, Inference and Learning [4]. This task is the so-called *"Miniature Language Acquisition"* (MLA) and was proposed to be used as a *touchstone* for the capabilities of systems of learning and understanding. Basically, the MLA task consists of correctly associating simple two-dimensional visual scenes with sentences which describe these scenes. A few geometric objects with different shape, shade and size, and located in different relative positions can be involved in these scenes and their corresponding descriptions. To implicitly constrain the conceptual domain of the descriptive English sentences of the MLA task, a simple phrase structure grammar —called L0— was given by Feldman et al. [4]. This grammar generates a large, but finite, language that has already been adopted for language understanding experiments [3, 13] (as many as $1.6 \cdot 10^8$ sentences).

Adequate adaptations and extensions of the MLA task for MT have also been considered in this work. The aim was to specify a MT task that, while being sufficiently constrained, is rich enough to be comparable to some real-world tasks. Furthermore, this task would allow itself to be increasingly extended to incorporate new difficulties, in a controlled manner. Descriptions of scenes in any given *Source Language* (SL) are to be associated with corresponding descriptions in any given *Target Language* (TL); that is, source and target sentences which describe the same scene (and which, therefore, are translations of one another) are to be paired. By using the (slightly modified) L0 grammar, descriptive English sentences adequate for these purposes can be obtained. In addition, two new grammars for Spanish and German had to be defined, which were constrained to be within the same conceptual domain as that of the L0 grammar. These three grammars, which are shown in Figure 1, allow for generating descriptive MLA sentences in three languages, and thus, for obtaining six different corpora of translations by considering each of the three languages (English, Spanish and German) as a SL, in some cases, and as a TL, in other cases. In what follows, we will refer to this generic task as the *"Descriptive MLA-MT"* task.

From the point of view of our transduction learning paradigm, examples of the scene descriptions in a SL paired with their translation into a TL will be given to OSTIA. Then, OSTIA will have to learn the relevant portion of the SL-to-TL translation by providing an appropriate transducer, so that given a new, previously unseen, SL sentence, the transducer can give a correct translation in the TL. Under such a setting, the transducers obtained by OSTIA are expected to appropriately model the underlying mapping as long as the transduction from SL sentences into their corresponding TL sentences exhibits a "subsequential behaviour". Intuitively speaking, subsequential transductions are those in which output substrings are generated only after having seen enough input symbols to guarantee a correct output. Moreover, the amount of symbols to wait for may be variable and context-dependent. Also, detecting the end of the input string may often be required to correctly generate a trailing output substring. Therefore, a good measure of the difficulty of a transduction to be learnt by OSTIA is the degree of *"asynchrony"* between the symbols of the source sentences and their corresponding translations in the target sentences.

In the experiments with the Descriptive MLA-MT task presented here below, English has been chosen as the SL and both Spanish and German as two different TLs. The choice of the two different TLs is to study the effect of different sources of asynchrony in the translations to be learnt. For instance, if the input English sentence is "a medium square and a large light triangle are far above a dark circle," the corresponding Spanish translation (output sentence) is "un cuadrado mediano y un triangulo grande y claro estan muy por encima de un circulo oscuro." Adjectives in English almost always precede the noun, while in Spanish they usually come after. Therefore, for translating the English subsentence "large light triangle", waiting for the word "triangle" is required to generate "triangulo

(a)

S	⇒	NPS | NPP | NPS VPS | NPP VPP
NPS	⇒	DT NP1
NPP	⇒	DT NP1 AND DT NP1
VPS	⇒	VIS OI | VTS OD
VPP	⇒	VIP OI | VTP OD
NP1	⇒	OBJ | SHADE OBJ | SIZE OBJ | SIZE SHADE OBJ
OI	⇒	REL NPS | REL NPP
OD	⇒	NPS | NPP
REL	⇒	REL1 | FAR REL1
DT	⇒	a
VIS	⇒	is
VTS	⇒	touches
VIP	⇒	are
VTP	⇒	touch
OBJ	⇒	circle | triangle | square
SHADE	⇒	light | dark
SIZE	⇒	small | medium | large
REL1	⇒	above | below | to the left of | to the right of
FAR	⇒	far
AND	⇒	and

(b)

S	⇒	NPS | NPP | NPS VPS | NPP VPP
NPS	⇒	DT NP1
NPP	⇒	DT NP1 AND DT NP1
VPS	⇒	VIS OI | VTS OD
VPP	⇒	VIP OI | VTP OD
NP1	⇒	OBJ | OBJ SHADE | OBJ SIZE | OBJ SIZE AND SHADE
OI	⇒	REL NPS | REL NPP
OD	⇒	NPS | NPP
REL	⇒	REL1 | REL2 | FAR1 REL1 | FAR2 REL2
DT	⇒	un
VIS	⇒	esta
VTS	⇒	toca a
VIP	⇒	estan
VTP	⇒	tocan a
OBJ	⇒	circulo | cuadrado | triangulo
SHADE	⇒	claro | oscuro
SIZE	⇒	pequeño | mediano | grande
REL1	⇒	encima de | debajo de
REL2	⇒	a la derecha de | a la izquierda de
FAR1	⇒	muy por
FAR2	⇒	muy
AND	⇒	y

(c)

S	⇒	NPS | NPP | NPS VPS | NPP VPP	NP1AM	⇒	OBJM | SHADEAM OBJM | SIZEAM OBJM | SIZEAM SHADEAM OBJM
NPS	⇒	DTN NP1N	NP1AN	⇒	OBJN | NP1NN
NPP	⇒	DTN NP1N AND DTN NP1N	NP1DSN	⇒	OBJN | SHADEAM OBJN | SIZEAM OBJN | SIZEAM SHADEAM OBJN
VPS	⇒	VIS OI | VTS OD			
VPP	⇒	VIP OI | VTP OD			
NP1N	⇒	OBJ | NP1NM | NP1NN	DTN	⇒	ein
OI	⇒	REL NP1D	DTAM	⇒	einen
OD	⇒	ODS | ODP	DTD	⇒	einem
OBJ	⇒	OBJM | OBJN	VIS	⇒	ist
NP1NM	⇒	SHADENM OBJM | SIZENM OBJM | SIZENM SHADENM OBJM	VTS	⇒	beruhrt
			VIP	⇒	sind
NP1NN	⇒	SHADENN OBJN | SIZENN OBJN | SIZENN SHADENN OBJN	VTP	⇒	beruhren
			OBJM	⇒	kreis
REL	⇒	REL1 | FAR REL1	OBJN	⇒	dreieck | viereck
NP1D	⇒	NP1DS | NP1DP	SHADENM	⇒	weisser | dunkler
ODS	⇒	DTAM NP1AM | DTN NP1AN	SIZENM	⇒	kleiner | mittlerer | grosser
ODP	⇒	DTAM NP1AM AND DTAM NP1AM | DTAM NP1AM AND DTN NP1AN | DTN NP1AN AND DTAM NP1AM | DTN NP1AN AND DTN NP1AN	SHADENN	⇒	weisses | dunkles
			SIZENN	⇒	kleines | mittleres | grosses
			SHADEAM	⇒	weissen | dunklen
NP1DS	⇒	DTD NP1AM | DTD NP1DSN	SIZEAM	⇒	kleinen | mittleren | grossen
NP1DP	⇒	DTD NP1AM AND DTD NP1AM | DTD NP1AM AND DTD NP1DSN | DTD NP1DSN AND DTD NP1AM | DTD NP1DSN AND DTD NP1DSN	REL1	⇒	uber | unter | links von | rechts von
			FAR	⇒	weit
			AND	⇒	und

Figure 1: Descriptive MLA-MT grammars: (a) English; (b) Spanish; and (c) German.

grande y claro" which is the correct Spanish translation. This kind of asynchrony involves at most three words and will make the transducer wait for the English noun in order to output the correct Spanish translation.

However, the German translation of the given English sentence, "ein mittleres viereck und ein grosses weisses dreieck ist weit uber einen dunklen kreis," exhibits a higher degree of input-output asynchrony; i.e., the system needs to wait for the English verb in order to establish the case of the different parts of the German sentence. Moreover, once the case has been determined, the translation of the adjectives cannot be done until the gender of the noun is known. Note that while in the English-to-Spanish translation the asynchrony is due to the different positions that adjectives take with regard to the noun,

(a)

S	⇒	NPSA VIS PPA |
		NPSA VIS PPA VP |
		NPSB VIS PPB
NPSA	⇒	DT1 NP1
VP	⇒	REL NPS | REL NPP
NPSB	⇒	NPS | NPS RELAT
NP1	⇒	OBJ | SHADE OBJ |
		SIZE OBJ |
		SIZE SHADE OBJ
REL	⇒	REL1 | FAR REL1
NPS	⇒	DT2 NP1
NPP	⇒	DT2 NP1 AND DT2 NP1
RELAT	⇒	WHICH VIS VP
DT1	⇒	a
DT2	⇒	the
VIS	⇒	is
PPA	⇒	added
PPB	⇒	removed
OBJ	⇒	circle | triangle | square
SHADE	⇒	light | dark
SIZE	⇒	small | medium | large
FAR	⇒	far
WHICH	⇒	which
REL1	⇒	above | below |
		to the right of |
		to the left of
AND	⇒	and

(b)

S	⇒	VIS PPA NPSA | VIS PPB NPSB
		VIS PPA NPSA VP |
NPSA	⇒	DT1 NP1
VP	⇒	REL NPS | REL NPP
NPSB	⇒	NPS | NPS RELAT
NP1	⇒	OBJ | OBJ SHADE | OBJ SIZE |
		OBJ SIZE AND SHADE
REL	⇒	REL1 | REL2 | FAR1 REL1 |
		FAR2 REL2
NPS	⇒	DT2 NP1
NPP	⇒	DT2 NP1 AND DT2 NP1
RELAT	⇒	WHICH VR VP
DT1	⇒	un
DT2	⇒	el
VIS	⇒	se
PPA	⇒	añade
PPB	⇒	borra
VR	⇒	esta
OBJ	⇒	circulo | triangulo | cuadrado
SHADE	⇒	claro | oscuro
SIZE	⇒	pequeño | mediano | grande
FAR1	⇒	muy por
FAR2	⇒	muy
WHICH	⇒	que
REL11	⇒	encima de | debajo de
REL12	⇒	a la derecha de | a la izquierda de
AND	⇒	y

(c)

S	⇒	VIS NPSA PPA | VIS NPSB PPB |	NP1DN	⇒	OBJN | SHADEAM OBJN |
		VIS NPSA VP PPA			SIZEAM OBJN |
NPSA	⇒	DT1N NPSAN | DT1M NPSAM			SIZEAM SHADEAM OBJN
VP	⇒	REL NP1D	VIS	⇒	man hat
NPSB	⇒	DT2AN NPSAN2 | DT2AM NPSAM |	VR	⇒	befindet
		DT2AN NPSAN2 RELATN |	PPA	⇒	hinzugefügt
		DT2AM NPSAM RELATM	PPB	⇒	entfernt
NPSAN	⇒	OBJN | SHADEAN OBJN |	DT1N	⇒	ein
		SIZEAN OBJN |	DT1M	⇒	einen
		SIZEAN SHADEAN OBJN	DT2AN	⇒	das
NPSAM	⇒	OBJM | SHADEAM OBJM |	DT2AM	⇒	den
		SIZEAM OBJM |	DT2D	⇒	dem
		SIZEAM SHADEAM OBJM	OBJN	⇒	dreieck | viereck
REL	⇒	REL1 | FAR REL1	OBJM	⇒	kreis
NP1D	⇒	NP1DS | NP1DP	SHADE	⇒	weisse | dunkle
NPSAN2	⇒	OBJN | SHADE OBJN |	SIZE	⇒	kleine | mittlere | grosse
		SIZE OBJN |	SHADEAN	⇒	weisses | dunkles
		SIZE SHADE OBJN	SIZEAN	⇒	kleines | mittleres | grosses
RELATN	⇒	WHICHN REL NP1D VR	SHADEAM	⇒	weissen | dunklen
RELATM	⇒	WHICHM REL NP1D VR	SIZEAM	⇒	kleinen | mittleren | grossen
NP1DS	⇒	DT2D NPSAM | DT2D NP1DN	REL1	⇒	uber | unter | rechts von |
NP1DP	⇒	DT2D NPSAM AND DT2D NPSAM |			links von
		DT2D NPSAM AND DT2D NP1DN |	FAR	⇒	weit
		DT2D NP1DN AND DT2D NP1DN |	WHICHN	⇒	das sich
		DT2D NP1DN AND DT2D NSAM	WHICHM	⇒	der sich
			AND	⇒	und

Figure 2: Grammars which generate sentences which are related to single object modification for the Extended MLA-MT task: (a) English; (b) Spanish; and (c) German.

in the English-to-German translation the asynchrony has nothing to do with this change of position. Actually, every piece of the German sentence has the same position as in the English sentence, but the difficulties are now case and gender, which are grammatical aspects of the TL that do not exist in the SL.

Although the Descriptive MLA-MT task is a good starting point for our experimentation purposes, we have further extended it in order to increase the difficulty in a controlled manner. Among the different variants proposed by Feldman et al. [4], we have chosen the one which involves single object modification; i.e., a single object can now be removed from or added to a scene. In both cases, the object can be identified by its shape and/or its relative position with respect to the other objects in the scene. For instance, the simplest sentences of this kind are: "a circle is added" or "the circle is removed". However, more detailed sentences are allowed: "a square is added far above the circle and the small triangle" or "the triangle which is to the left of the light square and the medium circle is removed".

To generate these new sentences three additional grammars, corresponding to the three languages considered in this work have been defined as shown in Figure 2. These new grammars only allow for generating sentences related to single object *modification*; i.e., they do not generate L0 sentences which are *descriptions* of scenes. Nevertheless, we have considered an *"Extended MLA-MT"* task which simultaneously includes both of these conceptual domains of MLA. The different global corpora of translations for this extended task have been obtained by joining the sentences generated through the grammars shown in Figure 2 with those of the Descriptive MLA-MT task (Figure 1).

In the Extended MLA-MT experiments, the choice of the SL and the TLs was the same as in the experiments with the Descriptive MLA-MT task. Our interest in this particular variant is because it introduces the use of the passive voice in English and thus allows for a large variety of asynchronous situations in the Spanish and German outputs. As an example, consider the English sentence "a large light circle is added far below the light triangle and the medium light square". In its corresponding translation into Spanish, "se añade un circulo grande y claro muy por debajo del triangulo claro y del cuadrado mediano y claro", the position of the verb "is added" shifts to the beginning of the Spanish sentence ("se añade"). On the other hand, the corresponding German translation is "man hat einen grossen weissen kreis weit unter dem weissen dreieck und dem mittleren weissen viereck hinzugefügt", and a new kind of asynchrony appears which simultaneously relates the verb "is added" to the beginning and the end of the German sentence ("man hat" and "hinzugefügt"). In these cases, the grammatical aspects of the languages involved result in high degrees of asynchrony which could make the automatic learning of such translations very difficult.

4 Experimental Setting

A series of experiments was carried out to test the capabilities of OSTIA for learning to translate Descriptive and Extended MLA-MT English sentences into both Spanish and German. For this purpose, a set of training input-output (English-Spanish/German) pairs is required from which the OSTIA will produce a subsequential transducer, τ. Also, in order to assess the degree to which this transducer accounts for the true transduction underlying the MT task, an *independent* test-set of input-output pairs is required. Let (x, y) be one of these test pairs. The input English sentence, x, is submitted to transduction by τ, resulting in a Spanish/German sentence $\hat{y} = \tau(x)$. This sentence is then compared with the true Spanish/German translation, y, and an error is counted whenever $\hat{y} \neq y$.

The generation of all these training and test sets of input-output pairs was governed by the English grammars (Figure 1(a) and Figure 2(a)), along with the associated Spanish/German grammars under a well-known mechanism called Syntax-Directed Translation Scheme [1]. Starting from the axiom, a random rewriting process was carried out to simultaneously produce each English sentence and the corresponding Spanish and German translations. This process assumed all rules which share the same non terminal to be equiprobable. Following this procedure, a large set of input-output pairs was initially generated for each of the two SL-to-TL translations in both of the two tasks, Descriptive and Extended MLA-MT. Each of these initial sets was further reduced by first removing repeated pairs and then randomly eliminating a number of pairs so as to yield a standard set of 100,000 pairs per SL-to-TL translation for the Descriptive MLA-MT task and 200,000 pairs per SL-to-TL translation for the Extended MLA-MT task. Examples of these pairs are shown in Figure 3.

English:	a medium light square and a circle touch a light circle and a medium square
Spanish:	un cuadrado mediano claro y un circulo tocan a un circulo claro y un cuadrado mediano
German:	ein mittleres weisses viereck und ein kreis beruhren einen weissen kreis und ein mittleres viereck
English:	a medium dark triangle and a dark circle are to the right of a large light circle
Spanish:	un triangulo mediano oscuro y un circulo oscuro estan a la derecha de un circulo grande claro
German:	ein mittleres dunkles dreieck und ein dunkler kreis sind rechts von einem grossen weissen kreis

English:	a large dark triangle is added far to the left of the square and the medium circle
Spanish:	se añade un triangulo grande y oscuro muy a la izquierda del cuadrado y del circulo mediano
German:	man hat ein grosses dunkles dreieck weit und links von dem viereck und dem mittleren kreis hinzugefügt
English:	the large circle which is above the square and the medium triangle is removed
Spanish:	se elimina el circulo grande que esta encima del cuadrado y del triangulo mediano
German:	man hat den grossen kreis der sich uber dem viereck und dem mittleren dreieck befindet entfernt

Figure 3: Examples of input English sentences of the Descriptive and Extended MLA-MT tasks, accompanied by their translation in each one of the two output languages: Spanish and German.

5 Learning MT Tasks with OSTIA: Experiments

For each of the two sets of 100,000 non-repeated input-output pairs (English-Spanish and English-German) of the Descriptive MLA-MT task, a *cross-validation* or leaving-k-out-like procedure [12] was used to evaluate the translation performance of OSTIA transducers. To this end, each global set of 100,000 pairs was randomly split into 5 sets of 20,000 pairs. Each of the two translation experiments consisted of 10 trials, each one having a different combination of 3 out of the 5 sets as a 60,000-sample training-set. In each trial, the training-set was supplied to OSTIA in accumulative blocks of 3,000 pairs, up to 60,000. Then, in each trial, a more detailed coverage of the first 9,000 samples of the training-set was carried out by taking accumulative blocks of 250 pairs. The remaining 2 sets not included in the training-set (40,000 test samples) were used to measure the accuracy of the learnt transducers. Finally, the results on each accumulated training block were averaged over the 10 trials.

For the Extended MLA-MT task, a similar experimental procedure was performed.

Both sets of 200,000 pairs corresponding to the English-to-Spanish and English-to-German translations were randomly split into sets of 40,000 pairs. In each trial of these experiments, the training and test sets consisted of 120,000 and 80,000 pairs, respectively, and the accumulative blocks were also composed of 3,000 pairs. Here, no smaller blocks of samples were considered for a more detailed study.

Afterwards, the whole experimental procedure described above was repeated to investigate the effect of the order of presentation of the training samples. For this purpose, the training-set of each trial was length-sorted on the input (English) sentences before it was supplied to OSTIA in increasing blocks. This was performed for both English-to-Spanish and English-to-German translations of the two MLA-MT tasks (Descriptive and Extended).

Figures 4 and 5 show the results for the Descriptive MLA-MT task for the English-to-Spanish and English-to-German translations, respectively. The results for the Extended MLA-MT task are presented in Figures 6 and 7, which also correspond to the English-to-Spanish and English-to-German translations, respectively. In each figure, part (a) presents the results obtained with the random presentation of the training samples, and part (b) corresponds to the length-sorted presentation. In all cases, three curves are presented: error rate, number of edges and number of states of the learnt transducers.

All the results with the Descriptive MLA-MT task, for both SL-to-TL translations and both modes of training data presentation, share the characteristic that a size of the training-set less than 9,000 pairs leads to very accurate transducers which have an error rate of less than 1%. However, for both translations, length-sorted presentation requires less training pairs to get extremely accurate transducers which have a 0.01% error rate (Figures 4(b) and 5(b)). Moreover, for the English-to-Spanish translation, perfect transducers for this task are obtained using the shortest 1,500 training samples (Figure 4(b)). On the other hand, the size of the learnt transducers is very small for the most accurate of them; namely, less than 25 states and 120 edges for the English-to-Spanish translation (Figure 4), and less than 40 states and 250 edges for the English-to-German translation (Figure 5). In the case of length-sorted presentation, the size of the transducers obtained is more stable for any given size of the training-set, while for random presentation the stability is reached when the size of the training-set is large enough to get accurate transducers.

The Extended MLA-MT task presents more similar results with regard to the error rates of the learnt transducers for the two translations. It clearly appears that it is more difficult this task to be automatically inferred than the previous one, because larger training-sets are required in order to obtain very accurate transducers. Figures 6 and 7 show that length-sorted presentation does not introduce important differences as compared with random presentation. Only in the English-to-German translation, does the length-sorted presentation require less training samples to get transducers with a 0.1% error rate (Figure 7(b)). For its part, the behaviour of the size of the learnt transducers is similar to that of the Descriptive MLA-MT task, though in the case of the Extended MLA-MT task the size of the most accurate transducers is obviously larger. Nevertheless, length-sorted presentation yields a smaller transducer size than random presentation; namely, less than 100 states and 1,000 edges for the English-to-Spanish translation (Figure 6), and less than 50 states and 750 edges for the English-to-German translation (Figure 7).

An example of the kind of mapping that has been inferred for the Extended MLA-MT task is shown in Figure 8, which displays a fragment of a transducer learnt by OSTIA along with the translation performed for an English sentence. Note that all the asyn-

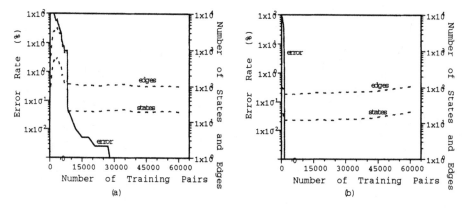

Figure 4: Evolution of the average error rate, number of edges and states of OSTIA-learnt transducers for the Descriptive MLA-MT English-to-Spanish translation task. (a) Random presentation of the training. (b) Length-sorted presentation of the training. Note that the logaritmic error scale has been augmented in order to enable the representation of 0% error rate.

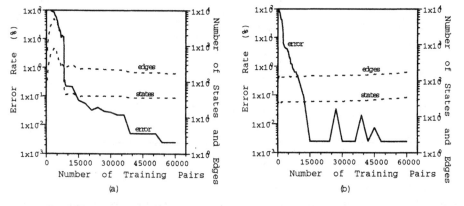

Figure 5: Evolution of the average error rate, number of edges and states of OSTIA-learnt transducers for the Descriptive MLA-MT English-to-German translation task. (a) Random presentation of the training. (b) Length-sorted presentation of the training.

chronies are solved by simply waiting for having seen enough input symbols to guarantee a correct output. On the other hand, it can be observed in this fragment of transducer that while exact transductions are generated for perfect input English sentences, quite disparate translations can be obtained for incorrect input. Although this is not in fact a problem if correct input is guaranteed, more reasonable behaviour can be obtained by imposing input and output language constraints on the OSTIA learning process, as shown in [11].

Finally, computation time patterns of OSTIA in learning these two tasks are comparable to those reported in [3, 9, 10]. These patterns (not presented here for the sake of brevity) once more show an almost linear growth with the size of the training-sets, with

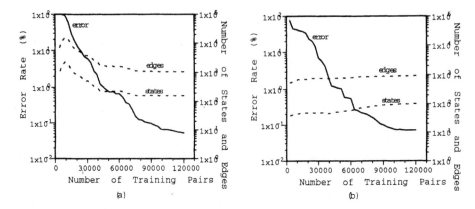

Figure 6: Evolution of the average error rate, number of edges and states of OSTIA-learnt transducers for the Extended MLA-MT English-to-Spanish translation task. (a) Random presentation of the training. (b) Length-sorted presentation of the training.

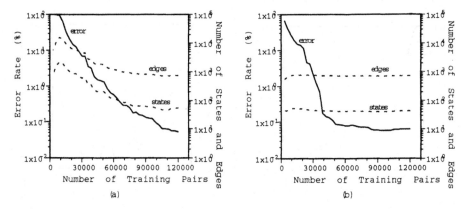

Figure 7: Evolution of the average error rate, number of edges and states of OSTIA-learnt transducers for the Extended MLA-MT English-to-German translation task. (a) Random presentation of the training. (b) Length-sorted presentation of the training.

computation times never exceeding 2 minutes for the larger sizes of the training-set with an HP-APOLLO/735 computer.

6 Concluding Remarks

Two rather challenging limited-domain Machine Translation tasks based on the Miniature Language Acquisition task proposed by Feldman et al. [4] have been established. Two related grammars for Spanish and German were specified from the English grammar which constrained the semantic scope of the MLA task. Then, the Descriptive MLA-MT task which associates English sentences of the basic MLA task to corresponding translations

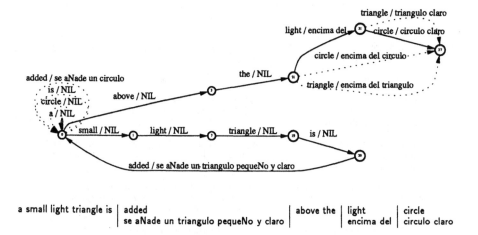

| a small light triangle is | added | | above the | light | circle |
| | se aNade un triangulo pequeNo y claro | | | encima del | circulo claro |

Figure 8: Part of a transducer learnt by OSTIA for the English-to-Spanish translation of the Extended MLA-MT task along with a symbol-by-symbol translation of an English sentence. Dotted lines in the transducer represent edges which are not used in this translation.

into Spanish and German was defined which involves basic translation "asynchronies". Afterwards, an extension of the MLA task was considered for increasing the degree of asynchrony. Consequently, three additional grammars were also specified to generate the new English sentences and their translation into Spanish and German of the Extended MLA-MT task.

Huge corpora of the English-to-Spanish and English-to-German translations for the Descriptive and Extended MLA-MT tasks were used in a series of exhaustive experiments for testing the capability of OSTIA to automatically learn such translations. The results show that the Descriptive MLA-MT task can be very accurately learnt through OSTIA from relatively small training-sets. On the other hand, the Extended MLA-MT task does not constitute a difficulty to OSTIA if large enough training-sets are available. In this case, the transducers learnt for the English-to-Spanish and English-to-German translations very accurately account for the increased difficulty due to the corresponding grammatical aspects of the languages involved.

Although the translation tasks presented here are very constrained, all these practical results encourage us to think that the OSTIA learning framework is a good starting point towards the efficient and effective application of formal transduction learning techniques in limited-domain MT tasks. A recent work which shows the enhanced performance of OSTIA when input and output language constraints are imposed on the learning process [11] reinforces this idea. Moreover, more recent results [5] go deeply into this question and show that Spoken-Language MT —a task which entails fundamental difficulties due to the noisy nature of the input— can be very appropriately approached through techniques such as those above mentioned based on OSTIA.

References

[1] A. AHO, R. SETHI, J.ULLMAN *Compilers. Principles, Techniques, and Tools.* Addison-Wesley Publishing Company, Reading, Massachusetts. 1986.

[2] J. BERSTEL. *Transductions and Context-Free Languages.* Teubner, Stuttgart. 1979.

[3] A. CASTELLANOS, E. VIDAL, J. ONCINA. "Language Understanding and Subsequential Transducer Learning". *1st International Colloquium on Grammatical Inference*, Colchester, England. Proceedings, pp. 11/1-11/10. April, 1993.

[4] J.A. FELDMAN, G. LAKOFF, A. STOLCKE, S.H. WEBER. "Miniature Language Acquisition: A touchstone for cognitive science". Technical Report, TR-90-009. International Computer Science Institute, Berkeley, California. April, 1990.

[5] V. JIMENEZ, E. VIDAL, J. ONCINA, A. CASTELLANOS. "Spoken-Language Machine Translation in Limited-Domain Tasks". *CRIM/FORWISS Workshop on Progress and Prospects of Speech Research and Technology.* Munich (Germany), September 1994. (to be published).

[6] P. LUNEAU, M. RICHETIN, C. CAYLA. "Sequential Learning from Input-Output Behaviour". *Robotica*, Vol. 1, pp. 151-159. 1984.

[7] J. ONCINA. *Aprendizaje de Lenguajes Regulares y Funciones Subsecuenciales.* Ph. D. dissertation, Universidad Politénica de Valencia. 1991.

[8] J. ONCINA, P. GARCIA. "Inductive Learning of Subsequential Functions". Technical Report, DSIC II/34/91. Dpto. Sistemas Informáticos y Computación, Univ. Politécnica de Valencia. 1991.

[9] J. ONCINA, P. GARCIA, E. VIDAL. "Transducer Learning in Pattern Recognition". *11th IAPR International Conference on Pattern Recognition*, The Hague, The Netherlands. Proceedings, Vol. II, pp. 299-302. 1992.

[10] J. ONCINA, P. GARCIA, E. VIDAL. "Learning Subsequential Transducers for Pattern Recognition Interpretation Tasks". *IEEE Transactions on Pattern Analysis and Machine Intelligence*, Vol. 15, No. 5, pp. 448-458. May, 1993.

[11] J. ONCINA, A. CASTELLANOS, E. VIDAL, V. JIMENEZ. "Corpus-Based Machine Translation through Subsequential Transducers". *Third International Conference on the Cognitive Science of Natural Language Processing.* Dublin (Ireland), July 1994.

[12] S.J. RAUDYS, A.K. JAIN. "Small Sample Size Effects in Statistical Pattern Recognition: Recommendations for Practitioners". *IEEE Transactions on Pattern Analysis and Machine Intelligence*, Vol. 13, No. 3, pp. 252-264. March, 1991.

[13] A. STOLCKE. "Learning Feature-based Semantics with Simple Recurrent Networks". Technical Report, TR-90-015. International Computer Science Institute, Berkeley, California. April, 1990.

[14] E. VIDAL, P. GARCIA, E. SEGARRA. "Inductive Learning of Finite-State Transducers for the Interpretation of Unidimensional Objects". *Structural Pattern Analysis.* R. Mohr, T. Pavlidis and A. Sanfeliu (eds.), World Scientific, pp. 17-35. 1990.

Inducing Probabilistic Grammars by Bayesian Model Merging

Andreas Stolcke
Stephen Omohundro
International Computer Science Institute
1947 Center St., Suite 600
Berkeley, CA 94707
E-mail: {stolcke,om}@icsi.berkeley.edu

Abstract

We describe a framework for inducing probabilistic grammars from corpora of positive samples. First, samples are *incorporated* by adding ad-hoc rules to a working grammar; subsequently, elements of the model (such as states or nonterminals) are *merged* to achieve generalization and a more compact representation. The choice of what to merge and when to stop is governed by the Bayesian posterior probability of the grammar given the data, which formalizes a trade-off between a close fit to the data and a default preference for simpler models ('Occam's Razor'). The general scheme is illustrated using three types of probabilistic grammars: Hidden Markov models, class-based n-grams, and stochastic context-free grammars.

1   Introduction

Probabilistic modeling has become increasingly important for applications such as speech recognition, information retrieval, machine translation, and biological sequence processing. The types of models used vary widely, ranging from simple n-grams to Hidden Markov Models (HMMs) and stochastic context-free grammars (SCFGs). A central problem for these applications is to find suitable models from a corpus of samples.

Most common probabilistic models can be characterized by two parts: a discrete structure (e.g., the topology of an HMM, the context-free backbone of a SCFG), and a set of continuous parameters which determine the probabilities for the words, sentences, etc. described by the grammar. Given the discrete structure, the continuous parameters can usually be fit using standard methods, such as likelihood maximization. In the case of models with hidden variables (HMMs, SCFGs) estimation typically involves expectation maximization (EM) (Baum *et al.* 1970; Dempster *et al.* 1977; Baker 1979).

In this paper we address the more difficult first half of the problem: finding the discrete structure of a probabilistic model from training data. This task includes the problems of finding the topology of an HMM, and finding the set of context-free productions for an SCFG. Our approach is called *Bayesian model merging* because it performs successive merging operations on the substructures of a model in an attempt to maximize the Bayesian posterior probability of the overall model structure, given the data.

In this paper, we give an introduction to Bayesian model merging for probabilistic grammar inference, and demonstrate the approach on various model types. We also report briefly on some of the applications of the resulting learning algorithms primarily in the area of natural language modeling.

2 Bayesian Model Merging

Model merging (Omohundro 1992) has been proposed as an efficient, robust, and cognitively plausible method for building probabilistic models in a variety of cognitive domains (e.g., vision). The method can be characterized as follows:

- **Data incorporation**: Given a body of data X, build an initial model M_0 by explicitly accommodating each data point individually such that M_0 maximizes the likelihood $P(X|M)$. The size of the initial model will thus grow with the amount of data, and will usually not exhibit significant generalization.

- **Structure merging**: Build a sequence of new models, obtaining M_{i+1} from M_i by applying a *generalization* or *merging* operator m that coalesces substructures in M_i, $M_{i+1} = m(M_i), i = 0, 1, \ldots$

The merging operation is dependent on the type of model at hand (as will be illustrated below), but it generally has the property that data points previously 'explained' by separate model substructures come to be accounted for by a single, shared structure. The merging process thereby gradually moves from a simple, instance-based model toward one that expresses structural generalizations about the data.

To guide the search for suitable merging operations we need a criterion that trades off the goodness of fit of data X against the desire for 'simpler,' and therefore more general models. As a formalization of this tradeoff, we use the *posterior probability* $P(M|X)$ of the model given the data. According to Bayes' rule,

$$P(M|X) = \frac{P(M)P(X|M)}{P(X)} \quad ,$$

the posterior is proportional to the product of a *prior probability* term $P(M)$ and a *likelihood* term $P(X|M)$ (the denominator $P(X)$ does not depend on M and can therefore be ignored for the purpose of maximizing). The likelihood is defined by the model semantics, whereas the prior has to be chosen to express the bias, or prior expectation, as to what the likely models are. This choice is domain-dependent and will be elaborated below.

Finally, we need a search strategy to find models with high (maximal, if possible) posterior probability. A simple approach here is

- **Best-first search**: Starting with the initial model (which maximizes the likelihood, but usually has a very low prior probability), explore all possible merging steps, and successively choose the one (greedy search) or ones (beam search) that give the greatest

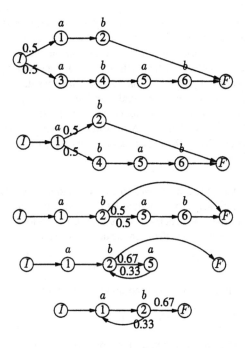

Figure 1: Model merging for HMMs.

immediate increase in posterior. Stop merging when no further increase is possible (after looking ahead a few steps to avoid simple local maxima).

In practice, to keep the working models of manageable size, we can use an *on-line* version of the merging algorithm, in which the data incorporation and the merging/search stages are interleaved.

We now make these concepts concrete for various types of probabilistic grammar.

3 Model merging applied to probabilistic grammars

3.1 Hidden Markov Models

Hidden Markov Models (HMMs) are a probabilistic form of non-deterministic finite-state mouels (Rabiner & Juang 1986). They allow a particularly straightforward version of the model merging approach.

Data incorporation. For each observed sample create a unique path between the initial and final states by assigning a new state to each symbol token in the sample. For example, given the data $X = \{ab, abab\}$, the initial model M_0 is shown at the top of Figure 1.

Merging. In a single merging step, two old HMM states are replaced by a single new state, which inherits the union of the transitions and emissions from the old states. Figure 1 shows four successive merges (where each new state is given the smaller of the two indices of its predecessors). The second, third and fifth models in the example have a smaller model structure without changing the generated probability distributions, whereas the fourth model effectively generalizes from the finite sample set to the infinite set $\{(ab)^n, n > 0\}$. The crucial point is that each of these models can be found by locally maximizing the posterior probability of the HMM, under a wide range of priors (see below). Also, further merging in the last model structure shown produces a large penalty in the likelihood term, thereby *decreasing* the posterior. The algorithm thus stops at this point.

Prior distributions. Our approach has been to choose relatively *uninformative* priors, which spread the prior probability across all possible HMMs without giving explicit preference to particular topologies. A model M is defined by its *structure* (topology) M_S and its continuous parameter settings θ_M. The prior may therefore be decomposed as

$$P(M) = P(M_S)P(\theta_M|M_S) \quad .$$

Model structures receive prior probability according to their *description length*, i.e.,

$$P(M_S) \propto \exp(-\ell(M_S)),$$

where $\ell(M_S)$ is the number of bits required to encode M_S, e.g., by listing all transitions and emissions. The prior probabilities for θ_M, on the other hand, are assigned using a Dirichlet distribution for each of the transition and emission multinomial parameters, similar to the Bayesian decision tree induction method of Buntine (1992). (The parameter prior effectively spreads the posterior probability as if a certain number of evenly distributed 'virtual' samples had been observed for each transition and emission.) For convenience we assume that the parameters associated with each state are *a priori* independent.

There are three intuitive ways of understanding why simple priors like the ones used here lead to higher posterior probabilities for simpler HMMs, other things being equal:

- Smaller topologies have a smaller description length, and hence a higher prior probability. This corresponds to the intuition that a larger structure needs to be 'picked' from among a larger range of possible equally sized alternatives, thus making each individual choice less probable *a priori*.

- Larger models have more parameters, thus making each particular parameter setting less likely (this is the 'Occam factor' (Gull 1988)).

- After two states have been merged, the effective amount of data per parameter increases (the evidence for the merged substructures is pooled). This shifts and peaks the posterior distributions for those parameters closer to their maximum likelihood settings.

These principles also apply *mutatis mutandis* to the other applications of model merging inference.

Posterior computation. Recall that the target of the inference procedure is the model *structure*, hence the goal is to maximize the posterior

$$P(M_S|X) \propto P(M_S)P(X|M_S)$$

The mathematical reason why one wants to maximize $P(M_S|X)$, rather than simply $P(M|X)$, is that for inference purposes a model with high posterior *structure* represents a better approximation to the Bayes-optimal procedure of averaging over all possible models M, including both structures and parameter settings (see Stolcke & Omohundro (1994:17f.) for details).

The evaluation of the second term above involves the integral over the parameter prior,

$$P(X|M_S) = \int_{\theta_M} P(\theta_M|M_S)P(X|M_S,\theta_M)d\theta_M,$$

which can be approximated using the common Viterbi assumption about sample probabilities in HMMs (which in our case tends to be correct due to the way the HMM structures are initially constructed).

Applications and results. We compared the model merging strategy applied to HMMs against the standard Baum-Welch procedure when applied to a fully parameterized, randomly initialized HMM structure. The latter represents one potential approach to the structure finding problem, effectively turning it into a parameter estimation problem, but it faces the problem of local maxima in the parameter space. Also, in a Baum-Welch approach the number of states in the HMM has to be known, guessed or estimated in advance, whereas the merging approach chooses that number adaptively from the data. Both approaches need to be evaluated empirically.

First, we tested the two methods on a few simple regular languages that we turned into HMMs by assigning uniform probabilities to their corresponding finite-state automata. Training proceeded using either random or 'structure covering' sets of samples. The merging approach reliably inferred these admittedly simple HMM structures. However, the Baum-Welch estimator turned out to be extremely sensitive to the initial parameter settings and failed on more than half of the trials to find a reasonable structure, both with minimal and redundant numbers of states.[1]

Second, we tested merging and Baum-Welch (and a number of other methods) on a set of naturally occurring data that might be modeled by HMMs. The task was to derive phonetic pronunciation models from available transcriptions in the TIMIT speech database. In this case, the Baum-Welch-derived model structures turned out to be close in generalization performance to the slightly better merged models (as measured by cross-entropy on a test set).[2] However, to achieve this performance the Baum-Welch HMMs made use of about twice as many transitions as the more compact merged HMMs, which would have a serious impact on potential applications of such models in speech recognition.

Finally, the HMM merging algorithm was integrated into the training of a medium-scale spoken language understanding system (Wooters & Stolcke 1994). Here, the algorithm also serves the purpose of inducing multi-pronunciation word models from speech data, but it is now coupled with a separate process that estimates the acoustic emission likelihoods for the HMM states. The goal of this setup was to improve the system's performance over a comparable

---

[1] Case studies of the structures, under-generalizations and overgeneralizations found in this experiment can be found in Stolcke & Omohundro (1994).

[2] argued that this domain is slightly simpler, since it contains, for example, no looping HMM structures.

system that used only the standard single-pronunciation HMMs for each word, while remaining practical in terms of training cost and recognition speed. By using the more complex, merged HMMs the word error was indeed reduced significantly (from 40.6% to 32.1%), indicating that the pronunciation models produced by the merging process were at least adequate for this kind of task.

3.2 Class-based n-gram Models

Brown *et al.* (1992) describe a method for building class-based n-gram models from data. Such models express the transition probabilities between words not directly in terms of individual word types, but rather between word categories, or classes. Each class, in turn, has fixed 'emission' probabilities for the individual words. One potential advantage of this approach is that it can drastically reduce the number of parameters associated with ordinary n-gram models, by effectively sharing parameters between similarly distributed words.

To infer word classes automatically, Brown *et al.* (1992) suggest an algorithm that successively merges classes according to a maximum-likelihood criterion, until a target number of classes is reached. From our perspective we can cast their algorithm as an instance of model merging, the essential difference being the non-Bayesian (likelihood-based) criterion guiding the merging and stopping. In fact, in retrospect, class merging in n-gram grammars can be understood as a special case of HMM merging. A class-based n-gram model can be straightforwardly expressed as a special form of HMM in which each class corresponds to a state, and transition probabilities correspond to class n-gram probabilities.

3.3 Stochastic Context-Free Grammars

Based on the model merging approach to HMM induction, we have extended the algorithm to apply to stochastic context-free grammars (SCFGs), the probabilistic generalization of CFGs (Booth & Thompson 1973; Jelinek *et al.* 1992). A more detailed description of SCFG model merging can be found in Stolcke (1994).

Data incorporation. To incorporate a new sample string into a SCFG we can simply add a top-level production (for the start nonterminal S) that covers the sample precisely. For example, the grammar at the top of Figure 2 arises from the samples $\{ab, aabb, aaabbb\}$. Instead of letting terminal symbols appear in production right-hand sides, we also create one nonterminal for each observed terminal, which simplifies the merging operators.

Merging. The obvious analog of merging HMM states is the merging of nonterminals in a SCFG. This is indeed one of the strategies used to generalize a given SCFG, and it can potentially produce inductive 'leaps' by generating a grammar that generates more than its predecessor, while reducing the size of the grammar.

However the hallmark of context-free grammars are the hierarchical, center-embedding structures they can represent. We therefore introduce a second operator called *chunking*. It takes a given sequence of nonterminals and abbreviates it using a newly created nonterminal, as illustrated by the sequence AB in the second grammar of Figure 2. In that example, one more chunking step, followed by two merging steps produces a grammar for the language

$$S \rightarrow AB$$
$$\rightarrow AABB$$
$$\rightarrow AAABBB$$
$$A \rightarrow a$$
$$B \rightarrow b$$

Chunk $(AB) \rightarrow X$:

$$S \rightarrow X$$
$$\rightarrow AXB$$
$$\rightarrow AAXBB$$
$$X \rightarrow AB$$

Chunk $(AXB) \rightarrow Y$:

$$S \rightarrow X$$
$$\rightarrow Y$$
$$\rightarrow AYB$$
$$X \rightarrow AB$$
$$Y \rightarrow AXB$$

Merge S, Y:

$$S \rightarrow X$$
$$\rightarrow ASB$$
$$X \rightarrow AB$$

Merge S, X:

$$S \rightarrow AB$$
$$\rightarrow ASB$$

Figure 2: Model merging for SCFGs.

$\{a^n b^n, n > 0\}$. (The probabilities in the grammar are implicit in the usage counts for each production, and are not shown in the figure.)

Priors. As before, we split the prior for a grammar M into a contribution for the structural aspects M_S, and one for the continuous parameter settings θ_M. The goal is to maximize the posterior of the structure given the data, $P(M_S|X)$. For $P(M_S)$ we again use a description length-induced distribution, obtained by a simple enumerative encoding of the grammar productions (each occurrence of a nonterminal contributes $\log N$ bits to the description length, where N is the number of nonterminals). For $P(\theta_M|M_S)$ we observe that the production probabilities associated with a given left-hand side form a multinomial, and so we use symmetrical Dirichlet priors for these parameters.

Language	Sample no.	Grammar	Search
Parentheses	8	$S \rightarrow ()\mid (S)\mid SS$	BF
a^{2n}	5	$S \rightarrow aa\mid SS$	BF
$(ab)^n$	5	$S \rightarrow ab\mid SS$	BF
$a^n b^n$	5	$S \rightarrow ab\mid aSb$	BF
$wcw^R, w \in \{a, b\}^*$	7	$S \rightarrow c\mid aSa\mid bSb$	BS(3)
Addition strings	23	$S \rightarrow a\mid b\mid (S)\mid S + S$	BS(4)
Shape grammar	11	$\begin{aligned} S &\rightarrow dY\mid bYS \\ Y &\rightarrow a\mid cY \end{aligned}$	BS(4)
Basic English	25	$\begin{aligned} S &\rightarrow \text{I am } A\mid \text{he } T\mid \text{she } T\mid \text{it } T \\ &\rightarrow \text{they } V\mid \text{you } V\mid \text{we } V \\ &\rightarrow \text{this } C\mid \text{that } C \\ T &\rightarrow \text{is } A \\ V &\rightarrow \text{are } A \\ Z &\rightarrow \text{man}\mid \text{woman} \\ A &\rightarrow \text{there}\mid \text{here} \\ C &\rightarrow \text{is a } Z\mid ZT \end{aligned}$	BS(3)

Table 1: Test grammars from Cook *et al.* (1976). Search methods are indicated by *BF* (best-first) or *BS(n)* (beam search with width *n*).

Search. In the case of HMMs, a greedy merging strategy (always pursuing only the locally most promising choice) seems to give generally good results. Unfortunately, this is no longer true in the extended SCFG merging algorithm. The chief reason is that chunking steps typically require several following merging steps and/or additional chunking steps to improve a grammar's posterior score. To account for this complication, we use a more elaborate *beam search* that considers a number of relatively good grammars in parallel, and stops only after a certain neighborhood of alternative models has been search without producing further improvements. The experiments reported below use small beam widths (between 3 and 10).

Formal language experiments. We start by examining the performance of the algorithm on example grammars found in the literature on other CFG induction methods. Cook *et al.* (1976) use a collection of techniques related to ours for inferring probabilistic CFGs from sample distributions, rather than absolute sample counts (see discussion in the next section). These languages and the inferred grammars are summarized in Table 1. They include classic textbook examples of CFGs (the parenthesis language, arithmetic expressions) as well as simple grammars meant to model empirical data.

We replicated Cook's results by applying the algorithm to the same small sets of high probability strings as used in Cook *et al.* (1976). (The number of distinct sample strings is given in the second column of Table 1.) Since the Bayesian framework makes use of the actual observed sample counts, we scaled these to sum to 50 for each training corpus.

The Bayesian merging procedure produced the target grammars in all cases, using different levels of sophistication in the search strategy (as indicated by column 4 in Table 1). Since Cook's algorithm uses a very different, non-Bayesian formalization of the data fit vs. grammar complexity trade-off we can conclude that the example grammars must be quite robust to a variety of 'reasonable' implementations of this trade-off.

A more difficult language that Cook *et al.* (1976) list as beyond the scope of their algorithm can also be inferred, using beam search: the palindromes $ww^R, w \in \{a, b\}^*$. We attribute this improvement to the more flexible search techniques used.

Natural Language syntax. An obvious question arising for SCFG induction algorithms is whether they are sufficient for deriving adequate models from realistic corpora of naturally occurring samples, i.e., to automatically build models for natural language processing applications. Preliminary experiments on such corpora have yielded mixed results, which lead us to conclude that additional methods will be necessary for success in this area. A fundamental problem is that available data will typically be *sparse* relative to the complexity of the target grammars, i.e., not all constructions will be represented with sufficient coverage to allow the induction of correct generalizations. We are currently investigating techniques to incorporate additional, independent sources of generalization. For example, a part-of-speech tagging phase prior to SCFG induction proper could reduce the work of the merging algorithm considerably.

Given these difficulties with large-scale natural language applications, we have resorted to smaller experiments that try to determine whether certain fundamental structures found in NL grammars can in principle be identified by the Bayesian framework proposed here. In Stolcke (1994) a number of phenomena are examined, including

Lexical categorization Nonterminal merging assigns terminal symbols to common nonterminals whenever there is substantial overlap in the contexts in which they occur.

Phrase structure abstraction Standard phrasal categories such as noun phrases, prepositional and verb phrases are created by chunking because they allow a more compact description of the grammar by abbreviating common collocations, and/or because they allow more succinct generalizations (in combination with merging) to be stated.

Agreement Co-variation in the forms of co-occurring syntactic or lexical elements (e.g., number agreement between subject and verbs in English) is induced by merging of nonterminals. However, even in this learning framework it becomes clear that CFGs (as opposed to, say, feature-base grammar formalisms) are an inadequate representation for these phenomena. The usual blow-up in grammar size to represent agreement in CFG form can also cause the wrong phrase structure bracketing to be prefered by the simplicity bias.

Recursive phrase structure Recursive and iterative productions for phenomena such as embedded relative clauses can be induced using the chunking and merging operators.

We conclude with a small grammar exhibiting recursive relative clause embedding, from Langley (1994). The target grammar has the form

```
S  --> NP VP
VP --> Verb NP
NP --> Art Noun
   --> Art Noun RC
```

```
RC --> Rel VP
Verb --> saw | heard
Noun --> cat | dog | mouse
Art --> a | the
Rel --> that
```

with uniform probabilities on all productions.

Chunking and merging of 100 random samples produces a grammar that is weakly equivalent to the above grammar. It also produced essentially identical phrase structure, except for a more compact implementation of the recursion through RC:

```
S -->' NP VP
VP --> V NP
NP --> DET N
    --> NP RC
RC --> REL VP
DET --> a
     --> the
N --> cat
  --> dog
  --> mouse
REL --> that
V --> heard
  --> saw
```

4   Related work

Many of the ingredients of the model merging approach have been used separately in a variety of settings.

Successive merging of states (or state equivalence class construction) is a technique widely used in algorithms for finite-state automata (Hopcroft & Ullman 1979) and automata learning (Angluin & Smith 1983); a recent application to probabilistic finite-state automate is Carrasco & Oncina (1994).

Bell *et al.* (1990) and Ron *et al.* (1994) describe a method for learning deterministic finite-state models that is in a sense the opposite of the merging approach: successive state splitting. In this framework, each state represents a unique suffix of the input, and states are repeatedly refined by extending the suffixed represented, as long as this move improves the model likelihood by a certain minimum amount. The class of models thus learnable is restricted, since each state can make predictions based only on inputs within a bounded distance from the current input, but the approach has other advantages, e.g., the final number of states is typically smaller than for a merging algorithm, since the tendency is to overgeneralize, rather than undergeneralize. We are currently investigating state splitting as a complementary search operator in our merging algorithms.

Horning (1969) first proposed using a Bayesian formulation to capture the trade-off between grammar complexity and data fit. His algorithm, however, is based on searching for the grammar with the highest posterior probability by enumerating all possible grammars (such that one can tell after a finite number of steps when the optimal grammar has been found). Unfortunately, the enumeration approach proved to be infeasible for practical purposes.

The chunking operation used in SCFG induction is part of a number of algorithms aimed at CFG induction, including Cook et al. (1976), Wolff (1987), and Langley (1994), where it is typically paired with other operations that have effects similar to merging. However, only the algorithm of Cook et al. (1976) has probabilistic CFGs as the target of induction, and therefore merits a closer comparison to our approach.

A major conceptual difference of Cook's approach is that it is based on an information-theoretic quality measure that depends only on the *relative frequencies* of observed samples. The Bayesian approach, on the other hand, explicitly takes into account the *absolute frequencies* of the data. Thus, the *amount* of data available—not only its distribution—has an effect on the outcome. For example, having observed the samples $a, aa, aaa, aaaa$, a model of $\{a^n, n > 0\}$ is quite likely. On the other hand, if the same samples were observed a hundred times, with no other additional data, such a conclusion should be intuitively unlikely, although the sample strings themselves and their relative frequencies are unchanged. The Bayesian analysis confirms this intuition: a 100-fold sample frequency entails a 100-fold magnification of the log-likelihood loss incurred for any generalization, which would block the inductive leap to a model for $\{a^n, n > 0\}$.

Incidentally, one can use sample frequency as a principled device to control the degree of generalization in a Bayesian induction algorithm explicitly (Quinlan & Rivest 1989; Stolcke & Omohundro 1994).

5 Future directions

Since all algorithms presented here are of a generate-and-evaluate kind, they are trivial to integrate with external sources of constraints or information about possible candidate models. External structural constraints can be used to effectively set the prior (and therefore posterior) probability for certain models to zero. We hope to explore more informed priors and constraints to tackle larger problems, especially in the SCFG domain.

In retrospect, the merging operations used in our probabilistic grammar induction algorithms share a strong conceptual and formal similarity to those used by various induction methods for non-probabilistic grammars (Angluin & Smith 1983; Sakakibara 1990). Those algorithms are typically based on constructing equivalence classes of states based on some criterion of 'distinguishability.' Intuitively, the (difference in) posterior probability used to guide the Bayesian merging process represents a fuzzy, probabilistic version of such an equivalence criterion. This suggests looking for other non-probabilistic induction methods of this kind and adapting them to the Bayesian approach. A promising candidate we are currently investigating is the transducer inference algorithm of Oncina et al. (1993).

6 Conclusions

We have presented a Bayesian model merging framework for inducing probabilistic grammars from samples, by stepwise generalization from a sample-based ad-hoc model through successive merging operators. The framework is quite general and can therefore be instantiated for a variety of standard or novel classes of probabilistic models, as demonstrated here for HMMs and SCFGs.

The HMM merging variant, which is empirically more reliable for structure induction than Baum-Welch estimation, is being used successfully in speech modeling applications. The SCFG version of the model algorithm generalizes and simplifies a number of related algorithms that have been proposed previously, thus showing how the Bayesian posterior probability criterion can combine data fit and model simplicity in a uniform and principled way. The more complex model search space encountered with SCFGs also highlights the need for relatively sophisticated search strategies.

References

ANGLUIN, D., & C. H. SMITH. 1983. Inductive inference: Theory and methods. *ACM Computing Surveys* 15.237–269.

BAKER, JAMES K. 1979. Trainable grammars for speech recognition. In *Speech Communication Papers for the 97th Meeting of the Acoustical Society of America*, ed. by Jared J. Wolf & Dennis H. Klatt, 547–550, MIT, Cambridge, Mass.

BAUM, LEONARD E., TED PETRIE, GEORGE SOULES, & NORMAN WEISS. 1970. A maximization technique occuring in the statistical analysis of probabilistic functions in Markov chains. *The Annals of Mathematical Statistics* 41.164–171.

BELL, TIMOTHY C., JOHN G. CLEARY, & IAN H. WITTEN. 1990. *Text Compression*. Englewood Cliffs, N.J.: Prentice Hall.

BOOTH, TAYLOR L., & RICHARD A. THOMPSON. 1973. Applying probability measures to abstract languages. *IEEE Transactions on Computers* C-22.442–450.

BROWN, PETER F., VINCENT J. DELLA PIETRA, PETER V. DESOUZA, JENIFER C. LAI, & ROBERT L. MERCER. 1992. Class-based n-gram models of natural language. *Computational Linguistics* 18.467–479.

BUNTINE, WRAY. 1992. Learning classification trees. In *Artificial Intelligence Frontiers in Statistics: AI and Statistics III*, ed. by D. J. Hand. Chapman & Hall.

CARRASCO, RAFAEL C., & JOSÉ ONCINA, 1994. Learning stochastic regular grammars by means of a state merging method. This volume.

COOK, CRAIG M., AZRIEL ROSENFELD, & ALAN R. ARONSON. 1976. Grammatical inference by hill climbing. *Information Sciences* 10.59–80.

DEMPSTER, A. P., N. M. LAIRD, & D. B. RUBIN. 1977. Maximum likelihood from incomplete data via the *EM* algorithm. *Journal of the Royal Statistical Society, Series B* 34.1–38.

GULL, S. F. 1988. Bayesian inductive inference and maximum entropy. In *Maximum Entropy and Bayesian Methods in Science and Engineering, Volume 1: Foundations*, ed. by G. J. Erickson & C. R. Smith, 53–74. Dordrecht: Kluwer.

HOPCROFT, JOHN E., & JEFFREY D. ULLMAN. 1979. *Introduction to Automata Theory, Languages, and Computation*. Reading, Mass.: Addison-Wesley.

HORNING, JAMES JAY. 1969. A study of grammatical inference. Technical Report CS 139, Computer Science Department, Stanford University, Stanford, Ca.

JELINEK, FREDERICK, JOHN D. LAFFERTY, & ROBERT L. MERCER. 1992. Basic methods of probabilistic context free grammars. In *Speech Recognition and Understanding. Recent Advances, Trends, and Applications*, ed. by Pietro Laface & Renato De Mori, volume F75 of *NATO Advanced Sciences Institutes Series*, 345–360. Berlin: Springer Verlag. Proceedings of the NATO Advanced Study Institute, Cetraro, Italy, July 1990.

LANGLEY, PAT, 1994. Simplicity and representation change in grammar induction. Unpublished mss.

OMOHUNDRO, STEPHEN M. 1992. Best-first model merging for dynamic learning and recognition. Technical Report TR-92-004, International Computer Science Institute, Berkeley, Ca.

ONCINA, JOSÉ, PEDRO GARCÍA, & ENRIQUE VIDAL. 1993. Learning subsequential transducers for pattern recognition interpretation tasks. *IEEE Transactions on Pattern Analysis and Machine Intelligence* 15.448–458.

QUINLAN, J. ROSS, & RONALD L. RIVEST. 1989. Inferring decision trees using the minimum description length principle. *Information and Computation* 80.227–248.

RABINER, L. R., & B. H. JUANG. 1986. An introduction to hidden Markov models. *IEEE ASSP Magazine* 3.4–16.

RON, DANA, YORAM SINGER, & NAFTALI TISHBY. 1994. The power of amnesia. In *Advances in Neural Information Processing Systems 6*, ed. by Jack Cowan, Gerald Tesauro, & Joshua Alspector. San Mateo, CA: Morgan Kaufmann.

SAKAKIBARA, YASUBUMI. 1990. Learning context-free grammars from structural data in polynomial time. *Theoretical Computer Science* 76.223–242.

STOLCKE, ANDREAS, 1994. *Bayesian Learning of Probabilistic Language Models*. Berkeley, CA: University of California dissertation.

——, & STEPHEN OMOHUNDRO. 1994. Best-first model merging for hidden Markov model induction. Technical Report TR-94-003, International Computer Science Institute, Berkeley, CA.

WOLFF, J. G. 1987. Cognitive development as optimisation. In *Computational models of learning*, ed. by L. Bolc, 161–205. Berlin: Springer Verlag.

WOOTERS, CHUCK, & ANDREAS STOLCKE. 1994. Multiple-pronunciation lexical modeling in a speaker-independent speech understanding system. In *Proceedings International Conference on Spoken Language Processing*, Yokohama.

Statistical Estimation of Stochastic Context-Free Grammars Using the Inside-Outside Algorithm and a Transformation on Grammars*

Francisco Casacuberta
Dpto. de Sistemas Informáticos y Computación
Universidad Politécnica de Valencia
Cno. de Vera s/n
46071 Valencia
SPAIN
E-mail: fcn@iti.upv.es

Abstract

A combination of a transformation algorithm between some Stochastic Context-Free Grammars and the Inside-Outside algorithm allows us to define a method for the estimation of the rule probabilities of Stochastic Context-Free Grammars with the same time complexity as the Inside-Outside algorithm. The transformation algorithm relates Stochastic Context-Free Grammars, whose characteristic grammar is proper and does not have single rules, to Stochastic Context-Free Grammars in Chomsky Normal Form

1 Introduction

Stochastic Context-Free Grammars (SCFG) form an important class of grammars widely used in Syntactic Pattern Recognition [7]. In particular, they have been used to represent syntactic constraints in Automatic Speech Recognition [9] [11]. Both components of the SCFGs can be learned from a set of training samples. Grammatical Inference techniques provide the mechanism for building the corresponding characteristic grammar [12], while Probabilistic Estimation techniques are necessary to infer the corresponding rule probabilities.

---

*Work partially supported by the Spanish CICYT under grant TIC 1026/92-C02

The most popular algorithm for Probabilistic Estimation of SCFG is the Inside-Outside Algorithm (IOA) [2] [6] [10]. However, for the application of this algorithm, the SCFG must be in Chomsky Normal Form. This is not a drawback, because in this paper we propose a method for the use of IOA in SCFGs which is based on a combination of a transformation from the SCFG to a SCFG in CNF and the IOA. This method guarantees that the likelihood of the training set increases in each iteration of the algorithm, since the likelihood is transmitted by the transformation from one type of grammar to another, and the IOA defines growth transformations for the likelihood with SCFGs [9][5]. Another approach has been proposed in [13] and is based on an extension of the concepts used in the estimation of parameters of Hidden Markov Models to a type of Recursive Transition Networks.

In the next section, a brief review of the IOA is presented. In the following section, the method for the application of the IOA to CFGs is introduced. Finally, some concluding remarks are presented.

2 Growth Transformations for Probabilistic Functions of Stochastic Context-Free Grammars

A CFG G is a four-tuple (N,Σ,R,S), where N is a finite set of non-terminal symbols, Σ is a finite set of terminal symbols $(N \cap \Sigma = \varnothing)$, R is a finite set of rewriting rules of the form $A \rightarrow \alpha$, $(A \in N$ and $\alpha \in (\Sigma \cup N)^{*})$ and S is the initial symbol $(S \in N)$.

A CFG G in Chomsky Normal Form (CNF) is a CFG in which the rules are of the form $A \rightarrow BC$ or $A \rightarrow a$ $A,B,C \in N$ and $a \in \Sigma$.

A (left-)derivation of $x \in L(G)$, $D(x)$, is a sequence of rules $(r_1, ..., r_m)$ such that $D(x):S \overset{*}{\Rightarrow} x$. $L(G)$ is the language generated by the grammar G.

A SCFG G_S is a pair (G,q), where G is a CFG and q is a function $q:R \rightarrow]0,1]$ such that

$$\forall A \in N, \quad \sum_{\alpha \in (N \cup \Sigma)^{*}} q(A \rightarrow \alpha) = 1$$

The grammars that verify this normalization condition are called "normalized" SCFG [11] or "proper" SCFG [8]. This last name can be confused with a proper CFG [1], that is, if it is cycle-free, is λ-free (λ is the empty string) and has no useless symbols. In this work, "normalized" SCFGs are always considered, while the term "proper" is reserved to the meaning indicated for CFG in [1].

The probability of a derivation $D(x)=(r_1, ..., r_m)$ is defined as

$$p(x,D(x)|G_s) = q(r_1)...q(r_m)$$

and the probability of generating $x \in \Sigma^*$ by G (likelihood) is

$$p(x|G_s) = \begin{cases} \sum_{\forall D(x)} p(x,D(x)|G_s) & \text{if } x \in L(G) \\ 0 & \text{otherwise} \end{cases}$$

Alternatively, the Viterbi-score of $x \in \Sigma^*$ by G_S can be defined in a similar way, but by using a max operator, instead of the addition for all possible derivations.

To compute $p(x|G_S)$ efficiently ($x = x_1 x_2 ... x_{|x|}$), when G_S is a SCFG in CNF, the following variables must be defined [2] [6] [10] [5]

$$e(i,j,A) = p(A \overset{\bullet}{\Rightarrow} x_i ... x_j | G_S) \qquad A \in N \quad 1 \leq i \leq j \leq |x|$$

that is, the probability of the non-terminal symbol A generating the substring $x_i...x_j$, and

$$f(i,j,A) = p(S \overset{\bullet}{\Rightarrow} x_1 ... x_{i-1} A x_{j+1} ... x_{|x|} | G_S) \qquad A \in N \quad 1 \leq i \leq j \leq |x|$$

that is, the probability of generating a sentential form composed of the prefix $x_1...x_{i-1}$ of x, the non-terminal symbol A and the suffix $x_{j+1}...x_{|x|}$ of x.

These definitions can be recursively presented as:

For all $A \in N$ and $x \in L(G)$

$$e(i,i,A) = q(A \to x_i) \qquad 1 \leq i \leq |x|$$

$$e(i,j,A) = \sum_{B,C \in N} \sum_{k=i}^{j-1} q(A \to BC) e(i,k,B) e(k+1,j,C) \qquad 1 \leq i < j \leq |x|$$

and

$$f(1,|x|,A) = \delta(A,S)$$

$$f(i,j,A) = \sum_{B,C \in N} (\sum_{k=1}^{i-1} f(k,j,B) q(B \to CA) e(k,i-1,C) +$$

$$\sum_{k=j+1}^{|x|} f(i,k,B) q(B \to AC) e(j+1,k,C)) \qquad 1 \leq i \leq j \leq |x|$$

where $\delta(A,B) = 1$, if $A=B$, and 0, if $A \neq B$. From the definition of e and f,

$$p(x|G_s) = e(1,|x|,S) = \sum_{A \in N} f(i,i,A)q(A \to x_i) \text{ for } 1 \leq i \leq |x|.$$

The values of these variables can be computed using the Inside and the Outside algorithms whose time complexities are $O(|x|^3 \cdot |N| \cdot Br)$, where Br is the maximum number of rules with the same non-terminal on the left side of the rule.

The Viterbi score, and the corresponding optimal derivation can be obtained by a modification of the Inside algorithm [5].

To estimate the rule probabilities of a SCFG in CNF, a training set T must be available as a finite subset of the language generated by the characteristic grammar (a SCFG without the rule probabilities). The function to be maximized is the likelihood

$$p(T|G_S) = \prod_{x \in T} p(x|G_S)$$

The kernel of the estimation algorithm is based on growth transformations [3] [4], which, in these cases, take the following form [2] [6] [10] [5].

INSIDE-OUTSIDE TRANSFORMATIONS

$\forall (A \to BC) \in R$

$$Q_T(q(A \to BC)) = \frac{\sum_{x \in T} \frac{1}{p(x|G_s)} \sum_{j=1}^{|x|-1} \sum_{l=j+1}^{|x|} \sum_{m=j}^{l-1} f(j,l,A)q(A \to BC)e(j,m,B)e(m+1,l,C)}{\sum_{x \in T} \frac{1}{p(x|G_s)} \sum_{j=1}^{|x|} \sum_{l=j}^{|x|} f(j,l,A)e(j,l,A)}$$

and $\forall (A \to a) \in R$

$$Q_T(q(A \to a)) = \frac{\sum_{x \in T} \frac{1}{p(x|G_s)} \sum_{i=1}^{|x|} f(i,i,A)e(i,i,A)\delta(a,x_i)}{\sum_{x \in T} \frac{1}{p(x|G_s)} \sum_{j=1}^{|x|} \sum_{l=j}^{|x|} f(j,l,A)e(j,l,A)}$$

where $Q_T(q(A \to BC))$ and $Q_T(q(A \to a))$ are the corresponding transformations of the rule probabilities. The numerator of these transformations corresponds to the expected number of times that the rule is used to parse the training strings and the denominator is the expected number of times that the corresponding left non-terminal symbol is used in the parsing of the strings [2].

As a consequence of the use of growth transformations, the likelihood of the training set increases when these transformations are used [4] [5].

If $|N|\geq|\Sigma|$, the time complexity of these transformations is $O(|T|\cdot LM^3\cdot|R|)$ for the computation of variables e and f and the computation of the transformations where $LM=\max_{x\in T}|x|$.

The iterative application of these transformations to a specific CFG gives the Inside-Outside algorithm [2] [6] [10]:

INSIDE-OUTSIDE ALGORITHM

input: A characteristic grammar $G=(N,\Sigma,R,S)$ and a training set T.

output: A normalized function q: $R\rightarrow]0,1]$.

method:

q:= initial values

repeat

$$q:= Q_T(q)$$

until convergence

end of method.

When the Viterbi score is chosen as the function to be maximized, the corresponding transformations can be found elsewhere [5]. As in the IOA, the iterative application gives the Viterbi re-estimation algorithm. However, it is not difficult to see that the corresponding growth transformations for maximizing the Viterbi score for any SCFG are very similar to those obtained for SCFG in CNF. These transformations have the following form [11]

$$\forall(A \rightarrow \alpha) \in R \qquad \hat{Q}_T(q(A \rightarrow \alpha)) = \frac{\sum_{x\in T} N(A \rightarrow \alpha,x)}{\sum_{x\in T} M(A,x)}$$

where $N(A\rightarrow\alpha,x)$ and $M(A,x)$ are the number of times that the rule $A\rightarrow\alpha$ and the non-terminal A are used, respectively, in the optimal derivation of x. The Viterbi score of the training set increases when these transformations are used [5].

A property of the statistical estimation of Unambiguous Stochastic Grammars is the following: in such grammars each $x \in L(G)$ has only one derivation $D(x)$ associated to it, therefore:

$$p(x|G_s) = \sum_{D'(x)} p(x, D'(x)|G_s) = \max_{D'(x)} p(x, D'(x)|G_s) = p(x, D(x)|G_s)$$

As a consequence of this fact, $Q_T = \hat{Q}_T$ and $\hat{Q}_T\hat{Q}_T = \hat{Q}_T$. Therefore, the application of one of these transformations lets us achieve a global maximum of the function $p(T|G_S)$, that is

$$Q_T(G_S') = \hat{Q}_T(G_S) = \arg\max_{G_s} p(T|G_S)$$

3 The Inside-Outside Algorithm and the Stochastic Context-Free Grammars

The equivalence of CFG and CFG in CNF is a well-known fact [1], that can be extended to the corresponding stochastic version in some cases. In [1], the algorithm for transforming a proper CFG without single rules $G=(N,\Sigma,R,S)$ into a CFG in CNF $G'=(N',\Sigma,R',S)$ can be found:

TRANSFORMATION ALGORITHM

input: A proper CFG G without single rules.

output: A CFG G' in CNF.

method:

a) For all rules in R of the form $A \rightarrow a$, $A \in N$, $a \in \Sigma$, add $A \rightarrow a$ to R'.

b) For all rules in R of the form $A \rightarrow BC$ $A,B,C \in N$, add $A \rightarrow BC$ to R'.

c) For all rules in R of the form $A \rightarrow B_1B_2...B_k$, $k > 2$, $B_i \in N \cup \Sigma$ $1 \le i \le k$, add the following rules to R':

$$A \rightarrow B_1' \langle B_2..B_k \rangle$$
$$\langle B_2..B_k \rangle \rightarrow B_2' \langle B_3..B_k \rangle$$
$$...$$
$$\langle B_{k-1}B_k \rangle \rightarrow B_{k-1}'B_k'$$

where $\langle B_j..B_k \rangle$ $2 \le j \le k-1$ are new non-terminals, and each B_j' $1 \le j \le k-1$ is B_j, if $B_j \in N$, or a new non-terminal B_j', if $B_j \in \Sigma$. These non-terminals and rules are different for each original rule of R.

d) For all rules in R of the form $A \rightarrow B_1B_2$ such that B_1 or B_2 is in Σ, or both, add the rule $A \rightarrow B'_1B'_2$ as in c) to R'.

e) For all non-terminals B' added in c) or d), such that the corresponding B is a$\in \Sigma$, add the rules $B' \rightarrow a$ to R'.

end of method.

For simplicity, we do not consider the case in which the empty string is generated by a CFG. The proposal of using the Inside-Outside algorithm with CFG G is:

ESTIMATION ALGORITHM FOR PROPER STOCHASTIC CONTEXT-FREE GRAMMARS WITHOUT SINGLE PRODUCTIONS.

input: A proper CFG $G=(N,\Sigma,R,S)$ without single rules and a training set T.

output: A normalized function $q:R \rightarrow]0,1]$

method:

1. Build a CFG in CNF G' using the above Transformation Algorithm.

2. Estimate the probabilities of G' using a re-estimation algorithm (Inside-Outside) and the set of training samples T.

3. Assign probabilities to G according to:

    3.1. For all rules r of R, such that r is of the type defined in a), b) or d), if r' is the corresponding rule of R' associated to r by the Transformation Algorithm, then let $q(r)=q(r')$.

    3.2. For all rules r of R, such that r is of the type defined in c), r'_i $1 \le i \le k-1$ being the corresponding rules in G' associated to r by the transformation algorithm, then let $q(r)=q(r'_1)$, where r'_1 is the first rule produced (i.e. $A \rightarrow B'_1\langle B_2..B_k\rangle$)

end of method.

Note that the rest of the rules generated in c) and e) will have probability one, since there is only one such rule with the same non-terminal symbol on the left side of the rule.

The equivalence of SCFGs G and G´ can be established through the following proposition.

Proposition: Let $G_S=(G,q)$ and $G'_S=(G',q')$ be two SCFGs such that G' is in CNF and is obtained from G by the Transformation Algorithm. Let q' be an arbitrary probabilistic distribution over R, q is obtained from q' by applying the assignation of probabilities of the Estimation Algorithm for CFGs (step 3). Then $\forall x \in \Sigma^*$, $p(x|G_S)=p(x|G'_S)$.

Proof. Let $L(G)\subseteq\Sigma^*$ be the language generated by G, $L(G)=L(G')$ by [1], then $p(x|G_S)=p(x|G'_S)=0$, $\forall x \notin L(G)$.

First, from the assignation of probabilities in the Estimation Algorithm for CFGs, for all $x \in L(G)$ and for all $D(x)$ in G, there is a $D'(x)$ in G' such that $p(x,D(x)|G_S)=p(x,D'(x)|G'_S)$. On the other hand, from the Transformation Algorithm it is not possible for two different derivations $D_1(x)$ and $D_2(x)$ to have the same derivation $D'(x)$ in G'. Finally, it is not possible for a derivation $D'(x)$ to exist in G' which cannot be obtained from a derivation in G.

As a conclusion, for all derivations $D(x)$ in G, there is one and only one derivation in G'. Thus $p(x|G'_S)=p(x|G_S)$.∎

To obtain the time complexity of the estimation algorithm, it is necessary to note that in a CFG in CNF there are more rules than in general form (although they are shorter). But only the probabilities of the rules generated in a), b) and d) and the first rule of c) must be estimated.

The rest of the probabilities always have probability one. Therefore, the number of rules whose probability must be re-estimated is the same as the CFG in general form, although the rest of the rules are necessary in the re-estimation of the ones that must be re-estimated. The number of these extra rules is bound by the size of the rules of CFG not in CNF (the number of symbols on the right side of the rule). Thus, if L_R is the maximum size of the rules in a CFG, the number of rules in the CFG in CNF is $O(L_R\cdot|R|)$.

The final time complexity in each iteration of the IOA that is embedded in the estimation algorithm for CFG is $O(|T|\cdot LM^3 \cdot L_R\cdot|R|)$.

Let us consider the following example, a CFG $G= (N,\Sigma,R,S)$ such that:

$$N = \{S,T,F\}; \Sigma = \{+,*,[,],a\} \text{ and}$$
$$R = \{ S \rightarrow S+T; S \rightarrow [S]; S \rightarrow a; T \rightarrow T*F; T \rightarrow a; F \rightarrow a \}$$

The corresponding CFG in CNF G' is:

$$R' = \{\ S \rightarrow SN_1; N_1 \rightarrow N_2T; N_2 \rightarrow +; S \rightarrow N_3N_4; N_4 \rightarrow SN_5; N_3 \rightarrow [; N_5 \rightarrow]; S \rightarrow a;$$
$$T \rightarrow TN_6; N_6 \rightarrow N_7F; N_7 \rightarrow *; T \rightarrow a; F \rightarrow a\ \}$$

and $N' = \{S, T, F, N_1, N_2, N_3, N_4, N_5, N_6, N_7\}$

Let us suppose that the application of the IOA to this new grammar, using an adequate training set, leads to the following probabilities:

$$q(S \rightarrow SN_1) = 0.25; \quad q(N_1 \rightarrow N_2T) = 1.00; \quad q(N_2 \rightarrow +) = 1.00;$$
$$q(S \rightarrow N_3N_4) = 0.50; \quad q(N_4 \rightarrow SN_5) = 1.00; \quad q(N_3 \rightarrow [) = 1.00; \quad q(N_5 \rightarrow]) = 1.00;$$
$$q(S \rightarrow a) = 0.25;$$
$$q(T \rightarrow TN_6) = 0.75; \quad q(N_6 \rightarrow N_7F) = 1.00; \quad q(N_7 \rightarrow *) = 1.00;$$
$$q(T \rightarrow a) = 0.25$$
$$q(F \rightarrow a) = 1.0$$

Then by application of the proposed algorithm, we can get:

$$q(S \rightarrow S+T) = 0.25; \quad q(S \rightarrow [S]) = 0.50; \quad q(S \rightarrow a) = 0.25$$
$$q(T \rightarrow T*F) = 0.75; \quad q(T \rightarrow a) = 0.25;$$
$$q(F \rightarrow a) = 1.00$$

As an exercise, this method can be applied to Stochastic Regular Grammars (SRG), and then the Baum-Welch reestimation formulae for SRG can be obtained [5]. In this case, a regular grammar has the rules of the form :

$$A \rightarrow aB \quad or \quad A \rightarrow a \quad with\ a \in \Sigma \quad and\ A, B \in N$$

The corresponding rules in CNF are:

$$A \rightarrow N_1B \quad and \quad N_1 \rightarrow a \quad for\ A \rightarrow aB \quad and \quad A \rightarrow a \quad for\ A \rightarrow a.$$

Using these particular forms of rules in the IOA, the following well known transformations can be achieved:

FORWARD-BACKWARD TRANSFORMATIONS

$$\forall (A \rightarrow aB) \in R$$

$$Q_T(q(A \rightarrow aB)) = \frac{\displaystyle\sum_{x \in T} \frac{1}{p(x|G_s)} \sum_{j=1}^{|x|-1} f(j, |x|, A) q(A \rightarrow aB) e(j+1, |x|, B) \delta(x_j, a)}{\displaystyle\sum_{x \in T} \frac{1}{p(x|G_s)} \sum_{j=1}^{|x|} f(j, |x|, A) e(j, |x|, B)}$$

and $\forall (A \rightarrow a) \in R$

$$Q_T(q(A \rightarrow a)) = \frac{\sum_{x \in T} \frac{1}{p(x|G_s)} f(|x|,|x|,A)q(A \rightarrow a)\delta(a,x_{|x|})}{\sum_{x \in T} \frac{1}{p(x|G_s)} \sum_{j=1}^{|x|} f(j,|x|,A)e(j,|x|,A)}$$

where the e and f variables in the Inside-Outside Transformations can be transformed to the forward (α) and backward (β) variables [5] (or [14] for Hidden Markov Models), whose definitions are, for all $A \in N$ and $x \in L(G)$

$$f(1,|x|,A) = \alpha(1,A) = \delta(A,S)$$

$$f(j,|x|,A) = \alpha(j,A) = \sum_{B \rightarrow aA \in R} q(B \rightarrow aA)\alpha(j-1,B)\delta(x_{j-1},a) \qquad 1 \leq j \leq |x|$$

and

$$e(|x|,|x|,A) = \beta(|x|,A) = q(A \rightarrow x_{|x|})$$

$$e(j,|x|,A) = \beta(j,A) = \sum_{A \rightarrow aB \in R} \beta(j+1,B)q(A \rightarrow aB)\delta(x_{j+1},a) = \qquad 1 \leq j \leq |x|$$

The time complexity of both transformations is $O(|T| \cdot LM \cdot |R|)$.

4 Conclusions

The probabilistic component of a SCFG can be learned from training samples using the well-known transformation algorithm and the Inside-Outside algorithm without a significant increase in the time complexity with respect to this last algorithm.

Acknowledgments

The author wishes to thank the anonymous reviewer for his suggestions.

References

[1] A.V.Aho; J.D.Ullman : "The Theory of Parsing, Translation and Compiling". Vol. 1. Prentice-Hall. 1972.

[2]   J.K.Baker: "Trainable Grammars for Speech Recognition". 50th Anniversary Celebration of the Acoustical Society of America, pp. 31-35. June 1979.

[3]   L.E.Baum, G.R.Sell : "Growth Transformations for Functions on Manifolds". Pacific Journal of Mathematics. Vol. 27 (2), pp. 211-227. 1969.

[4]   L.E.Baum: "An Inequality and Associated Maximization Technique in Statistical Estimation for Probabilistic Functions of Markov Processes". Inequalities. Vol. 3, pp. 1-8. 1972.

[5]   F.Casacuberta: "Growth Transformations for Probabilistic Functions of Stochastic Grammars". Submitted for publication. 1994.

[6]   L.Dodd: "The Inside/Outside Algorithm: Grammatical Inference applied to Stochastic Context-Free Grammars". Tec. Report RSRE Memorandum No. 4160. 1988.

[7]   K.S.Fu: "Syntactic Pattern Recognition and Applications". Prentice-Hall. 1982.

[8]   R.C.Gonzalez, M.G.Thomason: "Syntactic Pattern Recognition: an Introduction". Ed. Addison-Wesley. 1978.

[9]   F.R.Jelinek, J.D.Lafferty, R.L.Mercer: "Basic Methods of Probabilistic Context-Free Grammars" in "Speech Recognition and Understanding". Eds. P.Laface and R. De Mori. Springer Verlag, pp. 345-360. 1992.

[10] K.Lari and S.J.Young: "The Estimation of Stochastic Context-Free Grammars using the Inside-Outside Algorithm". Computer Speech and Language. Vol. 4, pp. 35-56. 1990.

[11] H.Ney: "Stochastic Grammars and Pattern Recognition" in "Speech Recognition and Understanding". Eds. P.Laface and R. De Mori. Springer Verlag, pp. 319-344. 1992.

[12] E.Vidal, F.Casacuberta, P.García: "Syntactic Learning Techniques in Language Modeling and Acoustic-Phonetic Decoding" in "New Advances and Trends in Speech Recognition and Coding". Springer-Verlag. In press. 1994.

[13] J. Kupiec: "Hidden Markov Estimation for Unrestricted Stochastic Context-Free Grammars". Proc. International Conference on Acoustic, Speech and Signal Processing. Vol. I. pp. 177-180. 1992.

[14] L.R.Rabiner : "A Tutorial on Hidden Markov Models and Selected Applications in Speech Recognition". Proc. IEEE. Vol.77 No. 2 . pp. 257-286. 1989.

Statistical Inductive Learning
of
Regular Formal Languages

Juan Andrés Sánchez and José Miguel Benedí

Departamento de Sistemas Informáticos y Computación
Universidad Politécnica de Valencia
Camino de Vera s/n, 46071 Valencia (Spain)
e-mail: jandreu@dsic.upv.es

Abstract

The estimation problem of probabilistic grammar through the forward-backward algorithm does not guarantee that a global maximum is achieved [12]. In this process, which is based on a gradient descent technique, the initialization is a crucial aspect. In this paper, we show experimentally how the results obtained by this method can be improved when structural information about the task is inductively incorporated in the initial models to be learnt.

1 Introduction

In the framework of Pattern Recognition (PR), the Formal Language Theory constitutes a robust and suitable formalism of specification and resolution of problems [9, 6]. However, in order to consider real problems of PR, where both the variability and noise of data and ambiguity and uncertain of knowledge are always present, a generalization has been proposed: *The stochastic structural models* [7, 6]. A stochastic structural model (e.g., a stochastic grammar (SG)) is defined through two main components: the structure (the characteristic grammar in SG) and the probabilistic-distribution functions (the set of production probabilities in a SG) [3, 20].

Independently of the specification formalism used, one of most important problems in PR is the training of models. There are two classical points of view for solving this problem: deductively by a human expert and inductively from samples. In difficult tasks, it is well-known that neither the deductive knowledge is sufficient to characterize the problem nor the implantation of this knowledge in the system is an easy task. Therefore, there exists a greater natural tendency to consider the inductive approach to the training of models [1, 10]. The inductive learning of stochastic grammars must consider two aspects: structural (Grammatical Inference (GI)) and probabilistic components (Probabilistic Estimation (PE)). The relative success of stochastic models in real tasks is due to the existence of robust techniques for automatic estimation of probabilistic-distribution functions [3, 8]. In certain cases, these can in fact, allow us to consider the learning of the structural component as a result of the PE process (productions with non-zero probabilities). On the other hand if, due to the nature of problem, the structural component is simple enough then this structure can be given deductively (e.g., the topology of Hidden Markov Models (HMM) [15]).

Based on the maximum likelihood criterion, two well-known algorithms of PE were proposed: forward-backward [2, 1] for stochastic regular grammars and inside-outside [11, 10] for stochastic context-free grammars. Both of them can be seen in the framework of the Grow Transformations [8]. These are iterative algorithms which are based on a gradient descent technique that allows for increasing the likelihood of the training sample in each step until a local maximum is reached [12]. Therefore, the initialization is a crucial aspect since it affects to the convergence process and the obtaining of good results [13].

The underlying conjecture throughout this paper is that the structural component of models and, therefore, their training (GI) is very important for the learning of stochastic models. The subject of this work is centered on the initialization problem. This initialization can be carried out by using of an automatic method of inductive inference which can obtain a first version of both structural and probabilistic components.

In this paper, we are only going to center on the stochastic regular grammars. The reasons for this are twofold. On the one hand, it is well-known that the behavior of the two PE algorithms (forward-backward and inside-outside) are quite similar [4]. On the other hand, we have currently available a GI method (ECGI: Error Correcting Grammatical Inference) [16, 17] which has demonstrated its utility in real PR problems [14, 19].

The rest of the paper is organized as follows. In the following section, several aspects of notation together with some comments about the (ECGI) GI algorithm used and a description of our proposal are presented. The validity of our new proposal is tested in the section on experiments and results. Finally, some conclusions are discussed.

2 Theoretical Issues

For PE, an adaptation of the well-known forward-backward algorithm initially developed for Hidden Markov Models [15] is an adequate iterative algorithm to infer the rule probabilities for stochastic regular grammars. This algorithm only takes into account positive training samples. The forward-backward PE algorithm can be implemented in different ways. In this work, the achievement of this is based on the concept of Grow Transformations of certain functions in probabilistic spaces [2, 8]. This iterative algorithm guarantees that the defined grow transformation achieves a local maximum. As in all the gradient descendent methods, the initialization aspect affects the convergence process. Therefore, good initial values can make that convergence easier, both in the sense of faster convergence and better maximums.

The aim of this paper is to show how the performance of this algorithm can be optimized if structural information is incorporated to the estimation process. In this work, we chose to incorporate this information in the initialization step, though other alternatives could be taken into account in the future. Several methods exist that are able to obtain structural information from a positive sample of the language. This information could be incorporated in the initialization of the forward-backward algorithm. For this work, we chose the ECGI algorithm [16] for two reasons: first, this algorithm has been successfully used for several inference tasks [16, 14, 19], and second, it provides both adequate structural and statistical information [17] to be used in the initialization process. As other GI methods, the ECGI algorithm over-generalizes from the positive sample of the language to be learned. The over-generalization problem (inherent to the inference algorithms which learn only from positive samples) may be solved (partially) by improving the statistical information through the reestimation process. This is why reestimation step make sense.

The ECGI algorithm is a GI algorithm based on a heuristic that is able to learn from positive samples. It is able to achieve an "abstraction ability" which reflects the variability present in the local substructures of the patterns being considered and their concatenation [17]. It runs in such a way that an automaton without loops is learnt and this is why it seems to be appropriate to model constraints based on the length of these substructures. The language generated by the learnt automaton is a generalization of the training set and it is finite. The ECGI algorithm also has a stochastic version [17] that makes it very attractive to us.

When there is an attempt to learn a distribution and a final model is proposed, some method should be able to evaluate the goodness of that model. To evaluate the results obtained in this work, an evaluation method based on the entropy concept was chosen. If we had the original source, the most adequate measure to be used would be the relative or cross entropy (sometimes refered as the *Kullback-Liebler divergence*) [5]. Given two probabilistic language models, M_1 y M_2, the relative entropy can be defined as:

$$D_L(M_1 \| M_2) = \sum_{\forall x \in L} P_{M_1}(x) \log \frac{P_{M_1}(x)}{P_{M_2}(x)}$$

where $P_{M_1}(x)$ and $P_{M_2}(x)$ are the probability that each model assigns to each string belonging to the language. This value is not a real metric since it does not accomplish the triangular inequality. This value is greater than zero and it is zero iff $P_{M_1}(x) = P_{M_2}(x) \forall x \in L$, that is, when both distributions are equal. A possible interpretation for this measure is to consider it as an inefficient measure for assuming the distribution generated by M_2 when the correct distribution is the one generated by M_1 [5]. This ratio was calculated experimentally and therefore the addition was carried out over the test corpus. That means that the reported results are approximations to the real relative entropy.

3 Experimental Work

In order to prove the previously mentioned conjecture, an experimental work was carried out. This work has three parts: first, we will show what results are obtained when an inference method is used to learn some probabilistic languages. Second, we will see what results are obtained when a PE method, without any structural information, is used to learn a probabilistic language. In both cases, it can be seen that the results suggest that some improvements could be made. Finally, in the third part, we will see how incorporating structural information to the PE leads to the best results.

For the experimentation process, a set of regular languages previously studied in other works was chosen. These languages [1] were the following:

---

[1]The first seven languages are related to the languages studied in [18].

- L1: 0^+,
- L2: $(01)^+$,
- L3: any string of 0's and 1's in which a consecutive odd number of 1's is followed by a consecutive even number of 0's,
- L4: any string of 0's and 1's without the "000" string as substring,
- L5: any string of 0's and 1's with an even number of 0's and an even number of 1's,
- L6: any string of 0's and 1's where the difference between 0's and 1's can be divided by 3,
- L7: $0^+1^+0^+1^+$
- L8: the simple Rebber grammar, which can be seen in Figure 1,
- L9: $01^*0 \cup 02^*0$.

$$
\begin{array}{ll}
S \rightarrow 0A & C \rightarrow 4E \\
A \rightarrow 1B & D \rightarrow 5C \\
A \rightarrow 3C & D \rightarrow 2F \\
B \rightarrow 2B & E \rightarrow 3D \\
B \rightarrow 5D & E \rightarrow 4F \\
C \rightarrow 1C & F \rightarrow 6
\end{array}
$$

Figure 1: Simple Rebber grammar.

Two corpora of 500 strings were generated for each language (one for training and another for testing) from a probabilistic regular grammar. A probability value was assigned to each rule of the grammar but guaranteeing that the grammar was proper [3]. Table 1 shows some characteristics of the generated corpus.

	L1	L2	L3	L4	L5	L6	L7	L8	L9
l	3.28	6.67	2.75	2.13	6.18	6.14	9.79	9.76	4.31
n	17	17	56	42	171	161	295	163	29
Σ	0.99	0.99	0.96	0.96	0.74	0.77	0.62	0.79	0.99
per	7.36	7.52	8.00	9.19	37.53	27.28	215.27	47.83	14.22

Table 1: Test corpus characteristics. The first row shows the medium length of the strings. The second one shows the number of different strings generated, while the third one shows the representativeness in probability of these strings. The fourth row shows the perplexity of the languages for a bigger corpus (experimentally calculated from the probability that the original grammar assigned to each string). The training corpus had the same characteristics.

We can note in the corpus which was generated that the most difficult distribution belongs to the language L7. We can see that the corpus generated for this language is the less representative (in probability) as well.

The inference method used in order to learn the previous languages was the ECGI algorithm. It is a grammatical inference algorithm that obtains a grammar G from a positive sample L' belonging to a language $L(L' \subseteq L)$, in such a way that $L' \subseteq L(G)$. The algorithm begins with an empty grammar (without rules), and for each sample adds the error rules (usually, insertion, deletion and substitution rules) belonging to the parsing sequence with the least number of error rules. This process provides a grammar without loops which is more and more general. Furthermore, a counting of the use of each rule can be carried out in the parsing process. It is clear that the statistical part is not reliable and better approximations could be used. Table 2 shows the relative entropy between the original grammar and the *probabilistic* grammar obtained by the ECGI algorithm.

L1	L2	L3	L4	L5	L6	L7	L8	L9
0.077	0.0025	0.70	0.26	1.78	1.20	0.55	1.08	0.7

Table 2: Relative entropy between the source grammar and the grammar obtained by the ECGI algorithm (with respect to the test).

We can observe that the languages L1 and L2 were learnt correctly (these languages had an easier structure) but the results were as good for the other languages. We must remember that the relative entropy is zero when both models induce the same distribution on the language. From these results it can be deduced that the grammar obtained from the ECGI algorithm can be improved by adjusting the distribution generated by it to the distribution induced by the training corpus. This process could be done with a PE process where the previous structural information would be used.

We will now see a PE process without any structural information for learning a probabilistic language, and we will see that these results improve when some structural information is incorporated to the initialization. In order to compare the results, the number of parameters to be estimated in both cases should be the same. Therefore, we will describe how the initial model with structural information was obtained and how the model without structural information was created with the same number of parameters.

The ECGI algorithm obtains a sansat [2] grammar (the associated automaton emits the terminal symbols in the states). This is not a drawback because the expressive ability of this sort of grammar is equal to the expressive ability of general regular grammars [17]. But the ECGI algorithm uses an error model in the parsing process to avoid the fact that a sample cannot be accepted by the grammar. To solve this problem all the necessary rules were added to the grammar to allow it to accept the positive closure: transiting to all other states (even itself) except to the initial state was allowed from each state (except for initial and final state); all states (except final state and itself) could be reached from initial state; the final state had no output transitions.

The counting process was used to initialize the probabilities associated to each rule and the new added rules were initialized with a small value. The remaining probability rules were adequately modified to keep the grammar proper. In this way, we got a grammar which was both structurally and statistically initialized.

This initialization was compared against a completely random initialization. The random grammar had the same number of non-terminals but the terminals were equally distributed among the right sides of the rules, but keeping the grammar as sansat. In this way a grammar with the same number of rules was obtained and the probabilities of those rules were randomly generated.

Both initializations were used with the reestimation forward-backward algorithm for learning the same training corpus. Figure 2 shows the relative entropy ratio after each

---

[2]A grammar $G = (N, V, P, S)$ is sansat if the following property is accomplished: $\forall A, B, C \in N, \forall b, a \in V$, if $(B \rightarrow aA)$ and $(C \rightarrow bA) \in P$ then $b = a$.

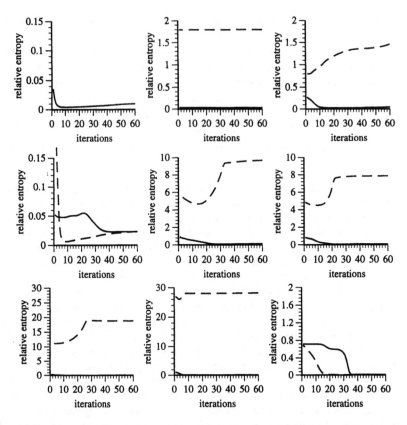

Figure 2: The relative entropy [3] with respect to the test corpus using the forward-backward algorithm with a random initialization (dashed lines) and using the grammar with structural information (continuous lines) for the languages L1-L9 appears from left to right and from top to bottom (It is important to note the different range of the y-axis).

iteration for all the languages mentioned.

We can see the better results obtained from the initialization with structural information (except L1 –taking into account the range and the simplicity of the language–, L4 where the results are the same at the end and L9 where the random initialization converges more rapidly). For the remaining languages the proposed initialization had better results. It is interesting to note that the results for the languages with a more complex structure (L5-L9) were better when structural information was used.

The bad results obtained from the random initialization could be due to the number of parameters to be estimated: the ECGI algorithm provides a grammar with a large number of non-terminals (when the length of the samples is big, the number of states increases quickly). Table 3 shows the difference of non-terminals between the source grammar and

---

[3]In some cases this value was less than zero. That was because strings not belonging to the training corpus could appear in the test corpus.

	L1	L2	L3	L4	L5	L6	L7	L8	L9
originals	1	2	4	3	4	5	5	7	3
ECGI	18	32	31	18	58	48	54	76	26

Table 3: Difference of non terminals between the grammar obtained from the ECGI algorithm and the source grammars. These were not necessarily sansat grammars.

the one obtained from the ECGI algorithm. With this large number of parameters the training corpus could have been over-learned. This was confirmed when the addition of probabilities of the training corpus (without repeated samples) was calculated with the learnt grammar and it was close to 1 for all languages.

In order to solve the over-learning problem, the training corpus was incremented for two of the languages in order to increase their representativeness. The same experimentation process was carried out again and Figure 3 shows the results.

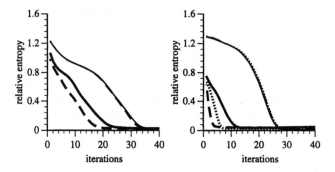

Figure 3: Results for L5 (left) and L7 (right) with a larger training corpora. For L5 two corpora were used: the first one had 1500 samples (continuous lines) and the second one had 5000 samples (dashed lines). For L7 three corpora were used: the first one with 1000 samples (continuous lines), the second one with 2000 samples (dashed lines) and the third one with 7000 samples (dotted lines). Thick lines correspond to the results obtained with PE with structural information and thin lines correspond to PE without structural information.

These figures showed that the anomalous behavior was due to a deficiency of samples. However, the results confirmed a better behavior when the grammar produced by the ECGI algorithm was used as initialization, that is, when structural information was incorporated to the estimation process. The results also show that when the number of samples is insufficient (quiet frequent in real tasks), incorporating some structural information can become very important.

Another possibility for solving the over-learning problem was pruning the initial grammar according to some criteria (e.g. deleting less used transitions or non-terminal symbols). The result (deleting up to 75 % of the states, which is not reported here) also improved without increasing the training corpus, but in one case the result was worse. This was because in the pruning process some structural information can be vital and it could be deleted.

Summarizing this section, we have seen on the one hand, that the results obtained by an inference method for learning a probabilistic language can be improved because the statistical part is quiet poor. On the other hand, we conjectured that a PE method, as the forward-backward algorithm, for learning a probabilistic language could improve if some structural information were incorporated to the process, and results confirmed this conjecture. The results also show that incorporating structural information can be very important when the number of samples of the training corpus is very small.

4 Conclusions

In this work we have shown how the PE can be improved through the forward- backward algorithm for learning a distribution of a formal language when structural information is incorporated in the process. For this purpose, we used the ECGI inference algorithm, and the information provided was adequately adapted and used as initialization by the forward-backward algorithm. The results obtained in this way were better than when a random initialization was used. We have also seen that incorporating structural information in the PE process can be very important when the number of available samples is insufficient.

For future research, these results suggest proving other non-heuristic inference methods to initialize the forward-backward algorithm that will allow us to confirm the results obtained in this work; other research would be proving the proposed method in real tasks where no knowledge about the task is available; finally, other proposed work would be applying the proposed method to other similar estimation algorithms such as the inside-outside algorithm for context free languages.

References

[1] *"Trainable Grammars for Speech Recognition"* J.K. Baker. 50th Anniversary Celebration of the Acoustical Society of America, pp. 31-35. June 1979.

[2] *"An Inequality and Associated Maximization Technique in Statistical Estimation for Probabilistic Function of a Markov Process"* L.E. Baum. Inequalities, Vol. III, 1972.

[3] *"Applying Probability Measures to Abstract Languages"* T.L. Booth, R.A. Thompson. IEEE Transactions on Computers, Vol. C-22, No. 5, pp. 442-450. May 1973.

[4] *"Growth Transformations for Probabilistic Functions of Stochastic Grammars"* F. Casacuberta. To be published. 1993.

[5] *"Information Theory"* T.M. Cover, J.A. Thomas. John Wiley & Sons. 1991.

[6] *"Syntactic Pattern Recognition and Applications"* K.S.Fu. Prentice Hall, 1982.

[7] *"Syntactic Pattern Recognition. An Introduction"* R.Gonzalez and M.Thomason. Addison- Wesley, 1978.

[8] *"An Inequality for Rational Functions with Applications to some Statistical Estimation Problems"* P.S. Gopalakrishnan, D.Kanevsky, A. Nadas, D. Nahamoo. IEEE Transactions on Information Theory, Vol. 37(1), pp. 107-113. 1991.

[9] *"Introduction to Automata Theory, Languages and Computation"* J.E. Hopcroft, J.D. Ullman. Addison-Wesly. 1979.

[10] *"Basic Methods of Probabilistic Context Free Grammars"* F. Jelinek, J.D. Lafferty, R.L. Mercer. Speech Recognition and Understanding. Ed. by P. Laface and R. De Mori, pp. 347-360. 1992.

[11] *"The Estimation of Stochastic Context-Free Grammars using the Inside-Outside Algorithm"* K. Lari, S. J. Young. Computer Speech and Language Vol. 4, pp. 35-56. 1990.

[12] *"On the Locality of the Forward-Backward Algorithm"* B. Merialdo. IEEE Trans. on Speech and Audio Processing, Vol. 1(2), pp. 255-257, 1993.

[13] *"Hidden Markov chains, the forward-backward algorithm and initial statics"* A. Nadas. IEEE Trans. Acoust., Speech and Signal Processing, vol. ASSP-31, pp. 504-506, 1983.

[14] *"Learning Language Models Though the ECGI Method"* N.Prieto and E.Vidal. Speech Communications, Vol.11, pp.299-309, 1992.

[15] *"Mathematical Foundations of Hidden Markov Models"* L.R.Rabiner. In Recent Advances in Speech Understanding and Dialog Systems. H.Niemann et al (eds). NATO ASI Series, Vo.F46, pp.183-205, 1988.

[16] *"Modeling (Sub)string-length-based Constraints through a Grammatical Inference Method"* H. Rulot, E. Vidal. Pattern Recogniton Theory and Applications, Devijver & Kittler Eds. Springer Verlag, pp.451-459. 1987.

[17] *"An Efficient Algorithm for the Inference of Circuit-Free Automata"* H. Rulot, E. Vidal. Syntactic and Structural Pattern Recognition. G. Ferrat Ed. Springer Verlag, pp.173-184. 1988.

[18] *"Dynamic Construction of Finite-State Automata from Examples Using Hill-Climbing"* M. Tomita. Proc. Fourth Annu. Cogn. Sci. Conf, pp. 105-108. 1982.

[19] *"Application of the Error-Correcting Grammatical Inference Algorithm (ECGI) to Planar Shape Recognition"* E.Vidal, H.Rulot, J.M.Valiente, G.Andreu. Grammatical Inference: Theory, Applications and Alternatives. S.24 (1-10), 1993.

[20] *"Probabilistic Languages: A Review and some Open Questions"* C.S.Wetherell. Computing Surveys, Vol.12, No.4, pp.361-379, 1980.

Learning Stochastic Regular Grammars by Means of a State Merging Method *

Rafael C. Carrasco
Jose Oncina
Departamento de Tecnología Informática y Computación
Universidad de Alicante, E-03071 Alicante
E-mail: (carrasco, joncina)@dtic.ua.es

Abstract

We propose a new algorithm which allows for the identification of any stochastic deterministic regular language as well as the determination of the probabilities of the strings in the language. The algorithm builds the prefix tree acceptor from the sample set and merges systematically equivalent states. Experimentally, it proves very fast and the time needed grows only linearly with the size of the sample set.

1 Introduction

Identification of stochastic regular languages (SRL) represents a highly interesting question within the field of grammatical inference. Indeed, most of realistic situations involve examples provided by a random source. The assumption of stochastic behaviour has important consequences on the learning process. Gold[1] introduced the criterion of *identification in the limit* for successful learning of a language. He also proved that regular languages cannot be identified if only *text* (i.e., only strings in the language) is given, but they can be identified if a *complete presentation* (where all strings are classified as belonging or not to the language) is provided. However, Angluin[2] proved that a wide range of distribution classes, including the SRL, are identifiable from *positive samples* (text) with probability one.

With this aim, some attempts to find suitable learning procedures have already been done. Maryanski and Booth[3] used a chi-square test in order to filter regular grammars provided by heuristic methods. Although convergence to the true one was not guaranteed, acceptable grammars were always found. The approach of van der Mude and Walker[4] merges variables in a stochastic regular grammar, where Bayesian criteria are applied. In that paper[4], convergence to the true grammar was not proved and the algorithm showed too slow for application purposes.

*Work partially supported under grant TIC93–0633–C02–02 from CICYT (Programa Nacional de Tecnologías de la Información y de las Comunicaciones)

In the last years, neural network models were used in order to identify regular languages [5, 6, 7, 8] and they have been applied to the problem of stochastic samples[9]. However, these methods share the serious drawback that long computational times and vast sample sets are needed. Hidden Markov models are used by Stolcke and Omohundro[10] in order to maximize the probability of the sample, but they include *a priori* probabilities in order to penalize the size of the automaton.

On the other hand, an algorithm is available[11] which allows for the correct identification in the limit of any regular language if a complete presentation is given. Moreover, the time needed by this algorithm in order to output an hypothesis grows at most as s^3, being s the size of the sample. Experimentally, its behaviour is in average linear in s. In the present paper, we will follow the same guidelines and present an algorithm (ALERGIA) which builds the prefix tree acceptor (PTA) from the sample and evaluates at every node the relative probabilities of the transitions coming out from the node. Next, it tries to merge couples of nodes, following a well defined order (essentially, that of the levels in the PTA or lexicographic order). Merging is performed if the resulting automaton is —within statistical uncertainty— equivalent to the PTA. The process ends when further merging is not possible. We will introduce some definitions in section 2, and comment on the difficulties related to stochastic regular languages identification in section 3. A more detailed description of ALERGIA can be found in sections 4 and 5. Finally, results and discussion will be presented in section 6.

2 Preliminaries

Let $\mathcal{A}$ be a finite alphabet, $\mathcal{A}^*$ the set of all strings on $\mathcal{A}$ and λ the empty string such that for every symbol a in $\mathcal{A}$ satisfies $a\lambda = \lambda a = a$. If w and x are strings of symbols in $\mathcal{A}^*$ and $w = xa$, then we will also write $x = wa^{-1}$. A *stochastic finite automaton* (SFA), $A = (\mathcal{A}, Q, P, q_1)$, consists of an alphabet $\mathcal{A}$, a finite set of nodes $Q = \{q_1, q_2, \ldots q_n\}$, with q_1 the initial node, and a set P of probability matrices $p_{ij}(a)$ giving the probability of a transition from node q_i to node q_j led by the symbol a in the alphabet. If we call p_{if} the probability that the string ends at node q_i, the following constraint applies:

$$p_{if} + \sum_{q_j \in Q} \sum_{a \in \mathcal{A}} p_{ij}(a) = 1. \tag{1}$$

The probability $p(w)$ for the string w to be generated by A is defined by:

$$
\begin{aligned}
p(w) &= \sum_{q_j \in Q} p_{1j}(w) \, p_{jf} \\
p_{ij}(w) &= \sum_{q_k \in Q} \sum_{a \in \mathcal{A}} p_{ik}(wa^{-1}) p_{kj}(a)
\end{aligned}
\tag{2}
$$

and the language generated by the automaton A is defined as:

$$L = \{w \in \mathcal{A}^* : p(w) \neq 0\} \tag{3}$$

Those languages generated by means of a SFA are called *stochastic regular languages*. In case the SFA contains no *useless nodes*[1], it generates a probability distribution for the

---

[1] A node q_i is useless if there are no strings $x, y \in \mathcal{A}^*$ such that $\sum_j p_{1i}(x)p_{ij}(y)p_{jf} \neq 0$.

strings in $\mathcal{A}^*$:

$$\sum_{w \in \mathcal{A}^*} p(w) = 1. \qquad (4)$$

Finally, two SRL are said to be *equivalent* if they provide identical probability distributions over $\mathcal{A}^*$. Note that it is not enough that two languages L_1 and L_2 include the same strings for them to be equivalent, also the probability of every string must be equal:

$$L_1 \equiv L_2 \iff p_1(w) = p_2(w) \ \forall w \in \mathcal{A}^*. \qquad (5)$$

In this work we will limit ourselves to *deterministic stochastic finite automata* (DSFA). This means that for every node $q_i \in Q$ and symbol $a \in \mathcal{A}$, there exists at most one node such that $p_{ij}(a) \neq 0$. In such cases, a transition function $k = \delta(i, a)$ can be defined. This function gives the final node q_k for the transition starting at q_i and driven by symbol a. The probability of this single transition will be denoted by $p_i(a)$. In contrast to nonstochastic automata, determinism is an effective restriction. Indeed, it is not generally possible to find a stochastic DFA equivalent to a given non-deterministic SFA.

3   Identifying Regular Languages

A complete sample S consistent with L consists of two subsets: S_+ with strings in L (*positive examples*) and S_- with strings not in L (*negative examples*). If only S_+ is presented, then S is a *positive sample* or *text*. The algorithm *identifies in the limit* L if adding new examples to S may only produce a finite number of changes of hypothesis. Negative examples play a relevant role, since they may be necessary in order to reject a language L' whose only difference with L lays on $L' - L$ (and such languages exist because an order which respects inclusion is not defined).

However, samples of SRL consist only of positive examples which appear repeatedly, according to the probability distribution expressed in eq. (2). Nevertheless, the statistical regularity is able to compensate the lack of negative data. As proved in ref.[2], many recursively numerable sets of distributions —in particular SRL when probabilities are restricted to rationals— are identifiable with probability one, again by means of enumerative algorithms.

Enumerative methods are experimentally unfeasible and the search of fast and reliable algorithms for identification becomes a challenging task.

The aim of this work is to find an algorithm which identifies in the limit stochastic regular languages and whose complexity does not grow exponentially with the size of S. Our approach will be based on the one proposed in ref.[11] for the identification of (non-stochastic) regular languages. For this reason, we will briefly describe it in the following.

Given a language L, the minimum DFA generating L is called the *canonical acceptor* $M(L)$. On the other hand, if S is a finite complete sample of L the prefix tree acceptor T of S is defined as the minimum automaton accepting only the (finite) set of strings S. For instance, the canonical acceptor of even valued binary strings is plotted in fig. 1 together with the prefix tree acceptor for the sample $S = \{\lambda, 00, 10, 110\}$

If π is a partition of the set Q of nodes of T, $\pi(T)$ is the automaton obtained by merging the nodes in the same block of the partition. For instance, in fig. 1, the canonical acceptor may be obtained from the prefix tree acceptor by merging states labelled with numbers in the same block of the partition $\tilde{\pi} = (\{1, 2, 4, 6, 7\}, \{3, 5\})$. Indeed, this is a particular example of a general well known fact: given a large enough sample S, there exists a partition $\tilde{\pi}$ of the nodes in T, such that $\tilde{\pi}(T)$ coincides with $M(L)$, the canonical acceptor. Therefore, the problem of identifying L is reduced to the simpler one of obtaining the partition $\tilde{\pi}$.

The language L_0 accepted by the PTA is always finite and coincides with the positive part of the sample set: $L_0 = S_+$. Any partition π leads to an enlarged accepted language $L_\pi \supset L_0$. Therefore, we are looking for a partition not including negative examples from S_-:

$$L_\pi \cap S_- = \emptyset. \tag{6}$$

The number of possible partitions in T grows exponentially with its size $t = |T|$, but a reasonable way to look for $\tilde{\pi}$ can be found. First, let us define an order of the nodes of T. The numerable set $\mathcal{A}^*$ —and therefore any language contained in $\mathcal{A}^*$— may be lexicographically ordered[2]. This allows one to define a similar order for the nodes of the automaton, as each node may be assigned the (lexicographically) first string leading from q_1 to that node. We will assume that the subindex i in q_i corresponds to this lexicographic order, as in fig. 1. Now, in order to find $\tilde{\pi}$, proceed as follows: merge (only if (6) still holds) nodes q_i and q_j, varying the subindex j from 2 to t and then, for every j, changing i from 1 to $j - 1$. In this way at most $\frac{1}{2}t(t-1)$ comparisons are done while convergence to the canonical acceptor is guaranteed. For a formal proof, see [11]. Convergence is achieved whenever S_- is large enough to reject any wrong merge and then, $M(L)$ is produced as output. Thus, once S_+ and S_- are large enough, the hypothesis automaton cannot be changed by adding new examples to S and identification is reached.

A similar procedure for stochastic languages, preserving the properties of identification and polinomial time complexity, is desirable. This is the subject of the next section.

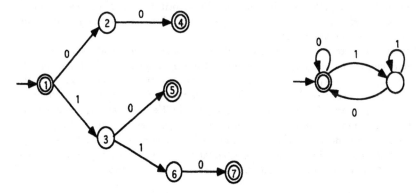

Figure 1: A prefix tree and the canonical acceptor for the regular set $(0 + 1)^*0$. Final states are doubled circled. Numbering of nodes follows the lexicographic order

---

[2]Sorted by length and then by alphabetical order within every length.

```
algorithm ALERGIA
input:
        S :    sample set of strings
        α :    1-confidence level
output:
        stochastic DFA
begin
        A = stochastic Prefix Tree Acceptor from S
        do (for j = successor( first node(A)) to lastnode(A))
           do(for i = firstnode(A) to j)
            : if compatible(i,j)
                 merge(A,i,j)
                 determinize(A)
                 exit (i-loop)
              end if
           end for
        end for
        return A
end algorithm
```

Figure 2: Algorithm ALERGIA.

4   The Algorithm

In the case of SRL, there are no negative examples in S, but the probability of appearance of every string follows a well defined distribution. Our algorithm ALERGIA takes advantage of this feature and performs merging of states when the resulting automaton is compatible with the observed frequencies of the strings in S.

The algorithm first builds the prefix tree T from S and evaluates at every node the relative frequencies of the outgoing arcs, incorporating this information in T (see fig. 9). We will write as n_i the (experimental) number of strings arriving at node q_i, $f_i(a)$ the number of strings following arc $\delta_i(a)$, and $f_i(\#)$ the number of strings ending at node q_i. The quotients $f_i(a)/n_i$ and $f_i(\#)/n_i$ estimate the probabilities $p_i(a)$ and p_{if} respectively.

Later, the algorithm compares couples of nodes (q_i, q_j), varying j from 2 to t and i from 1 to $j-1$. Two nodes in the same block of the partition $\tilde{\pi}$ are said to be *equivalent* ($q_i \equiv q_j$). As T is built, equivalent nodes have equal outgoing transition probabilities for every symbol $a \in \mathcal{A}$ and the destination nodes must be equivalent too:

$$q_i \equiv q_j \implies \forall a \in \mathcal{A} \begin{cases} p_i(a) = p_j(a) \\ \delta_a(i) \equiv \delta_a(j). \end{cases} \tag{7}$$

This provides a criterion in order to reject equivalence of nodes. However, experimental data are subjected to statistical fluctuations and equivalence must be accepted within a confidence range. In such case, the nodes will be called *compatible*.

A confidence range for a Bernoulli variable with probability p and observed frequency

f out of n tries is given by the Hoeffding bound[14]:

$$\left| p - \frac{f}{n} \right| < \sqrt{\frac{1}{2n} \log \frac{2}{\alpha}} \quad \text{with probability larger than } (1 - \alpha). \tag{8}$$

ALERGIA will reject equivalence if two estimated probabilities differ in an amount larger than the sum of confidence ranges (see fig. 3). In this way, the probability of a wrong rejection is kept below 2α because at least one of the estimations must lay out of its confidence range for them to be considered different. The check is done for the termination frequencies $f_i(\#)$ and for the frequencies of the outgoing arcs $f_i(a)$. Thus, $|\mathcal{A}| + 1$ comparisons are done at every node, being $|\mathcal{A}|$ the size of the alphabet. If two nodes are found to be similar, all destination nodes are checked recursively, as shown in fig. 4 (algorithm compatible).

algorithm different
input:

        n,n': number of strings arriving at each node
        f,f':number of strings ending/following a given arc
output:

        boolean
begin

        return $\left| \frac{f}{n} - \frac{f'}{n'} \right| > \sqrt{\frac{1}{2} \log \frac{2}{\alpha}} \left(\frac{1}{\sqrt{n}} + \frac{1}{\sqrt{n'}} \right)$
end algorithm

Figure 3: Algorithm different checks similitude of observed frequencies.

Recursion in algorithm compatible involves only a finite number of calls. Indeed, due to the order followed within the merging process, when (q_i, q_j) are compared, q_j is always the root of a subtree of the PTA and therefore, the language it generates is finite. In other words, there is no loop in the q_j-subtree and the recursion takes always a finite time. Another important point concerns indeterminism. When q_i and q_j are found to be compatible, q_i and q_j are merged and the resulting automaton could in principle be indeterministic. In practice, this is not the case because the successors responsible for the indetermination are merged too. The reason for this comes from the recursive character of compatible: the respective a-successors of two compatible nodes are also compatible. This feature also ensures that the defined (lexicographic) order of the nodes is preserved during the merging process, as the automaton remains deterministic. Finally, every time a merge is performed, the frequencies f_i and the numbers n_i are recalculated, consistently with the fact that more information is available at each node. A schematic representation of ALERGIA is shown in fig. 2. A detailed example showing how the whole process works can be found in the Appendix.

```
algorithm compatible
input:
       i,j :  nodes
output:
       boolean
begin
       if different(n_i, f_i(#), n_j, f_j(#))
         return false
       endif
       do(∀a ∈ A)
         if different(n_i, f_i(a), n_j, f_j(a))
            return false
         end if
         if not compatible(δ(i,a), δ(j,a))
            return false
         end if
       end do
       return true
end algorithm
```

Figure 4: Algorithm compatible checks $q_i \equiv q_j$.

5 Convergence of the Algorithm

In this section we will discuss the convergence of the algorithm. To this respect, the key point is the probability of finding the correct partition $\tilde{\pi}$ leading to the canonical acceptor. There are two different kinds of error where the algorithm could fail when looking for $\tilde{\pi}$:

1. (type α) rejection of compatibility between two equivalent nodes,

2. (type β) merge of two non-equivalent nodes.

Assume that S has a size $s = |S|$ large enough in the sense of section 3, while T —the prefix tree acceptor of S— is of size $t = |T|$ and the target (canonical) acceptor M has size $m = |M|$. Starting from T the algorithm should perform $t - m$ merges in order to successfully output M. Therefore, the global probability α_g for the first kind of error is bounded by the product $2\alpha(|A| + 1)t$, being α the parameter used in different (fig. 3). If one wants to keep α_g negligibly small as the size of the sample becomes large, one may take $\alpha = kt^{-1}$ with k a small constant. The value of k has a smooth influence on the results, as eq. (8) depends on $\log k$.

On the other hand, two non-equivalent nodes can (incorrectly) be found to be compatible if the difference of the observed frequencies is smaller than the confidence range. Once errors of type α are negligible, the resulting automaton must be a partition of M. In particular, the partition will be the trivial one and ALERGIA will output M if for every couple of blocks B_i and B_j of the partition $\tilde{\pi}$ of T there exist two incompatible nodes $q_i \in B_i$ and $q_j \in B_j$. Therefore, an upper bound for β_g is given by the probability that an error occurs when comparing representatives of each block. For this purpose, we may just select the first (in lexicographic order) node of the block as its representative. In this way, at most $\frac{1}{2}m(m-1)(|\mathcal{A}|+1)$ evaluations are needed in order to give an upper limit for β_g, each of those may contribute to β_g but all of them decrease with the size s. Therefore, β_g tends to zero as s grows. Recall that the error range behaves like:

$$\epsilon = \sqrt{\frac{1}{2}\log\frac{2}{\alpha}}\left(\frac{1}{\sqrt{n}}+\frac{1}{\sqrt{n'}}\right) \tag{9}$$

where n and n', the number of strings arriving at each node, grow linearly with s. Therefore, ϵ tends to zero as s grows, even if, as proposed here, α changes with t, as t cannot grow faster than s.

It is not difficult to write an upper bound for β_g. When comparing $\hat{f}_1 = f_1/n_1$ and $\hat{f}_2 = f_2/n_2$, the expected value and variance of the difference $\delta\hat{f} = \hat{f}_1 - \hat{f}_2$ are:

$$
\begin{aligned}
\mathrm{E}(\delta\hat{f}) &= \delta p = p_1 - p_2 \tag{10}\\
\mathrm{Var}(\delta\hat{f}) &= \mathrm{Var}(\hat{f}_1) + \mathrm{Var}(\hat{f}_2) = \\
&= \frac{p_1(1-p_1)}{n_1} + \frac{p_2(1-p_2)}{n_2} \le \frac{1}{4n_1} + \frac{1}{4n_2}. \tag{11}
\end{aligned}
$$

On the other hand, the probability $\beta = p(|\delta f| < \epsilon)$ that the observed difference is compatible with zero is smaller than $p(|\delta f - \delta p| > |\delta p| - \epsilon)$. Thus, using Chebychev's inequality[15], $\beta \le B$ with:

$$
B = \begin{cases} (|\delta p| - \epsilon)^{-2}\mathrm{Var}(\delta f) & \text{if } \epsilon < |\delta p| \text{ and } \mathrm{Var}(\delta f) < (\delta p - \epsilon)^2 \\ 1 & \text{otherwise} \end{cases} \tag{12}
$$

where B vanishes with s, because $\mathrm{Var}(\delta f)$ tends to zero (and so does ϵ). This bound B has to be evaluated less than $\frac{1}{2}m(m-1)(\mathcal{A}+1)$ times, and in all of them it tends to zero as the sample grows. Therefore, β_g vanishes in the limit of large sample sets.

It is also possible to choose a different functional dependence of α on t so that α_g also vanishes. However, this slows down convergence and the samples needed become larger. On the other hand, even if α_g is not very small, one obtains automata which are more complicated but equivalent (in the sense that the language is correctly identified) to the canonical one.

6 Results and Discussion

The performance of the algorithm has been tested with a variety of grammars. For each grammar, different samples were generated by the canonical stochastic automaton of the grammar and given as input for ALERGIA. For instance, the Reber grammar[16] of fig. 5 has been used in order to compare ALERGIA with previous works on neural networks which used this grammar as check[9].

In fig. 6 we plot the average number of nodes in the automaton found by ALERGIA as a function of the size of the sample set generated by the Reber grammar. The number of states is a measure of the complexity of the hypothesis. As seen in the figure, this

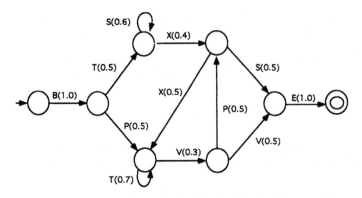

Figure 5: SFA corresponding to the Reber grammar

number always converges to the right value when the sample is large enough. We also checked that the structure of the automaton was correctly inferred. For small samples, the algorithm tends to propose hypothesis which are too complicated. However, when enough information is available it always finds the correct structure. The number of examples needed to achieve convergence is relatively small (about five hundred). This number compares rather favourably with the performance of recurrent neural networks[9] which cannot guaranty convergence for this grammar even after tens of thousands of examples.

In fig. 7, the time needed by the algorithm is plotted as a function of the number of examples in S. Although the temporal complexity could be in an extreme case be cubic, all the experiments showed a linear dependence. The algorithm proves very fast even for huge sample sets.

7 Conclusions

An algorithm has been proposed which identifies any stochastic regular language. Identification is achieved from stochastic samples of the strings in the language, and no information of the strings not belonging to the language is used. Experimentally, the algorithm needs very short times and comparatively small samples in order to identify the regular set. Even for large samples, only a linear time is needed (about one minute for a sample containing one million examples running on a Hewlett-Packkard 715). The algorithm is suitable for recognition tasks where noisy examples or random sources are common. In this line, applications to speech recognition problems are planned.

Acknowledgments

The authors want to acknowledge useful suggestions from E.Vidal and M.L.Forcada.

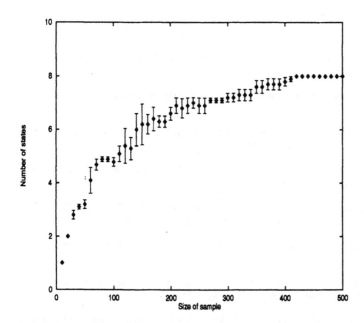

Figure 6: Number of nodes in the hypothesis for the Reber grammar as a function of the size of the sample.

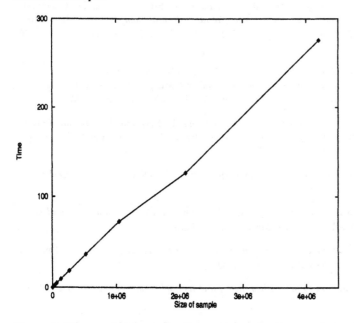

Figure 7: Time needed by our implementation of ALERGIA running on a Hewlett-Packard 715 as a function of the size of the sample.

References

[1] E.M. Gold: Complexity of Automaton Identification from Given Data. *Information and Control* **37** (1978) 302–320.

[2] D. Angluin: Identifying Languages from Stochastic Examples. Internal Report YALEU /DCS /RR–614 (1988).

[3] F.J. Maryanski and T.L. Booth: Inference of Finite-State Probabilistic Grammars. *IEEE Transactions on Computers* **C26** (1977) 521–536.

[4] A. van der Mude and A. Walker: On the Inference of Stochastic Regular Grammars. *Information and Control* **38** (1978) 310–329.

[5] A.W. Smith and D. Zipser: Learning Sequential Structure with the Real-Time Recurrent Learning Algorithm. *International Journal of Neural Systems* **1** (1989) 125–131.

[6] J.B. Pollack: The Induction of Dynamical Recognizers. *Machine Learning* **7** (1991) 227–252.

[7] C.L. Giles: Learning and Extracting Finite State Automata with Second Order Recurrent Neural Networks. *Neural Computation* **4** (1992) 393–405.

[8] R.L. Wartous and G.M. Kuhn: Induction of Finite-state Languages Using Second-Order Recurrent Networks. *Neural Computation* **4** (1992) 406–414.

[9] M.A. Castaño, F. Casacuberta, E. Vidal: Simulation of Stochastic Regular Grammars through Simple Recurrent Networks, in: *New Trends in Neural Computation* (Eds. J. Mira, J. Cabestany and A. Prieto). Springer Verlag, Lecture Notes in Computer Science **686** (1993) 210–215.

[10] A. Stolcke and S. Omohundro: Hidden Markov Model Induction by Bayesian Model Merging. To appear in: *Advances in Neural Information Processing Systems 5* (C.L. Giles, S.J. Hanson and J.D. Cowan eds.) Morgan Kaufman, Menlo Park, California (1993).

[11] J. Oncina and P. García: Inferring Regular Languages in Polynomial Time, in: *Pattern Recognition and Image Analysis* (N. Pérez de la Blanca, A. Sanfeliu and E. Vidal eds.) World Scientific (1992).

[12] K.S. Fu: *Syntactic Pattern Recognition and Applications.* Prentice Hall, Englewood Cliffs, N.J. (1982).

[13] J.E. Hopcroft and J.D. Ullman: *Introduction to Automata Theory, Languages and Computation.* Addison Wesley, Reading, Massachusetts (1979).

[14] W. Hoeffding: Probability inequalities for sums of bounded random variables. *American Statistical Association Journal* **58** (1963) 13–30.

[15] W. Feller: *An introduction to probability theory and its applications.* John Wiley and Sons, New York (1950)

[16] A.S. Reber: Implicit Learning of Artificial Grammars. *Journal of Verbal Learning and Verbal Behaviour* **6** (1967) 855–863.

A   Appendix

We will present a simple example to show how ALERGIA works. Assume that the automaton depicted in fig. 8 outputs the sample:

$$S = \{110, \lambda, \lambda, \lambda, 0, \lambda, 00, 00, \lambda, \lambda, \lambda, 10110, \lambda, \lambda, 100\}.$$

Only for illustration purposes, the parameter α will be arbitrarily set to 0.8. With this choice one has:

$$\gamma := \sqrt{\frac{1}{2} \log \frac{2}{\alpha}} \simeq 0.67$$

The algorithm starts by building the PTA, as shown in fig. 9. Each node is labelled with a number corresponding to its lexicographic order. In brackets, the number of strings arriving and terminating at that node are plotted. Every arc has a label with the symbol (0 or 1) inducing the transition, and in brackets appears the number of strings using that arc. Next, the algorithm checks if nodes q_2 and q_1 (labelled 2 and 1) are equivalent. This requires a comparison of the probabilities coming from these nodes. For instance, the termination probabilities are found to be similar:

$$|p - p'| = \left|\frac{1}{3} - \frac{1}{9}\right| \simeq 0.26 < \gamma(\frac{1}{\sqrt{n}} + \frac{1}{\sqrt{n'}}) \simeq 0.55$$

Also, the outgoing transitions have similar probabilities:

$$|p - p'| = \left|\frac{2}{3} - \frac{3}{15}\right| \simeq 0.46 < 0.55$$

In addition, equivalence of q_2 and q_1 also requires (due to the recursive definition) compatibility between destination nodes (namely q_4 and q_2). Proceeding in an analogous way, this is found to be the case and therefore $q_2 \equiv q_1$. The result after merging these two states is plotted in fig. 10.

In the next step the algorithm tries to merge the couple (q_3, q_1). However, they are found to be non-compatible when the termination probabilities are compared (0.6 and 0.0 respectively, whose difference is larger than 0.53)

Afterwards, comparison of q_5 and q_1 is done. The following similarities are accepted: $q_7 \equiv q_1$, $q_8 \equiv q_3$, $q_{10} \equiv q_6$, and $q_{11} \equiv q_9$. After the merges are performed one finds the automaton in fig. 11.

The merging of nodes q_6 and q_1 is rejected due to the difference in the transition probabilities labelled with 0 (0.75 being larger than 0.61). Instead, $q_6 \equiv q_3$ will be accepted, and the algorithm ends with the automaton plotted in fig. 12 as hypothesis. The estimated probabilities are shown in fig. 13 to be compared with 8.

The structure is the same but the probabilities have been only roughly estimated, due to the small size of the sample. Obviously one needs larger samples in order to find more accurate probabilities and in order to choose a reasonable confidence level (α).

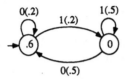

Figure 8: Stochastic finite automaton

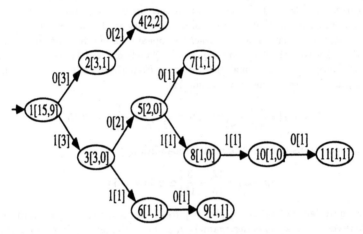

Figure 9: Prefix tree acceptor for the sample $S =\{$ 110, $\lambda, \lambda, \lambda$, 0, λ, 00, 00, $\lambda, \lambda, \lambda$, 10110, λ, λ, 100$\}$.

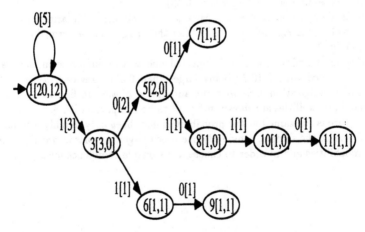

Figure 10: Prefix tree acceptor after merging q_2 and q_1.

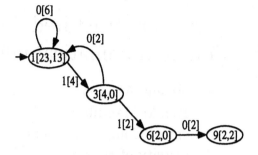

Figure 11: Automaton after merging q_5 and q_1.

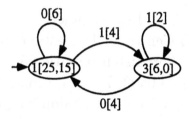

Figure 12: Automaton after merging q_6 and q_3.

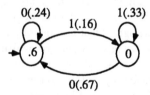

Figure 13: The final output.

Forming grammars for structured documents: an application of grammatical inference

Helena Ahonen
Heikki Mannila
Department of Computer Science
University of Helsinki
P.O. Box 26 (Teollisuuskatu 23)
FIN-00014 University of Helsinki, Finland
E-mail: {hahonen,mannila}@cs.helsinki.fi

Erja Nikunen
Research Centre for Domestic Languages
Sörnäisten rantatie 25
FIN-00500 Helsinki, Finland
E-mail: enikunen@domlang.fi

Abstract

We consider the problem of generating grammars for classes of structured documents — dictionaries, encyclopedias, user manuals, and so on — from examples. The examples consist of structures of individual documents, and they can be collected either by converting typographical tagging of documents prepared for printing into structural tags, or by using document recognition techniques. Our method forms first finite-state automata describing the examples completely. These automata are modified by considering certain context conditions; the modifications correspond to generalizing the underlying language. Finally, the automata are converted into regular expressions, and they are used to construct the grammar. In addition to automata, an alternative representation, characteristic k-grams, is introduced. Some interactive operations are also described that are necessary for generating a grammar for a large and complicated document.

1 Introduction

In recent years, writing, storing, and retrieving documents in electronic form has become popular. Most of the non-fiction documents are somehow structured, i.e., they consist of parts that usually form a hierarchy. For instance, a scientific article consists of a title, an abstract, a text body, and references. The text body consists of a list of sections, every section consists of subsections or paragraphs, and so on. Other typical examples of structured documents are dictionaries, encyclopedias, user manuals, and annual reports. Recent surveys of the research concerning structured documents are [AFQ89, Qui89]. The interest in the area has led to the creation of several document standards, of which the best known are Open Document Architecture (ODA) and Standard Generalized Markup Language (SGML) [ODA89, SGM86, Bro89, Gol90].

The common way to describe the structure of a document is to use context-free grammars. It is typical to use regular expressions on the right-hand sides of the productions of the grammar. For example, the following might describe the simplified structure of a dictionary entry:

Entry → Headword [Inflection]
    (Sense_Number Description
      [Parallel_form | Preferred_form] Example*)*,

which states that an entry consists of a headword followed by an optional inflection part and zero or more groups, each group consisting of a sense number, a description, a further optional part which is either a parallel form or a preferred form, and a sequence of zero or more examples.

Grammars can be used to facilitate transformations and queries that have structural conditions. The grammar also provides general knowledge of the text. It can be fairly complicated, however, to find the grammar that describes the structure of a given large text. A dictionary, for instance, may contain thousands of entries, and their structures may vary considerably.

Although it is difficult to construct a grammar for a set of documents, it is rather easy to name the parts of an individual document and construct simple productions from them. For instance the structure of the following dictionary entry:

delta: 1. a letter in the Greek alphabet. *2. (geographic)* land at the mouth of a river.

can be described with the simple productions:

Entry → Headword Sense Sense
Sense → Sense_number Description
Sense → Sense_number Technical_field Description

There are several ways to collect individual structures. When the sample is going to be rather small, or the user is just designing a new document structure, maybe the best way is to use an interactive program. Such a program is implemented in connection with the structured text database system HST [KLMN90]. It lets the user paint a part of a text with a pointing device and give a name to that part. The productions are constructed automatically from this information. The marking with a pointing device is inappropriate when the text considered is large and has a complicated structure. If this kind of text, like a dictionary, has been prepared for printing it is usually typographically tagged, i.e., parts of the text are marked by begin and end tags (e.g. begin bold – end bold). Since typographical means are used to make the structure clear to the reader, they can be used to make the structure explicit: tags can be changed to structural (SGML) tags (e.g. begin headword – end headword). The entries are further modified by removing the text and the end tags, and simple productions are formed. Nested tags form productions of their own. If the documents do not have any typographical tagging, it may be possible to use some document recognition techniques [TYS94, HI94, SEM94, SZ86] that try to recognize the parts using, for instance, keywords, fonts, or the physical layout of the text.

Since the simple productions are based on some specific parts of the text, they are overly restrictive and hence, they cannot be used as the grammar describing the structure of the whole set of documents. Thus, one should be able to generalize the productions in some meaningful way. For the generalization, we formulate the problem as a grammatical inference problem [AS83].

The method we have developed proceeds as follows.

1. The example productions are transformed to a set of finite automata, one for each nonterminal. These automata accept exactly the right-hand sides of the example productions for the corresponding nonterminal.

2. Each automaton is modified in isolation, so that it accepts a larger language. This language is the smallest one that includes the original right-hand sides and has an additional property called (k, h)-contextuality. This property states roughly that in the structure of the document what can follow a certain component is completely determined by the k preceding components at the same level. Steps 1 and 2 are based on the synthesis of finite automata presented in [Ang82, Mug90], specifically (k, h)-contextuality is a modification of k-reversibility [Ang82] and k-contextuality [Mug90].

3. The resulting automata are transformed to regular expressions, which form the right-hand sides of the productions for the corresponding nonterminals.

Practically our setting differs from the usual theoretical grammatical inference problems. The alphabet is not known beforehand. The user has not necessarily an underlying target language in mind: the target can change during the process, and the user can make errors. There are always a finite number of examples. In addition to (k, h)-contextuality, an important criterion of success is user's satisfaction that is affected by the clarity and compactness of the resulting grammar. Due to these practical reasons our automatic inference method is augmented by some interactive operations that allow the user to influence the learning process (See Section 6).

A related approach to the grammar generating problem is presented in [FX94]. While containing more developed environment for recognizing document structures it is not intended to be used with very large and complicated structures as our method is.

The rest of this paper is organized as follows. Section 3 describes our method of generalizing the right-hand sides of productions. Section 4 introduces an alternative representation to automata: a set of characteristic k-grams. Section 5 describes the conversion of generalized automata into regular expressions, and Section 6 interactive operations necessary in generating a grammar for a large document. Section 7 gives some experimental results. Finally, Section 8 contains some concluding remarks.

2   Basic definitions

Our method uses finite automata to represent and manipulate the collection of examples. We assume that the reader is familiar with finite-state automata, context-free grammars, and regular expressions (see, e.g., [HU79] for details), and just give the basic definitions for reference. A finite-state automaton is a quintuple $(Q, \Sigma, \delta, S, F)$, where Q is the set of states, Σ is the set of input symbols, $\delta : Q \times \Sigma^* \to Q$ is the transition function, $S \in Q$ is the start state and $F \subseteq Q$ is the set of final states. For an automaton A the language accepted by A is denoted by $L(A)$.

Regular expressions are defined as follows:

1. $\emptyset$ is a regular expression.

2. ϵ is a regular expression.

3. For each $a \in \Sigma$, a is a regular expression.

4. If r and s are regular expressions, then $(r|s)$, (rs), and (r^*) are regular expressions. A regular expression $(r|\epsilon)$ can be rewritten as $[r]$.

A context free grammar is denoted $G = (N, T, P, S)$, where N and T are finite sets of nonterminals and terminals, respectively. P is a finite set of productions. Each production is of the form $A \to \alpha$, where A is a nonterminal and α is a regular expression over the alphabet $(N \cup T)^*$. S is a special nonterminal called the start symbol.

3   Generalization of productions

The right-hand sides of productions obtained from the user's examples are represented by an automaton called a prefix-tree automaton. To construct a prefix-tree automaton we first take the set of sample productions that have the same left-hand side. The right-hand sides of these productions are added to the prefix-tree automaton one by one. For example, if the following productions are added into a prefix-tree automaton, the result is the automaton shown in Figure 1.

Entry → Headword Inflection Example Example
Entry → Headword Inflection Parallel_form Example Example Example
Entry → Headword Parallel_form Example Example
Entry → Headword Preferred_form Example
Entry → Headword Inflection Preferred_form Example Example

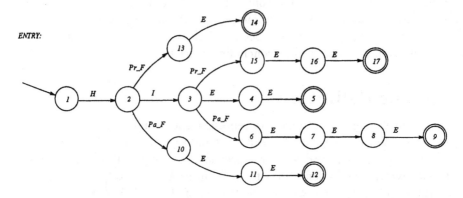

Figure 1: Prefix-tree automaton containing all the examples.

The prefix tree automaton accepts only the right-hand sides of the examples. To obtain useful grammars, we need some way of generalizing the examples, and the automaton describing them, in a meaningful way.

The examples of productions are all positive examples. To learn from positive examples, one needs some restrictions on the allowed result of the generalization. Namely, a consistent generalization of a set of positive examples would be an automaton accepting all strings! Thus we have to define a class of automata that are allowed as results of the generalization.

By merging some of the states we get an automaton which accepts more strings, i.e., this automaton generalizes the examples. Our assumption is that the grammars used in structured documents have only limited context in the following sense. If a sufficiently long sequence of nonterminals occurs in two places, the components that can follow this sequence are independent of the position of the sequence in the document structure. A language satisfying this condition is called k-contextual [Mug90]. The condition of k-contextuality can be described simply in terms of automata.

Definition 1 A regular language L is k-contextual if and only if there is a finite automaton A such that $L = L(A)$, and for any two states p_k and q_k of A and all input symbols $a_1 a_2 \ldots a_k$ we have: if there are states p_0 and q_0 of A such that $\delta(p_0, a_1 a_2 \ldots a_k) = p_k$ and $\delta(q_0, a_1 a_2 \ldots a_k) = q_k$, then $p_k = q_k$.

The above definition gives a way of constructing a k-contextual automaton containing language $L(C)$ for an automaton C. States of C satisfying the conditions in the implication of the definition are merged until no such states remain.

The intuition in using k-contextuality is that two occurrences of a sequence of components of length k implies that the subsequent components can be the same in both cases. We have relaxed this condition and generalized the k-contextual languages further to (k, h)-contextual languages. In these languages two occurrences of a sequence of length k implies that the subsequent components are the same already after h of these k characters. As for k-contextuality, we obtain an easy characterization in terms of automata.

Definition 2 A regular language L is (k, h)-contextual if and only if there is a finite automaton A such that $L = L(A)$, and for any two states p_k and q_k of A, and all input symbols $a_1 a_2 \ldots a_k$ we have: if there are states p_0 and q_0 such that $\delta(p_0, a_1) = p_1, \delta(p_1, a_2) = p_2, \ldots, \delta(p_{k-1}, a_k) = p_k$ and $\delta(q_0, a_1) = q_1, \delta(q_1, a_2) = q_2, \ldots, \delta(q_{k-1}, a_k) = q_k$, then $p_i = q_i$, for every i, where $0 \leq h \leq i \leq k$.

The algorithm for producing the automaton that acceps a (k, h)-contextual automaton is similar to the previous algorithm: one looks for states satisfying the conditions of the above definition, and then merges states. If similar paths of length k are found, not only the last states but also some of the respective states along the paths are merged. If $h = k$ only the last states are merged. If $h < k$ the paths have a similar prefix of length h before they are joined, i.e. $k - h + 1$ states are merged.

In Figure 2 we can see the final (2,1)-contextual automaton.

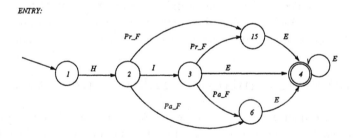

Figure 2: (2,1)-contextual automaton.

4   Characteristic k-grams

If an automaton is k-contextual, all the paths of length k that contain the same sequence of input symbols end at the same state. This feature illustrates the point that for any k-contextual language L there exists a finite set of strings of length $k + 1$ that uniquely identifies L. We call these strings *characteristic k-grams*, and they are formally defined as follows.

Definition 3 Let L be any (k, h)-contextual language. Then the set of *characteristic k-grams*, $grams_k(L)$, for L is the set

$$\{u \mid u \text{ is a substring of } \#^k w \#, \ |u| = k + 1, \ w \in L\}.$$

The definition extends to sets in a natural way. As any (k, h)-contextual language is also k-contextual, this definition applies also to (k, h)-contextual languages.

Example 4 The characteristic 2-grams of the language accepted by the automaton in Figure 2 are { # # H, # H Pr_F, # H I, # H Pa_F, H Pr_F E, I Pr_F E, H I Pr_F, H I E, H I Pa_F, H Pa_F E, I Pa_F E, Pr_F E E, Pa_F E E, I E E, E E E, Pr_F E #, Pa_F E #, I E #, E E # }

A set of k-grams can be used as a "machine", like automata and grammars.

Definition 5 Let CG be a set of k-grams over alphabet Σ. Then CG *generates* a language $L(CG) = \{w \mid grams_k(\{w\}) \subset CG\}$. A k-gram of the form $\#^k a$, where $a \in \Sigma$, is called an initial k-gram. Respectively, a k-gram of the form $u\#$, where $u \in \Sigma^k$ is called a final k-gram.

Any (k, h)-contextual automaton can be converted into a set of characteristic k-grams [Aho94]. Hence, the set of k-grams can be used as an efficient representation alternative to automata. Generalizing a set of examples to a k-contextual language can be done simply by adding all substrings of length $k + 1$ to the set of k-grams. The (k, h)-contextual languages require additionally that the set is the set of k-grams for some (k, h)-contextual language.

5 Conversion into a regular expression

After the generalization steps presented in the previous sections have been performed, we have a collection of (k,h)-contextual automata or k-grams. To obtain a useful description of the structure of the document, we still have to produce a grammar from these. An automaton can be converted into a regular expression by using standard dynamic programming methods [HU79]. The expressions produced by the standard method are not always so short as they could be, and therefore they have to be simplified. The simplified regular expressions form the right-hand sides of the productions for the corresponding nonterminals. Sample productions in Section 3 generate the production:

Entry → Headword
        (Inflection [Preferred_form | Parallel_form] |
        Parallel_form | Preferred_form)
        Example*

6 Interactive operations

Constructing a grammar for a large text may be quite a complex task. The sample text may, for instance, contain erroneous or rare structures, or the structures may be somehow insufficient. That is why it is important to offer — in addition to automatic learning — various interactive operations for influencing the learning process. These tools include displaying a list of examples of accepted structures and a possibility to remove some structures from this list. The user is also allowed to introduce more structure to make the resulting productions simpler. We also consider ways to use frequency information for separating exceptional cases from the more common ones.

If the user cannot understand the resulting grammar, it is often useful if the system can display a finite sample which somehow characterizes the grammar. The user can use the sample also to choose some structure to be removed.

Example 6 A characteristic sample constructed from the 2-grams of Example 4: H Pr_F E E E, H Pr_F E E, H Pr_F E, H Pa_F E E E, H Pa_F E E, H Pa_F E, H I E E E, H I E E, H I E, H I Pr_F E E, H I Pr_F E, H I Pa_F E E, H I Pa_F E.

It is quite usual that a large document contains some errors or very exceptional cases. Thus, the user may want to remove some structures. Some deletions, however, have to be refused, since the set of k-grams (or the automaton) has to be (k, h)-contextual also after operation.

If the document structure is very complicated, it is often useful to be able to introduce more nested structure than is present in the examples. For instance in our dictionary entries there are clearly nonterminals that form the first part of the entry (Headword, Inflection) and others that appear in the end (Parallel_form, Preferred_form, Example). Since both of these parts vary a lot, processing them separately reduces the complexity of the productions remarkably. The separation can be done by isolating a set of nonterminals to form a new nonterminal.

Generalizing to (k, h)-contextual languages does not necessarily produce a simple expression of the structure. Frequency information can be used for quantifying the importance of different types of structures for the component. It is desirable to get one or a few productions that cover most of the examples, and then several productions that correspond to the exceptions.

Frequency information can also be used in the following way. The user chooses the most common examples and let the learning program generate a grammar. The grammar is then used to parse rest of the example texts. If an example cannot be parsed, either the grammar is modified or the user changes the example. The latter gives the user a possibility to correct errors. The user should also be provided some statistical information, for instance the percentage of examples that the current grammar covers.

7 Experimental results

We have implemented the automatic generalization of the right-hand sides in C++ and, additionally, isolation of nonterminals and separation of common cases. As a representation of data we have used sets of $(2, 1)$-contextual 2-grams.

Our principal test data was the part $A - K$ of a Finnish dictionary [Suo90]. The dictionary was originally typographically tagged, i.e., parts of the text were marked by begin and end tags to show how certain parts should be

2470 EN → H S	1787 EN → H EX
1325 EN → H	1122 EN → H I S
1056 EN → H S EX	1031 EN → H I S EX
995 EN → H TF S	574 EN → H I CG S EX
549 EN → H I TF S	387 EN → H I EX
352 EN → H I CG S	329 EN → H R
258 EN → H I TF S EX	232 EN → H TF S EX
195 EN → H TF	171 EN → H I R
138 EN → H I CG TF S	125 EN → H I
117 EN → H TF EX	100 EN → H PrF
97 EN → H I CG TF S EX	94 EN → H I PI S
92 EN → H EX S	85 EN → H I CG R
84 EN → H TF R	66 EN → H I S EX TF EX
54 EN → H I PaF S EX	53 EN → H I TF R
51 EN → H I CG S EX TF EX	47 EN → H I CG PrF
46 EN → H I CG BW EX	45 EN → H I S EX TF S EX
44 EN → H I PrF	44 EN → H PI S
42 EN → H I EX S	39 EN → H TF EX S
34 EN → H I PaF S	34 EN → H I CG PaF S EX
34 EN → H I PI TF S	31 EN → H I S TF S
30 EN → H I TF TF S	29 EN → H I II TF S
29 EN → H I S EX S	29 EN → H I BW EX
28 EN → H I CG S EX TF S EX	24 EN → H I CG EX
24 EN → H S EX S	22 EN → H I R EX
22 EN → H I PI R	22 EN → H TF TF S
21 EN → H R EX	21 EN → H S TF S EX
21 EN → H S EX TF EX	20 EN → H I CG R EX
20 EN → H EX TF S	

Figure 3: Sample dictionary productions

printed (e.g. begin bold – end bold). We converted the typographical tags of
our data, which consist of about 16000 entries, to structural tags, and obtained
a set of 468 distinct productions. Every production also received a frequency,
i.e., the number of entries that the production covers. We chose 55 of the most
common productions (Figure 3), which together covered 14791 entries. As a
result of the automatic generalization we got the production shown in Figure 4.
The result is clearly unreadable and useless: some interactive operations are
needed.

EN → H[[I[CG]](PrF[[[S][EX(S EX)* [S]] TF ((([S] EX (S EX)* [S] | S) TF)*] R (EX (S EX)*
[S] TF ((([S] EX (S EX)* [S] | S) TF)* R)* EX [(S EX)* [[S] TF ((([S] EX (S EX)* [S] | S) TF)*
[S] EX [(S EX)* [S EX]] |S EX]] | [S] [[EX (S EX)* [S]] TF ((([S] EX (S EX)* [S] | S) TF)* [S]]
EX [(S EX)* [S EX]] | [[S] [EX (S EX)* [S]] TF ((([S] EX (S EX)* [S] | S) TF)*] [R (EX (S EX)*
[S] TF ((([S] EX (S EX)* [S] | S) TF)* R)* EX (S EX)* [[S] TF ((([S] EX (S EX)* [S] | S) TF)*
[[S] EX (S EX)*]] | [S] EX (S EX)* | S) |I [(II | [CG] (BW EX (S EX)* [S] | PaF S [EX (S EX)*
[S]])) TF [((([S] EX (S EX)* [S] | S) TF)* [R (EX (S EX)* [S] TF ((([S] EX (S EX)* [S] | S)
TF)* R)* EX (S EX)* [S] TF [(((S] EX (S EX)* [S] | S) TF)* [([S] EX (S EX)* [S] | S) TF]] |
([S] EX (S EX)* [S] | S) TF]] | II TF ((([S] EX (S EX)* [S] | S) TF)* (R (EX (S EX)* [S] TF
((([S] EX (S EX)* [S] | S) TF)* R)* EX [(S EX)* [[S] TF ((([S] EX (S EX)* [S] | S) TF)* [S] EX
[(S EX)* [S EX]] | S EX]] | [S] EX [(S EX)* [S EX]]) | [CG] (BW EX [(S EX)* [[S] TF ((([S] EX
(S EX)* [S] | S) TF)* (R (EX (S EX)* [S] TF ((([S] EX (S EX)* [S] | S) TF)* R)* EX [(S EX)*
[[S] TF ((([S] EX (S EX)* [S] | S) TF)* [S] EX [(S EX)* [S EX]] |S EX]] | [S] EX [(S EX)* [S
EX]]) |S EX]] | PaF S ([EX (S EX)* [S]] TF ((([S] EX (S EX)* [S] | S) TF)* R (EX (S EX)* [S]
TF ((([S] EX (S EX)* [S] | S) TF)* R)* EX [(S EX)* [[S] TF ((([S] EX (S EX)* [S] | S) TF)* [S]
EX [(S EX)* [S EX]] |S EX]] | [[EX (S EX)* [S]] TF ((([S] EX (S EX)* [S] | S) TF)* [S]] EX
[(S EX)* [S EX]])) | II TF ((([S] EX (S EX)* [S] | S) TF)* [R (EX (S EX)* [S] TF ((([S] EX (S
EX)* [S] | S) TF)* R)* EX (S EX)* [[S] TF ((([S] EX (S EX)* [S] | S) TF)* [[S] EX (S EX)*]]
| [S] EX (S EX)*] S | [CG] (BW EX (S EX)* [[S] TF ((([S] EX (S EX)* [S] | S) TF)* R (EX (S
EX)* [S] TF ((([S] EX (S EX)* [S] | S) TF)* R)* EX (S EX)*] [[S] TF ((([S] EX (S EX)* [S] |
S) TF)* [[S] EX (S EX)*]] S | PaF S [((EX (S EX)* [S]] TF ((([S] EX (S EX)* [S] | S) TF)* [R
(EX (S EX)* [S] TF ((([S] EX (S EX)* [S] | S) TF)* R)* EX (S EX)* [[S] TF ((([S] EX (S EX)*
[S] | S) TF)* [[S] EX (S EX)*]] | [S] EX (S EX)*] | EX (S EX)*) S])] | ([I] PI [((([S EX)* [S] TF
((([S] EX (S EX)* [S] | S) TF)*] R (EX (S EX)* [S] TF ((([S] EX (S EX)* [S] | S) TF)* R)* |
S) EX (S EX)*] [S] | [I [CG]] ([[S] [EX (S EX)* [S]] TF ((([S] EX (S EX)* [S] | S) TF)*] R (EX
(S EX)* [S] TF ((([S] EX (S EX)* [S] | S) TF)* R)* EX (S EX)* [S] | [S] [EX (S EX)* [S]])) TF
[((([S] EX (S EX)* [S] | S) TF)* [([S] EX (S EX)* [S] | S) TF]] | (I (II | [CG] (BW EX (S EX)*
[S] | PaF S [EX (S EX)* [S]])) TF ((([S] EX (S EX)* [S] | S) TF)* | [I] PI [(S EX)* [S] TF ((([S]
EX (S EX)* [S] | S) TF)*] | [I [CG]] [[S] [EX (S EX)* [S]] TF ((([S] EX (S EX)* [S] | S) TF)*
]) R [(EX (S EX)* [S] TF ((([S] EX (S EX)* [S] | S) TF)* R)* [EX (S EX)* [S] TF ((([S] EX (S
EX)* [S] | S) TF)* R]] | [I] PI ([(S EX)* [S] TF ((([S] EX (S EX)* [S] | S) TF)*] R (EX (S EX)*
[S] TF ((([S] EX (S EX)* [S] | S) TF)* R)* EX [(S EX)* [[S] TF ((([S] EX (S EX)* [S] | S) TF)*
[S] EX [(S EX)* [S EX]] |S EX]] | ((S EX)* [S] TF ((([S] EX (S EX)* [S] | S) TF)* [S] | S) EX
[(S EX)* [S EX]] | [((S EX)* [S] TF ((([S] EX (S EX)* [S] | S) TF)*] R (EX (S EX)* [S] TF
((([S] EX (S EX)* [S] | S) TF)* R)* EX (S EX)* [[S] TF ((([S] EX (S EX)* [S] | S) TF)* [[S] EX
(S EX)*]] | (S EX)* [S] TF ((([S] EX (S EX)* [S] | S) TF)* [[S] EX (S EX)*]) S | S (EX S)*)]

Figure 4: The result of the automatic generalization

We assume that the user has some knowledge of the target document. In the case of the dictionary, for instance, we assume that the user knows or notices that some parts of a dictionary entry always appear in the beginning of the entry, and some parts in the end. Hence, as the next step in the test we isolated parts *Headword (H)*, *Inflection (I)*, *Consonant_gradation (CG)*, *Inflection_instructions (II)*, and *Pronunciation_instructions (PI)* and constructed a new nonterminal *Headword_part (HP)*. In Figure 5 we can see the new production for *HP* and the production for *EN* where all the occurrences of *H*, *I*, *CG*, *II*, and *PI* are replaced by *HP*.

HP → H [I [II | CG] | [I] PI]

EN → HP [PrF| [([[PaF] S] [EX (S EX)* [S]] | BW EX (S EX)* [S]) TF (([S] EX (S EX)* [S] | S) TF)*] R [(EX (S EX)* [S] TF (([S] EX (S EX)* [S] | S) TF)* R)* [EX (S EX)* [S] TF (([S] EX (S EX)* [S] | S) TF)* R]] | (PaF S [EX (S EX)* [S]] | BW EX (S EX)* [S]) TF [(([S] EX (S EX)* [S] | S) TF)* [R (EX (S EX)* [S] TF (([S] EX (S EX)* [S] | S) TF)* R)* EX (S EX)* [S] TF [(([S] EX (S EX)* [S] | S) TF)* [([S] EX (S EX)* [S] | S) TF]] | ([S] EX (S EX)* [S] | S) TF]] | ([[S] [EX (S EX)* [S]] TF (([S] EX (S EX)* [S] | S) TF)*] R (EX (S EX)* [S] TF (([S] EX (S EX)* [S] | S) TF)* R)* EX (S EX)* [S] | [S] [EX (S EX)* [S]]) TF [(([S] EX (S EX)* [S] | S) TF)* [([S] EX (S EX)* [S] | S) TF]] | PaF S [[EX (S EX)* [S]] TF (([S] EX (S EX)* [S] | S) TF)* R (EX (S EX)* [S] TF (([S] EX (S EX)* [S] | S) TF)* R)* EX [(S EX)* [[S] TF (([S] EX (S EX)* [S] | S) TF)* [S] EX [(S EX)* [S EX]] |S EX]] | [[EX (S EX)* [S]] TF (([S] EX (S EX)* [S] | S) TF)* [S]] EX [(S EX)* [S EX]] | ([EX (S EX)* [S]] TF (([S] EX (S EX)* [S] | S) TF)* [R (EX (S EX)* [S] TF (([S] EX (S EX)* [S] | S) TF)* R)* EX (S EX)* [[S] TF (([S] EX (S EX)* [S] | S) TF)* [[S] EX (S EX)*]]] | [S] EX (S EX)*] | EX (S EX)*) S] | BW EX [(S EX)* [[S] TF (([S] EX (S EX)* [S] | S) TF)* (R (EX (S EX)* [S] TF (([S] EX (S EX)* [S] | S) TF)* R)* EX [(S EX)* [[S] TF (([S] EX (S EX)* [S] | S) TF)* [S] EX [(S EX)* [S EX]] |S EX]] | [S] EX [(S EX)* [S EX]]) |S EX]] | [[S] [EX (S EX)* [S]] TF (([S] EX (S EX)* [S] | S) TF)*] R (EX (S EX)* [S] TF (([S] EX (S EX)* [S] | S) TF)* R)* EX [(S EX)* [[S] TF (([S] EX (S EX)* [S] | S) TF)* [S] EX [(S EX)* [S EX]] |S EX]] | [S] [[EX (S EX)* [S]] TF (([S] EX (S EX)* [S] | S) TF)* [S]] EX [(S EX)* [S EX]] | (BW EX (S EX)* [[S] TF (([S] EX (S EX)* [S] | S) TF)* R (EX (S EX)* [S] TF (([S] EX (S EX)* [S] | S) TF)* R)* EX (S EX)*] [[S] TF (([S] EX (S EX)* [S] | S) TF)* [[S] EX (S EX)*]] | [[S] [EX (S EX)* [S]] TF (([S] EX (S EX)* [S] | S) TF)*] [R (EX (S EX)* [S] TF (([S] EX (S EX)* [S] | S) TF)* R)* EX (S EX)* [[S] TF (([S] EX (S EX)* [S] | S) TF)* [[S] EX (S EX)*]] | [S] EX (S EX)*]) S]

Figure 5: Headword_part (HP) has been isolated from Entry (EN).

The isolation process was continued further. In the next step we isolated parts *Sense*, *Example*, and *Technical_field*, and formed a new nonterminal *Sense_group (SG)*:

SG → ([S] ([EX (S EX)* [S]] TF [(([S] EX (S EX)* [S] | S) TF)* [([S] EX (S EX)* [S] | S) TF]] | [[EX (S EX)* [S]] TF (([S] EX (S EX)* [S] | S) TF)* [S]] EX [(S EX)* [S EX]]) | [[S] [EX (S EX)* [S]] TF (([S] EX (S EX)* [S] | S) TF)*] [[S] EX (S EX)*] S)

HP → H [I [II | CG] | [I] PI]

EN → HP [PrF | [[PaF | BW] SG] R (SG R)* | (PaF | BW) SG (R SG)* | [[SG] R (SG R)*] SG]

Sense_group looked still quite complicated, and there seemed to be repeating groups containing parts *Sense* and *Example* only. Therefore these nonterminals were isolated to form a new nonterminal *Sense_and_example (SE)*:

SE → ([S] EX (S EX)* | [[S] EX (S EX)*] S)

SG → ([SE] TF (SE TF)* | [[SE] TF (SE TF)*] SE)

HP → H [I [II | CG] | [I] PI]

EN → HP [PrF | [[PaF | BW] SG] R (SG R)* | (PaF | BW) SG (R SG)* | [[SG] R (SG R)*] SG]

Finally, some complexity of the production for *Entry* was possible to be removed by isolating the nonterminals *Sense_group* and *Reference*. They formed a new nonterminal *Sense_group_and_reference (SGR)*:

SGR → ([SG] R (SG R)* | [[SG] R (SG R)*] SG)

SE → ([S] EX (S EX)* | [[S] EX (S EX)*] S)

SG → ([SE] TF (SE TF)* | [[SE] TF (SE TF)*] SE)

HP → H [I [II | CG] | [I] PI]

EN → HP [PrF | [PaF | BW] SGR]

In a dictionary some structures are typically very common, and, on the other hand, most of the structures occur in one or two entries only. Hence, the rare cases can complicate the productions unnecessary. Therefore, the next step in the test was to separate the common cases. The threshold was 500, i.e., all the k-grams in a set describing the right-hand side had to appear at least 500 times in the examples. In the following the first production of each pair is the common one and the second one covers the exceptions.

SGR → (R | SG)
SGR → ([[SG] R (SG R)*] SG | [SG] R (SG R)*)

SE → ([S] EX | S)
SE → ([S] EX (S EX)* | [[S] EX (S EX)*] S)

SG → (TF | [TF] SE)
SG → ([[SE] TF (SE TF)*] SE | [SE] TF (SE TF)*)

HP → H [I [CG]]
HP → H (I II | [I] PI)

EN → HP [SGR]
EN → HP ((PaF | BW) SGR | PrF)

To check the correctness of the productions, the grammar was used to parse the examples, and the result was that it could parse all of them. Of the whole data of 15970 entries it could parse 15663 entries, which means that it covers 872 entries more than the original examples.

8   Conclusion

We have presented a method for generating a context-free grammar for a set of documents from the user's examples. The user provides names to the parts of existing texts. These names are used to form simple productions, which are then generalized and combined to form a grammar.

The following steps are taken:

1. The user describes the structure of the example text by extracting a part and giving it a name. These names form simple productions.

2. A prefix-tree automaton is built for every nonterminal that appears on the left-hand sides of the productions.

3. The automata are generalized by merging states.

4. The regular expressions are constructed which form the right-hand sides of the productions.

In the generalization of the examples we have first applied the idea of k-contextual languages and further developed them to (k, h)-contextual languages. These conditions seem to describe quite natural constraints in text structures. We have also presented an alternative representation for (k, h)-contextual automata: a set of (k, h)-contextual characteristic k-grams.

Additionally, we have presented some interactive operations that are necessary in generating a grammar for a large and complicated document. These operations include listing a characteristic sample, deletion of examples, and introducing more nested structure by isolating nonterminals to form new nonterminals. The possibility to use frequency information to separate rare and erroneous cases from the more probable ones is also considered.

We have implemented parts of the described method in C++, and experimented with several document types. Most challenging of these experiments was generating a grammar for a part of a Finnish dictionary. The experiments show that if documents are rather simple, the automatic generalization gives sufficient results. However, interactive operations are necessary, if the structures are more complicated, and especially if they contain iterations of slightly different combinations of parts. Although in the dictionary some parts can appear almost in any order and automatic generalization gives totally unreadable productions, breaking the problem to smaller pieces using isolation of nonterminals yields a small and readable grammar.

References

[AFQ89]   J. André, R. Furuta, and V. Quint. By way of an introduction. Structured documents: What and why? In J. André, R. Furuta, and V. Quint, editors, *Structured Documents*, The Cambridge Series on Electronic Publishing, pages 1–6. Cambridge University Press, 1989.

[Aho94]   Helena Ahonen. *Generating grammars for structured documents using grammatical inference methods*. Ph. Lic. thesis, University of Helsinki, Department of Computer Science, 1994.

[Ang82]   Dana Angluin. Inference of reversible languages. *Journal of the ACM*, 29(3):741–765, 1982.

[AS83]   Dana Angluin and Carl H. Smith. Inductive inference: Theory and methods. *Computing Surveys*, 15(3):237–269, 1983.

[Bro89]   Heather Brown. Standards for structured documents. *The Computer Journal*, 32(6):505–514, December 1989.

[FX94]   Peter Fankhauser and Yi Xu. Markitup! An incremental approach to document structure recognition. *Electronic Publishing - Origination, Dissemination and Design*, 6(4):447–456, 1994.

[Gol90]   C. F. Goldfarb. *The SGML Handbook*. Oxford University Press, 1990.

[HI94]   Tao Hu and Rolf Ingold. A mixed approach toward an efficient logical structure recognition from document images. *Electronic Publishing - Origination, Dissemination and Design*, 6(4):457–468, 1994.

[HU79]   John E. Hopcroft and Jeffrey D. Ullman. *Introduction to Automata Theory, Languages and Computation*. Addison Wesley, Reading, MA, 1979.

[KLMN90] Pekka Kilpeläinen, Greger Lindén, Heikki Mannila, and Erja Nikunen. A structured document database system. In Richard Furuta, editor, *EP90 – Proceedings of the International Conference on Electronic Publishing, Document Manipulation & Typography*, The Cambridge Series on Electronic Publishing, pages 139–151. Cambridge University Press, 1990.

[Mug90] Stephen Muggleton. *Inductive Acquisition of Expert Knowledge.* Addison Wesley, Reading, MA, 1990.

[ODA89] Information Processing – Text and Office Systems – Office Document Architecture (ODA) and Interchange Format. Technical Report ISO/IEC 8613, International Organization for Standardization ISO/IEC, Geneva/New York, 1989.

[Qui89] Vincent Quint. Systems for the manipulation of structured documents. In J. André, R. Furuta, and V. Quint, editors, *Structured Documents*, The Cambridge Series on Electronic Publishing, pages 39–74. Cambridge University Press, 1989.

[SEM94] Giovanni Semeraro, Floriana Esposito, and Donato Malerba. Learning contextual rules for document understanding. In *Proceedings of the Tenth IEEE Conference on Artificial Intelligence for Applications*, pages 108–115, 1994.

[SGM86] Information Processing – Text and Office Systems – Standard Generalized Markup Language (SGML). Technical Report ISO/IEC 8879, International Organization for Standardization ISO/IEC, Geneva/New York, 1986.

[Suo90] *Suomen kielen perussanakirja. Ensimmäinen osa (A–K).* Valtion painatuskeskus, Helsinki, 1990.

[SZ86] S.N. Srihari and G.W. Zack. Document image analysis. In *Proceedings of the Eighth International Conference on Pattern Recognition*, pages 434–436. IEEE Computer Society Press, 1986.

[TYS94] Yuan Yan Tang, Chang De Yan, and Ching Y. Suen. Document processing for automatic knowledge acquisition. *IEEE Transactions on Knowledge and Data Engineering*, 6(1):3–21, 1994.

A comparison of syntactic and statistical techniques for off-line OCR

S. Lucas*, E. Vidal**, A. Amiri*, S. Hanlon* and J.C. Amengual**
* Department of Electronic Systems Engineering,
University of Essex,
Colchester CO4 3SQ, UK
** Departamento de Sistemas Informaticos y Computacion,
Universidad Politecnica Valencia,
46071 Valencia, Spain

Abstract

This paper compares a number of different statistical and syntactic recognition methods on a difficult off-line OCR dataset. The motivation for such a test is to show that syntactic methods can perform as robustly as purely statistical techniques on noisy data. The main result is that, even given a very simplistic and idiosyncratic input coding, the syntactic method performs slightly better than any of the other methods. Furthermore, it is likely that the syntactic method could significantly outperform the other methods given a less idiosyncratic input coding.

1 Introduction

This paper compares a number of different statistical and syntactic recognition methods on a difficult off-line OCR dataset. The aim is to provide an account of the relative strengths and weaknesses of each approach.

One of the main motivations for such a test is the widespread belief within the pattern recognition community that while syntactic pattern recognition is a nice idea, for practical applications it is unsuitable due to:

- The need to extract 'primitives' – the terminals of the grammar in a robust manner;

- Problems in inferring a grammar once the samples are processed into strings/graphs of primitives;

- Parsing is traditionally seen as a rather cumbersome and slow process. Even given success with the above points, the final system will be too slow for practical use.

The first point can be circumvented by simply not bothering to extract any but the most low-level primitives. In this case, each image is coded as a string of over four possible orthogonal movements in two dimensions: North, East, South and West, as explained below. This process is extremely fast, simple and is explained in more detail below.

The second point is overcome by choosing to model the pattern classes as regular languages or other simple and theoretically adequate choices that have the benefit of fast, robust and accurate inference methods.

With respect to the third point, it should be pointed out that the most accurate syntactic methods employed in this paper seem not to be as fast as most of the statistical methods used, but well known techniques do exist to dramatically increase the speed of these syntactic methods (c.f. Section 4.2). Moreover, they do offer better recognition accuracy both on the training data, and especially on unseen test data.

The rest of this paper is structured as follows: the next Section describes the chain coding technique and the syntactic methods used, Section 3 outlines the feature extraction and statistical methods used, Section 4 describes the dataset and the results obtained, and finally, Section 5 concludes.

2 Syntactic Approaches

The very division into syntactic and statistical approaches is somewhat flawed, since in fact all the syntactic methods used here incorporate statistical techniques as well. In this sense, syntactic recognition techniques may be seen as a superset of statistical methods. Here, if the approach works with a chain code of the images, we describe it in this Section, while if it works with the raw image or some other type of (not string-based) features, we include it in the next Section.

2.1 The chain-coding procedure

The chain-coding procedure was designed to be as simple as possible. The procedure used uses just four direction vectors, and retains *all* the information in the original binary image – in fact, it is a type of lossless compression algorithm for this data, and compresses the images by a factor of about 10:1.

The procedure first detects all the edge transitions in the images, assigning four possible codes according to whether the transition is in a direction from top to bottom, or left to right, and whether it is going from white to black or black to white. These edges are then followed in specific directions, and connected up into strings. The starting point for each chain-code is found by scanning the image from top to bottom, left to right.

In fact, minor variations in the bitmap can cause rather dramatic changes in the chain-code, as illustrated in Figure 1. Here we see the omission of a single pixel changing two codes into one, and actually completely altering the symbol set of the coding of the interior edge. The first two numbers are the X and Y start positions of the chain, the rest is the chain code itself.

Most images consist of more than one chain code, but all the syntactic methods here are applied to build models of just one string for each pattern. We map a set of strings for a given image to a single string by removing the positional information (i.e. the X and Y start co-ordinates), and then concatenating the strings together. This operation destroys important information, and is only intended as a simple interim measure.

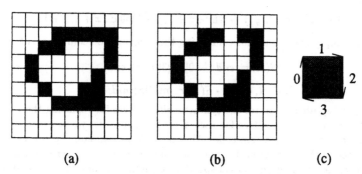

(a)　　　　　　　　(b)　　　　　　　(c)

Figure 1: The sensitivity of the chain-coding algorithm to minor changes in the bitmap. The two images above differ only in a single pixel, but the first one (a) produces the strings: (3 1 11111222322233330303001010) (4 1 233221211010100333) while the second one (b) produces the string: (3 1 11232332212110101003011222322233330303001010). (c) shows the coding of the edge transitions as movement symbols 0,1,2 and 3.

This sort of arbitrary sensitivity is enough to put one off applying this strategy further, but Vidal et al. [8] showed that grammatical inference techniques such as the ECGI were able to cope with such variations to a reasonable degree.

2.2　Syntactic Chain-coding

Instead of writing a special purpose piece of code for performing the task, it is instead possible to describe the rules of chain-coding as productions in an attribute grammar.

This way, the knowledge is specified in a fully declarative way, and is therefore easier to modify and maintain. Furthermore, it is possible in principle (though this has not yet been tried), to infer the grammar for the chain-code directly – hence, we could develop this part of the system without doing any programming at all!

For now, we just show the grammatical rules that take care of this part of the system. Consider the single pixel shown in Figure 1(c). This shows the direction vectors associated with each of the possible four edge transitions (black to white and white to black in either the vertical or horizontal axes). Assuming that each pixel is a square of side 2 units, and that we label pixel map edges with even co-ordinates, then we can specify how to label the edge-map with the following attribute grammar rules. The attribute of each pixel is the co-ordinate of its centre, while the attribute of each edge is the set of its start and end points. Pixel co-ordinates increase from bottom to top and from left to right. The white and black pixel colours are the terminals of this grammar, and are not divisible into any sub-components.

$$0(\{x,y\}, \{x,y+2\}) \rightarrow white(x-1,y+1)black(x+1,y+1)$$

$$1(\{x,y\}, \{x+2,y\}) \rightarrow white(x+1,y+1)black(x+1,y-1)$$

$$2(\{x,y\}, \{x,y-2\}) \rightarrow white(x+1,y-1)black(x-1,y-1)$$

$$3(\{x,y\},\{x-2,y\}) \rightarrow \text{white}(x+1,y-1)\text{black}(x+1,y+1)$$

Then, we simply need a rule for connecting these chain-code components together:

$$S(start,end) \rightarrow 0|1|2|3(start,end)$$

$$S(start,end) \rightarrow S(start,mid)S(mid,end)$$

where the '|' symbol separates the syntactic alternatives for replacing the LHS.

Then, having built a parse-tree for each distinct chain code, we can read off the leaf nodes in order to render the chain-code. Alternatively, we can add the concatenation of the chain-codes to the attribute rules, and build up the code as we perform the parse.

The advantage of the grammatical specification is that it only took twenty minutes to write (and it would take about this much time again to debug it), and it can then be used to drive a standard attribute grammar parser (or the rules can be almost directly implemented in Prolog, for example).

The advantage of the C program is that it gets the most out of the machine i.e. it is very fast and uses very little storage space; however, the grammatical approach is excellent for rapid prototyping.

2.3   ECGI

Error Correcting Grammatical Inference (ECGI) is a learning method that was introduced to obtain structural, finite-state models of (one-dimensional) objects from samples of these objects. The ECGI algorithm can be considered as a Grammatical Inference "heuristic", as opposed to other Grammatical Inference methodologies, often referred to as "characterizable" [4]. As an heuristic technique, ECGI explicitly incorporates certain task domain knowledge in its inference procedure. In particular, it was specially designed to capture relevant regularities exhibited by (the concatenation of) local substructures of the considered (one-dimensional) patterns, as well as by the lengths of these substructures. ECGI strongly relies on Error-Correcting Parsing and, as such, aims at learning not only syntactic or structural models of the patterns considered, but also *models of the errors or irregularities* that these patterns tend to present with respect to the learnt pattern models. ECGI completely builds these stochastic finite-state models throughout a single incremental pass over the training data. In the test phase, both the object-models and the corresponding error-models are cooperatively used to recognise new objects through stochastic error-correcting parsing. For more technical descriptions of ECGI see [5] [8]. ECGI has traditionally been applied to Automatic Speech Recognition problems and only recently has it started to be applied in the field of Image Processing and, more specifically, to Planar Shape Recognition tasks such as printed and handwritten digit recognition [7] [8].

2.4   MGGI

MGGI stands for Morphic Generator Grammatical Inference. The idea is that the stochastic kTSSLs (eg. BI-gram and TRI-gram) languages have nice properties in that they are theoretically learnable and there exist fast algorithms for inferring them in practice. However, when applied to many problems, the inferred models tend to be over-general. This can be overcome to some extent by passing the data through a re-naming function (the morphic generator). This expands the original alphabet of symbols, according to some criteria. For example, the renaming function used here, adds a subscript to each symbol depending on which tenth of the string the symbol occurs. For example,

$$00112233001122330011 \rightarrow 0_00_01_11_12_22_23_33_30_40_41_51_52_62_63_73_70_80_81_91_9$$

The use of the MGGI does not stop at this, and in fact, in our implementation we actually use another separate morphic generator to rename the symbols as bigrams. Then, whatever morphic generator we use, we use the same simplistic counter to estimate the monogram probability distribution of the transformed language. Hence, the language 'inference' algorithm is identical whether we are estimating bigram or trigram (or whatever) distributions, and this has a pleasing elegance.

2.5 Hidden Markov Models (HMMs)

Since HMMs are (more or less) theoretically equivalent to stochastic regular grammars (and these are what the ECGI method learns), we might expect the HMM and ECGI approaches to render similar results. As shown in the results below, however, this is not the case. The difference in perspective leads to different training algorithms. The HMM perspective leads us to re-estimate the statistics of a fixed model, while the grammatical inference perspective of the ECGI algorithm leads to models where the number of states (non-terminals) reflects the structure of the training data – the ECGI models for all the classes here have hundreds of states, with highly class-dependent state transition structures.

The HMMs used here had 10 hidden states, though we also experimented with alternative numbers up to 20 with no significant improvement. Beyond this size, training times become unreasonable compared to the other methods employed here.

2.6 Other syntactic possibilities

It should be pointed out that while statistical methods for OCR have been explored quite thoroughly, syntactic methods have only been the subject of sporadic bursts of interest.

Hence, although some of the syntactic methods reported here actually work rather well, there is still plenty of scope for improvement. In particular, the use of automatically inferred attribute grammars could provide generalisation power well beyond the limit of purely statistical methods.

Consider the image in Figure 2. Syntactic methods based on suitable attribute grammars have the potential to parse all the information in such images, recording all the structures that appear in different sizes, without ever having seen such multi-resolution images before. The syntactic methods employed in this paper do not offer the possibility of such generalisation power, but this is a very intersting avenue for future work.

Figure 2: What should the ideal recognition routine return in this case? At one level of resolution, we have the (times-roman) letters A – W in various positions. At a coarser level of resolution, we have perhaps a hand-written numeral '2'. Syntactic analysis has the potential to output all this information in a single parse of an image.

3 Statistical Approaches

In this Section we describe the statistical methods used in this paper. The techniques used are n-tuple sampling, which works on the images directly, and also, feature extraction methods, where the extracted features are then classified by a weighted Euclidean metric (this simple classifier is used as a baseline), and beyond this, a multi-layer perceptron (MPL) neural network, using the feature vectors as input.

3.1 N-tuple sampling

The n-tuple sampling method [1] is extremely attractive due to its simplicity and speed. The results shown in this paper were based on 100 10-tuples, each looking at a random 10 bits of the image bitmap. The present results incorporate no pre-processing at all, though we believe these can be improved by, for example centering each image be for presenting it to the n-tuple system, both for training and testing.

3.2 The Feature Extraction Methods

Each character in the database is stored as a $42 \times 50 = 2100$ bitmap. It was considered inappropriate to give this directly as input to the MLP, since this would lead to large networks (implying long training times), with the problem that as the number of weights in the network grows, so we need more training data to estimate the weights accurately.

The feature extraction methods used here are the radial transform, derived from the outermost-point method of Yamamoto and Mori [2], and a hard-wired version of the Hough transform.

The radial transform was adopted because it allows an enormous reduction in the number of features (in this case, from 2100 down to 16), while capturing much of the information necessary to describe a character (i.e. from a radial transform of a character we can perform an inverse transform, and in many cases obtain something recognisable as the original class).

The Hough transform was selected for its ability to pick out straight line information, something the radial transform is not particularly sensitive to; hence, it was expected to provide a useful complement.

3.3 Radial Transform

To take the radial transform of the input, we first find its centre of gravity, then place each point in a number of angularly defined bins around this centre, together with its distance from the centre.

Here we chose to use 16 bins – hence each bin corresponds to an angular range of 22.5 degrees. The procedure is illustrated in Figure 3.

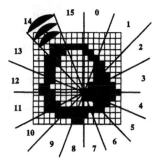

Figure 3: Constructing the radial mean vectors. After finding the centre-of-gravity of the image, we then place each pixel within an angular bin. Then, for each bin we find the mean distance of the black pixels from the centre of gravity. The means are then used to form a feature vector.

3.4 Hough Transform

The Hough Transform (HT) is a powerful method for extracting (usually simple) parametric figures such as lines or circles from images. The HT takes as input an image in pixel space, maps this to a signal in edge space, then maps this to a representation in parameter space. For example, if we are looking for straight lines, a possible parameter space (in fact, the one we adopt here) would be the 2-d space of orientation and distance from origin.

Here we adopt a very simple version of the HT where we only consider lines of 4 specific orientations, each one in 10 possible positions. This gives us 40-dimensional feature vectors, where each dimension consists of the evidence for that particular line.

This is illustrated in Figure 4, though this is not precisely what occurs in our current implementation; in fact, what actually happens is that we consider 40 central lines of each orientation, then sum the evidence of each adjacent set of 4 lines, to reduce the feature vectors to 10 dimensions for each orientation, or 40 in total.

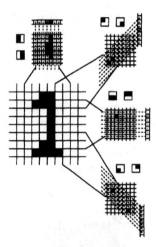

Figure 4: The hard-wired Hough Transform. Four edge maps are produced, by passing a convolution operator over the pixel image. The values in appropriate subsets of these maps are then summed to produce an accumulation of the evidence for a particular line segment.

3.5 MLPs

During the last ten years we have witnessed a great resurgence of interest in neural networks, and of the many different architectures the MLP has so far proved the most successful at a wide variety of pattern classification tasks, generally outperforming simple statistical approaches (eg. weighted Euclidean classifiers) and other types of neural net. While more advanced statistical techniques (e.g. based on classifiers that account for the co-variance between feature dimensions, such as those utilising Mahalanobis distance measures, for example) can rival MLP results, they are often more difficult to apply in practice and tend to make more assumptions about the distribution of the data.

In summary, MLPs are used a lot in practice because they usually perform at least as well as other techniques and are simpler to apply. The disadvantages are that training may be slow (though this was not really a problem in the work reported here), and that some kind of feature extraction is usually still necessary; here it was not considered feasible to work directly with the raw bit map of over 2000 pixels as the input vector.

The MLPs used below had a single hidden layer with 80 units in – this had the best performance both on the training and testing sets, when compared with MLPs with 10, 20 40 and 160 hidden units respectively.

4 Results

So far, we have obtained results on the University of Essex post office database The previous best results, on the same set of test characters were obtained by a PhD student who spent a good deal of time honing a statistical approach, that eventually produced results of about 81.2% accuracy, at a rate of about 1 seconds per character [3]. The characters consist of 42×50 bitmaps (2100 pixels), that have been automatically segmented from digitally scanned hand-written envelopes, from a large number of writers. The characters are divided into training and testing sets, with an average of 200 per class in the training set and slightly more than this in the test set. In fact, the separation was not done on a random basis, and the training characters were selected mostly as being reasonably good models. The reasons for this are historical, and this separation is probably to the detriment of all the methods under test here.

Hence, there is more variation in the test data than there is in the training data. Consider the MLP in Table 1. When we switch the training and test sets, we get a performance of 96.7% (c.f. 99.2%) on the training set and 86.8% (c.f. 79.1%) on the test set.

This effect was explored in some more detail; for the same numeric dataset (Table 1), we also reversed the datasets for the weighted Euclidean classifier. This reversal produced the most dramatic insight into the statistical differences between the training and test sets; with reversal we get 76.8% on the training set (c.f. 85.5%) and 76.6% on the test set (c.f. 60.5%).

An example of the difference between the sets is shown in Figures 5 and 6.

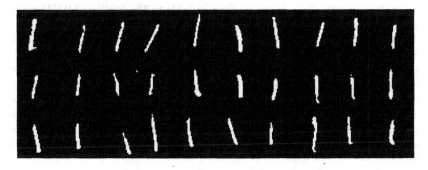

Figure 5: The first 30 ones in the training set.

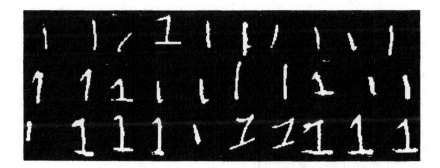

Figure 6: The first 30 ones in the test set.

All the results reported do not seem very high in absolute terms, but this is a very difficult set of data, and NTUPLE* for example, has already been applied to the large

METHOD	TRAINING-SET	TEST-SET
ECGI	95.8	85.8
MGGI	67.5	63.2
HMM	42.1	36.2
NTUPLE	91.7	41.2
NTUPLE*	100	85.6
EUC	85.5	60.5
MLP	99.2	79.2

Table 1: Recognition rates (in percent) for the various approaches.

CEDAR hand-written numeral database (supplied by the University of Buffalo, New York State) with results of over 90% accuracy on the test set.

4.1 Recognition Accuracy

The results for recognition accuracy are shown in Table 1. The ECGI and HMM methods were applied to exactly the same set of strings (chain codes derived from the images). The N-TUPLE row refers to a WISARD type system [1] applied to the raw image. N-TUPLE* shows the very significant improvement we get when we apply some pre-processing to the image (such as scale and translation normalisations) in addition to having specific n-tuple maps for each character. EUC denotes a weighted Euclidean classifier working in the space of combined radial mean and hough transform features, while MLP denotes an MLP with 80 hidden units working in this same feature space. Not only does the ECGI work best out of them all, but it worked as an *off the shelf* package, with no tuning or tweaking required at all (in fact, various options are possible, but these results just use the default options).

4.2 Training and Recognition Speed

Table 2 shows the average per-character training and classification times. Where feature extraction is used, this time added just once *not* to the training time, since it is a one-off process (for example, the MLPs were trained in 200 iterations, but the features only had to be extracted once – hence, for this case, the feature extraction time becomes negligible). However, for the recognition, we assume that it has to be performed once per classification, since each character to be classified in this phase will generally be novel. The average time to produce a chain code was 40 milli-seconds; to produce the combined radial and HT feature vectors was 90 milliseconds. As always with actual CPU timing results, these figures have to be treated with some degree of caution. For example, how much of the time taken is due to the essential cost of the algorithm, and how much due to inefficient programming techniques?

Nevertheless, given that all the algorithms here are implemented in C (and written by competent programmers) and the timings are based on running the algorithms on the same platform (SUN SPARC ELC rated at 22mips), we believe them to be of sufficient interest to publish.

METHOD	TRAINING	CLASSIFICATION
ECGI	810 + 40	12000 + 40
MGGI	11 + 40	16 + 40
HMM	24100 + 4	500 + 40
NTUPLE	34 + 0	34 + 0
NTUPLE*	34 + 120	34 + 120
EUC	1 + 90	1 + 90
MLP	1458 + 0	3 + 90

Table 2: Timing in milli-seconds for the training and recognition of per-character of each approach, plus the time taken for feature extraction or chain coding. MLP based on convergence in 200 iterations, HMMs converged in 10 iterations (other methods are non-iterative).

In fact, the speed obtained by most of the methods is quite reasonable, bearing in mind that each images consists of 2100 pixels, and most sentences (chain codes) are several hundred symbols long.

From the reported results, ECGI appears to be the slowest technique. However, one should take into account that the recognition algorithm used in this work was just the basic (and hence slowest) version of the Stochastic Error Correcting parser. In fact, orders of magnitude faster performance is possible, without (significantly) sacrificing the accuracy, by using more efficient parsing techniques such as those already used in [6] for ECGI-based Speech Recognition tasks. This has already been explored to some extent, by using a beam-search strategy to perform the error-correcting parse of each test pattern. The default is to effectively use an infinite width beam. By using a beam width of 15 (instead of infinite), the recognition time for each character reduces to about 2000 milliseconds. However, this reduced search also reduced the recognition rate to 80.4%. The time reflects the fact that each model (one per class) now takes about 200 millisecond to process an input string. A further significant improvement in time can be made by compiling all the class-models into a single model, but this has not yet been done.

5 Conclusions

We have shown syntactic recognition techniques to be of interest to practical off-line OCR problems. So far, the best method in terms of recognition accuracy has been the ECGI algorithm. As mentioned above, although the implementation of the algorithm used here is significantly slower than most of the other methods, this can be dramatically improved by the use of a beam search in the classification phase. Furthermore, the ECGI method has a powerful advantage over all the other techniques: it is much easier to apply. While with all the other methods, there are decisions to be made (for example, which features to extract, how many states to have in the HMM, how many hidden units to have in the MLP, which morphism to use in the MGGI), and hence the process of getting results is iterative and somewhat laborious, the ECGI method works out all the parameters (i.e. the number of states) for itself, and therefore requires less skill and insight on behalf of the user.

Finally, it is worth emphasising that the ECGI is just one possible syntactic pattern recognition method that performs well *despite* the idiosyncrasies of the input coding strategy. Work based on better input codings or superior grammatical structures (involving the use of attributes), which do not require any input pre-processing *at all* is already underway, and will be reported in a future paper.

Acknowledgements

This work was partially supported by SERC grant GR/J 52969, SERC grant GR/J 66959 under the DTI/SERC Speech and Language Technology (SALT) scheme and the Spanish CICYT, under grant TIC93-0633-C02-01

References

[1] I. Aleksander, "Wisard – a radical step forward in image recognition," *Sensor Review*, vol. July, pp. 120 – 124, (1984).

[2] K. Yamamoto and S. Mori, "Recognition of hand-printed characters by an outermost point method," *Pattern Recognition*, vol. 12, pp. 229 – 236, (1980).

[3] R. Tregidgio, "Parallel implementation of statistical classifiers for optical character recognition," *PhD Thesis, University of Essex*, (1992).

[4] D.Angluin, C.H.Smith: "Inductive Inference: Theory and Methods". Computing Surveys, Vol.15, N 3, 1983.

[5] H.Rulot, E.Vidal: "Modelling (Sub)string-Length-Based Constraints through a Grammatical Inference Method". In "Patter Recognition: Theory and Applications". Eds: Devijver and Kittler, pp. 451-459, Springer Verlag, 1987.

[6] F.Torro, E.Vidal, H.Rulot: "Fast and Accurate Speaker Independent Speech Recognition Using Structurals Models Learnt by the ECGI", in "Signal Processing V: Theories and Applications". L.Torres, E.Masgrav, M.A.Lagunas (Eds.). Elsevier Science Pub., 1990.

[7] E.Vidal, H.Rulot, J.M.Valiente, G.Andreu: "Font Independent Mixed-Size Digit Recognition Through Error-Correcting Grammatical Inference (ECGI)". ICPR-Proc., La Hague, pp.334-337, 1992.

[8] E.Vidal, H.Rulot, J.M.Valiente and G.Andreu: "Recognition of Planar Shapes Through the Error-Correcting Grammatical Inference Algorithm (ECGI)", First Int. Colloquium on Grammatical Inference: Theory, Applications and Alternatives, Proc. University of Essex, April 1993.

The algorithms RT and k-TTI: A first comparison.*

José Ruiz and Pedro García
Departamento de Sistemas Informáticos y Computación
Universidad Politécnica de Valencia

I.-INTRODUCTION

Recognizable tree sets are a generalization of regular languages [Gécsec and Steinby, 84]. The property that defines them is that they can be accepted by tree automata. Many properties of regular languages can be extended to recognizable tree sets in a very natural way. In particular, it is possible to obtain certain subfamilies of the class of recognizable tree sets as a generalization of subclasses of the class of regular languages. This is the case of two families that can be learned using positive data, the 0-reversible languages [Angluin, 82] and k-testable languages in strict sense [McNaughton, 74].

Learning recognizable tree sets or some of its subclasses is interesting for its relation to context-free languages. For any CFL, the set of skeletons of its derivation trees is a recognizable tree set, so CF languages can be learned from skeletons of their derivation trees with algorithms very similar to those used for regular languages.

We present here a first experimental comparison between two algorithms -RT and k-TTI algorithms- that learn recognizable tree sets. Both have the property that they identify in the limit a subfamily of recognizable sets from positive structural descriptions: the class of 0-reversible sets [Sakakibara, 92], and the class of k-testable sets [García, 92]. The comparison faces the possibility of aproximating languages generated from arbitrary context-free grammars using skeletons of its derivation trees.

II.-PRELIMINARIES AND NOTATION

Let N be the set of natural numbers and $(N^*, \cdot)$ the free monoid generated by N with λ as the identity. We define $u \leq w$ for $u, w \in N^*$ iff there exists $v \in N^*$ such that $w = u.v$ ($u<w$ if $u \leq w$ and $u \neq w$). For $x \in N^*$, we define the *length* of x denoted by $|x|$ as follows:

$$|\lambda| = 0$$
$$|x \cdot n| = |x| + 1 \text{ for } n \in N$$

$D \subseteq N^*$ is a *tree domain* iff it satisfies: a) $v \in D$ and $u < v$ implies $u \in D$ b) if $u.i \in D$, $i \in N$, then $u.j \in D$ for $1 \leq j \leq i$.

A *ranked alphabet* V is a finite set associated with a finite relation $r \subseteq (V \times N)$. V_n denotes the subset of V: $\{s \in V \mid (s, n) \in r\}$.

A tree t over a ranked alphabet V is a mapping $t : D \rightarrow V$ with D being a tree domain called domain of t and denoted by $dom(t)$. The set of finite trees over V will be called V^T. The alphabet can be seen as a set of function symbols having different arities in the way that V^T can be considered as the set of terms over V. For example, the tree shown in Figure 1 (left) can be represented as $S(A(a,b),B(c,C(c)))$.

---

*Work supported in part by the Spanish CICYT under grants TIC93-0633-CO2 and TIC1026/92-CO2.

Let $t \in V^T$ and $x \in dom(t)$. The *depth* of x is defined as $depth(x) = |x|$ and the depth of t as $depth(t) = max\{depth(x) \mid x \in dom(t)\}$. The *subtree* of t rooted at x, denoted as t/x is defined as : $dom(t/x) = \{y \mid x.y \in dom(t)\}$ and $(t/x)(y) = t(x.y) \quad \forall y \in dom(t/x)$. If $t \in V^T$, then $ST(t)$ is the set of subtrees of t, that is, $ST(t) = \{t/x \mid x \in dom(t)\}$ and for the set $T \subseteq V^T$, $ST(T) = \bigcup_{t \in T} ST(t)$. The *replacement* of the subtree t/x with $s \in V^T$ is defined as:

$$t(x \leftarrow s)(y) = \begin{cases} t(y) \text{ if } |y| \leq |x|; \ y \neq x \ ; y \in dom(t); \\ s(z) \text{ if } y = x.z; \ z \in dom(s) \end{cases}$$

A *skeletal alphabet* is a ranked alphabet with exactly one symbol that has arities greater or equal to one. If Sk denotes such an alphabet and V_0 is an alphabet of symbols whose arity is zero, a tree over $Sk \cup V_0$ is called a *skeleton* (all its inner nodes are labelled by σ and the leaves are symbols from V_0). If $t \in V^T$, $sk(t)$ denotes the *skeleton* of t, which is obtained labelling with σ all the inner nodes of t. For the set $T \subseteq V^T$, the set of skeletons associated to the trees in T is $sk(T) = \bigcup_{t \in T} sk(t)$.

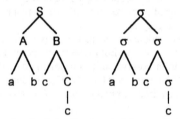

Fig.1. Example of a derivation tree and its associated skeleton

Let V be a ranked alphabet and m the greatest arity of the symbols in V. A *deterministic tree automaton* (DTA) is defined as the four-tuple $A = (Q, V, \delta, F)$ where Q is a finite set (states), $F \subseteq Q$ is the set of final states and $\delta = (\delta_0, \delta_1 \ldots \delta_m)$ the set of state transition functions defined by:

$\delta_k : (V_k \times Q^k) \to Q, \ k = 1, 2, \ldots, m$

$\delta_0(a) = a, \quad \forall a \in V_0$

δ can be extended to operate on trees as follows:

$$\delta(\sigma(t_1, \ldots t_n)) = \begin{cases} \delta_n(\sigma, \delta(t_1), \ldots \delta(t_n)) \text{ if } n > 0 \\ \delta_0(\sigma) \qquad\qquad \text{ if } \ n = 0 \end{cases}$$

A tree $t \in V^T$ is accepted by A if $\delta(t) \in F$. The set of trees accepted by A is defined as $T(A) = \{t \in V^T \mid \delta(t) \in F\}$

For a context-free grammar $G = (N, \Sigma, P, S)$ and for each symbol $X \in N \cup \Sigma$ we define the set of trees from G rooted at X as:

$$D_X(G) = \begin{cases} \{a\} \text{ if } X = a \in \Sigma \\ \{X(t_1, \ldots t_k) : X \to B_1 \ldots B_k, \ t_i \in D_{B_i}(G)(1 \leq i \leq k)\} \text{ if } A \in N \end{cases}$$

$DS(G)$ denotes the set of *derivation trees* of G. If $Sk = \{\sigma\}$, the set of trees over $Sk \cup \Sigma$ which are skeletons associated to trees in $DS(G)$ is denoted by $sk(D(G))$. Both $DS(G)$ and $sk(D(G))$ are regular tree sets.

Let $A = (Q, Sk \cup \Sigma, \delta, F)$ be a *DTA* for a set of skeletons. There exists a context-free grammar $G=(N, \Sigma, P, S)$ such that $sk(D(G)) = T(A)$ which can be obtained as follows:

$$N = Q \cup \{S\};$$

$$P = \{\delta_k(\sigma, q_1, \ldots, q_k) \to q_1, \ldots, q_k : k \geq 1, \ \sigma \in Sk_k, q_1, \ldots, q_k \in Q \}$$

$$\cup \{S \to q_1, \ldots, q_k : n \geq 1, \ \delta_k(\sigma, q_1, \ldots, q_k) \in F\}.$$

III. K-TESTABLE TREE SETS IN THE STRICT SENSE

Let (V, r) be a ranked alphabet, $k \geq 2$ and let V^T be the set of finite trees over V. For every $t \in V^T$, the *k-test vector* of t is defined as: $Test_k(t) = (r_{k-1}(t), \ l_{k-1}(t), \ p_k(t))$ where:

$$r_{k-1}(t) = \begin{cases} t \quad \text{if depth } (t) \leq k - 2 \\ t' : depth(t') = k - 2, dom(t') = dom_{k-2}(t), t'(y) = t(y) \forall y' \in dom(t') \\ \qquad \text{if depth } (t) > k - 2 \end{cases}$$

where $dom_k(t) = \{x \in dom(t) : |x| \leq k\}$.

$$p_k(t) = \begin{cases} \varnothing \quad \text{if} \quad depth(t) < k - 1 \\ \{r_k(t') : t' \in ST(t), depth(t') \geq k - 1\} \quad \text{if } depth(t) \geq k - 1 \end{cases}$$

$$l_{k-1}(t) = \{t' \in ST(t) : depth(t') \leq k - 2\}$$

Example 1. Let

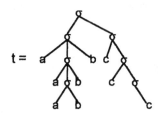

Then:

$$r_2(t)=$$

$$p_3(t) = \{ \qquad , \qquad , \qquad , \qquad , \qquad \}$$

$$l_2(t) = \{ \qquad , \qquad a, b, c \}$$

Let $\equiv_k$ be the equivalence relation in V^T defined as:

$\forall s, t \in V^T$, $s \equiv_k t \iff Test_k(s) = Test_k(t)$. Obviously $\equiv_k$ is a subtree invariant relation of finite index. A set $T \subseteq V^T$ is k-Testable (k-T) iff it is the union of some of the equivalence classes defined by $\equiv_k$. (so k-T sets are also regular sets). A set is *Locally Testable* (*LT*) if t is k-T for some k. A tree language is k-Testable in a *Strict* sense (k-TS) if there exist three finite sets R, L and P such that for every $t \in T$:

$$r_{k-1}(t) \in R, \quad l_{k-1}(t) \subseteq L, \quad p_k(t) \subseteq P.$$

The family of the k-T languages is the boolean closure of the k-TS family.

REMARK: An equivalence relation $\equiv$ defined over V^T is called *subtree invariant* if $t_1 \equiv t_2$ implies $\forall t \in V^T$, $\forall x \in D_t$, $t(x \leftarrow t_1) \equiv t(x \leftarrow t_2)$.

IV. THE k-TTI INFERENCE ALGORITHM

We can associate to the finite subset $S \subseteq V^T$ the four-tuple $Z_k(S) = (V(S), R_k(S), L_k(S), P_k(S))$ being $V(S)$ the ranked alphabet from S and

$R_k(S) = \{r_{k-1}(t): t \in S\}$, $L_k(S) = \bigcup_{t \in S} l_{k-1}(t)$, $P_k(S) = \bigcup_{t \in S} p_k(t)$.

The language defined by $Z_k(S)$ will be denoted as $T_k(S)$

Properties. Let S, S' be two finite tree sets, $k \geq 2$ and $T_k(S)$ and $T_k(S')$. Then:

a) $S \subseteq T_k(S)$

b) $T_k(S)$ is the smallest k-TS tree set containing S

c) $S \subseteq S \implies T_k(S') \subseteq T_k(S)$

d) $T_{k+1}(S) \subseteq T_k(S)$

e) If $k > 1 + \max_{t \in S} \{depth(t)\}$ then $T_k(S) = S$

k-TTI Inference Algorithm

INPUT:	$k \geq 2$, S finite set of skeletons.
OUTPUT:	DTA $A_k = (Q, V, \delta, F)$
METHOD:	$(V, R, L, P) := (V(S), R_k(S), L_k(S), P_k(S))$
	$Q := R \cup L \cup p_{k-1}(P)$
	$F := R$
	$\forall t \in L \;\; \delta(t) := t$
	$\forall \sigma(t_1, \ldots, t_n) \in P \;\; \delta_n(\sigma, t_1, \ldots, t_n) := r_{k-1}(\sigma(t_1, \ldots, t_n))$
	$A_k = (Q, V, \delta, F)$

Fig. 2. Inference algorithm

Example 2. Let k = 3 and S the positive structural sample:

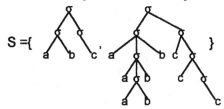

$A_3 = (Q, V, \delta, F)$, with:

$Q = \{$, a, b, c, ... $\}$

$F = \{$ ... $\}$

and the transition functions: $\delta_0(a) = a$; $\delta_0(b) = b$; $\delta_0(c) = c$; $\delta_1(\sigma, c) = \sigma(c)$;

$\delta_2(\sigma, a, b) = \sigma(a, b)$; $\delta_2(\sigma, \sigma(a, b), \sigma(c)) = \sigma(\sigma, \sigma)$; $\delta_2(\sigma, \sigma(a, \sigma, b), \sigma(c, \sigma)) = \sigma(\sigma, \sigma)$;

$\delta_2(\sigma, c, \sigma(c, \sigma)) = \sigma(c, \sigma)$; $\delta_2(\sigma, c, \sigma(c)) = \sigma(c, \sigma)$;

$\delta_3(\sigma, a, \sigma(a, \sigma, b), b) = \sigma(a, \sigma, b)$; $\delta_3(\sigma, a, \sigma(a, b), b) = \sigma(a, \sigma, b)$;

Example 4. Let $k=3$ and S be considered as a set of skeletons of a context-free grammar the same as Example 2. From the automaton A_3 obtained in Example 3, we obtain a context-free grammar $G=(N, \Sigma, P, S)$ such that $sk(D(G)) = T(A_3)$.

By renaming the states in $Q-\Sigma$ in order to simplify the notation: $\sigma(\sigma, \sigma) = A$, $\sigma(a, b) = A_2$, $\sigma(c) = B_2$, $\sigma(a, \sigma, b) = A_1$, $\sigma(c, \sigma) = B_1$, we obtain the following grammar:

$\Sigma = \{a, b, c\}$; $N = \{S, A_1, B_1, A_2, B_2\}$,

$P = \{S \to A_1 B_1 \mid A_2 B_2, A_1 \to aA_1 b \mid aA_2 b, B_1 \to cB_1 \mid cB_2, A_2 \to ab, B_2 \to c\}$

V. REVERSIBLE CONTEXT FREE GRAMMARS

DEFINITION. A context-free grammar $G = (N, \Sigma, P, S)$ is called *invertible* iff for any two productions of the form $A \to \alpha$ and $B \to \alpha$, then $A = B$. Invertible grammars constitute a normal form for CFGs.

DEFINITION. A context-free grammar $G = (N, \Sigma, P, S)$ is said to be *reset-free* if $\forall B, C \in N$, $\alpha, \beta \in (N \cup \Sigma)^*$, $(A \to \alpha B \beta$ and $A \to \alpha C \beta) \Rightarrow B = C$.

DEFINITION. A context-free grammar $G = (N, \Sigma, P, S)$ is *reversible* iff G is invertible and reset-free. Reversible grammars constitute a normal form for CFGs [Sakakibara, 92].

VI. RT LEARNING ALGORITHM FOR TREE AUTOMATA [Sakakibara, 92]

a) DESCRIPTION. The input to the algorithm is a finite set S of skeletons. It begins constructing the base tree automaton A for S and then generalizes by merging up states. Once it constructs the finest partition π_f of the set Q of states of A with the property that A/π_f is reversible, outputs A/π_f.

Begining with the trivial partition of Q, π_1, two distinct blocks B_1 and B_2 are merged in one of the stages of the process if any of the following conditions is satisfied:

1.- B_1 and B_2 contain final states of A. (A reversible tree automaton must contain just one final state).

2.-There exist $q \in B_1$ and $q' \in B_2$ with $q = \sigma(u_1, \ldots, u_k)$ and $q' = \sigma(u'_1, \ldots, u'_k)$ such that for $1 \le j \le k$, u_j and u'_j are in the same block or or the same terminal symbols. (Fig. 3)

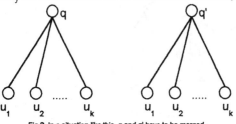

Fig 3. In a situation like this, q and q' have to be merged

3.- There exist two states q, q' with $q = \sigma(u_1, \ldots, u_k)$ and $q' = \sigma(u'_1, \ldots, u'_k)$ in the same block and an integer l ($1 \le l \le k$) such that $u_l \in B_1$ y $u'_l \in B_2$ and for $1 \le j \le k$ ($j \ne l$), u_j and u'_j are in the same block or the same terminal symbols.(Fig. 4)

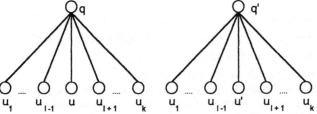

Fig 4.- If q and q' are in the same block, the blocks containing u and u' are merged

Next figure shows the algoritm RT as it is described in Sakakibara's article:

```
INPUT: a positive sample S of skeletons.
OUTPUT: a reversible skeletal tree automaton A.
METHOD:
        Let A = (Q, V, δ, F) the automaton SA(S);
        Let π₀ the trivial partition of Q;
        Choose q ∈ F;
        LIST = {(q,q'), ∀q' ∈ F - {q}};
        i = 0;
        While LIST ≠ ∅ do
                Remove the first element (q₁, q₂) from LIST;
                Let B₁ = B(q₁, πᵢ) and B₂ = B(q₂, πᵢ);
                If B₁ ≠ B₂ Then
                        πᵢ₊₁ = merge(πᵢ, B₁, B₂);
                        p-update (πᵢ₊₁) and s-update (πᵢ₊₁, B₁, B₂);
                        i++;
                end (if)
        end (while)
        f = i; Outputs A/π_f
end.
```

The two routines used in the algorithm are:

---

p-update(π_{i+1})

For all pairs of states $\sigma(u_1, \ldots, u_k)$ and $\sigma(u_1', \ldots, u_k')$ in Q with

$B(u_j, \pi_{i+1}) = B(u_j', \pi_{i+1})$ or $u_j = u_j' \in \Sigma$, $\forall 1 \le j \le k$ and

$B(\sigma(u_1, \ldots, u_k), \pi_{i+1}) \ne B(\sigma(u_1', \ldots, u_k'), \pi_{i+1})$

Add $(\sigma(u_1, \ldots, u_k), \sigma(u_1', \ldots, u_k'))$ a LIST.

---

s-update(π_{i+1}, B_1, B_2)

For all pair of states $\sigma(u_1, \ldots, u_k) \in B_1$ and $\sigma(u_1', \ldots, u_k') \in B_2$ such that

$u_l, u_l' \in Q$ and $B(u_l, \pi_{i+1}) \ne B(u_l', \pi_{i+1})$ for l, $1 \le l \le k$ and $\quad B(u_j, \pi_{i+1}) = B(u_j', \pi_{i+1})$ or

$u_j = u_j' \in \Sigma$, $\forall 1 \le j \le k$, $j \ne l$

Add the pair (u_l, u_l') a LIST

VII. EXPERIMENTAL RESULTS.

It has been theoretically proved that the algorithm k-TTI identifies the family of k-TS tree sets from positive structural information in the limit and so does the algorithm RT with CF reversible languages.

The experiments carried out so far are a first attempt to compare the behaviour of both algorithms when they are used to identify CFLs from structural descriptions of arbitrary (meaning that they need not be neither k-TS nor reversible) CF grammars. Those experiments are to be considered preliminary and we are currently doing a better comparison using more CFG grammars chosen in a random way.

We first chose 10 CFG in an arbitrary way from several "Formal Language Theory" books. For each of those grammars, appropiate sets of structural training and validation data were randomly generated. The training data consisted in a set of 100 skeletal trees obtained randomly from the grammar. The validation data -used to observe the evolution of the algorithm- consisted in a set of 400 of skeletal trees, also obtained from the grammar. These experiments were repeated 10 times for each grammar. The average of trainig sentences required for convergence of both algorithms is shown in Table 1 (1).

For each automata learned in this way, we obtained the corresponding CF grammar, as in II. Then we used Earley's algorithm to clasify the first 1000 sentences of Σ^* (in lexicographic order) with the target grammar and with the grammars obtained with the algorithms. The percentage of well classified sentences for different grammars is shown in Table 1.

The experiments have been done using Mathematica language [Wolfram, 91]. While RT has correctly classified about 5% more words than k-TTI (for k=3), the former seems to run much slower than the latter. For instance, training the fifth grammar of Table 1 with the same 50 skeletons took 18,89 seconds for the algorithm k-TTI and 795,49 seconds for the algorithm RT on a Next Station.

GRAMMARS	TSFC (1)		CCTS (2)	
	k-TTI	RT	k-TTI (K=3)	RT
S->AB A->aAb|ab, B->cB, B->c	7	5,6	100	100
S->aaA|bB|cbba, A->ab|B|abbA,B->cbc|aB|bA	13	9,6	98,7	100
S->aAaS|bSa|b, A->aaaB, B->bB|b	11	7,8	100	96
S->aSASb|Saa|b, A->caA|Ac|bca	22,3	8,5	100	100
S->SaB|Sa|aB|a, B->bB|b	30,8	6,6	100	100
S->aA|bA|b|a, A->bS|aS	11,3	4,8	49,4	100
S->AB|BC, A->AB|a, B->AA|CB|b,C->a|b	16	10	99,1	99,1
S->AbAbA|bAbA|AbbA|AbAb|bbA|bAb|Abb|bb,A->aA|a	2,8	3,7	100	100
S->aS|bA, A->aA|bB, B->aB|a	3,5	6	4,1	100
S->aB|bA, A->bAA|bA|a|aS, B->b|bS|aBB	7	11,5	100	10,94
AVERAGE	12,5	7,4	85,13	90,61

Table1. Rate of learning of the algorithms when tested with all the words of Σ^* up to length 10.
(1) Training sentences required for convergence.
(2) Correct clasification of the test set (%).

Some other features shown by the experiments done so far are:

(1) While the time needed by k-TTI is always increasing with the amount of data, RT may decrease some times (the time curves present some "saddle points").

(2) The grammars obtained with both algorithms classify correctly all the positive words of the language, they only may fail in overgeneralizing if the grammar is not of the correct type.

(3) The algorithm k-TTI achieves better classification rates for greater values of k, at the cost of less generalization (which means longer time of computation to get the definitive automata). The chosen value k = 3 is the one that gives better ratio: classification rate / learning-time.

VIII CONCLUSIONS

As it has been discussed, both the RT and k-TTI algorithms obtain similar results. They will hopefully work even better with CF grammars chosen randomly.

Our future experiments will try to measure in a more accurate way the classification rate and especially, the evolution of learning.

IX.-REFERENCES

[Angluin, 82] ANGLUIN, D. "Inference of reversible languages". Journal of the ACM, 29(3), 741-765, 1982.

[García, 90] GARCÍA, P. & VIDAL, E. (1990) "Inference of k-Testable Languages in the Strict Sense and Application to Syntactic Pattern Recognition". IEEE Transactions on Pattern Analysis and Machine Intelligence, Vol. PAMI-12(9), 920-925

[García,93] GARCÍA, P. (1993) "Learning K-Testable Tree Sets from positive data". Internal Report, U. P. Valencia DSIC-II/46/93.

[Gécseg, 84] GÉCSEG, F.-STEINBY, M. (1984) "Tree automata". Akadémiai Kiadó, Budapest.

[Mäkinen,92] MÄKINEN ERKKI (1992) "On the structural grammatical inference problem for some classes of context-free grammars", Information Processing Letters 42, 1-5. North-Holland.

[Mc Naughton, 74] MC NAUGHTON, R. "Algebraic decision procedures for local   testability" Mathematics Systems Theory, 8(1), 60-76, 1974.

[Sakakibara,92] SAKAKIBARA, Y. (1992) "Efficient Learning of Context-Free Grammars   from Positive Structural Examples", Information and Computation 97,   23-60.

[Wolfram, 91] WOLFRAM, S. "Mathematica, a system for doing Mathematics by computer", Addison Wesley, 1991.

Dynamic Grammatical Representations in Guided Propagation Networks

Martine Roques

LIMSI
BP 133
91403 ORSAY Cédex
France
E-mail: roques@limsi.fr

Abstract

This paper describes a connectionnist system which is able to build syntactic structures from examples. Inherent robustness to distortions and ability to complete internal representations in the course of processing allow noisy pattern parsing. Structured representations are obtained through extraction of syntactical substructures using different strategies. A comparison with classical grammar representation is presented.

Keywords: associative memory, unsupervised learning, syntax, automatic clustering

1 Introduction

The purpose of grammatical inference is to obtain a grammar, given a set of data it is supposed to generate, and occasionally a set it is supposed not to generate [1]. This way of teaching a system with both examples and counterexamples can be related to general computational strategies used in machine learning [2]. Moreover, the grammar should support generalization, in particular when faced with variable and noisy structures often encountered in natural language. This would fill the gap between paradigm and practice, a well-known drawback of grammatical inference [3]. The grammatical representation presented in this paper is built from examples, and its robustness to noisy patterns results from two properties: the occurrence of learning mechanisms during the processing, allowing the possible completion of internal representations; an associative memory which supports distortions of the input pattern (missing or supplementary items, inversion).

Links between Associative Memory models (sometimes called *connectionist systems* or *Neural Networks*) and grammatical inference have been established between Recurrent Neural Networks and stochastic regular grammars. The so-called backpropagation algorithm has thus been applied to layered networks in order to induce rewrite rules [4]. Some hybrid systems are able to decompose sentences into subject and predicate, then to detect the head of the subject [5]. But we are more interested in a memory model exhibiting grammatical inference. This does not seem to have been attempted yet [1].

The underlying associative memory is a Guided Propagation Network (GPN) [6]. This network of elementary processing units implements *coincidence detection* between input and internal signals in order to build and activate its internal representations. It has been developed for different Human-Machine Communication (HMC) tasks: our contribution to this work is to apply the model to representing syntactic structures of natural language, in close connection with speech processing. We are trying to represent the regularities of a training set of natural language sentences in a self-structuring network. A similar problem is presented in [7]. The initial syntactic knowledge required by the parsing system is a dictionary containing words and their respective classes. The system is then provided with a set of natural language sentences, from which grammatical structures are inferred. One can use the argument of "poverty of the stimulus" to assert that initial structures are necessary for processing natural language in a connectionist network [8], but our goal is to develop and study a device designed to be integrated inside a complete HMC system. Then the simultaneous cooperation of different such devices will imply the contribution of several stimuli.

This paper mainly describes the basic constituents and mechanisms involved in GPN, and focuses on the automatic extraction of syntactical substructures from examples using different connectionist strategies [9]. A comparison with a classical grammar representation is presented, and application to casual speech is then approached.

2 Presentation of the parser

2.1 Guided Propagation

Guided Propagation is a parallel and serial processing model which has been developed for HMC tasks, such as continuous speech recognition [10], model of reading [11], symbolic processing [12]. The complete system involves specialised modules, which are heavily interacting and are based on a unique computational architecture [13]. Within each module, processing units are able to detect coincidence in time and space between two flows of signals: predictions along internal memory pathways and incoming stimulation. Stimuli are represented by time-space patterns of activated Feature-Detectors (FD). Unexpected patterns are taken into account through the creation of new structures.

2.2   Basic constituents

2.2.1   Feature-Detectors

Feature-Detectors (FD) code the time-space distribution of punctual events. They stand at the network input. In speech processing, events are instantaneous representations of time-frequency signal analysis.

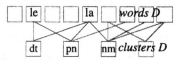

In Natural Language Processing (NLP), there are two sets of FDs: the word detector set is initially connected to the classe detector sets. Continuous speech processing gives ambiguous analysis, because of the different possible segmentations. These ambiguities might induce simultaneous word detector activations. As shown in the margin, a FD corresponds with "le", and an other one with "la". "la" can be a *determinant, pronoun* or *noun*; this is why it is connected with three classe-detectors. "le" can be a *determinant* or a *pronoun*.

Compared with formal language representations, a FD can be associated with an element of the alphabet (terminal vocabulary), which is the set of lexical classes, in the following NLP examples.

2.2.2   Context-Dependant Units

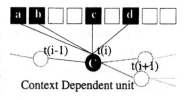

Context-Dependant unit (CD) performs coincidence detections by summing both internal (reference) and incoming (input pattern) signals. A CD codes for a pattern of syntactic classes which occur in a specific context. The corresponding set of activated FDs is connected to the CD. This CD is also linked with the CD which codes for the previous classes, and possibly with the CD coding for the next classe. An internal flow then propagates along this chain of units (so-called *memory pathway*), and receives progressively the contribution of activated FDs.

Compared with formal language representations, a CD can be considered as an occurrence of a non-terminal in a given context, i.e. in a given rule (for example, C in S--> ABCD), and this non-terminal is rewritten in a terminal rule (for example C --> a / b / c / d).

2.2.3 Memory pathways

The same type of representation is used for each series of word classes, thus forming a set of memory pathways. Each pathway initiates from a root unit, representing the initial context. Each pathway terminates in a FD, which codes for a given syntactic (sub)structure. The tree of pathways issued from the same root-unit forms a

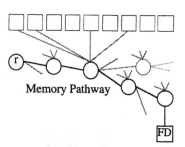

"module", which is the "brick" of the complete modular architecture. A FD can feed deeper modules containing memory pathways representing more abstract knowledge, such as combinations of syntactical substructures.

In the framework of formal languages, a pathway can be considered as a representation of a sentence existing in the training set, and the root is the initial non-terminal symbol.

2.2.4 Activity propagation

A decision threshold owned by the CDs may be crossed by these summed signals; in this

case, the unit delivers a signal towards other CDs in the network. Signals spreading along memory pathways are standard pulses which are delayed, weighted, and possibly modified in duration at the level of every unit input. Time-delays are aimed at synchronising every signal that reaches a given unit; weights are proportional to the number of signal occurrences. The signal duration facilitates its possible coincidence with other incoming signals and provides robustness to time distortions.

2.3 Never-Ending Learning in Guided Propagation

For each new sentence, the network to acquires the possible new informations it contains. Internal structures are not fixed, since they can be adapted throughout the processing [14]. The different mechanisms involved in this "Never-ending" learning are triggered depending on network's parameters: with high thresholds, the network is inclined to differentiation, with low thresholds, it is inclined to generalization.

2.3.1 Propagation mechanism

In the simplest case, the pattern presented (i.e. a set of word classes) is already represented in the network. The activity spreads along the pathway down to the final FD in the following way:

• the root unit sends a contextual signal to the first CD of the pathway. This signal is not strong enough to cross the CD's threshold. At the same time, the FDs that represent the pattern are activated (a);

• the first CD detects a coincidence between the contextual signal and stimuli, because its activity runs past the threshold (b). It thus emits a signal which preactivates the next CD in the pathway;

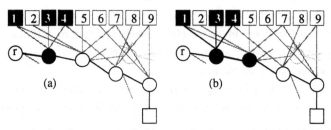

• since the pattern is already represented, this preactivation corresponds to a good prediction, which is confirmed by the next stimuli (c);

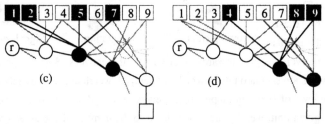

• in the same way, signals are guided along the memory pathway by incoming stimuli, step by step (d), (e).

• finally, the last CD unit activates the FD bounding the pathway (f). In this example, the configuration of events which is coded in the pathway is:

(1-3-4) (1-2-5-7) (4-8-9) (6-7-9), where (x-y-z) means "x or y or z".

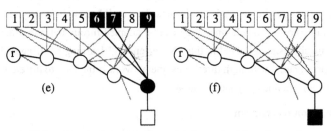

The grammar which subtends the network containing only this pathway is:

G = (X, V, P, S), where   X = {1, 2, 3, 4, 5, 6, 7, 8, 9}, V = {S, A, B, C, D}

and P = {S --> A B C D; A --> 1 / 3 / 4; B --> 1 / 2 / 5 / 7; C --> 4 / 8 / 9; D --> 6 / 7 / 9 }

More often, the pattern is not yet represented in the network. The network must be completed accordingly, following two basic building mechanisms: generalization and differentiation.

2.3.2 Generalization

Generalization is triggered when the current pattern activation coincides with at least an

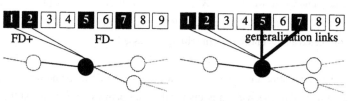

internal CD. This may occur due to a strong "expectation" of the network, which results not only in the usual preactivation of the CD, but in its full activation. In the case represented above, the unexpected FDs (FD-) occur at the same time as the expected FDs (FD+). Generalization consists in the enlargement of the FD set which may feed the CD. New links will connect the CD with every FD-.

Compared with formal language representations, generalization can be linked with the extension of a terminal rule of the grammar. In the example above, "5" and "7" are added to the terminal rule corresponding to the non-terminal in progress.

If the rule fired at the present time is: $X \rightarrow \alpha\ A\ \beta$, α and β in $X^* \cup V^*$, with $A \rightarrow 1\,/\,2$, generalization shown above consists in a modificaying the rule to: $A \rightarrow 1\,/\,2\,/\,5\,/\,7$

As may be noticed, generalization does not involve a new processing unit, i.e. a new rule in the grammar, but only modifications of the connectivity, i.e. a modification of an existing rule. The set of units (rules) is not extended, but the representation is completed.

2.3.3 Differentiation

Differentiation is triggered when the above coincidence criteria is not satisfied. In this case, none of the

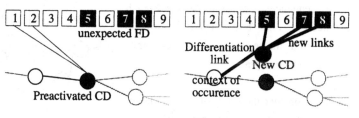

preactivated CDs become fully activated. Differentiation consists in creating a new pathway, a new branch sprouting from the pathway currently activated. This differentiation mechanism results in the tree-like structure of pathways.

Compared with formal languages representations, differentiation can be viewed as the insertion of a new rule in the set P. Let us assume that the rule in progress at the present time is: $X \dashrightarrow \alpha \, A \, \beta$, α and β in X^* U V^*, (α is the left context), with $A \dashrightarrow 1 \, / \, 2$

then, the expected non-terminal is A, i.e. the expected pattern is "1" or "2"

but the actual pattern is "5", "7" and "8"

Thus, a new rule will be $X \dashrightarrow \alpha \, A' \, ...$, α in X^* U V^*, with $A' \dashrightarrow 5 \, / \, 7 \, / \, 8$

This new rule is not yet complete, because the pattern is not yet finished. It will be completed as the entire pattern will be processed.

Differentiation thus involves a new processing unit in the network, that is a new rule in the grammar. This mechanism is involved for all pathway creations. At the beginning, there are no CDs in the network, but only a root unit, and a set of FDs. When the first part of the first pattern is presented, differentiation involves the creation of a new (and first) CD, in the context provided by the root unit.

3   Syntactic representations in NLP

3.1   Notations

In the examples presented here, we will use the following dictionary:

(le, pn/dt) (du, dt) (un, dt) (chat, nm) (lait, nn) (boit, vb) (est, vb) (petit, aj) (gentil, aj)[1]

And we will use the following set of sentences as learning corpus:

(Le chat boit du lait. Un chat est gentil.Le petit chat boit.)[2]

3.2   Example of elementary network

Within Guided Propagation networks, natural language sentences are represented by lexical classes sequences. For example, the French sentence "le chat boit du lait"[3] will be represented as the sequence "dt-nm-vb-dt-nm", as shown in the margin.

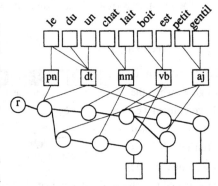

Let us consider the set X of lexical classes defined in the dictionary. All sentences that can

---

[1]Words are *the, some, a, cat, milk, drinks, is, small, nice,* clusters are *pronoun, determinant, noun, verb, adjective.*

[2]*The cat drinks the milk. A cat is nice. The small cat drinks.*

[3]*The cat drinks some milk.*

be defined on this vocabulary are in the X* set of combinations of words in X, but there is no network that can accept this infinite set of sentences, because there is no actual recursiveness in GPN.

3.3 Comparison with a Maximal Canonical Automaton

Let C be a set of examples such that all sentences are different. Let the system construct a distinct pathway for each sentence. Then, the network will have the same structure than the *Maximal Canonical Automaton* (MCA).

For example the network shown below (the word classes are not represented) is equivalent to the MCA just before it (in GPN, the terminal vocabulary is associated to units, and in automatons, the terminal vocabulary is associated to edges). Note that this automaton is not deterministic.

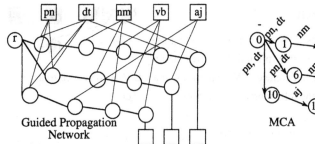
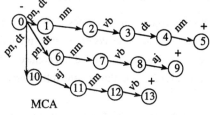

Guided Propagation Network

MCA

The grammar rules are:

S --> A1 A2 A3 A4 A5 / A5 A7 A8 A9 / A10 A11 A12 A13

A1 --> pn/dt	A2 --> nm	A3 --> vb	A4 --> dt	A5 --> nm
A6 --> pn/dt	A7 --> nm	A8 --> vb	A9 --> aj	
A10 --> pn/dt	A11 --> aj	A12 --> nm	A13 --> vb	

Or more simply:

S --> pn-dt nm vb dt vb / pn-dt nm vb aj / pn-dt aj nm vb

But if we compare this network with the preceding one, we notice that the beginning of the different pathways are shared if they do represent the same left-hand context. The root unit has three successor units that are connected to the same classes. If this network had been built with the mechanisms described in 2.3, the root had have only on successor unit, because it would have been used again for the second and third sentence.

On the other hand, it is not possible to share parts of pathways that represent the same right-hand context because of the Differentiation learning mechanism.

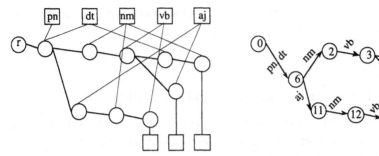

With the same principle, we can redraw the network and its associated automaton (simplified MCA), sharing the left context. The difference with the previous network lies only in the graphical representation,, because the language generated is the same (i.e. exactly the set of examples). This principle can be applied to produce a deterministic automaton from a non-deterministic one.

3.4 Equivalent grammar

Let us consider a given corpus C. With a single processing pass of each sentence, the system is able to build the corresponding tree of pathways, with shared left contexts. We can represent a CD (Ci) connected to a set of classes $c_1, c_2 \ldots c_n$, through the following rule: $Ci \rightarrow c_1 / c_2 / \ldots / c_n$

The most general network (in the margin) could be represented by the following grammar:
$G=(X, V, P, S)$, with $X= \{c_1, c_2, \ldots, c_i\}$, $V= \{A_1, \ldots, A_n, C_1, \ldots, C_n\}$,

and $P= \begin{vmatrix} S & \rightarrow \ldots / C1\ A1 / \ldots \\ \ldots & \\ An & \rightarrow \ldots / Cm / \ldots \\ C1 & \rightarrow \ldots / cp / \ldots \end{vmatrix}$

The rules of the grammar equivalent to the network example presented in 3.3 are (using notation defined on simplified CMA):

S	--> C6 A6	C6	--> pn / dt	C11	--> aj
A6	--> C2 A2 / C11 A11	C2	--> nm	C12	--> nm
A2	--> C3 A3	C3	--> vb	C13	--> vb
A3	--> C4 A4 / C9	C4	--> dt		
A4	--> C5	C5	--> nm		
A11	--> C12 A12	C9	--> aj		

Note that, from a static point of view, non-terminals C2, C5, C12, and C3, C13, and C9, C11 are equivalent, but the dynamic management of weights and time durations involves differences between the different occurrences of the same classes.

3.5 Representation and processing of ambiguity

In the topological representation implemented in a GPN, the ambiguity of an event is proportional to the size of the memory subset it activates. Lexical ambiguity is thus represented by the activation of several input classe detectors (FDs), which entails the propagation of a wide internal flow, not focused enough to perform accurate expectations. Contextual disambiguation, based on a simple probabilistic principle, has been developed in order to reduce lexical ambiguity [15]. Lateral inhibition between concurrent pathways is another mechanism introduced for this purpose.

However, these representations are not satisfying for representing large sets of sentences or rich syntactic structures. Indeed, the number of internal units does increase in a linear way with the number of words processed. Several strategies can be designed to obtain structured networks, by sharing duplicated sub-structures such as nominal or verbal phrases. Using the hierarchical organisation of the modules, we tried to map the different sub-structures of a sentence onto the different layers of the network: the deeper the layer, the higher the level of the structure. Since no boundary markers indicates syntactic limits, probabilistic criterions or teaching strategies are necessary.

4 Automatic construction of the network

Although some authors state that "a natural language cannot be theorised as a formal language", they also show that automatic parsers of linear complexity in time can be designed thanks to computer aided observations and statistics [16]. Unsupervised learning mechanisms have been investigated for the system to build structured networks [17, 18].

4.1 Unsupervised strategies

A strategy uses connection weights as a measure of co–occurrence probabilities. For example, the "dt-nn" connection may be enhanced in comparison with the other couples of CD units. If the strength of a connection reaches a certain value, the corresponding couple of CDs is extracted from this pathway (module 2), and put in a more peripheral module (module 1). Then, using generalization on coincident activations, every occurrence of this structure will be replaced by a single CD in module 2.

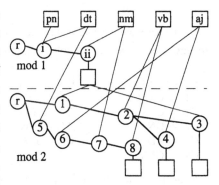

The network architecture that results from this strategy is equivalent to the following grammar rules:

S --> C1 A1 / C5 A5	C1 --> **GN**	**GN --> Ci Cii**
A1 --> C2 A2	C2 --> vrb	**Ci --> pn / dt**
A2 --> C3 A3 / C4 A4	C3 --> **GN**	**Cii --> nm**
A3 --> C3	C4 --> aj	
A4 --> C4	C5 --> dt	
A5 --> C6 A6	C6 --> aj	
A6 --> C7 A7	C7 --> nm	
A7 --> C8	C8 --> vb	

The noun phrase "dt-nm" has been automatically extracted, thanks to both reinforcement and generalization. But this strategy exhibits two main weaknesses:

• Due to the tree structure, the beginning of each pathway is always more reinforced than its end. Thus, there is a strong trend towards extraction of the structure beginnings.

• Due to the lack of explicit boundary marks in the processed sentences, and if reinforcement is carried out during the entire life-time of the system, extraction eventually transfers every structure from the central modules to the periphery. In a continuous speech processing system, prosody would be an helpful source of features for segmenting sentences.

The next strategy investigated consists in always using representations that already exist in the network. A deeper module is then added. For example, if the processed sentence is "Le chat boit du lait", the couple of CDs that represents the noun phrase "le chat" is reused to represent the NP "du lait".

The network architecture that results from this strategy is equivalent to the following grammar rules:

S --> C1 A1 / C4	GNV1 --> Ci Cii Ciii	Ciii --> vb
A1 --> C2 / C3	GNV2 --> Ci Cv Cvi Cvii	Civ --> aj
C1 --> GNV1	GN --> Ci Cii	Cv --> aj
C2 --> GN	AD --> Civ	Cvi --> nm
C3 --> AD	Ci --> pn / dt	Cvii --> vb
C4 --> GNV2	Cii --> nm	

Note that more structures are extracted than in the first strategy. But they are not linguistically significant. And a new layer is added each time a structure can be reused. The network is thus inclined to grow more and more deeply without control.

In their current version, unsupervised learning strategies such as the above ones are not adapted to large corpora (more than 100 sentences). It may not be realistic to design a fully unsupervised strategy, whereas syntax learning involves frequent interaction with a teacher. The "educational strategy" brings into play a series of corpora, presented in order to increase complexity. For example, the first corpus contains elementary noun phrases, such as "le chat" or "à Paris"; the second one contains more complex phrases, that are combinations of the previous ones ("à la maison" or "le chien ou le chat") and a third corpus contains full sentences. The structured representations obtained with this approach use a third less CDs than a non-hierarchical network.

4.2 Processing of unexpected words

When set in an "extended propagation" mode (low thresholds) a GPN performs stronger expectations concerning the next classes and to come. This ability has been used in two ways: *assimilation*, i.e. adding new words in the dictionary) or *accommodation*, i.e. extracting information of a syntactic structure ignoring "noisy" or unknown lexical items.

4.2.1 Assimilation

The unexpected word is considered as a significant item which must be represented in the network. Internal representations are used to infer its classe. The new word is represented by a new FD and both possible patterns of connection corresponding to generalization and differentiation are created. The correct structure is then automatically selected, depending on the next words, and thanks to the selective reinforcement of useful pathways. The network successfully categorized 73% of the unknown words in our test corpora (for more details, consult [18]).

4.2.2 Accommodation

The unexpected item is considered as a "noisy" word which occurs in a sentence that is already represented in the network. The resulting lack of input stimulation is then compensated by a stronger internal flow of expectations. Simulation tests have shown that the structure of more than 80% of sentences could be identified, despite the presence of noisy words. Accommodation allows more than dealing with unrecognised words. We are now investigating the treatment of other forms of noises such as inversions, delayed or missing words, in order to get the network structures to resemble the syntactic forms encountered in natural speech more closely.

5 Conclusion

The representations supported by a GPN can be described using non-recursive grammars, and can be obtained through several learning strategies. Simulation experiments carried out on unsupervised strategies have shown the limitations of a "purely unsupervised" approach, which should be helped by extra informations provided whether by a parallel flow of data (such as prosodic features) or by a teacher. An educational strategy has been applied to a large corpus of natural language sentences, with applications to natural speech sentences in mind. It is assumed that a GPN initially trained on a large set of "correct" sentences will be able to deal with casual speech, thanks to both inherent robustness to distortion and ability to complete its internal structures in the course of processing.

References

[1] **Lucas S.M.**, (1993) : *New Directions in Grammatical Inference*, IEEE Colloquium on Grammatical Inference, Colchester, Univ. of Essex, April 22-23 1993

[2] **Carbonell J.G., Michalski R.S., Mitchell, T.M.**, (1983) : *An Overview of Machine Learning* in "Machine Learning, An Artificial Intelligence Approach", Morgan Kaufman Publishers (Ed.)

[3] **Miclet L**, (1990) : *Grammatical Inference*, Series in Computer Sciences, **7**, Syntactic and Structural Pattern Recognition: Theory and Applications, World Scientific

[4] **Das S., Mozer M.C.**, (1993) : *A Connectionnist symbol manipulator that induces Rewrite Rules in Context-Free Grammars*, IEEE Colloquium on Grammatical Inference, Colchester, Univ. of Essex, April 22-23 1993

[5] **Lyon C.**, (1993) : *Using Neural Networks to Infer Grammatical Structures in Natural Language*, IEEE Colloquium on Grammatical Inference, Colchester, Univ. of Essex, April 22-23 1993

[6] **Béroule D.G.**, (1987) : *Guided Propagation inside a Topographic Memory*, IEEE First Conference on Neural Networks, San Diego, June 21-24 1987

[7] **Fletcher P.**, (1993) : *Neural Networks for Learning Grammars*, IEEE Colloquium on Grammatical Inference, Colchester, Univ. of Essex, April 22-23 1993

[8] **Sharkey A.J.C., Sharkey N.E.**, (1993) : *Connectionnism and Natural Language*, IEEE Colloquium on Grammatical Inference, Colchester, Univ. of Essex, April 22-23 1993

[9] **Roques M., Béroule D.**, (1991) : *Strategies of unsupervised learning for a parallel parsing architecture*, IJCNN91, Seattle, July 8-12 1991

[10] **Escande P.**, (1992) : *Reconnaissance de parole par un modèle connexionniste à détection de coïncidences*, Thèse de 3ème cycle, Orsay, Notes et Documents LIMSI n° 93-09

[11] **Béroule D., Von Hoe R., Ruellan, H.**, (1994) : *A Guided Propagation Model of Reading*, IPO Annual Report

[12] **Martin J-C.**, (1994) : *A connectionnist model using multiplexed oscillations and synchrony to enable dynamic connections*, Fourth International Conference on Artificial Neural Networks (ICANN'94), Sorrento, Italy, May 26-29 1994

[13] **Béroule D.G.**, (1990) : *Guided propagation: Current state of theory and applications*, NATO ASI Serie, F68, Neurocomputing, F.Fogelman-Soulié & J.Hérault, Springer-Verlag (Ed.), pp 240-260

[14] **Béroule D.G.**, (1988) : *The Never-Ending Learning* in "Neural Computers", NATO ASI Serie, Vol F41, pp 219-230, Springer Verlag (Ed.)

[15] **Roques M .**, **Béroule D .**, (1990) : *Traitement parallèle de séquences lexicales par propagation guidée*, 5èmes Journées Neurosciences et Sciences de l'Ingénieur, Aussois, May 7-10 1990

[16] **Vergne J.**, (1993) : *Syntactic properties of natural languages and application to automatic parsing*, Sociedad Española para el Procesamiento del Lenguaje Natural (SEPLN93), Grenade, September 1993

[17] **Roques M .**, (1992) : *Exemple d'analyse syntaxique dans une architecture connexionniste pour la communication homme-machine*, 6èmes Journées Neurosciences et Sciences de l'Ingénieur, Oléron, May 1992

[18] **Roques M.**, (1993) : *Apprentissage et reconnaissance de structures syntaxiques par une approche connexionniste*, Thèse de 3ème cycle, Orsay, Notes et Documents LIMSI n° 94-01

A Hybrid Connectionist-Symbolic Approach to Regular Grammatical Inference Based on Neural Learning and Hierarchical Clustering

R. Alquezar

A. Sanfeliu

Instituto de Cibernética

Universidad Politécnica de Catalunya - CSIC

Diagonal 647 2a planta, Barcelona, Spain

E-mail: alquezar@ic.upc.es, sanfeliu@ic.upc.es

Abstract

Recently, recurrent neural networks (RNNs) have been used to infer regular grammars from positive and negative examples. Several clustering algorithms have been suggested to extract a finite state automaton (FSA) from the activation patterns of a trained net. However, the consistency with the examples of the extracted FSA is not guaranteed in these methods, and typically, some parameter of the clustering algorithm must be set arbitrarily (e.g. the number of clusters in k-means method). In this paper we present a hybrid approach to regular grammatical inference based on neural learning and hierarchical clustering. The important new feature in the proposed method is the use of symbolic representation (*unbiased* FSA) and processing (*merge* operation) along with the clustering performed after neural learning, which allows to guarantee the extraction of a consistent deterministic FSA with the "minimal" size (with respect to the consistent FSA extractable by hierarchical clustering). Moreover, it is only required to define the cluster distance measure criterion.

1 Introduction

The problem of *regular grammatical inference* has been studied extensively in the past [1, 2]. Just a few of the existing symbolic methods are designed to induce grammars from positive and negative sample strings [3, 4, 5]. In the latest years, a variety of recurrent neural networks (RNNs) have been investigated as an alternative approach to learn grammars from examples (e.g. [6, 7]). In some of the works with RNNs, both positive and negative sample strings have been used to train the network to learn the classification task for a target regular language[7, 8]. The capability of RNNs to learn simple regular grammars have been shown, but the consistency of the obtained classifier with the given data cannot be guaranteed, e.g. because of local minima solutions. An attempt to combine neural and symbolic techniques in an active grammatical inference (AGI) methodology, which would always produce consistent solutions, has been recently reported by the authors [9, 13].

On the other hand, several works have shown that it is feasible to extract a FSA from a RNN [8, 10, 11]. It has been observed that RNNs develop an internal state representation in form of clusters in the activation space of the recurrent hidden units [6, 8]. Therefore, by using clustering techniques, a symbolic description of an (approximately simulated) FSA can be obtained from the network dynamics during or after learning. Different techniques have been suggested: dynamic clustering [11], search on a regular partition [10], and k-means algorithm [8]. For the last two, a subsequent FSA symbolic minimization has been recommended. Alternatively, a self-clustering RNN with discretized activations, that requires a "pseudo-gradient" training algorithm, can be employed to ease the FSA extraction [8]. However, due to the possibility of incomplete learning by the RNN, the consistency with the examples of the extracted FSA cannot be guaranteed in the above methods. Furthermore, at least one key parameter of each algorithm must be set arbitrarily, such as the minimal inter-cluster distance (for dynamic clustering), the cell width (for regular partition search algorithm), and the number of clusters or states (for k-means algorithm).

We present here an FSA extraction method based on hierarchical clustering [6], that always yields a consistent deterministic FSA, whose number of states is minimal with respect to the consistent FSA reachable through hierarchical clustering from the network activation data over the training set. In addition, no arbitrary parameter is involved. The new feature in our method is the use of symbolic representation (*unbiased* FSA [5]) and processing (*merge* operation) along with the clustering process after neural learning, so that the algorithm can be regarded as a *neural-network guided merging of states from the sample prefix tree*. Hence, this hybrid approach may be included in the class of grammatical inference (GI) methods based on finding a partition of the states of a canonical automaton [2, 4, 5]. Actually, it has been conceived as a step in the active GI paradigm presented in [9], which is summarized in the next section. *Unbiased* FSA and their use in GI from both positive and negative data [9] are briefly reviewed in Section 3. The FSA extraction algorithm is explained in detail in Section 4.

2 Active Grammatical Inference

Active grammatical inference (AGI) is a methodology which allows to guide the learning process of a grammar to accomplish with demanded constraints or heuristic criteria [9]. The guiding procedure can be applied iteratively after a neural learning stage (or *neural run*), in which a recurrent neural network (RNN) is used to induce a classifier from a set of positive and negative string examples (by finding a local or global minimum of the classification error function over the training set). At the end of every *neural run*,

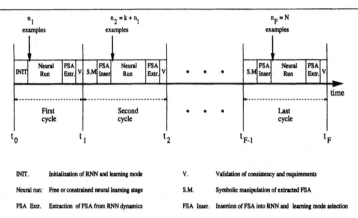

INIT.	Initialization of RNN and learning mode	V.	Validation of consistency and requirements
Neural run:	Free or constrained neural learning stage	S.M.	Symbolic manipulation of extracted FSA
FSA Extr.	Extraction of FSA from RNN dynamics	FSA Inser.	Insertion of FSA into RNN and learning mode selection

Fig. 1 *Time diagram of an Active Grammatical Inference process*

a grammar is extracted in the form of a FSA. Then, this grammar can be modified through symbolic procedures according to a-priori knowledge of the target grammar or to include specific rules. The modified FSA can be totally or partially inserted into a new RNN with computable weights, and subsequent neural training can be selected to be free or constrained (i.e. keeping the inserted rules). The inference process ends when the extracted grammar generates all the positive strings, does not generate any of the negative strings, and meets the requirements.

The whole learning process, shown in Figure 1, can take several cycles, each one ended in a validation step. The initial weights (and possibly the size) of the RNN vary from one cycle to another. The available positive and negative sample can be used integrally as training set in all runs, or (as in Fig.1) it can be supplied incrementally during some cycles until completely satisfied. In the simplest cases, a single cycle may be enough to obtain a proper grammar. A key phase in AGI is the extraction of a consistent FSA from the dynamics of a trained net, which is discussed hereinafter.

3   Unbiased Finite State Automata (UFSA) and their use in Grammatical Inference (GI)

An *unbiased finite state automaton* (or UFSA) is defined as a six-tuple $U = (\Sigma, Q, \delta, q_0, F_P, F_N)$, where Σ is a finite set of input symbols (alphabet), Q is a finite set of states, $q_0 \epsilon Q$ is the initial state, $F_P \subseteq Q$ and $F_N \subseteq Q$ are sets of positive and negative final states respectively, which satisfy the constraint $F_P \cap F_N = \emptyset$, and $\delta : (Q \times \Sigma) \rightarrow 2^Q$ is a state transition (partial) function. The language of strings *accepted* by U is defined as $L_A(U) = \{\alpha \epsilon \Sigma^* \mid \Delta(q_0, \alpha) \cap F_P \neq \emptyset\}$, where $\Delta : (Q \times \Sigma^*) \rightarrow 2^Q$ is the transition function extended to strings of symbols. Symmetrically, the language *rejected* by U is defined as $L_R(U) = \{\beta\epsilon\Sigma^* \mid \Delta(q_0, \beta) \cap F_N \neq \emptyset\}$. The language of strings from Σ^* that are neither included in $L_A(U)$ or $L_R(U)$ is said to be *ignored* by U. We denote the languages $L_S(U) = L_A(U) \cup L_R(U)$ and Σ^* as the *scope* and the *domain* of U, respectively. An UFSA U is *consistent* iff $L_A(U) \cap L_R(U) = \emptyset$; if, in addition, $L_S(U) = \Sigma^*$, then U is said to be *complete*. An UFSA $U = (\Sigma, Q, \delta, q_0, F_P, F_N)$ is *deterministic* iff $\delta : (Q \times \Sigma) \rightarrow Q$. Similarly to the FSA case, there is an algorithm to transform any given non-deterministic UFSA into an equivalent deterministic UFSA [5]; that algorithm is also used to check the consistency of non-deterministic UFSA[1].

It is obvious that "classical" FSA and complete UFSA have the same classification power, that of recognizing the class of regular languages. Note, however, that UFSA are unbiased with respect to positive and negative information, since both types of data are explicitly and symmetrically represented. Furthermore, the class of consistent UFSA has more representational power than FSA, since it tackles the existence of strings that cannot be classified with certainty using the available knowledge. These simple properties make UFSA well suited to the task of GI from both positive and negative examples, as it was discussed in [5]. Nonetheless, the available theory about FSA and GI [12, 1] can be easily extended to deal with the UFSA representation.

Given two UFSA U_2 and U_1, we say that U_2 *extends* the scope of U_1 iff $L_A(U_2) \supseteq L_A(U_1) \wedge L_R(U_2) \supseteq L_R(U_1)$; and U_2 *covers* U_1, iff $U_2 = U_1/\pi$, i.e. U_2 is a quotient UFSA[2] for some partition π of the states of U_1. If, in addition, U_2 is consistent, then *consistently-extends*(U_2, U_1) and *consistently-covers*(U_2, U_1) are true, respectively. It is directly deducible from automata theory that *covers*$(U_2, U_1) \Rightarrow$ *extends*(U_2, U_1), so *consistently-covers*$(U_2, U_1) \Rightarrow$ *consistently-extends*(U_2, U_1). Given an UFSA $U = (\Sigma, Q, \delta, q_0, F_P, F_N)$ and two states $q_i, q_j \in Q$, a merge operation is defined as $U_{Mij} = \text{merge}(U, q_i, q_j) = U/\pi_{ij}$, where the partition $\pi_{ij} = \{\{q \in Q\} \mid q \neq q_i, q \neq q_j\} \cup \{q_i, q_j\}$. It is clear that U_2 *consistently-covers* U_1, iff U_2 results from zero or more successive consistent merge operations starting on the states of U_1.

Let $S = (S_+, S_-)$ be a sample of a language L on an alphabet Γ, where $S_+ \subseteq L$ (positive sample) and $S_- \subseteq \Gamma^* - L$ (negative sample). $S = (S_+, S_-)$ is said to be *structurally complete* for an UFSA $U = (\Sigma, Q, \delta, q_0, F_P, F_N)$, if $\Gamma = \Sigma$, $L_A(U) \supseteq S_+$, $L_R(U) \supseteq S_-$, and every transition of δ is used at least once in the generation of a string of S_+ or S_-. The *prefix tree* UFSA of a sample $S = (S_+, S_-)$ is defined as $PT(S) = (\Sigma, Pr(S), \delta, \lambda, S_+, S_-)$, where $Pr(S)$ is the set of prefix over the finite language $S_+ \cup S_-$, λ is the string of length zero, and δ is given by: $\forall u \in Pr(S), \forall a \in \Sigma, \delta(u, a) = ua$ if $\exists ua \in Pr(S)$. Let $U(L)$ be the minimum-size deterministic complete UFSA that accepts a regular language L. By analogy with the FSA case, it can be concluded that, if S is structurally complete for the UFSA $U(L)$, then there exists a partition π on the states of $PT(S)$ such that $PT(S)/\pi = U(L)$. In terms of UFSA, the problem of regular GI can be stated as: given a sample $S = (S_+, S_-)$, find a consistent UFSA U that satisfies $L_A(U) \supseteq S_+ \wedge L_R(U) \supseteq S_-$. If one assumes that S is *structurally complete* for the unknown target solution U_T, then the search can be restricted to the UFSA that *consistently-cover*

---

[1] For a deterministic UFSA $U = (\Sigma, Q, \delta, q_0, F_P, F_N)$, U is consistent iff $F_P \cap F_N = \emptyset$.

[2] The definition of a quotient UFSA [5] is similar to that for FSA [4].

$PT(S)$. In practice, an inductive bias is needed to select just one or a few plausible solutions.

4 Method for regular GI from positive and negative examples using neural learning and hierarchical clustering

The method involves two stages: in the former, a RNN is trained to classify the strings of a sample $S = (S_+, S_-)$; in the latter, the internal state representation developed by the trained net is used through hierarchical clustering to guide a state merging process which starts on the sample prefix tree $PT(S)$. The consistency analysis, that provides the stop criterion, is eased by using UFSA. For a review of how to train a RNN for a GI task (architectures, learning algorithms, data representation, training scheme) see for example [7, 8, 9]. Here, we just assume that a certain RNN with n recurrent hidden units and 1 output unit is trained to classify a sample S until a (maybe local) stable minimum of the total error function is reached. It is not required that the whole sample be correctly classified by the final net, but in any case, it is expected that the net has developed its own states in the form of clusters of the hidden unit activation patterns [8]. This information, together with a size-minimization heuristic, can be employed as inductive bias in the selection of an UFSA U that *consistently-covers* $PT(S)$. Our UFSA extraction method is formalized in Algorithm 1.

ALGORITHM 1: *Consistent UFSA extraction from RNN dynamics*
Inputs: *net* is a trained RNN with one output unit giving activation values in [0,1].
       sample is a training set consisting of pairs (*string,class*) where *class* is "+" or "-".
Outputs: *U* is a consistent deterministic UFSA derived from the sample prefix tree
    through hierarchical clustering of the RNN unit activations over the training set.
Internal Var: *PT* is the sample prefix tree UFSA.
       nc is the number of clusters.
       mean_clus is an array with the mean vectors of each cluster.
       npt_clus is an array with the number of points of each cluster.
begin_algorithm
cluster_initialization_and_prefixtree_buildup (net,sample; **returns** *PT*,nc,mean_clus,npt_clus);
hierarchical_clustering_and_state_merging (*PT*,nc,mean_clus,npt_clus; **returns** *U*);
end_algorithm

Algorithm 1 consists of two procedures. In the first one, the prefix tree UFSA is built, and, at the same time, single-point clusters are initialized with the activations of the net hidden units resulting after each symbol transition of the strings in the sample. There is a one-to-one correspondence between the initial clusters and the states of the prefix tree. However, in order to improve the final result, the single-point clusters associated with incorrectly classified strings (under a tolerance $\epsilon \leq 0.5$) are deleted; but the corresponding states in the prefix tree are not pruned.

208

function *cluster_initialization_and_prefixtree_buildup* (net,sample; **returns** PT,nc, mean_clus,npt_clus)

$n = 0$; $\quad PT_n = (\emptyset, \{\lambda\}, \emptyset, \lambda, \emptyset, \emptyset)$; $\quad nc = 1$;

fill_with_reset_activations (net; **returns** mean_clus[0]); $\quad$ npt_clus[0] = 1;

while $\quad n <$ number_of_strings_in_training_set (sample) **do**

$\quad n = n + 1$;

$\quad$ get_example (sample,n; **returns** s,$class$);

$\quad\quad$ {where s is a string and $class$ is "+" or "-"}

$\quad PT_n$ = expand_prefix_tree (PT_{n-1},s,$class$; **returns** $tpath$,$tplen$,$plns$);

$\quad\quad$ {where $tpath$ is the path of states of PT_n visited by s, $tplen$ is its length, and $plns$ is the position in $tpath$ of the lowest new state due to s}

$\quad$ **for** $\quad i = 1$ **to** $\quad tplen$ **do**

$\quad\quad p$ = compute_net_output (i,$s[i]$,net);

$\quad\quad\quad$ {where p is the activation value of the only output unit}

$\quad\quad$ **if** $i \geq plns$ **then**

$\quad\quad\quad st = tpath[i]$;

$\quad\quad\quad$ fill_with_hidden_unit_activations (net; **returns** mean_clus[st]);

$\quad\quad\quad$ npt_clus[st] = 1; $\quad nc = nc + 1$;

$\quad\quad$ **end_if**

$\quad$ **end_for**

$\quad$ error = $(p < (1 - \epsilon) \wedge class = $ "+"$) \vee (p > \epsilon \wedge class = $ "-"$)$;

$\quad$ **if** error **then**

$\quad\quad$ **for** $\quad i = plns$ **to** $\quad tplen$ **do**

$\quad\quad\quad st = tpath[i]$;

$\quad\quad\quad$ clear (mean_clus[st]); $\quad$ npt_clus[st] = 0; $\quad nc = nc - 1$;

$\quad\quad$ **end_for**

$\quad$ **end_if**

end_while

end_function

Next, a hierarchical clustering is carried out, in which the two closest clusters are determined and merged at each step. Each time two clusters are merged into a new one, a parallel merging of their associated states is performed in the UFSA representation. This is repeated until the state merging yields an inconsistent UFSA. Once an inconsistency occurs, any further merge will not remove it, so the process must be stopped and the last consistent UFSA U (or its deterministic equivalent one) is returned. By construction, U is the minimum-size UFSA which *consistently-covers* $PT(S)$ among the UFSA extractable from the trained RNN through hierarchical clustering, and it can be obtained without the need of defining any parameter, except that a distance measure between clusters is required (e.g. centroid euclidean distance).

Figure 2 illustrates the method by showing an example with real data. A first-order RNN with 3 hidden units and 1 output unit was trained to classify all the binary strings of length ≤ 4 according to the odd-parity predicate. After learning, the parallel process of clustering and state merging led to a 3-state UFSA equivalent to the target (2-state) odd-parity recognizer.

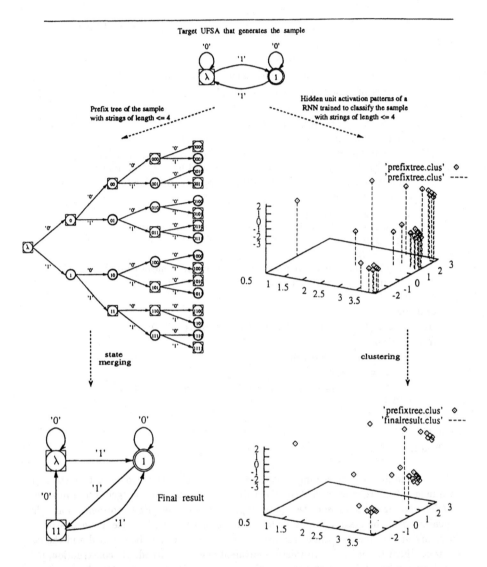

Fig. 2 *Diagram of the hybrid grammatical inference method, using as example the odd-parity recognizer and a trained first-order RNN with 3 recurrent hidden units.*

```
function hierarchical_clustering_and_state_merging (PT,nc,mean_clus,npt_clus; returns U)
consistency = TRUE;   n = 0;   Uₙ = PT;
while consistency do
        find_closest_clusters (mean_clus,npt_clus; returns cl1,cl2);
        merge_clusters (cl1,cl2; returns mean_clus,npt_clus);
        nc = nc − 1;   n = n + 1;
        Uₙ = merge_states (Uₙ₋₁,cl1,cl2);
        consistency = check_consistency (Uₙ);
end_while
if   deterministic (Uₙ₋₁) then   U = Uₙ₋₁;
else                             U = transform_to_deterministic (Uₙ₋₁);
end_if
end_function
```

5   Conclusions

A hybrid connectionist-symbolic approach to regular GI from positive and negative examples has been described, that involves two phases: neural learning for sample classification, and automaton extraction through hierarchical clustering of network activation data. The second phase is actually a symbolic state merging process, which starts on the sample prefix tree and is guided (biased) by the network's state representation. By construction, the result is guaranteed to be a consistent generalization[3] of the given sample, and its size is as small as the cluster information and the consistency constraint permits. The method has been implemented and tested, yielding successful results.

The use of *unbiased* FSA allows a symmetric consistency analysis and facilitates to establish a parallelism between the connectionist and symbolic representations. Finally, this method can be employed in an iterative and controlled hybrid methodology to infer complex grammars, called *active grammatical inference*, that has been outlined.

6   Acknowledgements

This work has been partially supported by a grant of the Government of Catalonia.

---

[3]Properly speaking, a consistent extension of both positive and negative data.

References

[1] D. Angluin and C.H. Smith, "Inductive inference: theory and methods," *ACM Computing Survey* **15** (3), pp.237-269, 1983.

[2] L. Miclet, "Grammatical inference," in *Syntatic and Structural Pattern Recognition: Theory and Applications*, H.Bunke and A.Sanfeliu, Eds., World Scientific, 1990.

[3] E.M. Gold, "Complexity of automaton identification from given data," *Information and Control* **37**, pp.302-320, 1978.

[4] J. Oncina and P. Garcia, "Identifying regular languages in polynomial time," in *Advances in Structural and Syntactic Pattern Recognition, Proc. of the 2nd IAPR Int. Workshop on SSPR, Bern, Switzerland, August 1992*, H.Bunke, Ed., World Scientific, 1992, pp.99-108.

[5] R. Alquezar and A. Sanfeliu, "Incremental grammatical inference from positive and negative data using unbiased finite state automata," in *Proc. of the 3rd IAPR Int. Workshop on Structural and Syntactic Pattern Recognition, SSPR-94, Nahariya, Israel, October* 1994.

[6] A. Cleeremans, D. Servan-Schreiber and J.L. McClelland, "Finite-state automata and simple recurrent networks," *Neural Computation* **1**, pp.372-381, 1989.

[7] C.B. Miller and C.L. Giles, "Experimental comparison of the effect of order in recurrent neural networks," *Int. Journal of Pattern Recognition and Artificial Intelligence* **7** (4), pp.849-872, 1993.

[8] Z. Zeng, R.M. Goodman and P. Smyth, "Learning finite state machines with self-clustering recurrent networks," *Neural Computation* **5** (1993), pp.976-990, 1993.

[9] A. Sanfeliu and R. Alquezar, "Active grammatical inference combining neural and symbolic techniques," in *Proc. of the 3rd IAPR Int. Workshop on Structural and Syntactic Pattern Recognition, SSPR-94, Nahariya, Israel, October* 1994.

[10] C.L. Giles and C.W. Omlin, "Extraction, insertion and refinement of symbolic rules in dynamically-driven recurrent neural networks," *Connection Science*, spec. issue on "Architectures for Integrating Symbolic and Neural Processes", 1993.

[11] S. Das and R. Das, "Induction of discrete-state machine by stabilizing a simple recurrent network using clustering," *Computer Science and Informatics*, vol.21, no.2, pp.35-40, 1991.

[12] J.E. Hopfcroft and J.D. Ullman, *Introduction to Automata Theory, Languages and Computation.* Addison-Wesley, Reading MA, 1979.

[13] A. Sanfeliu and R. Alquezar, "Understanding neural networks for grammatical inference and recognition," in *Advances in Structural and Syntactic Pattern Recognition, Proc. of the 2nd IAPR Int. Workshop on SSPR, Bern, Switzerland, August 1992*, H.Bunke, Ed., (World Scientific, 1992), pp.75-98.

Inference of Context-free Grammars by Enumeration: Structural Containment as an Ordering Bias

Jean-Yves Giordano

Institut de Recherche en Informatique et Systèmes Aléatoires
Campus de Beaulieu 35042 Rennes, FRANCE

Abstract

The problem of inferring grammars from examples and counter-examples has been mostly studied for regular languages. Here we apply a classical approach, said by enumeration, to context-free grammars. Structural containment is used as an ordering relation, and associated operators are defined. Special attention is paid to computation time, hence our system cannot always reach all the solutions for a given problem. Though, our system is able to generalize efficiently, and the solutions found constitute a good description of the sample.

1 Introduction

Grammatical inference is often seen as the identification of a formal language, given a set of words of this language, and possibly a set of words not belonging to this language. However, asking for a system to identify a given language is a very strong constraint, since this problem is known to be NP-complete, and the number of words required for the identification is often too large. In practice, the user might be more interested in a system that finds one or more possible descriptions of a sample in most cases, even if sometimes it does not.

The system we propose aims at a good compromise between the ability to generalize a grammar from a set of words, and the computation time required. Our approach is based on the same principles as the early enumeration methods. We first define a partial ordering on the set of grammars to be explored. The structure of the ordered set is then analysed, in order to produce operators that speed up the enumeration by pruning the search space and avoiding redundancy. Though every grammar cannot be reached, it is possible to quickly infer complex descriptions of the sample set.

In a previous article ([Gio93]), we set the basic ideas of our approach. Here we embed it in a more formal framework by analyzing the structure of the search space, present its last improvements (in particular with respect to speeding up the enumeration) and draw its limitations (some grammars cannot be produced without questioning the efficiency of the system).

2 Enumeration methods and version space

One of the first techniques suggested for grammatical inference is simple enumeration of all possible grammars in the class of interest until a suitable grammar is found. According to Gold ([Gol67]), in the learning situation where a new string is presented and a new grammar is guessed at each instant of time, no other algorithm can uniformly reach a steady correct guess in less time for all grammars in the class and for all information sequences.

In practice, the enumeration methods use pruning techniques to increase the efficiency of the enumeration. In these methods, a partial ordering (covering) is defined on the set of grammars, which allows deleting classes of incompatible grammars on the basis of a test on one of them. Indeed, if a grammar G does not generate a string in the language, all the grammars covered by G will have the same behavior and can be discarded. Many inference methods make use of this pruning technique ([Fel72b],[Fel72a],[Mic80],[Gar92]).

The formalism developed by Mitchell ([Mit82]) allows a systematic exploration of a set of hypotheses that potentially describe the examples and counter-examples (instances) given so far. It integrates the pruning technique used by the enumeration methods, and eliminates some of the redundancy by retaining only the most general and specific descriptions at each step of the presentation.

Let M be a predicate matching the hypotheses and the instances. A partial ordering relation called generalization is defined on the set of hypotheses. It is derived from the matching predicate M (an hypothesis g1 is less general than an hypothesis g2 if g1 matches a subset of the elements matched by g2). Then, the set of hypotheses is explored by means of generalization/specialization operators. These operators allow the current set of hypotheses to be consistent with the instances presented so far, by producing the most general specialization (the most specific generalization) of a given hypothesis.

Through the presentation, the algorithm maintains the coherence between the sets of minimal (S) and maximal (G) hypotheses, which respectively cover the examples presented so far in the most specific and in the most general way. Here are the steps of the algorithm for an example i (the processing of a counter-example is symmetrical):

Candidate Elimination Algorithm   % a positive instance i is given %

1. Remove from G the hypotheses that do not match i.
2. Generalize the elements of S until they match i, while remaining more specific than an element in G.
3. Retain the most specific hypotheses of S.

If only specialization operators are available, the algorithm can be used to find the set G:

Algorithm   % a negative instance i is given %

1. Specialize the elements of G that match i, until they do not match i, while matching all the positive instances.
2. Retain the most general hypotheses of G.

Within this framework, we specify a set of hypotheses, a generalization relation efficiently computable, and a set of specialization operators.

3 Structural containment

Among the classical grammatical coverings ([Nij80]), weak containment compares the strings in the language, structural containment compares the structures of the derivation trees, and Reynolds covering compares the productions. Weak containment is undecidable for context-free grammars. Enumeration using Reynolds covering was studied in [Bal87], but gave poor results. Here we investigate the possibilities offered by structural containment, which is computable in polynomial time on a normal form of context-free grammars.

3.1 Definition

A *structure* generated by a grammar is a derivation tree with all non-terminal labels deleted. A grammar G1 is *structurally contained* in (resp. *structurally equivalent* to) a grammar G2 if the set of structures generated by G1 is contained in (resp. equal to) the set of structures generated by G2. Structural containment implies weak containment.

	G1	G2
	S → S1 S2	S → S S1
Example:	S1 → S1 S1	S → S S
	S1 → a	S → a
	S2 → b	S1 → b

G2 produces the words of G1 in the same way, such as the word "aab" which derivation is shown above.

3.2 Computability

Structural containment is computable in exponential time on the set of context-free grammars ([McN67]), but in polynomial time on one of their normal forms ([Ros80]): uniquely invertible grammars.

A grammar G is *uniquely invertible* iff no two productions in G have the same right-hand side, i.e. for all productions X → u and Y → u, we have X = Y.

Example:	S → S S1	
	S → a	is uniquely invertible
	S1 → b	

The following results are valid whatever normal form is chosen initially. For the sake of simplicity, we consider grammars under Chomski normal form, i.e. a grammar which productions are all of the form:

$$\langle \text{non-terminal} \rangle \rightarrow \langle \text{non-terminal} \rangle \langle \text{non-terminal} \rangle,$$
$$\text{or} \langle \text{non terminal} \rangle \rightarrow \langle \text{terminal} \rangle.$$

According to McNaughton, there is an exponential time algorithm that converts any context-free grammar into a structurally equivalent uniquely invertible grammar ([McN67]). Hence the set of uniquely invertible grammars is equivalent to the whole set of context-free grammars, and applying the version space algorithm to the inference of uniquely invertible grammars does not restrict the capacity of the system. Moreover, structural containment can be computed in polynomial time. Indeed, Hunt and Rosenkrantz give ([Ros80]) a polynomial time algorithm that determines if an uniquely invertible grammar is structurally contained in an other:

Algorithm Structural_containment (G1,G2) = True iff G1 $\subseteq$ G2

% Let G1 = (M,Σ,P,S) and G2 = (N,Σ,Q,T) be two uniquely invertible grammars %

1. % The grammars are transformed so as to have a single initial production

   Let \$, S', T' be symbols not appearing in G nor in H. Construct grammars G1' = (M',Σ',P',S') and G2' = (N',Σ',Q',T'), where Σ' = $\Sigma \cup$ {\$}, M' = M $\cup$ {S'}, N' = N $\cup$ {T'}, P' = P $\cup$ {S' $\rightarrow$ S \$} and Q' = Q $\cup$ {T' $\rightarrow$ T \$}.

2. % The set MATCHING STRUCTURES is the set of pairs (A,B) such that A $\in$ M', B $\in$ N', and there is a common structure generated by A and B %

   Initially, MATCHING STRUCTURES is empty. The pair (A,B) is added to MATCHING STRUCTURES if P' has a production A $\rightarrow \alpha_1\alpha_2...\alpha_k$ and Q' has a production B $\rightarrow \beta_1 \beta_2 ... \beta_k$ such that, for $1 \leq i \leq k$, either α_i and β_i are identical terminals, or α_i and β_i are both non-terminals and (α_i,β_i) has already been determined to belong to MATCHING STRUCTURES.

3. % Test %

   For all A $\rightarrow \alpha_1\alpha_2...\alpha_k$ in P' and every sentence $\beta_1\beta_2...\beta_k$ such that for $1 \leq i \leq k$, either α_i and β_i are identical terminals, or $(\alpha_i,\beta_i) \in$ MATCHING STRUCTURES, there must be a production in Q' having $\beta_1\beta_2...\beta_k$ as its right-hand side.

	G1	G2
	T $\rightarrow$ S \$	T $\rightarrow$ S \$
	S $\rightarrow$ S1 S2	S $\rightarrow$ S S1
Example:	S1 $\rightarrow$ S1 S1	S $\rightarrow$ S S
	S1 $\rightarrow$ a	S $\rightarrow$ a
	S2 $\rightarrow$ b	S1 $\rightarrow$ b

MATCHING STRUCTURES (G1,G2) = {(S2,S1), (S1,S), (S,S), (T,T)}, G1 is structurally contained in G2.

To summarize, the set of context-free grammars is equivalent to the set of uniquely invertible grammars. On the latter a generalization relation can be computed in polynomial time. Therefore, within the frame of version space, it makes sense to consider uniquely invertible grammars as hypotheses and structural containment as a generalization relation.

4 Structure of the search space

4.1 Inductive leap

Learning from instances implies the production of a description that generalizes the set of examples in some way. We obtain this inductive leap by putting a constraint on the number of non-terminals of the considered grammars, which corresponds to the idea of structural complexity of the strings generated. Furthermore this allows to limit the size of the search space.

4.2 Equivalence classes and their representatives

Enumeration methods have to deal with the problem of equivalent grammars, which is a source of redundancy. We firstly study the nature of the equivalence classes induced by structural containment on the search space (uniquely invertible grammars with no useless symbol and a fixed number of non-terminals). Then we define representatives of these classes, so that the system processes these grammars only.

4.2.1 Equivalent symbols

To determine whether two uniquely invertible grammars are structurally equivalent, Mc-Naughton develops in [McN67] the notion of equivalent symbols.

Let $G = (X,V,P,S)$ be an uniquely invertible grammar. Two non-terminals N1 and N2 of G are *equivalent* iff a structurally equivalent grammar is obtained by replacing every occurrence of N1 and N2 in P by a symbol not belonging to $V \setminus \{N1,N2\}$.

Example:

T	→ S $	
S	→ S S1	S1 et S2 are equivalent,
S	→ S S2	the grammar can be simplified into:
S	→ S1 S1	
S	→ S1 S2	T → S $
S	→ S2 S1	S → S S1
S	→ S2 S2	S → S1 S1
S1	→ a	S1 → a
S2	→ b	S1 → b

Two non-terminals are equivalent iff they have the same contexts ([McN67]):

Let $G = (M,\Sigma,P,T)$ be a uniquely invertible grammar, N a non-terminal of G. Let $(G) = (M,\Sigma',(P),T)$ be the parenthesized version of G, obtained by enclosing the right-hand sides of its productions with parentheses ($\Sigma'=\Sigma \cup \{(,)\}$). We call contexts of N, and we note C(N), the set:

$$\{(w1,w2) \in \Sigma'^* \times \Sigma'^* \mid T \Rightarrow^*_{(G)} w1 \ N \ w2\}.$$

We established the following proposition to determine the equivalent symbols in polynomial time:

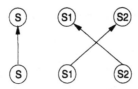

Figure 1: Relation between non-terminals

Proposition (1)

Let N1 and N2 be non-terminals of a uniquely invertible grammar G.
$C(N1) \subseteq C(N2)$ iff $\forall\ X \to U\ N1\ V \in G, \exists\ Y \to U\ N2\ V \in G$, with $C(X) \subseteq C(Y)$.

4.2.2 Representatives of the equivalence classes

The operators will apply on representatives of the equivalence classes. Thus, it is important that we determine them in a way that the operators are simple. We distinguish between the case where the grammars of the class has equivalent symbols or not.

a) Grammars with no equivalent symbols

If two uniquely invertible and reduced grammars G1 and G2 have no equivalent symbols, they are structurally equivalent iff they are isomorphic ([McN67]).

Example:

S → S1 S2	S → S2 S1
S1 → S1 S1	S2 → S2 S2
S2 → S2 S1	S1 → S1 S2
S1 → a	S2 → a
S2 → b	S1 → b

These two grammars are structurally equivalent, the relations between their non-terminals is shown in figure 1.

The equivalence class of a grammar G with no equivalent symbols is the set of grammars isomorphic to G. Any of them can be chosen as a representative.

b) Grammars with equivalent symbols

If G1 and G2 have equivalent symbols, they are structurally equivalent iff two isomorphic grammars are obtained by eliminating the equivalent symbols from G1 and G2 ([McN67]). In this case several representatives are necessary to easily determine the maximal specializations of a grammar, as the following example shows:

	H	G
	$T \rightarrow S\ \$$	$T \rightarrow S\ \$$
	$T \rightarrow S1\ \$$	$S \rightarrow S\ S$
	$S \rightarrow S\ S$	$S \rightarrow S\ S1$
	$S \rightarrow S\ S1$	$S \rightarrow S\ S2$
Example:	$S \rightarrow S1\ S1$	$S \rightarrow a$
	$S1 \rightarrow S\ S2$	$S1 \rightarrow b$
	$S1 \rightarrow S1\ S2$	$S2 \rightarrow c$
	$S \rightarrow a$	
	$S2 \rightarrow b$	
	$S2 \rightarrow c$	H is a maximal specialization of G

In order to determine efficiently the most general specializations of such a grammar, we choose as its representatives a maximal set of grammars equivalent to it, and not isomorphic between them. Then every element in the class of G is isomorphic to one of them, and its specializations can be computed easily.

These representatives are obtained by applying proposition (1). Though, their number may be exponential with the number of equivalent symbols and the number of rules. In such cases, in order to reduce complexity it should be preferable to apply heuristics that select a few of them as representatives of the class.

5 Specialization procedures

In this section we address the problem of what kind of transformations have to be operated on a grammar G in order to obtain its most general specializations. Here again two cases have to be distinguished, whether G has equivalent symbols or not.

a) G has no equivalent symbols

Let H be a most general specialization of G. We have shown that in this case there exists a uniquely invertible grammar H' such that:

- H' is reduced
- H' is structurally equivalent to H
- H' has no equivalent symbols
- the right-hand sides of the productions of H' are right-hand sides of productions of G.

Then all the maximal specializations of G can be obtained by changing left-hand sides of productions or deleting productions.

b) G has equivalent symbols

In this case there exists a representative G' of the class of G, such that the right-hand sides of H are right-hand sides of G'. Then H can be obtained by the same operations as in the previous case.

Every maximal specialization can be obtained by the above operations. Though, every combination of substitutions on left-hand sides and deletions of rules does not lead to a maximal specialization. In order to run the enumeration algorithm efficiently, we need to determine substitutions and deletions producing grammars that are both specializations of the initial grammar and the most general ones.

Two kinds of maximal specializations are examined: those obtained by deletion, and those obtained by substitution. We do not consider the maximal specializations that require substitutions and deletions to be executed in parallel.

The problem concerning the substitutions on left-hand sides of productions is to determine appropriate substitutions. The following result makes it possible to compute a large class of maximally specializing substitutions.

Proposition (2)

Let $A1...An$, $B1...Bn$ be non-terminals of G, not necessarily distinct, such that $\forall$ i, $C(Bi) \subseteq C(Ai)$, and (Ai,Wi) are productions of G. Then $H = G \setminus \{(Ai,Wi)\} \cup \{(Bi,Wi)\}$ is structurally contained in G.

In other words, if there are in G two non-terminals such that $C(B) \subseteq C(A)$, a specialization of G is obtained by changing A into B in the left-hand side of any rule of G. This is worth for several rules, and several substitutions with different non-terminals can be operated in parallel.

For a given grammar G, there is a polynomial algorithm that determines the pairs (A,B) of non-terminals satisfying $C(B) \subseteq C(A)$. It derives from proposition (1).

Algorithm

1. $D := \{\{S\}\}$

2. For all $X \rightarrow U$ N1 V Do $D := D \cup \{\{N2 \in N \mid \exists Y \in N, Y \rightarrow U$ N2 V $\in P\}\}$

3. $E0 := \{(N1,N2) \in N \times N \mid \forall M \in D, N1 \in M \Rightarrow N2 \in M\}$; $n:=0$

4. Repeat
   For all $\{(N1,N2)\} \in$ En Do
       For all $X \rightarrow U$ N1 V, $Y \rightarrow U$ N2 V $\in P$, Do
           If $X \equiv Y$ and $\{(X,Y)\} \notin$ En then En+1 := En $\setminus \{(N1,N2)\}$
   Until En+1 = En

5. Result R := E.

Given a grammar G and a set of possible substitutions, the maximal specializations of G are determined by a constraint propagation algorithm. The specializations obtained by substitution are organized in a lattice, each level n corresponding to n substitutions. This lattice is explored breadth-first. For each grammar produced, the set of specializing substitutions are computed and constitutes a constraint for the inferior levels. The search stops when all the grammars of the current level contradict a constraint, i.e. are not maximal specializations.

Concerning the deletion of rules, the most general specializations are obtained by deleting only one rule, unless its left-hand side may be changed.

The case where one of these transformations leads to a grammar with useless symbols corresponds to a change in the number of non-terminals (equivalent symbols). The produced grammar then has to be reduced, and equivalent grammars with the proper number of non-terminals are reintroduced into the system.

6 Conclusion

Enumerating the grammars in the class of interest is a classical way of inferring grammars. However existing algorithms only deal with regular languages. We show here that enumeration can be used for inferring context-free grammars. In order to keep a reasonable complexity, the requirement that the system identifies any language in the limit has to be relaxed, and heuristics should be used to limit the growth of the search space. Though, the system proposed is a first attempt at being able to generalize complex descriptions from strings, realizing a good compromise between efficiency and computation time. We still have to run experiments to determine its efficiency on significant samples. However, the number of descriptions produced and the flexibility of the system should make it possible to produce enough grammars to characterize the samples in most cases.

References

[Bal87]   K. Vanlehn & W. Ball. A version space approach to learning context-free grammars. *Machine learning*, 2:39–74, 1987.

[Fel72a] A.W. Biermann & J.A. Feldman. On the synthesis of finite-state machines from samples of their behaviour. *IEEE Transactions on Computers*, 1972.

[Fel72b] A.W. Biermann & J.A. Feldman. A survey of results in grammatical inference. In *Frontiers of pattern recognition*, Academic Press, 1972.

[Gar92]   J. Oncina & P. Garcia. Inferring regular languages in polynomial updated time. In *IVth Spanish Symposium on Pattern Recognition and Image Analysis*, 1992.

[Gio93]   J-Y. Giordano. Version space for learning context-free grammars. In *First International Colloquim on Grammatical Inference*, 1993.

[Gol67]   E. Gold. Identification in the limit. *Information and control*, 10:447–474, 1967.

[McN67]   R. McNaughton. Parenthesis grammars. *Journal of the association for computing machinery*, 14:490–500, 1967.

[Mic80]   L. Miclet. Regular inference with a tail clustering method. *IEEE Transactions on SMC*, 1980.

[Mit82]   T.M. Mitchell. Generalization as search. *Artificial Intelligence*, 18:203–226, 1982.

[Nij80]   A. Nijholt. *Context-Free Grammars : Covers, Normal Forms and Parsing.* Volume 93 of *Lecture Notes in Computer Science*, Springer Verlag, 1980.

[Ros80]   H.B. Hunt & D.J. Rosenkrantz. Efficient algorithms for structural similarities of grammars. In *Conference record of the 7th ACM Symposium on principals of programming languages*, pages 213–219, 1980.

Representational Issues for Context Free Grammar Induction Using Genetic Algorithms

Peter Wyard,
Natural Language Group,
Systems Research Division,
BT Laboratories,
Martlesham Heath,
Ipswich IP5 7RE, UK.
email: pwyard@bt-sys.bt.co.uk

Abstract

This paper describes results on the inference of two classes of context free grammar (CFG), using a genetic algorithm (GA). The first class is that of n-symbol palindromes, where n = 2 to 4; the second class is small natural language grammars. The use of different normal forms of the grammars was compared experimentally. The use of different encodings of the grammars in the chromosomes of the GA, and the implications of these different representations within the genetic search are discussed. It is concluded that by paying attention to representational issues, worthwhile results may be achieved using a GA.

1   Introduction

The general grammatical induction problem consists of inferring an underlying grammar from a sample of strings from the language generated by the grammar (called positive strings), and possibly a sample of strings not in the language as well (i.e. negative strings) (see [1] for further details). Automatic grammatical inference has great potential benefits in a number of fields, for example:

- natural language processing, where much effort is currently spent on hand-crafting grammars

- speech recognition, for the inference of more varied speech models than are normally used

- syntactic pattern recognition in general (e.g. visual image classification)

- automatic computer program synthesis.

Grammatical inference has proved to be a complex problem in practice. The problem of grammatical induction from legal and illegal strings is known to be NP-complete even for finite state grammars [2]. For context free grammars, which correspond to finite state automata with a push-down stack, the problem cannot be any easier.

Many grammar inference methods have been devised, of widely varying type:

• "AI" methods, where a set of production rules is typically built up incrementally as the strings of the sample are presented, according to a detailed logical procedure

• probabilistic methods, where for instance a stochastic CFG is inferred using the inside-outside algorithm

• neural nets, where no explicit rules are learnt at all but similar functionality is obtained at the end.

Some of these methods are surveyed in [1] , [3], [4] and [5].

Many of these methods suffer from one or more of the following limitations:

1. The class of grammar inferred is limited, e.g. to regular grammars or a subset of regular grammars, and the inference method is often tailored to the characteristics of that class.

2. More information is required than a set of positive and negative strings, e.g. a set of skeleton parse trees.

3. They run in greater than polynomial time, so the inference of large-scale grammars is computationally infeasible.

Genetic algorithms (GAs) [6] , which are a class of search methods based on ideas from biological evolution, provide a general method of inferring any class of grammar, given only a set of positive and negative strings. This is a major advantage over methods suffering from limitations 1 or 2 above.

A GA has a population of individuals, sometimes called chromosomes, which represent solutions to the problem under consideration. The population evolves over a number of generations. Broadly speaking, in each generation the fittest chromosomes as determined by an evaluation function are allowed to reproduce, using the genetic operators of crossover and mutation, while the least fit are eliminated from the population.

Due to the genetic operators the GA achieves an "implicit parallelism" [6], which should make it much more efficient at searching than a standard hill-climbing algorithm , and *a fortiori* a random walk. This implicit parallelism has nothing to do with physical parallel processing, although GAs do lend themselves naturally to this , since all individuals in a population may then be evaluated in parallel to determine their fitness. Implicit parallelism refers to so-called "hyperplane searching" *within* a serial search, whereby many subsections of a chromosome are implicitly evaluated in the act of evaluating the chromosome as a whole.

The GA only works in this effective way if suitable building blocks (schemata) can be created and built together during the search to create a high-scoring individual. These building blocks are useful combinations of alleles within a chromosome which contribute something to an individual's overall fitness on their own, for example a building block in an animal's genotype for light-sensitivity in cells . The creation of suitable schemata is dependent on the representation chosen for the grammars in the chromosomes of the GA. The challenge is to devise representations for the grammars such that the genetic search operates in an effective manner, and this is the theme that is addressed, in a preliminary way, in this paper.

The reason that GAs have not been more widely used for the problem of grammatical inference is that because they are a general-purpose search method, it is not easy to use the sort of extra knowledge which many grammatical inference methods use, such as the characteristics of a particular class of languages, or structural information about the parse trees. This means that the GA is somewhat blind in its search, although over a wide range of problems [7] this has not proved to be a disadvantage, if the building block mechanism is working properly.

The motivation of the experimental work presented in this paper was to begin to explore the representational issues mentioned above, in order to have some raw material from which to construct a theory of the relationship between genetic search and representation. Although this exploration is still at a preliminary stage, we have achieved some experimental results for the inference of CFGs from a sample of strings which are at least as good as any other GA results (e.g. [9], discussed below in Section 1.1) in terms of the complexity of the language learnt, and are at least comparable with the best alternative methods applied to this task (here we refer to results on inferring CFGs as opposed to regular languages, e.g. [14], discussed below in Section 4.2, and [15], discussed in Section 4.3).

1.1 Related Work

The use of GAs for grammatical inference is still a small field. The most closely related work is that of Lucas [8], who describes the use of "biased" chromosomes for grammatical inference. He uses a bit-string representation for the grammars, in which there is a bit for every possible rule which can be generated from the set of left-hand side (LHS) variables and right-hand side (RHS) variables and terminals used in the grammar concerned. The most difficult grammar learnt by Lucas using this approach is that for 2-symbol palindromes, for which the total number of bits in each string was 75. Using what he calls "embedded normal form" to represent the grammars [9], Lucas has also successfully learnt 3-symbol palindromes.

Other related work is that of Kitano [10] and Gruau [11] who have published results on the use of GAs to infer generation grammars for neural nets. In this work, the candidate grammars are not evaluated directly on their ability to parse a string sample, but on their ability to generate neural nets which in turn perform well on the target problem. It is somewhat difficult to compare the difficulty of the problems tackled by Gruau, for example, and those tackled in this paper. The overall problem tackled by Gruau is learning a family of neural nets to solve a family of Boolean functions, such as the decoder with L inputs. It is not clear whether one should attempt to compare the natural language (NL) grammars of this paper with the decoder problem itself (and if so, how), or with the generation grammars which are learnt by Gruau's GA. The latter are fairly simple 3-rule grammars, for example, and appear to be rather simpler than those tackled in this paper.

Koza [12] has used a GA to learn a LISP S-expression which is equivalent to a grammar which can accept a language of just 4 strings, each of length 5, and reject all other strings of this length over a 4-symbol alphabet. Although this task is somewhat artificial as a language learning task, we achieved successful results at it, as reported in Section 4.2.

This paper builds on previous work by the author [13], in which a genetic algorithm was successfully used to infer grammars for the language of correctly balanced and nested brackets.

The rest of the paper is structured as follows: Section 2 discusses the representational issues which were explored experimentally, Section 3 describes the GA used and the experimental methodology, Section 4 gives the results and Section 5 concludes.

2. Representational Issues

As we have already mentioned in Section 1, one of the key issues in the effective use of GAs is choosing a suitable representation for the problem in the structures (chromosomes) which are being evolved. At least three factors are interrelated: the representation of the problem, the choice of genetic operators and parameters (e.g. the type of crossover, the degree of mutation, the selection of the next generation), and the evaluation function chosen to determine the fitness of the chromosomes. Very often, GAs are used in a somewhat routine fashion, e.g. variables or structures in the problem are encoded as binary strings using a simple and obvious mapping from symbol to bit string. Although the fact that they may be used as general purpose "off the shelf" problem solvers is one of their attractions, if insufficient thought is given to the factors above, the performance of the GA will sometimes be disappointing.

What is really needed is theoretical work which relates the known theory of genetic search, schemata, etc., e.g.[6], to the three factors mentioned above. It is very likely that the optimal choice of representation, for example, is problem and domain dependent. Nevertheless, it may be hoped that some theoretical results can be abstracted which are problem independent, and which may then be applied to different problems.

We are some way from having such a theory at the present time. However, in this section we discuss some of the representational issues for the problem of grammar induction, which we hope may feed into a proper theory in the future.

When it comes to choosing a representation for the problem of grammar induction, there are two main degrees of freedom: the formalism of grammar used, and the encoding of the grammar into a chromosome.

Taking the grammar formalism issue first, there are several different context-free grammar (CFG) formalisms, such as Greibach Normal Form (GNF), Chomsky Normal Form (CNF) and standard CFG, all of which may be used with GAs. Two of the main considerations are the size of the resulting grammar search space and the fraction of the total number of rules in a grammar which are needed on average to parse a string. GNF and CNF tend to have more rules and more variable symbols than the equivalent grammar in general CFG form, so the size of the grammar search space is larger, which would normally be a disadvantage for any search method. For example, the small natural language grammar for which results are reported in Section 4 has 7 rules, 4 variables and 4 terminals in general CFG form, giving a search space size of $(4*(4+4)^2)^7 \sim 10^{16}$, if we assume only 2 symbols on the RHS of a rule. The equivalent grammar in CNF has 11 rules, 7 variables and 4 terminals, giving a search space size of $(7*(7+4)^2)^{11} \sim 10^{32}$. However, this is not necessarily the most important issue, since GAs are good at searching vast search spaces by means of their implicit parallelism, mentioned in Section 1. Probably more important is the possibility of building up a high-scoring solution from building-blocks. What this means in the present case is that there should be a good chance, using the chosen representation, of throwing up individuals which have *some* of the properties of the target grammar and are also able to correctly accept some of the positive sample and reject some of the negative sample. This is the criterion used to assess fitness by the evaluation function. They can do this, crudely speaking, because part of their chromosome is right. Different individuals will have different parts right, and the normal process of the GA will build up a good solution. If the representation is such that, for example, no positive strings at all can be parsed unless all the rules of the grammar are present in an individual, then we are reduced to a "needle in the haystack" search, and the GA will be unlikely to be better than a random search. Two ways of avoiding this problem are to have excess rules in the chromosome (see Section 4 for an example), and to use a grammar formalism in which many of the positive strings only require a fraction of the total number of rules in the grammar to be parsed. This is dependent on the language being inferred, but for example, with general GNF many of the NL strings in Section 4 require 6 or 7 out of 7 of the rules to be parsed, whereas with CNF, only about 7 out of 11 are needed. The choice of evaluation function is also relevant at this point. If some credit could be given to chromosomes which have *some* of the right rules, or in some other way are approaching the solution, without actually being able to accept positive strings or reject negative strings, this would be beneficial. To do this without giving the evaluation function access to the target grammar (only to strings generated by the target grammar) is difficult, but might be possible if the evaluation function and the representation were suitably co-adjusted.

Regarding the second issue, the encoding of the grammar into a chromosome, we use a direct encoding as a list of rules, with the symbols of the grammar explicitly appearing in the chromosome, because this has previously shown good results, and we wished to hold one of the factors constant. For example, a simple grammar with four rules would be encoded as the string

S->AB,S->a,A->bA,B->ab

where "->" denotes the "rewrites as" symbol, and a comma is a rule delimiter.

Other encodings of grammars, which may be used with GAs, are as bit strings (one bit per possible rule [8,9], or rewriting the grammar symbols in binary form), various tree or graph representations [12, 17], and recursive transition networks. For all of these encodings, the key issues are again search space size and the building block issue. We have begun experiments using a bit string representation, to provide a comparison with the symbolic coding we have used hitherto. Ultimately we would like a thorough theoretical and empirical comparison of these encodings for grammar inference.

3. The GA Program

3.1 Representation

Each individual chromosome in the population was a complete grammar, and was represented as a symbol string, as described in Section 2 above. We experimented with different normal forms for the grammars, as described in Section 4 below.

3.2 Generation of the Initial Population

All chromosomes in the initial population were generated with n rules, where n was sometimes equal to the number of rules in the target grammar, and sometimes greater (Section 4 gives details). Each rule in each chromosome was generated randomly, but conforming to the normal form chosen for that run. The set of variables and terminals used to generate the rules was the same as in the target grammar, and the maximum number of symbols on the RHS of a rule was the same as in the target grammar. This was either two or three in our experiments. It would be possible not to use knowledge of the target grammar in this way (which violates our paradigm of learning only from the string sample), but the infringement is minor and does serve to restrict the search space size.

3.3 The Genetic Operators

A fairly standard GA was used, with one-point crossover and mutation as genetic operators. Mutation of a chromosome involved mutating each of its rules with a probability of 1 in 200, and mutating a rule involved randomly changing one of its symbols for another one that was legal in that position. Care was taken to ensure that after crossover the two offspring were both legal grammars, by ensuring that the breakpoints in the two parents were of the same type (e.g. both breakpoints between rules, or both between LHS and RHS). Chromosomes were able to change length (i.e. increase or decrease their number of rules) through crossover.

3.4 Evaluation of the Chromosomes

Evaluation of individuals at the end of each generation was done by testing their ability to accept a random sample of positive strings (generated from the target grammar) and to reject a random sample of negative strings. This test set of strings was fixed throughout each run of the GA for the results reported here, since experiments with a moving target of test strings showed no significant improvement (we have in general found this to be the case if the test set is large enough). The size of the test set turns out to be an important parameter, and we present results for different test set sizes. The standard scoring, used in all experiments unless stated otherwise, was as follows: a chromosome scores +1 for accepting a positive string or rejecting a negative string, and scores -1 for rejecting a positive string or accepting a negative string. There is also a penalty of 1 for each rule in excess of the number of rules in the target grammar, which is desirable to prevent the genetic search favouring grammars with large numbers of rules, which are therefore able to accept a large number of positive strings, although they wildly overgenerate. Finally we introduced a penalty of 1 for each RHS variable in a chromosome in excess of the total number of RHS variables in the target grammar, in order to favour more compact grammars giving shorter derivations of the positive strings.

A fast chart parser was used in the evaluation phase. The time required for evaluating the fitness of each population of chromosomes is a large fraction of the overall time for running the GA (typically 80-90%), because every chromosome (candidate grammar) must be used to parse every test string. For a typical run with a population size of 1000 and 500 test strings, this means 500,000 parses per generation. Our parser is fast for its type, and can cope with any grammar, however unusual, whatever form of CFG is used, and however many epsilon-rules (rules with an empty right hand side) there are. However, it was really designed for natural language parsing with much larger grammars than we use in the current work, and has not been optimised for this task. It typically performs between 30 and 100 parses per second in our experiments on a SPARCstation 10, depending on the number of rules in the grammar (typically 4 to 12) and the distribution of test string length. In some cases we used a maximum string length of 40, in order to obtain a reasonable number of positive strings, which of course makes the parsing slow. The fact that one generation may thus take a number of hours to evaluate has been the major limiting factor in our experiments, and it is the reason why we have had to sample GA parameter space fairly sparsely, although we hope in an intelligent fashion. It has not been possible to perform exhaustive and systematic sets of runs using each combination of parameter values.

Lucas [9] quotes fast evaluation times for his GA approach, so it is worth making some brief comparisons. He uses a CYK-type parser in conjunction with a variant of CNF for his grammars, which leads to faster parsing for ambiguous grammars than a chart parser. He also uses a maximum string length of 7, which greatly reduces parsing time. We did not wish to be restricted to a particular normal form, since investigation of different grammar formalisms for genetic search is one of the aims of our research. Lucas uses a positive sample with strings of length 2-4, which means that the sample is small. We have found it necessary to use many more, and hence longer, strings in our positive sample than Lucas. It is not clear how generally one can learn CFGs from such short strings.

3.5 The Overall Operation of the GA

An initial population of chromosomes was produced as in Section 3.2. The production of each succeeding generation from the current one was done in a somewhat unusual way, which was arrived at in the course of the experimentation. After scoring each member of the population in the current generation as described in Section 3.4, the next generation was formed as follows: the top 10% was mutated, the top 30% were reproduced using crossover but no mutation (each pair of chromosomes producing two offspring regardless of their fitness), and the top 60% went through unchanged. We have found that GAs are usually insensitive to these details, but it would be advisable in the future to re-examine this aspect of our method. In an attempt to maintain diversity in the population, we screened the population for duplicate grammars. If a duplicate was found, one of its rules was randomly selected for unconditional mutation, although if it was still a duplicate after this process, it was allowed to go through to the next generation anyway. For most of the runs to be described in Section 4, two chromosomes were regarded as duplicates if they were identical strings, i.e. they had the same rules in the same order. For some of the later runs, two chromosomes were regarded as duplicates if they had the same rules, but not necessarily in the same order (called "rule set screening" in Section 4). Screening adds to the overall amount of mutation.

The GA was either left to run for a predetermined number of generations, typically 20 or 30, or its progress was monitored manually, and it was terminated if it learnt a perfect solution or had clearly got stuck in a local maximum.

3.6   Implementation

The program was implemented in a mixture of ML and C, and run on a SPARCstation 10.

4.   Results

As discussed in Section 3, we have not been able to perform an exhaustive or systematic set of GA runs for each of the grammars studied due to the CPU intensive nature of the evaluation phase. Instead, we present a series of results which show the achievements of this kind of GA at inferring grammars, and highlight the pros and cons of different representations. We begin with some of the simple CFGs which have been the subject of inference experiments in the literature. We then move to palindromes, which are regarded as a more difficult challenge, partly because they cannot be cast as deterministic CFGs. These have been studied particularly by Lucas [8,9]. Finally we present results for a simple NL grammar.

In the following sections, P= population size, L = number of rules in each chromosome, pos = number of positive strings, neg = number of negative strings.

4.1   Simple CFGs

The first experiment aimed to infer the language of strings containing equal numbers of "a" and "b", e.g. "ba", "abba", "abab", etc.

For this experiment, the target grammar was expressed in GNF. It has 7 rules:

S->aAS, S->bBS, S->e, A->aAA, A->b, B->a, B->bB.

This proved too difficult to learn when GNF was used as internal representation in the GA (i.e. every rule is of the form LV -> RT RVlist, where LV is variable, RT is a terminal and RVlist is a possibly empty list of variables), using a maximum population size of 1000 and a maximum of 30 generations.

We then switched to using general CFG as internal representation, i.e. there is no restriction on the form of the RHS of the rules. A first run used {P=1000, L=7, pos=150,neg=150} and allowed each rule to have up to 3 symbols on the RHS. By 12 generations a perfect solution had been found, namely:

A->baS, A->aSb, A->bSa, A->A, B->b, S->AS, S->e.

On inspection, the 4th and 5th rules were redundant, so another run was performed, with {P=1000, L=5, pos=150,neg=150} and only using 2 variables S and A. This also learnt a perfect solution by the 12th generation, namely:

A->aa, S->SS, S->aSb, S->e, S->bSa.

On inspection, the first two rules are redundant (the first could be eliminated by a very simple algorithm). Thus the GA has learnt this grammar, and nearly learnt the minimal CFG form. It would be easy to repeat this run with L=3, to see if the GA could learn the minimal grammar directly, but this was not done, due to processing time limitations.

This experiment seems to be a case where reducing the grammar search space size by changing from GNF to general CFG has been very beneficial.

4.2 Two languages with few positive strings

The next two languages learnt were cases where the language to be learnt consisted of an unusually small fraction of the total number of strings which could be generated from the set of terminal symbols and the length of string used. In both cases, the positive strings in the test set were greatly outnumbered by the negative strings. The scoring function was therefore modified to weight the ability to accept an individual positive string more highly than the ability to reject a negative string, such that a perfect grammar would gain a reasonable fraction of its score both from accepting positives and from rejecting negatives. If this is not done, grammars quickly evolve which have a near perfect score, because they are perfect at rejecting negatives, but there is very little evolutionary pressure to learn the positives.

The first case was the language $b^n a b^{n-1}$, $n>=1$, used by Giordano in his version space grammar inference experiments [14]. This was learnt in 5 generations, using {P=500,L=4,pos=10,neg=200}, and with positives weighted 20 times more than negatives. The internal representation was general CFG. The grammar found by the GA was: S->bA, A->Sb, A->a, A->a. The last rule is redundant, so the GA has learnt the minimal CFG form of this grammar, with only 3 rules and 2 variables. The GA could be run again with these settings, to see if this minimal grammar could be learnt directly.

The second case comes from Koza [12], and was mentioned in Section 1. As presented by Koza, the task is to accept just four 5-symbol strings, namely {aaatt, aattt, aactt, aagtt}, and to reject all other 5-symbol strings over the alphabet of these 4 terminals.

A target grammar was drawn up which had seven rules: S->AMT, A->aa, T->tt, M->a|t|c|g.

When the GA was run with chromosomes having 7 rules, it failed to learn {P=500,L=7,pos=4, neg =500}, positives weighted 25 times more than negatives. The best score obtained was just over 500, with all negatives correctly rejected but no positives accepted. It was noted that the population moved towards a state in which there were hardly any variables left in the RHS of the rules, making the chances of further evolution towards the correct grammar remote. It was speculated that the reason for this may have been that the large score available merely for rejecting negatives may have been an evolutionary pressure which drove the variables out of the population, as this is an easy way of rejecting strings.

Another run was then done with 4 excess rules in the chromosomes. It was hoped that there would then be more chance that some of the rules in some of the individuals would be useful in accepting positives, and that the other rules would change during evolution to become merely redundant, rather than harmful. The values used were {P=500, L=11, pos=4, neg=500}. After 11 generations, a grammar was learnt which achieved a perfect performance on the Koza task, as far as the author can determine, namely:

S->At, A->aM, A->t, A->aA, A->ct, A->at, M->At, M->gt, M->t, T->e, T->c.

The last 2 rules are redundant, because they are never reached. Thus the GA has learnt a 9-rule grammar for the Koza task. What it has not done is to learn a grammar which can reject *all* strings except the 4 positive ones, which our target grammar does. It only rejects all negative strings of length 5. This is not surprising, because there are no other negative strings in the test set.

4.3 Palindromes

The languages of n-symbol palindromes seem to be regarded as a common test case for the effectiveness of various grammatical inference methods. Lari and Young [15] tackled the palindrome problem using stochastic CFG inference by means of the Inside-Outside algorithm, an extension of the Forward-Backward algorithm used in training Hidden Markov Models, which are equivalent to stochastic regular grammars. They successfully learnt a stochastic CFG for 2-symbol palindromes, and although the Inside-Outside algorithm failed to learn 3-symbol palindromes on its own, it was successful when interleaved with a procedure which detected and reallocated redundant symbols in the grammars thrown up by the Inside-Outside algorithm.

We ran a number of experiments to compare different grammar formalisms. For 2-symbol palindromes, the GNF target grammar has 7 rules: S->0, S->1, S->e, S->0SA, S->1SB, A->0, B->1. A general CFG target grammar has only 5 rules: S->0S0, S->1S1, S->0, S->1, S->e.

Using GNF in the chromosomes, a 2-symbol palindrome grammar was learnt in 19 generations, using a population of 1000, but could not be learnt using a population of 500 (both these runs used {L=7, pos=150, neg=150}). Using a general CFG, a perfect grammar was learnt in 18 generations, using {P=500, L=5, pos=150, neg=150}, again showing the advantage of smaller search space size.

Using a general CFG, a 3-symbol palindrome grammar was learnt in 12 generations using a population of 1000 {P=1000, L=7, pos=150, neg=150}, but not learnt at all with a population of 700, or with {pos=75, neg=75}. This shows the critical role played by population size and test set size in determining whether learning is successful. We have found experimentally that when evolution gets "stuck", the answer is usually to increase P, although the test string set must also be big enough to give a faithful representation of the language to be learnt.

We failed to learn the 4-symbol palindrome grammar, which has 9 rules in general CFG form, using a population of 1000 or 2000, and {pos=neg=200}. Computing resources for bigger runs were not available. The best performance on the test of 200 positive and 200 negative strings was 313/400, and the difference in performance when P was increased from

1000 to 2000 was not thought to be statistically significant for a single run (the GA involves several random processes). The percentage of positive strings accepted was similar to that of negative strings rejected, so it seems that the test set was doing its job, but it did not appear that evolution was likely to succeed by using more generations, because useful (essential?) rules such as S->tSt, where t is one of the terminals, had been eliminated from all the high-scoring chromosomes by 30 generations. Such rules had been present earlier in the evolution, which suggests that the GA had become stuck in a local maximum.

4.4   A Simple Natural Language Grammar

Ultimately, we should like our GAs to learn grammars useful for natural language processing (NLP). As a first step towards this, we performed some experiments on a very small natural language grammar, using just 4 terminal symbols, [adjective = a, determiner = d, noun = n, verb = v]. The 7 rules captured a basic noun-phrase, verb-phrase structure of the English language: S->AC, A->dB, A->B, B->aB, B->n, C->v, C->A.

Using a general CFG representation in the chromosomes, we performed four runs as shown below. All used 30 generations. Rule set screening, as described in Section 3, was introduced at this point, and used hereafter.

Pop Size	No. of test strings	L	Best Score Reached
700	200+/100-	9	292/300
1000	200+/200-	9	367/400
1000	200+/300-	7	482/500
2000	200+/300-	7	434/500

All of the above runs failed to learn this language, although one grammar had a score of 482/500, and had learnt some of the structure of the target grammar, such as a broad distinction between NP and VP, and a recursive rule for adjectives:
S->CC, C->dC, C->v, C->B, B->aB, B->n, B->nv. B and C correspond moderately well to A and C in the target.

A second set of experiments was performed, using the idea of two-stage evolution. This has some resemblance to Lucas's use of a gene pool. The idea was to begin the search with a test set of positive strings only, to find rules which could accept positive strings, even if they badly overgenerated, and then continue with positive and negative strings, to steer the population towards the desired grammar.

In the first stage, we used {P= 700, pos = 100, neg = 0, L = 9}. After 7 generations, a score of 98/100 had been reached. This population was then used as seed population for a run with {P= 700, pos = 200, neg = 100, L = 9}, but the best score after a further 20 generations was only 277/300, and the grammars were no better than those found in the previous set of experiments. The problem is that in the first stage the grammars learnt are far too general, i.e. the GA finds grammars which can accept positive strings the "easy way", by having rules with lots of variables. Unfortunately, these rules wildly overgenerate, and are not a useful starting point for further evolution towards a correct grammar.

A third set of experiments was performed, using Chomsky Normal Form (CNF) as the representation. The motivation for this was that although the grammar search space size becomes larger, because the number of rules in a CNF grammar for a given language is usually larger than in a minimal CFG form, the fraction of rules in a grammar used to parse a particular string is lower than in the CFG representation, where most of the rules are needed to parse most strings (for the small NL grammar, at least). This makes it very hard for "building-blocks" (useful subsets) of rules to appear in chromosomes in the population with the CFG representation, as discussed in Section 2.

The target grammar (equivalent to the minimal CFG grammar above) was: S->AC, A->DB, A->EB, A->n, B->EB, B->n, D->d, C->v, C->FA, E->a, F->v. This was generated by a standard transformation [16] from the general CFG representation.

Two runs were performed, both using 30 generations.

Results were as follows:

Pop Size	No. of test strings	Best Score Reached	Comment
1000	200+/200-	399/400	1
1000	250+/350-	600/600	2

Comments:

1. The best grammar found was:

S->EA, S->BD, S->FE, E->n, E->CE, E->CF, A->v, D->v, F->EA, C->d, C->a.

The second rule is redundant because there is no B-rule. Although this grammar only failed to reject one of the negative strings, it is easy to find negative strings which it will not reject, e.g. "adav". It appeared that the 200 negative strings were insufficient to find its weaknesses, so more negative strings were used in the second experiment.

2. The best grammar found (in fact the only perfectly-scoring one in the population, found on the 30th generation!) was: S->AE, S->ED, A->ED, B->BE, D->v (twice), E->n, E->FE, F->d (twice), F->a.

The B-rule is redundant, and two of the rules are duplicates, so the GA has actually found an 8-rule CNF grammar. It appears that the GA has nearly found a clever and correct solution. Unfortunately, the grammar is not quite perfect, because there is still a small class of short negative strings which the grammar fails to reject, e.g. "adnv", which can be derived by: S->ED->Ev->FEv->FFEv->adnv. None of this class of strings appeared in the randomly generated test set. However, a perfect score has been obtained on a large test set, which may be regarded as a very encouraging result.

In conclusion, this grammar appears to be a case where the advantage of a small search space is outweighed by the need for building blocks to work properly.

5 Conclusion

It is concluded that by paying attention to the representational issues of grammar formalism and chromosome encoding, encouraging results on the inference of small CFGs from a sample of positive and negative strings using a GA have been achieved. In particular, a perfect grammar for 3-symbol palindromes was learnt, and a grammar which captures the noun-phrase verb-phrase structure of English was learnt which achieved a perfect score on the 600-string test set. These results are at least as good as any other GA results [9] in terms of the complexity of the language learnt, and are at least comparable with the best alternative methods [14,15].

The results indicate that GAs may be a very effective general method for grammatical inference, which may be applied to any class of language learning problem. However, the challenge remains to devise suitable representations to enable the GA to operate effectively on any new language which it may face, and to learn large grammars in reasonable time, which may require a form of modular or incremental learning.

Avenues of future work which look particularly promising include:

• a critical evaluation of the relative merits of string and tree encoding of grammars

• controlled use of the test strings to guide the genetic search in sub-populations

• the use of a classifier system [18], where the population is a market economy of co-operating rules rather than standalone grammars.

6 References

[1]   Fu, K, and Booth, T, Grammatical Inference: Introduction and Survey, IEEE Transactions on Pattern Analysis and Machine Intelligence, vol. 8, pp. 343-375, 1986.

[2]   Gold, E.M., Complexity of automaton identification from given data, Information and Control, 37, 302-320.

[3]   Angluin, D., and Smith, C.H. , "Inductive inference: theory and methods". Computing Surveys, vol. 15, no.3, September 1983.

[4]   Cohen, P.R., and Feigenbaum, E.A. ,"The handbook of artificial intelligence: volume 2". Los Altos, California. Publ. Morgan Kaufmann, 1983.

[5]   Lucas,S, New Directions in Grammatical Inference, Proc. IEE Colloq. on Grammatical Inference: Theory, Applications and Alternatives, 1993, Digest No. 1993/092, London.

[6]   Holland, J.H. "Adaptation in natural and artificial systems", Univ. of Michigan Press, Ann Arbor, 1975.

[7]   Goldberg, D., Genetic Algorithms in Search, Optimization and Machine Learning, Addison-Wesley, 1989.

[8]   Lucas, S, Biased Chromosomes for Grammatical Inference, Proc. of Natural
Algorithms in Signal Processing, IEE Workshop at Danbury Park, UK, 1993.

[9]   Lucas,S, Structuring Chromosomes for Context-Free Grammar Evolution, First
International Conference on Evolutionary Computing, pp. 130-135, 1994.

[10]   Kitano, H, Designing neural networks using genetic algorithm with graph generation
system, Complex Systems, vol. 4, pp. 461-476, 1990.

[11]   Gruau, F, Cellular Encoding as a Graph Grammar, Proc. IEE Colloq. on Grammatical
Inference: Theory, Applications and Alternatives, 1993, Digest No. 1993/092, London.

[12]   Koza, J, Genetic Programming, MIT Press, 1992.

[13]   Wyard, P J, Context Free Grammar Induction Using Genetic Algorithms, Proc. IEE
Colloq. on Grammatical Inference: Theory, Applications and Alternatives, 1993, Digest No.
1993/092, London.

[14]   Giordano, J-Y, Version Space for Learning Context-Free Grammars, Proc. IEE
Colloq. on Grammatical Inference: Theory, Applications and Alternatives, 1993, Digest No.
1993/092, London.

[15]   Lari, K. and Young , S.J., The estimation of stochastic context-free grammars using
the Inside-Outside algorithm, Computer Speech and Language, vol. 4, no. 1, 1990.

[16]   Hopcroft, J. and Ullman, J, Introduction to Automata Theory, Languages and
Computation, Addison-Wesley, 1979.

[17]   Dunay,D, Petry, F, and Buckles, B, Regular Language Induction with Genetic
Programming, First International Conference on Evolutionary Computing, pp. 396-400,
1994.

[18]   Goldberg, D, Genetic Algorithms in Search, Optimization and Machine Learning,
Addison-Wesley, 1989.

Regular Grammatical Inference from Positive and Negative Samples by Genetic Search : the GIG method

Pierre Dupont
France Télécom CNET/LAA/TSS/RCP
2, route de Trégastel BP40 - 22301 Lannion Cedex France
E-mail: dupont@lannion.cnet.fr

Abstract

We recall briefly in this paper the formal theory of regular grammatical inference from positive and negative samples of the language to be learned. We state this problem as a search toward an optimal element in a boolean lattice built from the positive information. We explain how a genetic search technique may be applied to this problem and we introduce a new set of genetic operators. In view of limiting the increasing complexity as the sample size grows, we propose a semi-incremental procedure. Finally, an experimental protocol to assess the performance of a regular inference technique is detailed and comparative results are given.

1 Introduction

Grammatical Inference is an instance of the *Inductive Learning* problem which can be formulated as the task of discovering common structures in examples which are supposed to be generated by the same process. In this particular case, the examples are sentences defined on a specific alphabet and the common structures are represented by a grammar or an equivalent machine. Once the grammar has been inferred from the learning data, the induced language is identified.

A set of negative information, i.e. a set of examples not respecting the common structures, may also help the language induction. This is theoritically motivated by the Gold's results of language identification in the limit [5]. He shows that the class of languages which are identifiable in the limit, given positive information only, is the class of *non superfinite*[1] languages. On the contrary, given a complete (positive and negative) information, the class of *admissible*[2] grammars are identifiable in the limit.

---

[1] A superfinite class of languages denotes any class which contains all the languages of finite cardinality and at least one of infinite cardinality. Consequently, the regular class is superfinite.

[2] A class C of grammars is admissible if C is countable and for any grammar G in C, the language membership problem is decidable. The context-sensitive grammars are admissible since the context-sensitive languages are accepted by nondeterministic linearly space-bounded Turing machines for which the language membership problem is decidable [8].

In section 2, we review the formal theory of the regular inference problem and we state it as a search through a boolean lattice. In this framework, regular inference is viewed as the discovery of an optimal state merging operation in a canonical finite automaton built from the positive information. We show how the negative information may be used to control the grammar induction by means of an evaluation function of each potential solution. The proposed grammatical inference by genetic search is detailed in section 3. As the search space dramatically grows with the size of the positive sample, the correct inference becomes more difficult while getting a larger positive information on the language to be identified. This seemingly paradoxical situation motivates the semi-incremental procedure exposed in section 4. The experimental assessment is exposed in section 5 followed by comparative results with another inference method.

In the following sections of this paper, we assume the reader familiar with the usual notations of formal language theory (see, for instance, [1]).

2   The Regular Inference Problem

2.1   Definitions and notations

A regular language L may be referred to by $L(R)$, $L(A)$ or $L(G)$, depending on whether this language is respectively, but equivalently, specified by a regular expression R, a finite automaton A or a regular grammar G.

A finite automaton is a 5-tuple $(Q, \Sigma, \delta, q_0, F)$ where Q is a finite set of *states*, Σ is an *alphabet*, δ is a *transition function*, i.e. a mapping from $Q \times \Sigma$ to 2^Q, q_0 is the *initial state* and F is a subset of Q identifying the *final* or *accepting states*. If for any q in Q and any a in Σ, $\delta(q, a)$ has at most one member, respectively exactly one member, the automaton A is said to be *deterministic*, respectively *complete*. Given a finite automaton $A = (Q, \Sigma, \delta, q_0, F)$, let $\Pi = (\pi_0, \ldots, \pi_{r-1})$ be a partition of the set Q. Let $A_\Pi = (\Pi, \Sigma, \gamma, \pi_0, F_\Pi)$ be the *derived automaton* with respect to the partition Π. It is defined as follows:

(1) $q_0 \in \pi_0$.

(2) $F_\Pi = \{\pi_i \in \Pi \mid \exists q_j \in F, q_j \in \pi_i\}$.

(3) $\gamma(\pi_i, a) = \{\pi_j \in \Pi \mid \exists a \in \Sigma, \exists q_k \in \pi_i, \exists q_l \in \pi_j \text{ such that } q_l \in \delta(q_k, a)\}, 0 \leq i \leq r - 1$.

Hence, the automaton A_Π is obtained by merging the states of A belonging to the same subset π_i, for each subset $\pi_i, 0 \leq i \leq r - 1$. The finite automaton A_Π is said to be *derived from A with respect to the partition* Π. Note the important property that $L(A)$ is included in $L(A_\Pi)$ as a consequence of the construction of A_Π [4].

Let I_+ and I_- be two disjoint finite subsets of Σ^*. They respectively denote the positive and negative learning samples of the inference algorithm. A sample I is said to be *structurally complete* with respect to a finite automaton A if the two following conditions hold:

(1) every transition of A is used at least once when accepting the strings of I.

(2) every element of F (the final state set of A) is an accepting state of at least one string of I.

Let $MCA(I_+)$ denote the *maximal canonical automaton with respect to I_+* [11]. It is the automaton having the largest number of states with respect to which I_+ is structurally complete, since each transition of $MCA(I_+)$ is used exactly once when accepting the strings of I_+. The $MCA(I_+)$ is generally non-deterministic. Let $PTA(I_+)$ denote the *prefix tree acceptor with respect to* I_+ [2]. It is necessarily deterministic and may be derived from the $MCA(I_+)$ by merging states sharing the same prefixes. Let UA denote the *universal automaton*. It accepts all the strings defined over the alphabet Σ, i.e. $L(UA) = \Sigma^*$, and it is the smallest automaton with respect to which every sample of Σ^* is structurally complete. Let $mDFA(L)$ denote the minimal deterministic automaton accepting the language L. It is unique up to a renumbering of its states.

2.2 Fundamental theorems of the regular inference

Theorem 1 *Let I_+ be a positive sample of any regular language L and let A be any automaton accepting exactly L. If I_+ is structurally complete with respect to A, then A may be derived from the $MCA(I_+)$ for some partition Π [11].*

Theorem 2 *Let I_+ be a positive sample of any regular language L and let A be an automaton isomorphic to the minimal DFA accepting L. If I_+ is structurally complete with respect to A, then A may be derived from the $PTA(I_+)$ for some partition Π [2].*

These theorems, revisited in [3], form the basis of a family of inference methods (see, for instance, [12, 2]) by state merging technique, since they amount either to heuristically discover the partition Π or to explicitly construct this partition for some specified subclass of regular languages. Our method aims at discovering the partition Π under the control of the negative sample I_-, like in [14], but here the problem is considered as an explicit search toward an optimal partition.

Let us mention that the first theorem is more general than the second one in the sense that it only suppose the structural completeness of I_+ with respect to any automaton accepting a language L, not necessarily with respect to the minimal DFA for L. In other respects, as the $PTA(I_+)$ generally contains less states than the $MCA(I_+)$, starting from the $PTA(I_+)$ allows for reducing the search space.

2.3 Statement of the regular inference problem

Given the positive and negative samples I_+ and I_-, a finite automaton A is a solution of the regular inference problem if the three following conditions are satisfied:
(1) I_+ is structurally complete with respect to A.
(2) $I_- \subseteq \Sigma^* - L(A)$.
(3) A is an automaton having the fewest number of states, which fulfils the two preceding conditions.

We may also restrict the possible solutions to deterministic automata. In that particular case, we search for the minimal DFA consistent with I_+ and I_-. That is, we take the simplicity of the inferred automaton as generality criterion but there is no guarantee that the identified language includes all the languages agreeing with I_+ and I_-. Unfortunately, the minimal DFA consistency problem is known to be NP-complete [6]. However we shall see that when looking for an optimal automaton as defined in section 2.4, we may correctly identify a set of typical regular languages, in practice.

2.4 Search for the optimal partition

Let Q denote the set of states of the $MCA(I_+)$, let N denote the cardinality of Q and let $P(I_+)$ be the set of all partitions of Q. Let $r(\Pi_i)$, or simply r_i, denote the number of elements, or *blocks*, of the partition Π_i. Let $\Pi_1 = \{\pi_{11}, \ldots, \pi_{1r_1}\}$ and Π_2 be two partitions of $P(I_+)$. We say that Π_2 *directly derives from* Π_1 if the partition Π_2 is constructed from Π_1 as follows: $\Pi_2 = \{\pi_{1j} \cup \pi_{1k}\} \cup \Pi_1 \setminus \{\pi_{1j}, \pi_{1k}\}$, for some j, k between 1 and r_1, $j \neq k$. Consequently, $r_2 = r_1 - 1$.

This derivation operation defines a partial order relation on $P(I_+)$, which we shall denote $\preceq$. In particular, we have $\Pi_1 \preceq \Pi_2$. Let $\ll$ denote its transitive closure. We already known the language inclusion property [4] which may be reformulated as follows: $\Pi_i \ll \Pi_j$ if $L(A_{\Pi_i}) \subseteq L(A_{\Pi_j})$.

Note that the set $P(I_+)$ ordered by the relation $\preceq$ is a boolean lattice of which $MCA(I_+)$ and UA are respectively the null and universal elements. Hence the regular inference problem may be stated as a search through this lattice where each potential solution may be evaluated by the function f_{I_+, I_-} defined as follows.

$f_{I_+, I_-} : P(I_+) \to \mathbf{R}^+, f_{I_+, I_-}(\Pi) = g(r_{I_+}(\Pi), k_{I_-}(\Pi))$, where g is a positive penalty function of two integer arguments:

$r_{I_+}(\Pi)$, the number of blocks of the partition Π, and

$k_{I_-}(\Pi)$, the number of strings from I_- being accepted by the derived automaton A_Π.

One possible definition of the function g is as follows:

$g(a, 0) = a, g(a, b) = N + 1$ if $b > 0, a \geq 1$.

We may now consider the minimal DFA problem as an optimization problem, that is, the search through the lattice $P(I_+)$ for the partition Π for which f_{I_+, I_-} is minimal. In other words, if $d(\Pi)$ denotes the *depth* of an automaton A_Π in the lattice, i.e. $d(\Pi) = N - r(\Pi)$, we are looking for an automaton at maximal depth and compatible with the positive and negative samples. In the same theoretical framework, Tomita proposed a heuristic search by hill-climbing [16] and already mentioned the potential advantage of adaptive search technique. Another search technique, called BRIG, which relies on a random pruning of the boolean lattice has been recently proposed by Miclet [13]. In the section 3, we detail the Grammatical Inference by Genetic search (GIG) method.

3 The GIG method

3.1 Overview of genetic algorithms

We follow here the presentation of Genetic Algorithms (GAs) given in [7]. A GA is a parallel search technique in which a set, namely the *population*, of potential solutions, called *individuals* is progressively updated through a *selection mechanism* and *genetic operations*, i.e. the *crossover* and the *mutation*. Each individual is coded as a fixed length bit string, called a *chromosome*.

Starting from a randomly generated initial population, i.e. at the first *generation*, each individual is evaluated by the *fitness function* to be optimized. The population of the next generation is obtained in three steps. Firstly, a random selection with repetitions is performed, usually on the whole population. The probability of a given individual to be selected, possibly several times, is obtained from the ratio between its fitness value and the average fitness value computed over the whole population. This is the fitness proportionate reproduction mechanism which promotes the fittest individuals to be reproduced. Secondly, a given percentage, i.e. at a given *crossover rate*, of this temporary population is selected by pairs. Each pairs of *parents* gives rise to two *children* which are constructed by taking alternative subparts from their parent chromosomes. After the crossover operation, the parents are replaced by their children in the temporary population. Thirdly, some individuals are selected at a given *mutation rate*. One position in the associated chromosome of each selected individual is randomly chosen and the corresponding bit value is swapped. The final population of the next generation is made of the individuals obtained after fitness proportionate reproduction, crossover and mutation. This process is iterated until some termination criterion is met[3].

The use of a GA for solving the regular grammatical inference problem is motivated by the three following considerations. Firstly, we would like to take advantage of an implicitly parallel search technique. Secondly, a GA offers a way to numerically optimize data represented in a symbolic form. Thirdly, since a GA aims at continuously improving potential solutions, it should offer the possibility to rapidly converge to a new solution after updating the learning samples.

A very preliminary work on the use of GA for grammatical inference has been recently proposed [17]. However, the theoretical framework was not stated, a lot of a priori knowledge was used (number of rules, maximal rule length, sets of terminals and nonterminals of the unknown grammar supposed to be known) and the experimental assessment was very limited.

In the sequel, we detail the representation scheme and the genetic operators of the GIG method. Besides, we consider the function f_{I_+, I_-} introduced in the section 2.4 as the fitness function to be optimized[4].

3.2 Classical partition representation scheme

Each individual in the population corresponds to a partition of the state set of the $MCA(I_+)$, that we represent by its *group-number encoding*. Formally, each partition Π is encoded as a string of N integers $(i_1, \ldots, i_N)$ where $i_j \in \{1, \ldots, r(\Pi)\}, 1 \leq j \leq N$. The $j - th$ integer i_j indicates the group number, or block index, assigned to the state j. For example, the encoding $(2, 1, 2, 3, 2)$ represents the partition $\{\{1, 3, 5\}, \{2\}, \{4\}\}$ of the set $\{1,2,3,4,5\}$.

The group-number encoding satisfies the closure property of the representation, that is, every chromosome may be interpreted as a valid partition. However, this coding is largely redundant since there are $r(\Pi)!$ equivalent representations. For this reason, a *left-to-right canonical group-number encoding* [9] has been introduced. Formally, the groups are numbered in such a way that their are in the same left-to-right order as their state of minimal rank. For example, $(2, 1, 2, 3, 2)$ will be renumbered as $(1, 2, 1, 3, 1)$.

---

[3]Usually the search is stopped when the number of distinct evaluated individuals reaches a maximal value or when the population has converged to a few distinct individuals.

[4]The value of f_{I_+, I_-} assigned to any derived automaton not compatible with I_-, i.e. accepting at least one string from I_-, is equal to $N + 1$. As a consequence, such an automaton may be selected for reproduction although with a lower probability than a compatible automaton

3.3 Genetic operators

We define here the genetic operators in the *phenotype space*, that is, the space of possible partitions. Note that these operations are actually performed on the associated representation, i.e. the *genotype*, in such a way that the resulting individuals remain canonically numbered.

3.3.1 Structural Mutation

The structural mutation consists of a random selection of a state in some block of a given partition followed by the random assignment of this state to a block. Consider, for instance, the partition $\{\{1,\mathbf{3},5\},\{2\},\{4\}\}$ and supposed that the state **3** is randomly selected for mutation. Suppose, moreover, that the randomly selected block is the second one. The resulting partition is $\{\{1,5\},\{2,\mathbf{3}\},\{4\}\}$. In that particular case, the number of blocks has not been changed. However, we may similarly obtain a partition with a cardinality increased or decreased by one. In other words, the depth of the derived automaton obtained after mutation differs at most by 1 from the original one. This is a particular feature of our problem, since classical GAs applied to partitioning problems often use repair function to insure that the fixed number of blocks remains constant during the search [10]. Here, we try to find the partitions having the smallest cardinality, i.e. the derived automaton at maximal depth, under the control of the negative sample[5].

3.3.2 Structural Crossover

The structural crossover consists of the union in both parent partitions of a randomly selected block. For example, let the two following partitions be selected for crossover, $\{\{\mathbf{1,4}\},\{2,3,5\}\}$ and $\{\{\mathbf{1,3}\},\{2\},\{4\},\{5\}\}$, and let the first block be randomly selected in both parents. The union of the selected blocks is $\{\mathbf{1,3}\}\cup\{\mathbf{1,4}\}=\{\mathbf{1,3,4}\}$ and the two resulting partitions are $\{\{\mathbf{1,3,4}\},\{2,5\}\}$ and $\{\{\mathbf{1,3,4}\},\{2\},\{5\}\}$. The derived automata obtained after crossover share a common block, i.e. a common subset of states merged together. Moreover, the depth of each new automaton is either equal to the original one or increased by 1.

4 A semi-incremental procedure

As mentioned in the section 1, we are faced with a paradoxical situation. Indeed, the search space size dramatically increases with the size of the $MCA(I_+)$, i.e. with the size of the positive sample, making the correct identification more difficult when we have a larger positive information on the language to be identified. For this reason, we propose a semi-incremental inference procedure. It is not purely incremental in the sense that it assumes that we dispose of some fixed positive and negative samples, but it makes use of the positive information in an incremental way. We first sort the positive sample I_+ in lexicographical order. Consequently, the shortest strings are first taken into account. Starting with the first sentence of I_+, we construct the associated $MCA(I_1^+)$ and we search for the optimal partition of its state set under the control of the whole negative

---

[5]Remind that the derived automaton should not accept any strings from I_-.

sample I_-. Let A_1 denote the derived automaton with respect to this optimal partition. Let s_{next} denote the next string in I_+. If s_{next} is already accepted by A_1, we skip it. Otherwise, the automaton A_1 is extended in such a way that $L(A_1^{ext}) = L(A_1) \cup s_{next}$. The search is then restarted from the extended automaton A_1^{ext} under the control of I_-. We pursue this incremental procedure till all the strings of I_+ had been considered.

Note that the proposed technique is a heuristic way of reducing the computational complexity of the inference problem, with no guarantee of getting the correct solution. It is not only useful for the GIG method but may be applied to other search algorithms.

5 Experimental Assessment

5.1 Protocol

The following experimental protocol has been proposed to evaluate regular inference methods. We test a set of typical regular languages [16, 13]. Associated to each language L, we automatically build the corresponding $mDFA(L)$. The learning samples are then generated as follows:

(1) I_+ consists of a set of strings randomly generated from the $mDFA(L)$, with the property that I_+ is structurally complete. Let $|I_+|_c$ be the sample size required to randomly get such a sample. Depending on the value of a parameter denoted M, we pursue the random generation until the sample size $|I_+|$ is equal to $M.|I_+|_c$.

(2) I_- is constructed in the same way but from the complementary automaton, i.e. the automaton accepting $\Sigma^* - L$.

Remark that there is no guarantee that the optimal solution, defined in section 2.4, exactly accepts the target language. In order to evaluate the quality of the proposed solutions, we compute the correct classification rate on Σ^l, the set of all the positive and negative strings up to a given length l, according to the target automaton[6].

The set of 15 test languages are defined hereafter. The 7 languages L_1 to L_7 are those defined by Tomita [16]:

$L_1 : a^*$

$L_2 : (ab)^*$

$L_3 :$ any sentence without an odd number of consecutive a's after an odd number of consecutive b's.

$L_4 :$ any sentence over the alphabet a,b without more than two consecutive a's.

$L_5 :$ any sentence with an even number of a's and an even number of b's.

$L_6 :$ any sentence such that the number of a's differs from the number of b's by 0 modulo 3.

$L_7 : a^*b^*a^*b^*$

$L_8 : a^*b$

$L_9 : (a^* + c^*)b$

$L_{10} : (aa)^*(bbb)^*$

---

[6]It is very important to distinguish the positive and negative classification rate. Otherwise, the empty automaton would have a nearly perfect score in the case of a very small proportion of positive strings in Σ^l. Similarly, the universal automaton would have a nearly perfect score in the case of a very small proportion of negative strings in Σ^l.

L_{11} : any sentence with an even number of a's and an odd number of b's.
L_{12} : $a(aa)*b$
L_{13} : any sentence over the alphabet a,b with an even number of a's.
L_{14} : $(aa)*ba*$
L_{15} : $bc*b + ac*a$

5.2 Comparative results with the RPNI method

Grammatical inference evaluations often lack practical comparisons between alternative techniques. Here, the RPNI method has been chosen as "state of the art" technique, since it has been proved to identify any regular language in the limit [14]. Besides, there is a theoretical link with our method since the RPNI may be viewed as an ordered search in the boolean lattice following a single path of increasing depth with a limited possibility of backtracking.

The results presented here have been obtained according to the very same experimental protocol, learning and test data for both methods.

	st/tr	L	+class	-class	class	max	best
L_1	1/1	9	100.0	100.0	100.0	100.0	100.0
L_2	2/2	9	99.7	100.0	99.8	100.0	100.0
L_3	4/7	9	91.9	98.8	95.3	99.4	94.6
L_4	3/5	9	68.0	79.7	73.9	90.6	81.2
L_5	4/8	9	74.6	63.4	69.0	83.5	80.5
L_6	3/6	9	92.0	86.3	89.2	95.0	95.0
L_7	4/7	9	96.3	93.3	94.8	100.0	99.2
L_8	2/2	9	100.0	100.0	100.0	100.0	100.0
L_9	4/7	7	99.4	98.5	99.0	99.6	99.2
L_{10}	5/6	9	93.9	99.1	96.5	99.9	96.6
L_{11}	4/8	9	78.6	42.7	60.7	72.2	70.8
L_{12}	3/3	9	100.0	99.6	99.7	99.8	99.8
L_{13}	2/4	9	98.8	97.7	98.2	100.0	100.0
L_{14}	3/4	9	89.2	96.4	92.8	99.9	99.8
L_{15}	4/6	7	94.2	98.7	96.4	99.5	99.4
$Mean$	-	-	91.8	90.3	91.0	96.0	94.4

Table 1: Classification results of the GIG method with semi-incremental search

The parameters of the GIG method are not specifically tuned before each experiment but they have been chosen after a few tests. Their value is listed hereafter: Population size = 100, Max number of evaluations = 2000, Crossover rate = 0.2, Mutation rate/bit = 0.01. The initial population is constructed as follows: the first chromosome corresponds to the currently extended automaton (see section 4). Let N be the number of its states. Up to 50% of the initial population is made of partitions randomly selected from the $N.(N-1)/2$ partitions having $N-1$ elements. The remaining part of the population is randomly generated.

For each pair of samples, we performed 10 independent runs. The first column of table 1 refers to the number of states and transitions of the $mDFA(L)$ associated to each language, i.e. the target automaton. The test sets are made of all strings (except the strings contained in the learning samples) up to the maximal length[7] given in the second column. The third column refers to the correct classification rate of positive sample (according to the target automaton), averaged over 10 runs. The fourth column refers to the correct classification rate of negative sample, averaged over 10 runs. The fifth column gives the total classification rate computed as the arithmetic mean of the two previous features. The sixth column indicates the maximal total classification rate obtained over 10 runs and the last column indicates the total classification rate obtained with the solution automaton having the minimal number of states over the 10 runs[8]. All these results are averaged over the 10 independent (I_+, I_-) samples, randomly generated for each language with the M parameter being set equal to 3. They have been obtained with the semi-incremental procedure described in section 4.

M	RPNI	GIG	GIG_{inc}
1	80.5	82.3	82.2
3	93.9	85.4	94.4

Table 2: Comparative results

We show in table 2 the comparative results between the RPNI method and the GIG method (i.e. we refer here to the correct classification rate of the automaton having the minimal number of states over 10 runs). The two last columns refer to the results obtained without and with the semi-incremental procedure, respectively. These are averaged results over the 15 test languages and over 10 (I_+, I_-) samples for each language, with two different data set depending on the value of the M parameter. Note that for M being equal to 1, we observed that the minimal DFA agreeing with the samples did not always correspond to the target automaton. This explains the worse results obtained with these learning data. Besides, the semi-incremental procedure is very effective, in particular when the sample size grows (M being equal to 3 instead of 1).

6 Acknowledgments

I am indebted to L. Miclet for having taught me the topic of grammatical inference. I would like to thank E. Vidal for the many fruitful discussions we had about this work and for having performed the tests with the RPNI method. I also thank J. Oncina for having made his programs available.

---

[7]We may characterize the language of an $mDFA$ having N states by considering all the strings up to the length L, with L being at most $2N - 1$ [15]. Seeing that the alphabet of the languages $L9$ and $L15$ contains 3 symbols instead of 2, we get a similar test set size by setting L equal to 7.

[8]Remark that this particular solution may be selected without knowing the target automaton.

References

[1] A. Aho and J. Ullman, *The Theory of Parsing, Translation and Compiling, Vol. 1: Parsing*, Series in Automatic Computation, Prentice-Hall, Englewood, Cliffs, 1972.

[2] D. Angluin, *Inference of Reversible Languages*, Journal of the ACM, Vol. 29, No. 3, pp. 741-765, 1982.

[3] P. Dupont, L. Miclet and E. Vidal, *What is the search space of the regular inference ?*, to be published in the Proc. of the 2nd ICGI, 1994.

[4] K.S. Fu and T.L. Booth, *Grammatical Inference: Introduction and Survey*, IEEE Transactions on SMC, Part 1: Vol. 5, pp. 85-111, Part 2: Vol. 5, pp. 409-423, 1975.

[5] E.M. Gold, *Language Identification in the Limit*, Information and Control, Vol. 10, No. 5, pp. 447-474, 1967.

[6] E.M. Gold, *Complexity of Automaton Identification from Given Data*, Information and Control, Vol. 37, pp. 302-320, 1978.

[7] D.E. Goldberg, *Genetic Algorithms in Search, Optimization & Machine Learning*, Addison-Wesley, Reading, Massachusetts, 1989.

[8] M.A. Harrison, *Introduction to Formal Language Theory*, Addison-Wesley, Reading, Massachusetts, 1978.

[9] D.R. Jones and M.A. Beltrano, *Solving Partitioning Problems with Genetic Algorithms*, Proc. of the 4th ICGA, Morgan Kaufmann Pub., CA, pp. 442-449, 1991.

[10] Z. Michalewicz, *Genetic Algorithms + Data Structures = Evolution Programs*, Springer-Verlag, Berlin, 1992.

[11] L. Miclet, *Inférence de Grammaires Régulières*, Thèse de Docteur-Ingénieur, E.N.S.T., Paris, France, 1979.

[12] L. Miclet, *Regular Inference with a Tail-Clustering Method*, IEEE Trans. on SMC, Vol. 10, pp. 737-743, 1980.

[13] L. Miclet and C. de Gentile, *Inférence Grammaticale à partir d'Exemples et de Contre-Exemples : deux Algorithmes Optimaux (BIG et RIG) et une Version Heuristique (BRIG)*, Actes des JFA-94, Strasbourg, France, pp. F1-F13, 1994.

[14] J. Oncina and P. Garcia, *Inferring Regular Languages in Polynomial Update Time*, Pattern Recognition and Image Analysis, N. Perrez de la Blanca, A. Sanfeliu and E. Vidal (editors), Series in Machine Perception and Artificial Intelligence, Vol. 1, pp. 49-61, World Scientific, 1992.

[15] B. Trakhtenbrot and Ya. Barzdin, *Finite Automata: Behavior and Synthesis*, North Holland Pub. Comp., Amsterdam, 1973.

[16] M. Tomita, *Dynamic Construction of Finite-Automata From Examples Using Hill-Climbing*, Proc. of the 4th Annual Cognitive Science Conference, USA, pp. 105-108, 1982.

[17] P. Wyard, *Context Free Grammar Induction Using Genetic Algorithms*, Proc. of the 4th ICGA, Morgan Kaufmann Pub., CA, pp. 514-518, 1991.

TRAINING AND APPLICATION OF INTEGRATED GRAMMAR/BIGRAM LANGUAGE MODELS

J.H.Wright*, G.J.F.Jones[†] and H.Lloyd-Thomas*

* Department of Engineering Mathematics, University of Bristol,
Queen's Building, University Walk, Bristol BS8 1TR, U.K.
and Ensigma Limited, Turing House, Station Road, Chepstow,
Gwent, NP6 5PB, U.K.
E-mail: j.h.wright@bristol.ac.uk, harvey@ensigma.com
† Department of Engineering, University of Cambridge,
Trumpington Street, Cambridge CB2 1PZ, U.K.
E-mail: gjfj@eng.cam.ac.uk

Abstract

This paper discusses a robust language model consisting of context-free grammar rules and symbol bigrams, integrated into a single framework. The aim is to remove the sharp grammatical/ungrammatical distinction by exploiting whatever grammar structure is present in every sentence, and hence to achieve continuity of scoring across the language. Both training and scoring are based on a similar principle: summing over paths that span the sentence. In addition to finding the overall score, a procedure for finding the best interpretation is described. Efficiency is maximised by the use of node-based (rather than path-based) procedures.

1. Introduction

Robustness is an important objective of language models, but if a grammar-based model is sufficiently robust to parse a high proportion of sentences presented to it then ambiguity is likely to be a serious problem. Even then, if the probabilities associated with the model are well-adapted then the highest-scoring alternative parse may have a sound syntactic structure for that sentence, but there is another problem. The grammar may also be able to parse many sentences which a user of the language would regard as highly implausible (or plain wrong). This may not be regarded as a problem for the parsing of text corpora, but if the model is used to score multiple (N-best) hypotheses in a speech recognition system then it may be of little assistance in isolating the correct sentence.

Bigram and trigram statistical models are robust and have been used more widely than higher forms of grammar for speech applications. Their lack of structure appears to be outweighed by their avoidance of ambiguity and by their computational efficiency. Despite their problems, context-free grammars (CFGs) have qualities that can complement the low-level statistical models in an overall model. Although by definition the CFG generalises upon the n-gram, in practice the two tend to operate in orthogonal directions — the n-gram from left to right and the CFG from top down. The integrated approach described in this paper fully recognises this fact and exploits it, first in a training procedure for symbol bigram probabilities and grammar-rule probabilities (but not yet for the rules themselves), and then in a scoring procedure appropriate for applications. By placing the emphasis upon phrasal syntactic structure, and removing the requirement that a sentence parse overall for the grammar to be employed, the aim is to minimise ambiguity while maintaining high robustness and computational efficiency.

In previous work [1,2,6] we have demonstrated the advantages that using a CFG can bring to speech recognition, and we have reported results for a hybrid system in which sentences within the language covered by the grammar are scored by that model, with remaining sentences scored by a conventional bigram model. Sentences are therefore partitioned into two classes, with consequent problems for interpreting and comparing scores for sentences in different classes. We have also experimented with long-distance or "extended" bigrams and trigrams [3-5], which further emphasise the importance of structures wider in scope than conventional trigrams, and other researchers have reached similar conclusions [7-10]. Positive results from combining n-gram and CFG models have been noted by Meteer and Rohlicek [11], and the approach taken in this paper is similar but more general in scope.

2. Training procedure

2.1 Subtree paths

For both training and scoring, a substring parser is used to spot all possible subtrees within a sentence, even when the sentence does not parse overall. This algorithm is derived from an LR parser, enhanced so that every nonterminal symbol is accessible from the initial state and applied to every subphrase within the sentence. The subtrees are stored (shared as far as possible), and in general there may be many ways of finding a left-to-right path through them that spans the sentence. An example is shown in figure 1. The dotted lines are bigram links that join the subtrees.

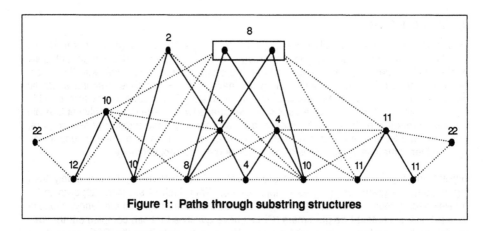

Figure 1: Paths through substring structures

There are 22 possible paths through the subtrees for this 7-word sentence, and above each node are shown the numbers of these paths that pass through that node. Similarly (but not marked) there are numbers of paths that pass along each bigram link. These totals are found using a two-pass algorithm (see below). The number of possible paths can be very large, especially for a long sentence when the grammar is rich in structure, but the algorithm is node-based and does not have to follow every path, and is therefore reasonably fast. The proportions of the total paths that use each bigram link are added to overall totals for the appropriate symbol pairs, and similarly the proportions of the total paths that pass through each node are added to overall totals for the appropriate CFG rules. A special procedure handles null rules. In outline the procedure is as follows:

(1)   Initialise overall bigram and rule counts.
(2)   For each training sentence,
    (2.1)   run substring parser,
    (2.2)   initialise temporary bigram and rule counts,
    (2.3)   run two-pass algorithm to find total number of paths and to set bigram and rule counts (including null rules),
    (2.4)   normalise bigram and rule counts and increment overall counts.
(3)   Apply smoothing algorithm to infer bigram and rule probabilities.

2.2 Two-pass algorithm

In the description that follows, a parse forest node (referred to as $X, Y,$ or Z) is not identified with the symbol there because for a left- or right-recursive grammar a symbol may occur more than once on a branch. Let X be a packed node in the parse forest containing R rules, (if $R > 1$ this represents a local ambiguity [12], where part of the sentence can be derived in more than one way from the symbol at the node). Let the RHS nodes for the rth rule be $Z_1, \cdots, Z_{N_r}$ (N_r = length of RHS for this rule), and let

$$d(X, r) = \prod_{n=1}^{N_r} a(Z_n)$$

denote the number of possible derivations from X, starting from the rth rule, where $a(Z_n)$ is the total ambiguity at the daughter node Z_n, and then

$$a(X) = \sum_{r=1}^{R} d(X, r)$$

is the total ambiguity at X. If X is a terminal node then $a(X) = d(X) = 1$. Also let $f(X), b(X)$ denote the numbers of forward and backward paths through node X, and $\mathrm{span}(X) = (k_1, k_2)$ denote the part of the sentence spanned by node X, where $1 \le k_1 \le k_2 \le L$ for sentence length L. Let $\$$ denote an end-of-sentence marker, so the actual sentence string is $\$w_1 w_2 \cdots w_L \$$.

Forward pass (see figure 2)

(1)   Initial step: for each node Y such that $\mathrm{span}(Y) = (1, m)$ for some m,

$$f(Y) = a(Y)$$

(2)   Recurrence step: for all j from 2 to L, and for each node Y such that $\mathrm{span}(Y) = (j, m)$ for some m,

$$f(Y) = a(Y)\sum_{i=1}^{n} f(X_i)$$

where X_i $(i = 1,\cdots,n)$ are all the nodes such that $span(X_i) = (k, j-1)$ for some k.

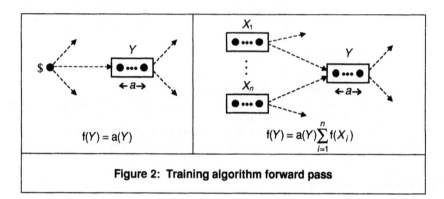

$$f(Y) = a(Y) \qquad\qquad f(Y) = a(Y)\sum_{i=1}^{n} f(X_i)$$

Figure 2: Training algorithm forward pass

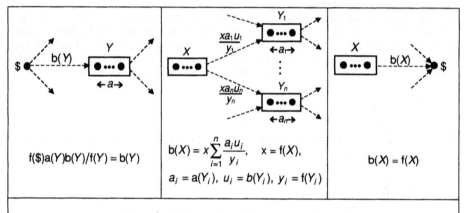

$$f(\$)a(Y)b(Y)/f(Y) = b(Y) \qquad b(X) = x\sum_{i=1}^{n}\frac{a_i u_i}{y_i}, \quad x = f(X), \qquad b(X) = f(X)$$

$$a_i = a(Y_i), \ u_i = b(Y_i), \ y_i = f(Y_i)$$

Figure 3: Training algorithm backward pass

Backward pass (see figure 3)

(1) Initial step: for each node X such that $span(X) = (k, L)$ for some k,

    (a) $b(X) = f(X)$

    (b) add $b(X)$ to the bigram count from symbol at X to $\$$

    (c) add $d(X,r)b(X)/a(X)$ to the rule count for the rth rule at X, $(r = 1,\cdots,R)$.

(2) Recurrence step: for all j from $L-1$ down to 1, if $Y_1,\cdots,Y_n$ are all the nodes such that $span(Y_i) = (j+1, m_i)$ for some m_i and X is a node such that $span(X) = (k, j)$ for some k, then

(a) $b(X) = f(X) \sum_{i=1}^{n} \dfrac{a(Y_i)b(Y_i)}{f(Y_i)}$

(b) add $f(X)a(Y_i)b(Y_i)/f(Y_i)$ to the bigram count from symbol at X to symbol at Y_i

(c) as (1)(c).

(3) Final step: for each node Y such that $span(Y) = (1, m)$ for some m, add $b(Y)$ to the bigram count from \$ to symbol at Y.

The principle behind this procedure is quite simple: each path through a node found during the forward pass is subsequently inflated by a factor depending on the structures to the right of that node, and this factor is applied during the backward pass. Paths are allocated to temporary symbol bigram counts and rule counts, (for ambiguous nodes the paths are allocated to the rules in proportion to their numbers of derivations). After normalisation with respect to the total number of paths, each symbol bigram count becomes the proportion of paths through the sentence that use that bigram (this could in fact exceed 1 if the bigram occurs more than once in a sentence), and each rule count becomes the proportion of paths passing through nodes expanded using that rule. Accumulating these proportions over many training sentences (in the overall bigram and rule counts) gives a measure of their relative utility, which naturally produces probability distributions after smoothing and final normalisation.

Null rules are treated separately. Symbols with empty span do not feature in the bigram count procedure because there is little purpose in invoking a bigram step to a nonterminal symbol which is then nulled out. In the present implementation, if a null rule occurs between words w_k and w_{k+1} then the total of all (backward pass) paths exiting nodes above w_k (or entering nodes above w_{k+1}) is found and allocated to the null rule. Normalisation over all rules with a common LHS (including any null rule) then gives an appropriate rule probability.

It would be possible to weight paths in the temporary counts, to give greater weight either to those that are close to the words or to those that pass through higher structural levels, but this is not done at the present time.

2.3 Smoothing

In practice, and as usual in language modelling, it is essential to do some smoothing of the estimated probabilities, in order to reduce the variability for events that have been observed and to extrapolate to events that have not. Unigram symbol probabilities can be used to smooth the bigram probabilities, and a method we often find useful is a pseudo-Bayes optimal procedure [13], in which the smoothing parameters are optimised over the training set without reference to test data.

If C_{ij} is the count of bigram transitions from the ith to the jth symbols in the vocabulary of total size V, with $N_i = \sum_{j=1}^{V} C_{ij}$ and $N = \sum_{i=1}^{V} \sum_{j=1}^{V} C_{ij}$, then

$$r_j = \frac{1}{N}\sum_{i=1}^{V} C_{ij}$$

is the unigram probability estimate for the jth symbol, and

$$\hat{P}(j|i) = \frac{C_{ij} + \lambda_i r_j}{N_i + \lambda_i}, \quad 1 \le i,j \le V$$

is the smoothed (and normalised) bigram probability, where

$$\lambda_i = \frac{N_i^2 - \sum_{j=1}^{V} C_{ij}^2}{\sum_{j=1}^{V}\left[C_{ij} - N_i r_j\right]^2}$$

is the smoothing parameter. It can be shown [13] that this minimises the mean square error

$$E\left\{\sum_{j=1}^{V}\left[\hat{P}(j|i) - P(j|i)\right]^2\right\}$$

provided the counts $\{C_{ij}: j = 1,\cdots,V\}$ follow a multinomial distribution.

In the absence of a suitable lower-order probability estimate for the rules, the rule probabilities are smoothed simply by adding a small constant to each count before normalising. The language model then consists of the CFG rules with estimated probabilities, and the estimated symbol bigram probabilities. The latter exist for every pair of symbols in the vocabulary, and not just for the terminal symbols as in conventional bigrams.

3. Scoring Procedure

Sentence scoring starts from the subtrees as in training, and is based on path scores. Each path score is a product of derivation probabilities (of rules used within subtrees below nodes passed through by the path) and of bigram probabilities (of links used by the path). In this way the top-down grammar scoring and the left-to-right bigram scoring are brought together in a natural way, and the language model is correctly normalised overall.

The first part of the scoring procedure simply uses the trained symbol bigram and rule probabilities to assign an overall score to a sentence. The second part finds the best interpretation.

3.1 Sentence score

Assuming that the substring parser has recorded all syntactic structures in a sentence, the following algorithm (very similar to the hidden Markov model forward algorithm) finds the overall score.

(1) Initial step: for each node Y such that $\mathrm{span}(Y) = (1,m)$ for some m,

$$\alpha(Y,m) = P(Y|\$)P(Y \overset{*}{\Rightarrow} w_1 \cdots w_m)$$

(2)   Recurrence step: for all j from 2 to L, and for each node Y such that $span(Y) = (k, j)$ for some $k > 1$, if $X_1, \cdots, X_n$ are all the nodes such that $span(X_i) = (m_i, k-1)$ for some m_i (equivalently such that $\alpha(X_i, k-1)$ exists) then

$$\alpha(Y, j) = \left[\sum_{i=1}^{n} \alpha(X_i, k-1) P(Y | X_i) \right] P(Y \stackrel{*}{\Rightarrow} w_k \cdots w_j)$$

(3)   Final step: if $X_1, \cdots, X_n$ are all the nodes such that $span(X_i) = (m_i, L)$ for some m_i (equivalently such that $\alpha(X_i, L)$ exists) then the sentence score is

$$P(\$w_1 w_2 \cdots w_n \$) = \sum_{i=1}^{n} \alpha(X_i, L) P(\$ | X_i)$$

Derivation probabilities of the form $P(X \stackrel{*}{\Rightarrow} x)$ where X is a nonterminal node and x is a substring from the sentence include the sum over all local ambiguities within the subtree(s) dominated by X, and are inferred from the output of the substring parser. If X is a terminal node then this probability can either be set to 1 (for perplexity calculations) or to the word acoustic likelihood (for recognition). A transition probability of the form $P(Y | X)$ represents the smoothed bigram probability from the symbol at X to that at Y.

3.2 Subtree path totals

There are paths through the structures at all levels but we can distinguish (as a "trail", or perhaps "Bergweg" in German!) a path that passes at the highest levels through the structure. Each trail has a score (the sum of the scores for all paths bounded above by the trail, including all local ambiguity) and provides a segmental interpretation of the sentence. A full interpretation could then be found by partitioning the trail scores over the ambiguous alternatives within the subtrees, a fairly simple procedure that will not be discussed here. The sentence score is not in general the sum of the trail scores because trails can share paths.

The first part of the procedure is the computation (from the bottom up) of total scores through subtrees, for particular pairs of entry and exit nodes and stored at the apex of each subtree, see figure 4. Essentially as part of the reduce action for the A-rule, the symbols $B_1, \cdots, B_N$ on the RHS are scanned and the path totals for each subtree are joined by appropriate bigrams and added. Part of the way through this process, the total score for paths from X to U will have been found, and the total score from V to Y can be accessed. The product of these is multiplied by the bigram probability from U to V, and these are summed over all U and V to give the total score from X to Y. Eventually a node (Z) on the right-most branch is reached, and the score stored at A. In addition to these path-based scores, a purely syntactic score (top-down derivation) is also stored at A, and the entry and exit nodes for this item are recorded as A itself. These syntactic scores can then be treated in the same way as all the others that span the same words, with paths passing through the apex node A as well as lower down (X to Z).

Define $\phi_{i,j}^A(X, Y)$ as the total score for all paths through a subtree with apex symbol A, spanning words $w_i, \cdots, w_j$, entering through X (a node on the left branch) and exiting

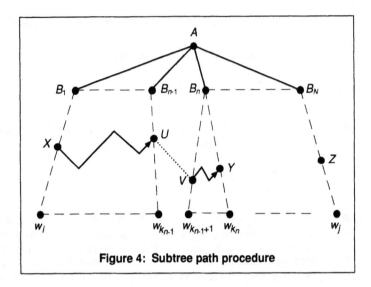

Figure 4: Subtree path procedure

through Y (on the right branch). In particular, $\phi_{i,j}^A(A,A)$ represents the total syntactic score (which may be a sum over locally ambiguous derivations). These are stored at the apex node A. When the rule $A \rightarrow B_1 B_2 \cdots B_N$ is reduced, the daughter nonterminals B_n ($n = 1, \cdots, N$) span words from $k_{n-1}+1$ to k_n respectively, where $k_0 = i-1$ and $k_N = j$. For the syntactic score (ignoring local ambiguity),

$$\phi_{i,j}^A(A,A) = P(A \rightarrow B_1 \cdots B_N)\prod_{n=1}^{N}\phi_{k_{n-1}+1,k_n}^{B_n}(B_n,B_n)$$

The remaining total scores are found by the following procedure which works across the subtrees, summing over all nodes down the branches from B_{n-1} to $w_{k_{n-1}}$ and from B_n to $w_{k_{n-1}+1}$:

(1) $\psi_{i,k_1}(X,U) = \phi_{i,k_1}^{B_1}(X,U)$ for all X,U

(2) $\psi_{i,k_n}(X,Y) = \sum_U \sum_V \psi_{i,k_{n-1}}(X,U)P(V\,|\,U)\phi_{k_{n-1}+1,k_n}^{B_n}(V,Y)$
    for all X,Y ($n = 2, \cdots, N$)

(3) $\phi_{i,j}^A(X,Z) = \psi_{i,j}(X,Z)$ for all X,Z

This bottom-up procedure is concluded when no further reductions are possible. To find the interpretation scores, it is now sufficient to find the paths linking the top-level nodes. If the sentence parses overall then there is nothing further to be done. In general, however, the sentence may not parse overall, there may be local ambiguities within the structure, and there will almost certainly be many shared nodes. Extracting the correct scores is not quite as simple as might at first appear.

3.3 Trail scores

In figure 5 there is an illustration of the step of joining up the top-level structures (dotted arrows). The upper trail is obvious, connecting three unreduced nodes that together span the sentence. The lower trail is less obvious, because it passes through several nodes that have actually been reduced to higher levels. Trails pass through "marked" nodes, and a two-pass algorithm (this time with the backward pass first) marks the appropriate nodes and finds the scores.

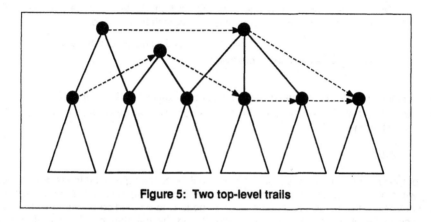

Figure 5: Two top-level trails

Define "L-reduced" and "R-reduced" nodes as those reduced as (respectively) a left-most subtree and a right-most subtree to a higher structure. The algorithm also refers to "L-flags" and "R-flags" for each position in the sentence, of Boolean type, initially false.

Consider a node as "marked" if any of the following hold:

 (i)   it is unreduced,

 (ii)   it is not R-reduced in an R-flagged position (from step (1) below),

 (iii) it is not L-reduced in an L-flagged position (from step (3)(a) below).

With each node there is associated a list of numbered trails, and for each trail t a list of scores $\alpha_t(Z, j)$ for all nodes Z down the right branch(es) from that node, spanning words up to w_j.

(1)   Backward pass: for all j from L down to 2, and for each marked node Y such that $span(Y) = (k, j)$ for some k, consider each non-R-reduced node X such that $span(X) = (m, k-1)$ (for some m) as marked, by setting the R-flag for position $k-1$.

(2)   Initial step: $\alpha_1(\$, 0) = 1$, and consider the initial $\$$ to be a marked node.

(3)   Forward pass: for all j from 1 to L, and for each marked node Y such that $span(Y) = (k, j)$ for some k,

(a) if it either unreduced or not L-reduced in an L-flagged position (cases (i) or (iii) above) then consider each non-L-reduced node Z such that $\text{span}(Z) = (j+1, m)$ (for some m) as marked, by setting the L-flag for position $j+1$,

(b) for each marked node X such that $\text{span}(X) = (i, k-1)$ for some i, and for each trail t at X,

$$\alpha_{t'}(Z, j) = \sum_U \sum_V \alpha_t(U, k-1) P(V|U) \phi_{k,j}^Y(V, Z)$$

where U is a node down the right branch from X, V is a node down the left branch from Y, Z is a node down the right branch from Y, and

$$t' = \begin{cases} t & \text{if this is the first continuation of trail } t \text{ beyond } k-1 \\ \text{new trail number} & \text{otherwise} \end{cases}$$

(4) Final step: for each marked node Y such that $\text{span}(Y) = (k, L)$ for some k, and for each trail t at Y, the trail score for t is the sum over all symbols U down the right branch(es) from Y:

$$\sum_U \alpha_t(U, L)$$

The purpose of the L-flags is to propagate the marking to the right in the forward pass, but only when new scores are being carried forward. In figure 6(a), nodes A, B are marked on the backward pass, but it would be an error for node C to be marked on the forward pass because nodes A, B, C are spanned by node D, and the trail through D is therefore the appropriate one. Node C is not marked because the L-flag applicable for node B is not set (even though that for A, D is set). In figure 6(b) in contrast, node C is correctly marked on the forward pass because the L-flag applicable for node B is set. This is controlled by step (3)(a). Marked nodes are indicated by the larger circles in figure 6(a),(b).

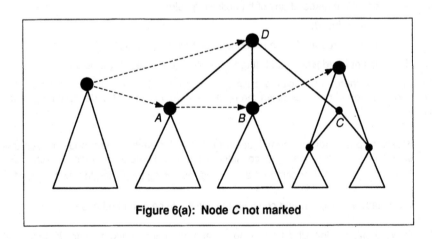

Figure 6(a): Node C not marked

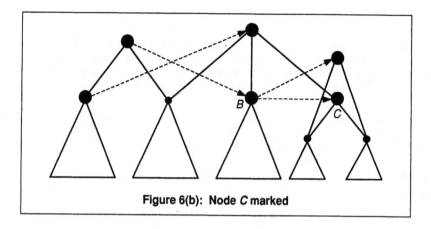

Figure 6(b): Node *C* marked

Because each trail consists of a unique sequence of nodes it would be possible to apply either higher-order *n*-grams or long-distance *n*-grams [3-5] to score this sequence. This may improve the capability of the system to find the best interpretation and will be the subject of future work.

4. Results

Results have been obtained using a corpus of Airborne Reconnaissance Mission (ARM) reports [14]. These have a fixed vocabulary of 511 words, and each report consists of a series of sentences of standard types. There is a full grammar for these reports, which we have adapted into context-free form, and now consists of 226 structural rules, in addition to the rules for converting preterminal to terminal symbols. This allows us to study the effect of using a hierarchy of grammars, from very limited coverage to full coverage. Previous work using this material [3-5] has shown that significant reductions in test corpus perplexity are achieved using "extended" bigrams and trigrams, compared with their conventional counterparts.

4.1 Corpus perplexity

Perplexity of a test corpus is measured by $[\text{corpus score}]^{-1/N}$ where *N* is the total number of words in the corpus, including the final end-marker $ for each sentence. This measure can be used to compare two or more language models for the same corpus (with smaller figures normally indicating better models), and to compare one corpus with another (scored using the same model). Table 1 contains perplexity figures for a test corpus of ARM sentences, scored using a hierarchy of *n*-gram models from basic unigram to extended bigram and trigram (the latter results based on the procedures described in [3-5] but now improved, and smoothed using the method described in section 2.3). The perplexity 10.0 obtained using the full-coverage grammar compares well with the best results obtained using *n*-grams. When the top-level rules are removed from the grammar so that only 1% of the sentences parse overall, the perplexity remains low (in fact falls marginally to 9.5).

Corresponding figures are shown for a second corpus generated at random using the smoothed bigram model, and a third corpus generated using the smoothed trigram model. Although these sentences have the same local statistics as the real ARM sentences they lack the overall structure (and very few of them parse overall). When scored by the integrated grammar/bigram system the perplexity behaves as expected, with the highest figure (24.2 for the bigram corpus) well in excess of that for the test corpus.

Language model	Test corpus perplexity	Bigram corpus perplexity	Trigram corpus perplexity	Word replacement
Unigram	116.5	106.4	103.9	2.19
Bigram	17.1	16.7	13.4	1.16
Trigram	12.9	25.0	9.1	1.15
Extended bigram	12.3	43.7	19.0	1.14
Extended trigram	8.9	94.8	18.3	1.15
Grammar, full	10.0	24.2	14.9	1.13
Grammar, no top-level	9.5	–	–	1.11

Table 1: ARM corpus results

4.2 Word-replacement tests

Word-replacement tests are intended to simulate a speech recognition situation where the aim is to pick out the correct sentence from a set of very similar candidates. For each sentence in the test corpus, a word is chosen at random and replaced with another word (again at random) to generate another sentence, a set of 10 sentences are generated this way, then all 11 sentences are scored and the rank of the score of the correct sentence found, starting from the highest. The mean rank over the corpus should be low (ideally 1.0) for a good model. The grammar/bigram system very slightly outperforms the n-gram models on this test, as shown in the last column of table 1. This outperformance persists when the top-level rules are removed so that the correct sentence does not parse overall.

5. Conclusions

We have described training and scoring procedures for a probabilistic language model consisting of bigrams and context-free grammar rules, integrated into a single structure. The speed of the current implementation is encouraging, and further gains in this respect can be envisaged. For the latest version, training and scoring (including substring parsing) require respectively five and one seconds per sentence on average (on a multi-user UNIX system). The trail-scoring procedure (sections 3.2,3.3) requires three seconds per sentence on average, although these are initial experiments. Results for test corpus perplexity and from word replacement tests indicate that the model is working successfully and is usually able to spot valid sentences, even when they don't parse overall. Work is in progress using reduced grammars and different smoothing procedures, and on a full implementation of the trail-scoring procedure.

Although the model has been applied to a task for which a full-coverage grammar exists (for testing and assessment purposes) we believe that the important benefits will be seen in applications to tasks where a relatively compact but high utility partial-coverage grammar exists. The motivation for this arises from the observation that many complex sentences are constructed from phrases that have a standard structure. This is especially important for speech applications because the overall linguistic structure of freely-spoken speech tends to be far less regulated than that of written text, and language models have to be driven by (and adapted to) actual data rather than being fabricated *a priori*. Furthermore, although direct application of CFG models to speech data gives better recognition [6], this is intractable for tasks of realistic size, and the consequent need for re-scoring *N*-best lists (derived from a preliminary *n*-gram model and preferably compacted into a lattice) is a task to which the approach described in this paper should be well suited.

6. Acknowledgements

We would like to thank the Speech Research Unit, Defence Research Agency, Malvern, for supporting this work and for providing the ARM corpus, with special thanks to Dr M.J.Russell. The work is also supported by the Engineering and Physical Sciences Research Council.

References

[1] J.H.Wright, G.J.F.Jones and E.N.Wrigley, "Hybrid grammar-bigram speech recognition system with first-order dependence model", *Proc. ICASSP-92*, San Francisco, pp I-169-172.

[2] G.J.F.Jones, J.H.Wright and E.N.Wrigley, "The HMM interface with hybrid grammar-bigram language models for speech recognition", *Proc. ICSLP-92*, Banff, pp 253-256.

[3] G.J.F.Jones, H.Lloyd-Thomas and J.H.Wright, "Adaptive statistical and grammar models of language for application to speech recognition", *Proc. I.E.E. Colloquium on Grammatical Inference: Theory, Applications and Alternatives*, University of Essex, April 1993.

[4] J.H.Wright, G.J.F.Jones and H.LLoyd-Thomas, "A consolidated language model for speech recognition", *Proc. European Conference on Speech Communication and Technology*, Berlin, 1993, pp 977-980.

[5] J.H.Wright, G.J.F.Jones and H.Lloyd-Thomas, "A robust language model incorporating a substring parser and extended *n*-grams", *Proc. ICASSP-94*, Adelaide, pp 361-364.

[6] G.J.F.Jones, "Application of Linguistic Models to Continuous Speech Recognition", PhD Thesis, University of Bristol, 1994.

[7] X.Huang, F.Alleva, H-W Hon, M-Y Hwang, K-F Lee, and R.Rosenfeld, "The SPHINX-II speech recognition system: an overview", *Computer Speech and Language* 7, 1993, pp 137-148.

[8] R.Rosenfeld, "A hybrid approach to adaptive statistical language modelling", *Proc. ARPA Workshop on Human Language Technology*, Plainsboro, U.S.A., March 1994, pp 76-81.

[9] R.Iyer, M.Ostendorf and J.R.Rohlicek, "Language modelling with sentence-level mixtures", *Proc. ARPA Workshop on Human Language Technology*, Plainsboro, U.S.A., March 1994, pp 82-86.

[10] H.Ney, U.Essen and R.Kneser, "On structuring probabilistic dependencies in stochastic language modelling", *Computer Speech and Language*, vol 8 (1994), pp 1-38.

[11] M.Meteer and J.R.Rohlicek, "Statistical language modelling combining *n*-gram and context-free grammars", *Proc. ICASSP-93*, Minneapolis, pp II-37-40.

[12] M.Tomita, "Efficient Parsing for Natural Language", Kluwer Academic Publishers, Boston, 1986.

[13] Y.M.Bishop, S.E.Fienberg and P.W.Holland, "Discrete Multivariate Analysis: Theory and Practice", M.I.T.Press, 1975.

[14] M.J.Russell, K.M.Ponting, S.M.Peeling, S.R.Browning, J.S.Bridle and R.K.Moore, "The ARM continuous speech recognition system", *Proc. ICASSP-90*, Albuquerque.

Learning unification-based grammars using the Spoken English Corpus

Miles Osborne and Derek Bridge

Department of Computer Science, University of York, Heslington,
York YO1 5DD, U. K.
{miles,dgb}@minster.york.ac.uk

July 12, 1994

Abstract

This paper describes a grammar learning system that combines model-based and data-driven learning within a single framework. Our results from learning grammars using the Spoken English Corpus (SEC) suggest that combined model-based and data-driven learning can produce a more plausible grammar than is the case when using either learning style in isolation.

1 Introduction

In this paper, we present some results of our grammar learning system acquiring unification-based grammars using the Spoken English Corpus (SEC). The SEC is a collection of monologues for public broadcast and is small (*circa* 50,000 words) in comparison to other corpora, such as the Lancaster-Oslo-Bergen Corpus [JLG78], but sufficiently large to demonstrate the capabilities of the learning system. Furthermore, the SEC is tagged and parsed, thus side-stepping the problems of constructing a suitable lexicon and of creating an evaluation corpus to determine the plausibility of the learnt grammars.

In contrast to other researchers (for example [BMMS92, GLS87, Bak79, LY90, VB87]), we try to learn competence grammars and not performance grammars. We also try to learn grammars that assign linguistically plausible parses to sentences. Learning competence grammars that assign plausible parses is achieved by combining model-based and data-driven learning within a single framework [OB93b, OB93a]. The system is implemented to make use of the Grammar Development Environment (GDE) [CGBB88] and it augments the GDE with 3300 lines of Common Lisp.

Our aim in this paper is to show that combining both learning styles produces a grammar that assigns more plausible parses than is the case for grammars learnt using either learning style in isolation. Plausibility is important in Natural Language Processing as it is very rare that applications need just to determine whether a sentence is grammatical: applications need also to determine the internal structure of sentences (a plausible parse). A grammar that assigns plausible parses is therefore preferable over one that does not assign plausible parses.

The structure of this paper is as follows. Section 2 gives an overview of the combined model-based and data-driven learner. Section 3 then describes the method used to generate the results, which are then presented in section 4. Section 5 discusses these results and points the way forward.

2 System overview

2.1 Architecture

We assume that the system has some initial grammar fragment, G, from the outset. Presented with an input string, W, an attempt is made to parse W using G. If this fails, the learning system is invoked. Learning takes place through the interleaved operation of a parse completion process and a parse rejection process.

In the parse completion process, the learning system tries to generate rules that, had they been members of G, would have enabled a derivation sequence for W to be found. This is done by trying to extend incomplete derivations using what we call *super rules*. Super rules are the following unification-based grammar rules:

$$[\,] \to [\,]\,[\,] \quad \text{(binary)}$$
$$[\,] \to [\,] \quad\quad \text{(unary)}$$

The binary rule says (roughly) that any category rewrites as any two other categories, and the unary rule says (roughly) that any category rewrites as any other category. The categories in unification grammars are expressed by sets of feature-value pairs; as the three categories in the binary super rule and two categories in the unary super rule specify no values for any of the grammar's features, these rules are the most general (or vacuous) binary and unary rules possible. These rules thus enable constituents found in an incomplete analysis of W to be formed into a larger constituent. In unifying with these constituents, the categories on the right-hand side of the super rules become partially instantiated with feature-value pairs. Hence, these rules ensure that at least one derivation sequence will be found for W.

Many instantiations of the super rules may be produced by the parse completion process described above. Linguistically implausible instantiations must be rejected and we interleave this rejection process with the parse completion process. Rejection of rules is carried out by the model-driven and data-driven learning processes described below. Note that both of these processes are modular in design, and it would be straightforward to add other constraints, such as lexical co-occurrence statistics or a theory of textuality, to help select correct analyses.

If all instantiations are rejected, then the input string W is deemed ungrammatical. Otherwise, surviving instantiations of the super rules used to create the parse for W are regarded as being linguistically plausible and may be added to G for future use.

2.2 Model-driven learning

A grammatical *model* is a high-level theory of syntax. In principle, if the model is complete, an 'object' grammar could be produced by computing the 'deductive closure' of the model (e.g. a 'meta'-rule can be applied to those 'object' rules that account for active sentences to produce 'object' rules for passive sentences). An example of purely model-based language learning is given by Berwick [Ber85]. More usually, though, the model is incomplete and this leads us to give it a different rôle in our architecture.

Our model currently consists of GPSG Linear Precedence (LP) rules [GKPS85], semantic types [Cas88], a Head Feature Convention [GKPS85] and X-bar syntax [Jac77].

- *LP rules* are restrictions upon *local trees*. A local tree is a (sub)tree of depth one. An example of an LP rule might be [GKPS85, p.50]:

  $$[\text{SUBCAT}] \prec \sim [\text{SUBCAT}]$$

  This rule should be read as 'if the SUBCAT feature is instantiated (in a category of a local tree) then the SUBCAT feature of the linearly preceding category should not be instantiated'. The SUBCAT feature is used to help indicate minor lexical categories, and so this rule states that verbs will be initial in VPs, determiners will be initial in NPs, and so on. In our learning system, any putative rule that violates an LP rule is rejected.

- We construct our syntax and semantics in tandem, adhering to the *principle of compositionality*, and pair a semantic rule to each syntactic rule [DWP81]. Our semantics uses the typed λ-calculus with extensional typing. For example, the syntactic rule:

  $$S \to NP\ VP$$

  is paired with the following semantic rule:

VP(NP)

which should be read as 'the functor **VP** takes the argument **NP**'[1]. The functor **VP** is of type[2]:

$$<<< e, t >, t >, t >$$

and the argument **NP** is of type:

$$<< e, t >, t >$$

The result of functionally applying **VP(NP)** has the type:

$$t$$

For many newly-learnt rules, we are able to check whether the semantic types of the categories can be functionally applied. If they cannot, then the syntactic rule can be rejected. For example, the syntactic rule:

$$VP \rightarrow VP\ VP$$

has the semantic rule **VP(VP)**, which is ill-formed because the type

$$<<< e, t >, t >, t >$$

cannot be functionally applied with itself.

- Head Feature Conventions (HFCs) help instantiate the mother of a local tree with respect to immediately dominated daughters. For example, the verb phrase dominating a third person verb is itself third person.

- X-bar syntax specifies a restriction upon the space of possible grammar rules. Roughly speaking, the RHS of a rule contains a distinguished category called the *head* that characterises the rule. The LHS of the rule is then a *projection* of the head. Projecting the head category results in a phrasal category of the same syntactic class as that of the head. For example, the rule $NP \rightarrow Det\ N1$ has a nominal head and a NP projection.

Model-based learning consists of filtering out instantiations of the super rules that violate any aspect of the model, or refining instantiation of a super rule such that they comply with some aspect of the model. LP rules and semantic types filter instantiations, whilst the Head Feature Convention and X-bar syntax refine instantiations.

---

[1] Syntactic categories are written in a normal font and semantic functors and arguments are written in a **bold** font.

[2] The exact details of these types is not important to understanding the thrust of this section and so they are not given any detailed justification.

2.3 Data-driven learning

Our data-driven component can prefer learnt rules that are 'similar' to rules previously seen by the parser. For this to work at all well, the system will need some prior training using a pre-training corpus. This can then be used in subsequent learning to score instantiations of the super rules.

In pre-training the frequencies of mother-daughter pairs (MDPs) found in parses of sentences taken from the pre-training corpus are recorded [LG91]. For example, the tree (S (NP Sam) (VP (V laughs))) has the following MDPs:

$$<S,NP>$$
$$<S,VP>$$
$$<VP,V>$$

The frequencies of these MDPs in the parse trees of the pre-training corpus are noted. From these frequencies, the score of each distinct MDP can be computed: if pair <A, B> occurs with frequency n out of a total number of N MDPs, then the MDP's score, f, is:

$$f(< A, B >) = n/N$$

The set of MDP frequencies is computed in advance of using our system for learning. During learning, after parse completion by the super rules, local trees in completed parses can be scored. The score is computed recursively, as follows:

- For local trees of the form (A (B C)) whose daughters are leaves, the score of the local tree is:

$$score(A) = gm(f(< A, B >),$$
$$f(< A, C >))$$

  where gm is the geometric mean. We take the geometric mean, rather than the product, to avoid penalising local trees that have more daughters over local trees that have fewer daughters [MM91].

- For interior trees of the form (B (C D)), the score of the local tree is:

$$score(B) = gm(score(C) \times f(< B, C >),$$
$$score(D) \times f(< B, D >))$$

(This does leave the problem of dealing with MDPs that arise in completed parses but which did not arise in the pre-training corpus. These can be given a low score. Giving them a score ensures that all trees can be scored, and thus the data-driven learner is 'complete', i.e. it can always make a decision.)

After scoring, instantiations of the super rule that have daughters whose scores exceed some threshold can be accepted. Other instantiations can be rejected. The higher the threshold, the fewer the number of rules accepted[3].

The approach we have described is a generalisation of the work of Leech, who uses a simple phrase structure grammar, whereas we use a unification-based grammar [Lee87].

3   Method

We predicted that the plausibility of grammars learnt using both model-based and data-driven learning would be better than the plausibility of grammars obtained by using either learning style in isolation. Plausibility is determined as how 'close', for the same sentence, a test parse is to a benchmark parse, taken (in our case) from the SEC. The following algorithm defines closeness between the test tree (T) and the benchmark tree (B):

- Each tree is normalised to use the same labelling scheme.

- The list L_T is a preorder walk of T and the list L_B is a preorder walk of B.

- Construct the set of lists M as follows. Find β, the longest list that is common to both L_T and L_B and add β to M. Remove β from L_T. Repeat removing lists until either L_T is the empty list or no list can be found that is both in L_T and L_B.

- Closeness is then the arithmetic mean of the list lengths of M divided by the list length of L_B. The nearer this figure is to unity, the better the match. A figure of 0 indicates no match at all.

For example, if L_T was the list (a b c d) and L_B the list (c a b c), then β would initially be (a b c). Removing β from L_T results in L_T becoming the list (d). As there are no lists common to both L_T and L_B, matching halts, with M being {(a b c)}. The closeness score would then be 3/4.

The matching algorithm is designed to allow a certain degree of fuzziness in matching. For example, it is the case that manually produced trees in the SEC are relatively shallow, whilst those generated using the learnt grammars are steep. However, taking a preorder of the trees and searching for longest common lists helps overcome this in-built mismatch. The matching algorithm is our attempt to strike a pragmatic balance between computational efficiency and achieving reliable matches.

To test the prediction, the following steps were taken:

---

[3]We have not investigated the effect of varying the threshold. Clearly, this would be interesting future work.

- Three disjoint sets of sentences were arbitrarily selected from the SEC. These were *pretrain* (less than 20 sentences), *train* (60 sentences) and *test* (60 sentences).

- A grammar, G, was used as the initial grammar. This was manually constructed and consisted of 97 unification-based rules with a terminal set of the CLAWS2 tagset [BGL93].

- The Model was configured to consist of 4 LP rules, 32 pairings of semantic types and corresponding syntactic categories, and a Head Feature Convention.

- *Pretrain* was used to calculate scores of MDPs, thus providing an initial estimate of grammaticality for the data-driven learner.

- *Train* was then processed using interleaved parsing and learning with the following configurations of the learner:

Configuration	Grammar produced
(A) No learning	G
(B) Data-driven learning only	G1
(C) Model-based learning only	G2
(D) Both learning styles together	G3

Note that X-bar syntax is such a vital aspect of acquiring plausible grammars that it is not optional and hence all configurations used this aspect of the model. Configuration A is the base case for comparison with the other configurations.

- *Test* was then parsed, without learning, using each of these grammars and the number of sentences successfully parsed was recorded.

- The set of sentences *plausible* was created as being 15 sentences in *test* that could be generated by grammars G1, G2 and G3. *Plausible* contained no sentence that could be generated by grammar G and hence guaranteed that each sentence needed at least one learnt rule in order to be generated. As a yardstick, 15 other sentences (*yardstick*) that could be generated using G were selected from *test*.

- *Plausible* was then parsed using grammars G1, G2 and G3 and the first 10 parses produced for each sentence was sampled. Out of these 10 parses, the score of the most plausible parse was noted.

- *Yardstick* was parsed using grammar G and the same process was carried out to derive 10 plausibility scores.

Learning grammars in the manner outlined previously is computationally intractable. For example, using the binary super rule may lead to a number of parses equal (at least) to the Catalan series with respect to sentence length. This is because, as a worst case, the binary super rule will create all possible binary branching parses for some sentence [CP82]. In order to generate results therefore, steps were taken to place resource bounds upon the learning process. These bounds were to halt when n parses or m edges had been generated (n=1, m=3000) for some sentence. Increasing n leads to more ambiguous attachments being learnt. The motivation for the m limit follows from Magerman and Weir who suggest that large numbers of edges being generated might correlate with ungrammaticality [MW92]. In effect, the parser spends a lot of time searching unsuccessfully for a parse and this is reflected in the large number of edges generated. The other constraint upon the system was that we only used the binary super rule during interleaved parsing and learning. This is because use of the unary rule greatly increases the search space that needs to be explored. The effect of only learning binary rules, however, will be to decrease the plausibility of the parses produced.

4 Results

In the following table, showing some characteristics of the various grammars, the size column is the number of rules in the grammar, coverage is the percentage of sentences in *test* generated by each grammar, and plausibility is the arithmetic mean of the closeness scores of *yardstick* using G and *plausible* with G1, G2 and G3.

Configuration	Size	Coverage	Plausibility
A	97	26.7	0.103
B	129	75.0	0.086
C	128	65.0	0.095
D	129	75.0	0.098

5 Discussion

From the previous table, it is clear that extending the initial grammar G using learning reduced G's undergeneration considerably. For example, G could only parse 26.7% of the sentences in *test*, but G3 could parse 75.0% of these sentences. As predicted, combining model-based and data-driven learning produces a grammar that assigns more plausible parses than do grammars learnt using either approach in isolation (as shown by the plausibility score for configuration D being higher than the score for configuration B or C). Learnt grammars are less plausible than the original manually constructed grammar (again, as shown by comparing the plausibility score for configuration A with that of the other configurations). The low score given to grammar plausibility is due to difficulties in matching the fine-grained, steep parses produced by the unification-based grammar with the coarse-grained, shallow parses that were manually constructed for the SEC sentences. The uneven quality of the SEC parses does not help in plausibility determination. However, the plausibility results are encouraging and suggest that using both learning styles together is a viable way of allowing formal grammars to be used for corpus parsing.

Future work will evaluate how much the learnt grammars overgenerate. We also intend investigating other constraints upon grammaticality, such as to be found in Government and Binding Theory [Cho81], punctuation [Num90], or textuality [HH76, dBD81]. Furthermore, we intend to consider using a lexically-based formalism in place of the current rule-orientated formalism currently used.

6   Acknowledgements

We would like to thank Eric Atwell (Leeds University) for allowing access to the SEC, the anonymous referee for providing comments upon this paper, and Ted Briscoe (Cambridge University) for supplying the grammar G. The first author is supported by a Science and Engineering Research Council grant.

References

[Bak79]   J. K. Baker. Trainable grammars for speech recognition. In D. H. Klatt and J. J. Wolf, editors, *Speech Communication Papers for the 97th Meeting of the Acoustical Society of America*, pages 547–550. 1979.

[Ber85]   Robert C. Berwick. *The acquisition of syntactic knowledge.* MIT Press, 1985.

[BGL93]   Ezra Black, Roger Garside, and Geoffrey Leech, editors. *Statistically driven computer grammars of English the IBM-Lancaster approach.* Rodopi, 1993.

[BMMS92] Eric Brill, David Magerman, Mitchell Marcus, and Beatrice Santorini. Deducing Linguistic Structure from the Statistics of Large Corpora. In *AAAI-92 Workshop Program: Statistically-Based NLP Techniques, San Jose, California*, 1992.

[Cas88]   Claudia Casadio. Semantic Categories and the Development of Categorial Grammars. In Richard T. Oehrle, editor, *Categorial Grammars and Natural Language Structures*, pages 95–123. D. Reidel, 1988.

[CGBB88] John Carroll, Claire Grover, Ted Briscoe, and Bran Boguraev. A Development Environment for Large Natural Language Grammars. Technical report number 127, University of Cambridge Computer Laboratory, 1988.

[Cho81] Noam Chomsky. *Lectures on Government and Binding.* Dordrecht: Foris, 1981.

[CP82] K. Church and R. Patil. Coping with syntactic ambiguity or how to put the block in the box on the table. *Computational Linguistics*, 8:139–49, 1982.

[dBD81] Robert de Beaugrande and Wolfgang Dressler. *Introduction to Text Linguistics.* Longman, 1981.

[DWP81] D.R. Dowty, R.E. Wall, and S. Peters. *Introduction to Montague Semantics.* D. Reidel Publishing Company, 1981.

[GKPS85] G. Gadzar, E. Klein, G.K. Pullum, and I.A. Sag. *Generalized Phrase Structure Grammar.* Harvard University Press, 1985.

[GLS87] R. Garside, G. Leech, and G. Sampson, editors. *The Computational Analysis of English: A Corpus-based Approach.* Longman, 1987.

[HH76] M. A. K. Halliday and Ruqaiya Hasan. *Coherence in English.* Longman, 1976.

[Jac77] Ray S. Jackendoff. *X-Bar Syntax: A Study of Phrase Structure.* The M.I.T Press, 1977.

[JLG78] S. Johansson, G. Leech, and H. Goodluck. Manual of Information to Accompany the Lancaster-Oslo/Bergen Corpus of British English, for Use with Digital Computers. Technical report, Department of English, University of Oslo, 1978.

[Lee87] Fanny Leech. *An approach to probabilistic parsing.* MPhil Dissertation, 1987. University of Lancaster.

[LG91] Geoffrey Leech and Roger Garside. Running a grammar factory: The production of syntactically analysed corpora or "treebanks". In Stig Johansson and Anna-Brita Stenström, editors, *English Computer Corpora: Selected Papers and Research Guide.* Mouten de Gruyter, 1991.

[LY90] K. Lari and S. J. Young. The estimation of stochastic context-free grammars using the Inside-Outside Algorithm. *Computer Speech and Language*, 4:35–56, 1990.

[MM91]   D. Magerman and M. Marcus. Pearl: a probabilistic chart parser. In *Proceedings of the 2nd International Workshop on Parsing Technologies, Cancun, Mexico*, pages 193–199, 1991.

[MW92]   David Magerman and Carl Weir. Efficiency, Robustness and Accuracy in Picky Chart Parsing. In *Proceedings of the 30th ACL, University of Delaware, Newark, Delaware*, pages 40–47, 1992.

[Num90] G. Numberg. *The linguistics of punctuation.* Center for the Study of Language and Information, 1990.

[OB93a] Miles Osborne and Derek Bridge. Inductive and deductive grammar learning: dealing with incomplete theories. In *Grammatical Inference Colloquim, Essex University*, 1993.

[OB93b] Miles Osborne and Derek Bridge. Learning unification-based grammars and the treatment of undergeneration. In *Workshop on Machine Learning Techniques and Text Analysis, Vienna, Austria*, 1993.

[VB87]   Kurt Vanlehn and William Ball. A Version Space Approach to Learning Context-free Grammars. *Machine Learning*, 2.1:39–74, 1987.

Stochastic Optimization of a Probabilistic Language Model

M.D. Dennis
A.M. Wallington
G.R. Sampson

School of Cognitive and Computing Sciences
University of Sussex
Brighton BN1 9QH
UK

E-mail: milesd@cogs.susx.ac.uk

Abstract

The system described generates a language model for use in the APRIL natural-language parser. The APRIL language model takes the form of a set of typical productions (pairings of mother label with sequence of daughter labels) for each non-terminal category; the system analyses an input by seeking a labelled tree over the words of the input which offers the best fit between each production in the tree and some production of the language model. Previous versions of APRIL used hand-designed language models, but this became a serious research bottleneck. This paper presents a system which uses stochastic optimization to reduce a large set of observed productions to a set of "prototype productions" which are few in number but which nevertheless successfully typify the large observed set.

1   The APRIL Parser

This paper discusses a system which automatically derives a language model, for use in a robust statistically-based natural-language parser, from a grammatically-analysed sample of the relevant natural language.

The parser which the system is intended to serve is the APRIL parser, an early version of which was described in Sampson et al. (1989). APRIL treats the problem of finding a satisfactory grammatical analysis of an input text as a statistical optimization problem. Given an input string, it looks for the labelled tree over the units of the string which maximizes a continuous measure of grammatical plausibility, where plausibility is assessed by comparing the various local configurations jointly making up a tree with the incidence of identical or similar configurations in a database of correctly-parsed natural-language material. The stochastic optimizing technique of simulated annealing is used to locate the best solution within the solution-space for an input. This space contains all possible tree structures having the appropriate number of terminal nodes, with all possible assignments of labels to the nonterminal nodes of the structures; no labelled tree is ruled out as grammatically "illegal", instead an analysis that a linguist would view as absurd is rejected because it is quantitatively less plausible than other analyses, by reference to the statistics of the parsed database. (Simulated annealing — see e.g. Aarts & Korst (1989) — involves executing a random walk through a solution space, subjecting the individual steps of the walk to an initially weak but steadily increasing bias against steps from better to worse solutions: in a wide range of problem domains this allows a system to converge on the global optimum solution while avoiding being trapped by local optima.)

In this way, the APRIL parser addresses the problem that rule-based parsers are often fragile when confronted with messy real-life language data that do not always conform perfectly to well-defined rules. By the nature of the simulated annealing algorithm, APRIL must yield some solution for any input, even a highly ungrammatical input: APRIL seeks the most plausible available analysis, without caring whether the absolute degree of plausibility of that analysis is high or (as is likely in the case of an ungrammatical input) relatively low.

For early versions of the APRIL system, inputs consisted of individual English sentences which an analyst had segmented into words and tagged (that is, wordclass codes had been assigned to the words). The current phase of Project APRIL[1] is producing a system whose inputs are paragraphs of English in the form of raw character strings lacking any analytic information. Using an electronic dictionary, the system begins by forming a word-hypothesis lattice whose arcs span segments of the input which may constitute words (not always obvious, e.g. in the case of punctuation or idioms) and which are labelled with candidate wordtags and tag-frequency information. The parse annealer then seeks the optimum labelled tree whose terminal nodes constitute some path through this lattice. (The word-hypothesis lattice structure is formally similar to data structures typically generated by speech-recognition systems; because of research-resource availability, Project APRIL is currently working with written English, but the system is designed for ease of transfer in due course to the speech domain, where problems of grammatically-messy usage are even more salient.)

The APRIL approach requires a language model capable of assigning a numerical measure of plausibility to any "production" — that is, any pairing of a mother label, drawn from an agreed vocabulary of

---

[1]Project APRIL is currently sponsored jointly by the UK Engineering and Physical Sciences Research Council and Ministry of Defence, under grant GR/J06108, "A full natural-language annealing parser".

nonterminal categories, with a finite sequence of daughter labels each drawn from the union of that vocabulary with the agreed vocabulary of wordtags. The current phase of Project APRIL uses as its categories those of the SUSANNE annotation scheme (Sampson 1994), a set of symbols and rules for applying them to difficult cases which has been designed as an explicit, comprehensive taxonomic scheme for representing written and spoken, surface and logical English grammar. The statistics of the APRIL language model are derived from the 130,000-word SUSANNE analysed Corpus, omitting a subset reserved for testing.[2]

2   The Use of Prototype Productions

Because of the complexity and unpredictability of real-life usage, the range of grammatical configurations found in the SUSANNE Corpus is immensely diverse. Even using simplified category labels which omit many of the details of the full SUSANNE annotation scheme, the parse-trees of the SUSANNE Corpus embody on the order of 14,000 distinct productions, some of which recur many times but many of which are hapax legomena. Furthermore it is sure that other samples of English would throw up other productions again. It would be unreasonable to treat the production-set of the SUSANNE Corpus as a definitive grammar of English for parsing purposes. Rather, it must be treated as a source from which a smaller, more tractable language model is to be distilled. Furthermore, this tractable language-model needs not only to be able to assign some measure of plausibility to productions that actually occur in English: the nature of the APRIL algorithm means that the system will repeatedly have to evaluate crazy, randomly-labelled parse-trees, so the language model needs to be able to assign some (often low) plausibility figure to any production whatsoever, provided only that mother and daughter labels are drawn from the agreed vocabularies.

APRIL solves this problem via the concept of "prototype" daughter sequences. For any given mother label, say "noun phrase",[3] there will be very many distinct daughter sequences in the data, but these will be groupable into families of sequences, such that each member of a particular family can be seen as deriving from a single prototype sequence for the family by insertion of extra labels into the sequence and/or omission of some of the elements from the sequence. Thus, for "noun phrase", one prototype sequence might be the single element "personal-pronoun", another might be "article + adjective-phrase + common-noun". Once a set of prototype sequences is chosen for each mother category, the APRIL language model is constructed automatically as a set of transition networks of the form shown in Figure 1. A prototype sequence supplies the labels for successive arcs on the "spinal route" through a network, and

---

[2]The SUSANNE Corpus is distributed free of charge via anonymous ftp by the Oxford Text Archive. To obtain a copy, log in by anonymous ftp to black.ox.ac.uk, move to the directory ota/susanne, and follow the instructions in the README file in that directory.

[3]For the sake of clarity, the technical codes of the SUSANNE annotation scheme are replaced in the bulk of this paper by self-explanatory descriptive terms.

these arcs are supplemented in a standardized manner with skip arcs allowing any arc on a spinal route to be omitted, and loop arcs allowing extra elements to be inserted at any point. Thus, Figure 1 shows the network that would be constructed for a prototype sequence A B C. Arcs labelled ε are jump arcs transited without consuming input; labels such as "V–BC" mean "the full vocabulary of labels, omitting B and C":

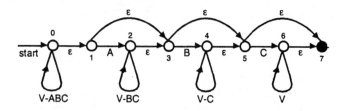

Figure 1 Skip-and-Loop transition network

Probabilities are assigned to the arcs, and to alternative symbols on the loop arcs, by running the parsed data over the network system; and the resulting model is used to evaluate productions during the parsing process by driving the daughter sequence of a production over the networks for the different prototype sequences for the relevant mother label, multiplying the probabilities of the various arcs transited and of the particular prototype, and taking the highest of the resulting products for the various prototypes. The arrangement of skip and loop arcs guarantees that any label sequence whatever will be accepted deterministically on any prototype network.[4]

The adequacy of the language model, and hence the performance of the APRIL parser, is therefore crucially dependent on the quality of the prototype sequences for various nonterminal categories. In earlier phases of Project APRIL, prototype sequences were derived from lists of observed productions by hand. Although the parsed corpus then used was much smaller than the SUSANNE Corpus and used less detailed grammatical categories (so that the number of observed productions was smaller), this proved to be a very serious bottleneck in system development. It seemed highly desirable to automate the process of deriving prototypes from observed productions.

3   Optimization of Prototypes

In the current phase of the project, the process of deriving prototypes from data is itself treated as an optimization problem to be solved by simulated annealing. For any given nonterminal category, a list is formed of the

---

[4]The skip-and-loop network concept as used in the APRIL parser is due to Robin Haigh, now of the University of Leeds Computing Service.

observed daughter sequences, with one entry for each sequence type, together with a record of the number of observed instances (tokens) for each type. A data structure is created which has a slot for each element in each daughter sequence, as in Figure 2 (the labels and figures in which are illustrative only). An annealing run involves a random walk through the space of alternative combinations of assignments of the values On and Off to the slots in such a structure. At each step of the run, a randomly-chosen slot is changed from On to Off or vice versa. In the situation illustrated, the current solution is assigning to the mother label M the prototype set {X Y Z, X B Y, P Y Z, P C Y Z, Q R S U}.

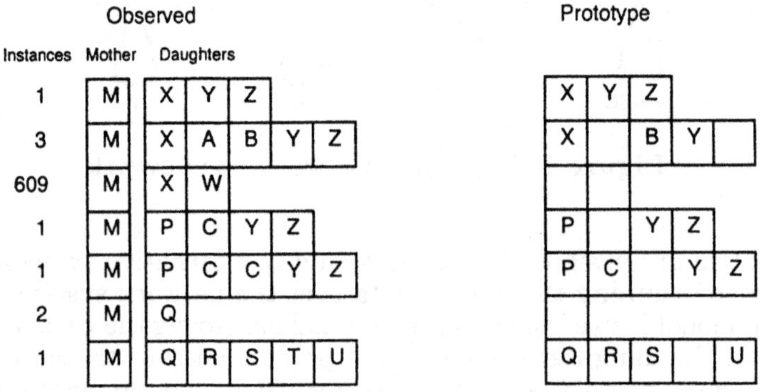

Figure 2 Data structure for observed/prototype sequences

Since we are concerned with generating a prototype set of daughters for a specific mother, no On/Off slots are needed for the mother label.

For a prototype set to be useful as part of a language model for the APRIL parser, it needs to contain few sequences, but there should be a good degree of similarity between each observed sequence and some prototype sequence. These requirements tend to conflict. The evaluation metric used in annealing a prototype set balances the requirements in a manner now to be described.

We first define a cost for an individual prototype sequence relative to an individual observed sequence. Consider the prototype sequence A B C (which gives rise to the skip-and-loop network of Figure 1), relative to the observed sequence X B Y C. The observed sequence is driven over the network, and a counter is incremented by 2 for each traversal of a loop arc or a skip arc (i.e. a jump arc between two odd-numbered states), by 1 for each traversal of an arc labelled with an element of the prototype sequence, and by 0 for each traversal of a jump arc from an even- to an odd-numbered state. In the case quoted, the result is 8, the transitions being as shown in the following table:

Input	Move	Cumulative Sum
start	go to state 0	0
X	loop V-ABC	2
B	edge ε from state 0 to 1	2
B	edge ε from state 1 to 3	4
B	edge B from state 3 to 4	5
Y	loop V-C	7
C	edge ε from state 4 to 5	7
C	edge C from state 5 to 6	8
end	edge ε to final state 7	8

Table 1 Transitions for a Skip-and-Loop network

A prototype has a higher cost, the more dissimilar it is from the observed sequence, but it has a positive cost even if identical to the observed sequence (since we want prototype sequences to be few). The resulting figure is "normalized" by being divided by the summed lengths of the prototype and observed sequences, and the normalized figure is squared. Normalization is intended to prevent figures for long observed or prototype sequences from swamping figures for short sequences in evaluating a set of prototypes; the squaring step was introduced as an empirical response to the need to make prototype-sequence cost increase more than linearly with increase in dissimilarity between the respective symbol-strings. Thus the cost of prototype A B C relative to observed XBYC is $(8 \div (3 + 4))^2 = 1.306$.

Having defined the cost of an individual prototype sequence relative to an individual observed sequence, we now define the cost of a *set* of prototype sequences relative to a *set* of observed sequences. For each observed sequence, that prototype sequence is found whose cost relative to the observed sequence is lowest, and this cost is multiplied by the frequency of instances of the observed sequence within the data. The resulting figures for all observed sequences are summed, and the sum is multiplied by the number of those prototype sequences within the prototype set which are lowest-cost sequences relative to at least one observed sequence.

It is this product which the language-model annealer seeks to minimize during an annealing run; and, on termination of the run, the set of prototypes output consists of just those prototype sequences whose cost contributed to the value of the final solution, omitting "useless" prototypes whose slots are currently On but which are not the cheapest prototype relative to any observed sequence.

Evidently, this evaluation metric implies a great deal of processing at each step of a language-model annealing run. The code has been carefully designed to minimize the amount of recalculation required; this is essential for the generation of a language model in a reasonable time.

Currently the time taken to generate a prototype set for the mother label "sentence" (the label for which our data give the largest solution space) is about two days on a Sun Sparc 10. (For this label there are just over 10,000 On/Off slots, hence the solution space has over 2^{10000} elements to be searched.)

4 Performance of the Language-Model Annealer

The results discussed here were generated after the language-model annealer had been implemented for only about a fortnight, and (as normal with simulated annealing applications) much of that time was devoted to empirical experimentation with different annealing schedules and different weightings attached to various aspects of the evaluation metric. Nevertheless, the system already appears likely to be able to generate a suitable language model for APRIL purposes. Almost all the prototype-sequences generated at current settings of the language-model annealer look sensible, and, where a particular sequence seems clearly unsuitable for inclusion in the language model, it normally belongs to a class (for instance, one-element sequences consisting just of a punctuation mark) which could be mechanically identified. (In practice, there would be no reason to rule out a limited use of manual post-editing in compiling the APRIL language model; but initial impressions are that this will possibly not be needed.)

The nature of the prototype sets generated is not wholly similar to what was initially expected. We saw above that the last step in measuring the cost of an individual prototype sequence relative to an individual observed sequence consists of squaring the normalized figure derived from the transition network. One can modify the evaluation function by taking the normalized figure to a power lower or higher than two. However, this tends simultaneously to affect both the length and the number of prototype sequences generated. Using a low power such as one, individual sequences become too short to be adequate (it is unlikely that a language model would function satisfactorily if the great majority of prototype sequences contained only a single daughter symbol). A power of two is large enough to give reasonably long daughter sequences typically containing two, three, or four symbols and give not unreasonable numbers of prototypes. For example, 190 observed "verb group" sequences were reduced to 17 prototype sequences, 165 observed "adjective phrase" sequences were reduced to nine, 242 "prepositional phrases" were reduced to nine, and 2844 "noun phrases" were reduced to 88 (the latter figure is rather higher than was envisaged). Higher powers still give much larger numbers of prototypes.

Another obvious way of adjusting the evaluation function is, when deriving the cost of prototype set relative to observed-sequence set, to multiply the summed individual costs not by the number of "useful prototypes" but by some power of that number. From preliminary experiments it seems likely that we might achieve a reasonable reduction in the number of prototypes, without reducing their typical length, by taking the number of useful prototypes to a fractional power somewhere between one and two before multiplying into the summed individual costs — though this would be at the expense of a considerable increase in processing time. (Using a power as high as two gives far too few prototypes.)

However, although the numbers of prototypes generated by the current evaluation criterion are, on occasions (as in the case of the "noun phrase" category quoted above), rather larger than initially envisaged, on examining the sequences generated we are at this early stage inclined to think that we should perhaps not give priority to increasing the subtlety of the prototype-set evaluation function, and that the system may be telling us that our original intuitive guesses underestimated the number of sequences needed for an adequate language model in these cases.

It is particularly noteworthy that a number of the prototype sequences generated would be quite unlikely to occur to a human analyst executing the task using his linguistic intuition and scanning the many observed sequences — some of them seem at first sight peculiar or implausible, and yet on reflection they may well be empirically satisfactory. One example for the mother category "noun phrase" is the daughter sequence "article + noun + comma + comma". Two commas will never occur without something inserted between them, and a human analyst would be far more likely to include the intervening element in a prototype than to include the commas and omit what separates them. Yet it is true that English noun postmodifiers include many diverse grammatical categories, but that these are often surrounded by commas; it may be that in practice the commas are a better cue to the nature of the construction than is the identity of the intervening element. Another example for the "noun phrase" mother category is the one-element daughter sequence "attributive-only adjective", such as *former*. At first sight, it seems quite undesirable to give good marks to a parse-tree in which an adjective is categorized as a noun phrase — if a single adjective is analysed as forming a phrase at all, under the SUSANNE scheme it would normally be an adjective phrase. However, the rules of the SUSANNE scheme insert adjective-phrase nodes above single adjectives only in predicative position, which is precisely where a word like *former* cannot occur. And, although *former* alone is unlikely to occur as a noun phrase, a phrase such as *the former* will indeed be labelled as a noun phrase with understood noun. So again the prototype may serve its purpose well although to a human analyst it initially looks misleading.

5   A Sample Category

In order to give a clearer impression of the nature of the observed data used by the system and of the relationship between input and output, we now give details of input and output for one non-terminal category, adjective phrase, in the experiments discussed in the preceding section.

2	AT	DA	JJ			
1	AT	DA	Tn			
2	AT	JJ	P			
2	AT	JJ				
1	D	JA	P	Fc		
3	D	JJ	Fc			
1	D	JJ	J+	P		
1	D	JJ	P	R	Fc	
2	D	JJ	P			
8	D	JJ				
1	D	YH	JJ			
1	DA	FB	YH	Tn		
5	DA	JJ	Fc			
2	DA	JJ	P	P		
20	DA	JJ	P			
1	DA	JJ	Ti	Fc		
2	DA	JJ	Ti			
74	DA	JJ				
1	DA	RR	JJ	P		
1	DA	Tg	P	P		
1	DA	Tg	P			
3	DA	Tg				
1	DA	Tn	Fc			
5	DA	Tn				
1	DA	YH	JJ			
1	DA1	JJ	Fc			
6	DA1	JJ	P			
6	DA1	JJ				
1	DD	DA	JJ	P	Fc	
2	DD	JJ				
1	DD1	JJ	P			
6	DD1	JJ				
1	FB	YH	FA			
3	FB	YH	JB			
21	FB	YH	JJ			
3	FB	YH	N			
5	FB	YH	NN1			
1	FB	YH	Tn			
3	FB	YH	ZZ1			
1	FB					
3	FO	YH	FA			
1	Fc	AT	DA	JJ		
1	Fc	YC	AT	DA	Tn	
1	Fc	YC	AT	JJ		
1	J	JJ				
1	J	YH	J			
4	J					
1	JA	P	P			
6	JA	P				
9	JA	Ti				
15	JA					
1	JB	YH	P			
5	JB					
6	JJ	Fc				
18	JJ	Fn				
1	JJ	Fn?				
1	JJ	J+	Ti			
2	JJ	JJ	JJ			
24	JJ	JJ				
3	JJ	P	Fc			
5	JJ	P	P			
1	JJ	P	Ti			
222	JJ	P				
10	JJ	R				
1	JJ	RG				
2	JJ	RR	P			
2	JJ	RR				
2	JJ	Tf				
1	JJ	Ti	Fc			
64	JJ	Ti				
1	JJ	Tn+	Ti			
1	JJ	YC	A			
1	JJ	YC	J-	YC	J+	P
1	JJ	YC	J-	YC	P	
1	JJ	YC	J-	YC	RR	
1	JJ	YC	J-	YC	Ti	
1	JJ	YC	R	YC		
1	JJ	YC	R			
1	JJ	YC	Tg			
1	JJ	YD	J+	YQ	YD	
1	JJ	YD	RR			
1	JJ	YH	FA			
1	JJ	YH	IO			
24	JJ	YH	JJ			
2	JJ	YH	P			
1	JJ	YP	JJ	YP		
1	JJ	YP	RE			
800	JJ					
1	LE	FB	YH	ZZ1		
1	LE	JB				
9	LE	JJ				
2	LE	MD				
1	MC	YH	FA			
1	MC	YH	JJ			
3	MC	YH	MD			
2	MD	JJ				
1	MD	P				
1	MD	YH	P			
5	MD					
1	N	JA				
5	N	JJ	P			
20	N	JJ				
1	N	ND1	P			
1	N	RG	JJ			
1	N	YH	FA			
9	N	YH	JJ			
4	ND1	JJ				
1	NN	YH	FA			
1	NN	YH	JJ			
13	NN1	JJ				
6	NN1	YH	FA			
29	NN1	YH	JJ			
1	R	DA	JJ			
1	R	JJ	Fc			
2	R	JJ	P			
1	Ř	JJ	P			
1	R	JJ	Tf			
2	R	JJ	Ti	Fc		
1	R	JJ	YC	R	YC	Fc
6	R	JJ				
1	R	Tn	Fc			
1	RG	JB	Tg			
1	RG	JB				
1	RG	JJ	Fc	P		
17	RG	JJ	Fc			
2	RG	JJ	Fn?			
1	RG	JJ	P	Fc		
30	RG	JJ	P			
1	RG	JJ	RG			
1	RG	JJ	RR			
2	RG	JJ	Tf			
1	RG	JJ	Ti			
103	RG	JJ				
1	RG	RG	JJ	Fc		
1	RG	Tg	Fc			
1	RG	Tg	P			
1	RG	Tg				
3	RG	Tn	Fc			
1	RG	Tn	J+	P		
1	RG	Tn	P	Fc		
2	RG	Tn	Ti			
1	RG	Tn				
1	RG	YH	JJ			
1	RR	IC	Tg			
1	RR	J				
1	RR	JA	P			
2	RR	JA				
1	RR	JJ	Fc			
3	RR	JJ	Fn			
1	RR	JJ	P	P		
1	RR	JJ	P	YC	Fa	
27	RR	JJ	P			
1	RR	JJ	R			
2	RR	JJ	Ti			
1	RR	JJ	YC	R		
197	RR	JJ				
1	RR	RG	JJ	P		
1	RR	RG	Tn	JJ	P	Fc
1	RR	RR	JJ			
2	RR	Tn				
1	RR	YH	JB			
4	RR	YH	JJ			
1	Tn	JJ				
2	XX	JJ				
1	XX	JJ	JJ			
1	XX	YH	RR	YH	JJ	

Table 2 Observed sequences for mother-label J (adjective phrase)

Table 2 shows the 165 daughter-label sequences observed below the mother-label J, "adjective phrase", in our data; the leftmost column gives the number of instances of each production in the data. In the experiment discussed, the system derived from these the following set of nine prototype sequences:

```
JJ
Tn
JA
JJ    P
YH
Tg
JB
RR    JJ
P
```

Space precludes giving a complete set of translations of the simplified SUSANNE symbols here, but the following list gives brief definitions of a number of them, including all those appearing in the above prototype sequences:

AT	article
D	determiner phrase, e.g. *so many*
DA	determiner capable of following article, e.g. *more*
FB	prefix
Fc	comparative clause, e.g. *than we have*
JB	attributive adjective, e.g. *former*
JJ	general adjective
N	noun phrase
NN1	singular common noun
P	prepositional phrase
R	adverb phrase
RG	qualifier, e.g. *very*
RR	general adverb
Tg	present-participle clause, often one-word, e.g. *depressing*
Tn	past-participle clause, e.g. *beaten*
XX	*not*
YH	hyphen

6   Closing Remarks

It must be pointed out that, at the time of drafting this paper, it is not yet possible to say how successful an automatically-generated language model will turn out to be at the task of preferring correct analyses to incorrect ones. It will be some time yet before a complete automatically-generated language model can be included in a functioning parse-annealer. We expect to have reached this stage, and to be in a position to discuss at least some early results from this version of the APRIL parser, by the time of the Alicante meeting.

If the technique does prove successful in practice, it offers an attractively re-usable method for generating grammatical models for natural languages. We do not assert that every natural language is necessarily as amenable as English to the APRIL system of parsing by reference to prototype sequences. (Languages with very free word order, or with very large ranges of inflexional forms, might lend themselves less well than English to this approach.) But many modern European languages would prima facie appear as suitable as English for this approach. If a satisfactory language model for English can be generated in the manner described here, it should equally be possible to generate a model for another such language, given only a grammatically-analysed corpus — and the latter is surely a sine qua non for most serious NLP-oriented research.

References

E. Aarts and J. Korst 1989 *Simulated Annealing and Boltzmann Machines*. Wiley.

G.R. Sampson 1994 *English for the Computer: The SUSANNE Corpus and Analytic Scheme*. Forthcoming from Oxford University Press.

G.R. Sampson et al. 1989 "Natural language analysis by stochastic optimization". *Journal of Experimental and Theoretical Artificial Intelligence* 1.271-87.

Computer Assisted Grammar Construction

S.J. Young and H-H. Shih
Cambridge University Engineering Department
Trumpington Street, Cambridge CB2 1PZ, England
E-mail: sjy@eng.cam.ac.uk

June 29, 1994

Abstract

This paper presents a system for computer assisted grammar construction (CAGC). The CAGC system is designed to generate broad-coverage grammars for large natural language corpora by utilizing both an extended inside-outside algorithm and an automatic phrase bracketing (AUTO) system, which is designed to provide the extended algorithm with constituent information during learning. This paper demonstrates the capability of the CAGC system to deal with realistic natural language problems and the usefulness of the AUTO system in the inside-outside based grammar re-estimation. Performance results including an analysis of degree of coverage and bracketing precision are presented for a grammar constructed for the Wall Street Journal (WSJ) corpus.

1 Introduction

In natural language processing (NLP), a grammar is often required for a new corpus. The conventional way of generating a new grammar is to ask linguists to design a set of production rules by hand parsing the text corpus. However, to develop a useful grammar which covers the whole corpus is almost impossible, unless the size of the corpus is small. Additionally, a grammar is usually developed under the assumption that the sentences in the corpus are well-formed, but this is not true for most naturally-occurring corpora. Because of these factors, only limited coverage can be achieved by a hand-written grammar. Furthermore, as more sentences are added to the corpus, re-tuning the grammar becomes necessary to maintain coverage. This is usually done by asking linguists to re-write some of the production rules and adding new ones. Development and later modification of a grammar by this means are labour intensive, time consuming and often introduce unwanted rule interactions.

To overcome these problems, automatic algorithms are needed to infer a grammar for a given corpus. Techniques for grammar inference (GI) [FB86] [Luc93] can be used to replace or augment the conventional manual grammar construction. Given a set of training data, the aim of GI is to estimate or infer a grammar G such that the language L(G) generated by G includes all sentences in the training set, and more importantly, the inferred G is able to generalise unseen members of the overall language L. Several algorithms have been explored for this purpose, for example, genetic algorithms [Wya93], the error correcting grammar inference (ECGI) algorithm [RPV89] and the inside-outside algorithm [Bak79, LY90].

In the inside-outside algorithm, there are two approaches for GI, namely explicit and implicit. The explicit approach [BLR92] is to manually produce a set of production rules for a language corpus and then use the inside-outside algorithm to estimate the required rule probabilities. The implicit approach [LY91, PS92] starts with a grammar containing all possible rules, given a set of non-terminals and (pre)terminals. The grammar is then trained on a large training corpus, in the hope that the learning process will converge to a linguistically-motivated grammar which fits the training corpus.

However, two inherent problems of the inside-outside algorithm inhibit its practical application in NLP. Firstly, the algorithm has a high complexity of $O(n^3m^3)$, where n is the length of sentences and m is the number of non-terminals in the grammar. With a complexity of $O(n^3m^3)$, only inference of simple toy grammars is practicable if all the possible rules are allowed in the learning process as in the implicit approach. Secondly, the algorithm does not guarantee convergence on a linguistically-motivated maximum. As the number of non-terminals increases, the convergence property of the algorithm degrades due to the insufficiency of data. Also, it becomes clear that the raw training text corpus from which the grammar is trained provides insufficient linguistic information.

To overcome the first problem, a hybrid method integrating the explicit and implicit approaches is necessary[BW93, Wae93]. The hybrid method integrates a core grammar (explicit rules) and a set of constrained implicit rules to reduce the size of the rule set as well as to maintain a good coverage. The second problem of insufficiency of linguistic knowledge can be diminished by utilizing phrase bracketing information during learning as proposed in [PS92, BLR92]. Further improvement can be obtained by giving high initial probabilities to the explicit rules to obtain better bootstrapping during learning.

This paper describes a complete system for computer assisted grammar construction. It includes a new algorithm for automatic phrase bracketing and an evaluation of its usefulness within the context of grammatical inference using the inside-outside algorithm. It also demonstrates that inside-outside based inference can be extended to deal with realistic problems using only tagged text data for training. It concludes with an experimental evaluation using a subset of the Wall Street Journal (WSJ) text corpus.

2 Overview of the CAGC system

The CAGC system is designed to infer linguistically-motivated SCFGs with broad-coverage for large corpora. The system takes advantages of both heuristic and stochastic approaches. Heuristic knowledge provides powerful and important constraints to the system, whereas stochastic information deals with situations which are too complex or too trivial for heuristic rules to handle. A block diagram of the system is shown in Figure 1. The first part of the system consists of two parallel stages: construction of an initial SCFG and phrase-bracketing of the raw text data. In the second part of the system, a grammar is inferred by utilizing the inside-outside algorithm to re-estimate the initial SCFG from the bracketed text data.

The initial SCFG is derived from the core grammar (explicit part) and a set of CF rules (implicit part). The explicit part was manually developed using a grammar development environment tool (GDE) [BGBC87] to form a skeleton of the SCFG. The implicit part consists of all possible rules which do not appear in the core grammar but which are nevertheless linguistically plausible. This is done by filtering all possible rule forms using headedness constraints[BW93]. The explicit and implicit rules are then integrated into a hybrid SCFG along with an appropriate set of initial probabilities. In order to bias the learning process towards a linguistically-motivated optimum, the explicit rules are given higher initial probabilities than the implicit rules. Details of the grammar development and the calculation of the initial probabilities are described in [SY94]. Before the raw training data can be used with the inside/outside algorithm, it must have phrase structure bracketing information added. For this a system called AUTO is used which combines both top-down and bottom-up heuristics to perform surface bracketing.

In the second part of the CAGC system, the inside-outside learning procedure, incorporating a bottom-up chart parser [GM88], iteratively re-estimates the probabilities of the production rules. The updated probabilities are calculated according to the weighted frequency counts of the rules used in parses licensed by the grammar and generated at the previous iteration. At the end of each iteration, the rules with probabilities falling below a pre-defined threshold are discarded. This reduces the size of the inferred grammar and the computational expense of further re-estimation. The re-estimation process continues until either the change in the total log probability (sum of log probabilities of all possible parses generated for all the training data) between iterations is less than a minimum or the number of iterations reaches a maximum (set to 10). Both limiting values and the rule elimination threshold were determined empirically in the system development. The final inferred grammar is generated when either criteria is met.

3   Automatic Phrase Bracketing System (AUTO)

In inside-outside based GI, constituent information about the training data provides an effective constraint during the re-estimation process, as stated in the introduction. However, generating a hand-parsed training corpus such as the Penn treebank [Mar91] used in [PS92] is very labour-expensive and this manual work must be repeated each time that a new training corpus is required. In order to overcome this problem, an automatic algorithm is needed to derive the constituent information for the training corpus. The AUTO system has been designed for this purpose. The output of the AUTO bracketing of the corpus is used to assist the inside-outside based grammar re-estimation in the CAGC system.

The AUTO system is a surface-bracketing technique, which employs heuristic knowledge about the phrase structure of sentences, to group various kinds of constituents within a tagged sentence. The system applies the heuristic knowledge in a manner that combines both top-down and bottom-up approaches. It is observed that some of the constituent information is easier to capture from a global view (the top-down approach) such as the subject and predicate relation, whereas other information can be identified locally (bottom-up approach) such as a noun phrase starting with a determiner or a verb phrase beginning with an auxiliary. Because of this, the AUTO system applies heuristic rules in

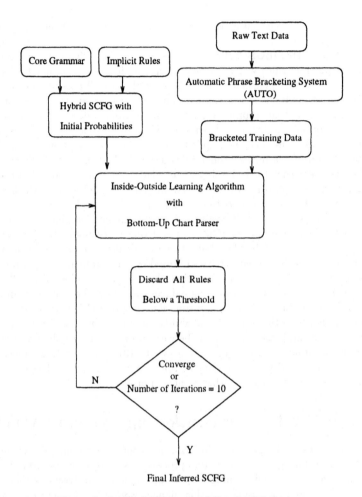

Figure 1: A Block Diagram of the CAGC System

both a top-down and a bottom-up fashion, whichever is more appropriate to deal with each type of constituent.

The various types of constituent cannot all be processed independently. Some larger constituents such as clauses rely on smaller constituents to be formed in advance. Also, interaction between two different constituents sometimes happen. As a consequence, the rules used in the AUTO system are applied in a prescribed order which has been determined empirically. The AUTO system is described in detail in [SY94].

4 Grammatical Inference Procedure

As noted above, grammatical inference is performed by using an extended form of the inside-outside algorithm. In its basic form, the inside-outside algorithm applies only to grammars in Chomsky Normal Form (CNF) and it performs an exhaustive evaluation of all possible derivations. In practice, a very large number of these possible derivations are linguistically implausible and carry a very small probability. The use of the phrase-bracketing information supplied by the AUTO algorithm filters out a great many of these yielding both a computational speed-up by a factor of 30 or more and fewer spurious rules in the final grammar.

The use of CNF is also limiting. In our work we avoid this by using a bottom-up left-right chart parser [Wae93]. The chart is built first and then the set of parses encoded by the chart are used to accumulate the inside and outside probabilities. The inside probabilities are computed bottom-up. First the terminal edges corresponding to pre-terminal rules are assigned the probability of the associated rule. For a general edge, the inside probability is calculated as the sum over all the sets of edges dominated by that edge, where the probability of each set is computed as the product of the constituent inside probabilities and the associated rule probability in the usual way. Outside probabilities are calculated top-down. Initially, the fully spanning edge corresponding to the start symbol is given an outside probability of 1 and all other outside probabilities are set to zero. The outer probability of each edge corresponding to a non-terminal B in a dominated set of edges of the form wBx corresponding to the rule $A \rightarrow wBx[p]$ is then incremented by the product of the outside probability of A, the rule probability p and all of the inner probabilities corresponding to w and x. This is repeated for each spanning edge working from top to bottom until all combinations have been processed. As with all re-estimation algorithms of this kind, numerical underflow has to be guarded against by scaling.

5 Experimental Evaluation

Training and Testing data were chosen from the Wall Street Journal(WSJ) text corpus. There were 1521 training sentences and 500 testing sentences in our WSJ subset which was selected so that no sentences contained punctuation. Instead of lexical entries, parts-of-speech (POSs) are used in our experiments to reduce computation. In order to capture more detailed syntactic information, some of the POSs used in the WSJ text corpus were subcategorized. This increased the number of POSs from 48 to 62. Detailed subcategorization is stated in [SY94].

5.1 Training Grammars with/without Constituent Information

Three experiments were carried out to investigate the extent to which bracketing information is utilized during the inside-outside re-estimation process and its effect on the final trained grammar. In the first two experiments, the explicit and hybrid (ie. explicit + implicit) grammars were trained from the raw corpus (NULL_BC i.e. no bracketing constraint). In the third experiment, the hybrid grammar was trained from the AUTO bracketed corpus (AUTO_BC).

Table 1 shows the results for these three trained grammars. It records the number of SCF rules which survived after training, the ratio of explicit and implicit trained rules, the number of test sentences parsed by each trained grammar, and the performance evaluation in terms of Recall, Precision and Crossings [BAF+91, Tho92]. Recall is the percentage of standard bracketings (in the Penn treebank) present in the most likely (Viterbi) parse of the each sentence. Precision is the percentage of bracketings in the Viterbi parse also present in the Penn treebank sentence. One crossing error occurs for every instance of a bracket pair from the Viterbi parse which partially overlaps one or more bracket pairs in the Penn treebank. The Crossings measure is the average number of these crossing errors per sentence. The table also records the number of test sentences successfully parsed by all three grammars and the performance based on these sentences only.

Grammar Types	Explicit	hybrid + NULL_BC	hybrid + AUTO_BC
Rules Remaining	33.99%	40.91%	18.54%
After Training	(2022/5949)	(6029/14736)	(2733/14736)
Exp:Imp rules	2022:0	3290:2739	1316:1417
Sent. Parsed	89.80% (449)	98.60% (493)	97.20% (486)
Recall	76.02%	70.76%	84.66%
Precision	58.56%	54.55%	62.50%
Crossings	2.86	3.49	2.14
Sent. All Parsed	89.20% (446)	89.20% (446)	89.20% (446)
Recall	76.11%	71.35%	85.58%
Precision	58.59%	55.23%	63.43%
Crossing	2.87	3.35	2.00

Table 1: Performance of the Explicit and Hybrid Grammars Trained From Raw/Bracketed Corpus

From Table 1, it can be seen that both the hybrid grammars achieved significantly greater coverage than the explicit grammar. The Recall and Precision results for the NULL_BC grammar are lower than those for the original explicit grammar, however, the AUTO_BC grammar shows considerable improvement of about 9% for Recall and 4% for Precision. In addition, the crossing errors are significantly reduced for the AUTO_BC grammar, particularly with respect to the NULL_BC grammar, where Crossings is reduced by 38%. What is more, the AUTO_BC grammar has less than half the number of rules of the NULL_BC grammar. Its only disadvantage is a slightly reduced coverage.

5.2 Complexity of the Original and Extended Inside-Outside Algorithm

The complexities of the original and extended inside-outside algorithms were recorded and a comparison is shown in Table 2. The NULL_BC hybrid grammar was used for calculating the CPU time of the original algorithm and the AUTO_BC grammar for that of the extended algorithm. Both were trained on an HP series 735 workstation.

Algorithm	Original	Modified
CPU Time in Minutes	507.34	17.37

Table 2: Complexities of Original and Extended Inside-Outside Algorithm

As shown in the table, the original algorithm spent 8 hour and 27 minutes CPU time whereas the extended algorithm took less then 18 minutes. This significant improvement indicates that the additional bracketing constraint overcomes the main weakness of the inside-outside algorithm by making it computationally tractable for use in grammatical inference.

5.3 Training the Hybrid Grammar from Hand-Parsed Corpus

In order to compare the effectiveness of the AUTO generated brackets with the Penn treebank brackets,the hybrid grammar was trained using the hand-parsed Penn treebank (PENN_BC) training corpus. Table 3 shows the performance comparison between these two approaches. As can be seen, the size of the AUTO_BC grammar remains the smallest and its recall, precision, crossings and coverage are very competitive with the performance of the PENN_BC grammar.

Types of Training Corpora	AUTO_BC	PENN_BC
Rules Remaining After Training	18.54% (2733/14736)	21.29% (3137/14736)
Exp:Imp rules	1316:1417	1482:1655
Sent. Parsed	97.20% (486)	97.80% (489)
Recall	84.66%	84.65%
Precision	62.50%	64.06%
Crossings	2.14	1.92
Sent. Both Parsed	96.20% (481)	96.20% (481)
Recall	84.76%	84.76%
Precision	62.67%	63.98%
Crossings	2.13	1.93

Table 3: A Performance Comparison between AUTO_BC and PENN_BC Grammars

6 Conclusions

A system for computer assisted grammar construction has been presented in this paper. The aim in developing this system was to efficiently infer a broad-coverage and linguistically-motivated grammar for a large corpus without relying on significant manual labour. The experimental results demonstrate that the CAGC system can successfully infer a grammar for a subset of the WSJ corpus which has acceptable coverage and precision. Two techniques employed in the system contributed to this success.

Firstly, the method of generating an initial SCFG ensures broad-coverage of the inferred grammar and provides good bootstrapping for the learning process. The initial SCFG includes a set of explicit rules (the core grammar), which is hand-produced, and a set of implicit rules that compensates for the limited coverage of the core grammar. Additionally, giving high initial probabilities for the explicit rules and low probabilities for the implicit rules means that the system is biased towards a linguistically-motivated grammar.

Secondly, the extended inside-outside algorithm used for the grammar re-estimation utilizes constituent information derived by the AUTO bracketing system to constrain the training process. The bracketed training data not only provides essential information for the extended algorithm to consider only the set of rules whose spans are compatible with the *a priori* bracketings, but also establishes similar constituent structures in the inferred grammar.

A variety of experimental results have been presented which show that, although the AUTO bracketing system does make errors, these errors do not appear to significantly degrade the inference procedure compared to the use of manually bracketed data. The use of automatically generated implicit rules allows coverage to be substantially increased and the introduction of bracketing constraints generated from the AUTO system significantly improves performance and maintains this coverage. Finally, unlike the standard inside-outside inference procedure, the system described here is computationally tractable when applied to realistic tasks.

References

[BAF⁺91] E. Black, S. Abney, D. Flicknger, C. Gdaniec, R. Grishman, P. Harrison, D. Hindle, R. Ingria, F. Jelinek, J. Klavans, M. Liberman, M. Marcus, S. Roukos, B. Santorini, and T. Strzalkowski. A procedure for quantitatively comparing the syntactic coverage of English grammar. In *DARPA Speech and Natural Language Workshop*, pages 306–311, 1991.

[Bak79] J.K. Baker. Trainable grammar for speech recognition. In *Speech Communication Papers for the 97th Meeting of the acoustical Society of America (D. Klatt and J. Wolf, eds)*, pages 547–550, 1979.

[BGBC87] E. Briscoe, C. Grover, B. Bogurraev, and J. Carroll. A formalism and environment for the development of a large grammar of english. In *Proceedings of the 10th International Joint Conference on Artificial Intelligence*, pages 703–708, Milan, Italy, 1987.

[BLR92] E. Black, J. Lafferty, and S. Roukos. Development and evaluation of a broad-coverage probabilistic grammar of English-language computer manuals. In *Proceedings of the 30th Annual Meeting of the Association for Computational Linguistics*, pages 185–192, June 1992.

[BW93] E. Briscoe and N. Waegner. Undergeneration and robust paring. In J. Arts, P. de Haan, and N. Oostdijk, editors, *English language corpora: design, analysis and exploitation*, pages 14–19. Rodopi, Amsterdam, 1993.

[FB86]   K. Fu and T. Booth. Grammatical inference: Introduction and survey. *IEEE Transactions on Pattern Analysis and Machine Intelligence*, 8:343–375, 1986.

[GM88]   G. Gazdar and C. Mellish. *Natural Language Processing in PROLOG*. Addison-Wesley, 1988.

[Luc93]   S.M. Lucas. New directions in grammatical inference. In *Colloquium on Grammatical Inference: Theories, Applications and Alternatives*, 1993.

[LY90]   K. Lari and S.J. Young. The estimation of stochastic context-free grammars using inside-outside algorithm. *Computer Speech and Language*, pages 35–56, 1990.

[LY91]   K. Lari and S.J. Young. Application of stochastic context-free grammars using inside-outside algorithm. *Computer Speech and Language*, pages 237–257, 1991.

[Mar91]   M. Marcus. Very large annotated database of american english. In *DARPA Speech and Natural Language Workshop*, page 430, 1991.

[PS92]   F. Pereira and Y. Schabes. Inside-outside re-estimation for partially bracketed corpora. In *Proceedings of the 30th Annual Meeting of the Association for Computational Linguistics*, pages 128–135, June 1992.

[RPV89]   H. Rulot, N. Prieto, and E. Vidal. Learning accurate finite-state structural models of words through the ECGI algorithm. In *Proceedings of the ICASSP 89*, volume 2, pages 643–646, 1989.

[SY94]   H-H. Shih and S.J. Young. A system for computer assisted grammar construction. Technical Report TR.170, Engineering Department, Cambridge University, England, June 1994.

[Tho92]   H.S. Thompson. Parseval workshop. In *ELSNews Vol.1(2)*, 1992.

[Wae93]   N. Waegner. *Stochastic Models for Language Acquisition*. PhD thesis, Cambridge University, England, 1993.

[Wya93]   Peter Wyard. Context free grammar induction using genetic algorithm. In *Colloquium on Grammatical Inference: Theories, Applications and Alternatives*, 1993.

Springer-Verlag
and the Environment

We at Springer-Verlag firmly believe that an international science publisher has a special obligation to the environment, and our corporate policies consistently reflect this conviction.

We also expect our business partners – paper mills, printers, packaging manufacturers, etc. – to commit themselves to using environmentally friendly materials and production processes.

The paper in this book is made from low- or no-chlorine pulp and is acid free, in conformance with international standards for paper permanency.

Lecture Notes in Artificial Intelligence (LNAI)

Lecture Notes in Computer Science